TM

References for the Rest of Us!™

BESTSELLING BOOK SERIES

Do you find that traditional reference books are overloaded with technical details and advice you'll never use? Do you postpone important life decisions because you just don't want to deal with them? Then our *For Dummies®* business and general reference book series is for you.

For Dummies business and general reference books are written for those frustrated and hard-working souls who know they aren't dumb, but find that the myriad of personal and business issues and the accompanying horror stories make them feel helpless. *For Dummies* books use a lighthearted approach, a down-to-earth style, and even cartoons and humorous icons to dispel fears and build confidence. Lighthearted but not lightweight, these books are perfect survival guides to solve your everyday personal and business problems.

"More than a publishing phenomenon, 'Dummies' is a sign of the times."

— The New York Times

"...you won't go wrong buying them."

— Walter Mossberg, Wall Street Journal, on For Dummies books

"A world of detailed and authoritative information is packed into them..."

— U.S. News and World Report

Already, millions of satisfied readers agree. They have made For Dummies the #1 introductory level computer book series and a best-selling business book series. They have written asking for more. So, if you're looking for the best and easiest way to learn about business and other general reference topics, look to For Dummies to give you a helping hand.

Wiley Publishing, Inc.

5/09

The SAT® I For Dummies,® 5th Edition

VERBAL

Analogy Question Review

The approach

1. **Use both words in a descriptive sentence.**
2. **Use the exact same sentence on each answer choice.**

Tips and tricks

- Turn a verb into an infinitive.
- Identify which part of speech (noun, verb, or adjective) the question word is.
- Try assuming that unknown words are synonyms.
- Use roots, prefixes, and suffixes.
- Identify the salient feature of a word — what makes it stand out.
- Remember the common relationships: cause and effect, characteristics, greater to lesser, location, member to group (or specific to general), opposites, part to whole, position, purpose or function, and synonyms.

Sentence Completion Question Review

The approach

1. **Read the entire sentence for its gist.**
2. **If possible, predict words to fit into the blanks.**
3. **Insert *every* answer choice into the blanks and reread the sentence.**

Tips and tricks

- Look for key connecting words that may change the meaning of the sentence (words such as *because, although, despite, therefore*).
- Predict whether you need positive or negative words to fit in the blanks.
- Skip questions with answers that depend entirely on unknown vocabulary.
- Use a few basic RPS (roots, prefixes, and suffixes) to figure out the killer vocabulary.

Critical Reading Question Review

- Be positive or neutral, not negative.
- Choose answers containing key words.
- Be wishy-washy, not dramatic.
- Look for answers above or below the key words or indicated line numbers.

General Verbal Tips

- Use RPS (roots, prefixes, and suffixes) to decode unfamiliar words.
- Skip Sentence Completion questions that depend entirely on unknown vocabulary.
- In Critical Reading answers, think positive or neutral, not negative.

General Tips for SAT Success

- Keep in mind that half right is average.
- Remember that wild guessing can hurt your score. Most questions subtract points for wrong answers.
- Mark your answers in the booklet *and* on the grid.
- Skip around within a section.
- Double-check easy and medium questions and don't obsess over hard ones.
- Note that the SAT doesn't test grammar or require an essay. (The PSAT does, however, test grammar.)

Item 5472-7.
For more information about Wiley Publishing, call 1-800-762-2974.

***This SAT is rated PG (Proctor Guarded).** Proctors have been genetically altered to have eyes in the backs of their heads, and they'll catch you if you peek at this Cheat Sheet during the SAT. Learn it, and then burn it.

The SAT® I For Dummies,® 5th Edition

MATH

Quantitative Comparison Question Review

The approach

1. **Solve for the quantity in Column A.**
2. **Solve for the quantity in Column B.**
3. **Compare the two quantities.**
4. **Choose answers as follows:**

   Choose A if the quantity in Column A is greater than the quantity in Column B.

   Choose B if the quantity in Column B is greater than the quantity in Column A.

   Choose C if the quantity in Column A is equal to the quantity in Column B.

   Choose D if you don't have enough information to determine the relationship between the quantities.
5. **Don't fill in an answer E under any circumstances.**

   Quantitative comparisons have no answer choice E.

Tips and tricks

- Bear in mind that if the columns look equal, there's usually a trap.
- Remember that if a figure is not drawn to scale, the answer is often choice D. If a picture is drawn to scale, the answer is rarely D.
- When the answer depends on how you draw the figure, choose D.
- Cancel quantities that are identical in both columns.
- Compare each part of Column A to its counterpart in Column B.
- When plugging in numbers, use 1, 2, 0, –1, –2, and ½, in that order.
- Plug in 100 for dollars and percentages.
- Plug in consecutive terms first and then non-consecutive terms.

Three FOIL Expressions to Memorize

- $(a + b)^2 = a^2 + 2ab + b^2$
- $(a - b)^2 = a^2 - 2ab + b^2$
- $(a - b)(a + b) = a^2 - b^2$

The Problem Solving Question Review

The approach for Problem Solving questions with multiple-choice answers provided

1. **Read the problem through carefully and circle what the question is asking for.**
2. **Predict how hard the problem is or how time-consuming it will be to solve.**
3. **Preview the answer choices.**
4. **Solve the problem forward and backward (plugging in the multiple-choice answers).**

The approach for Problem Solving questions without multiple-choice answers

1. **Read the problem through carefully and circle what the question is asking for.**
2. **Predict how hard the problem is or how time-consuming it will be to solve.**
3. **Solve the problem, double- and triple-checking your equations and calculations.**
4. **Darken in your answer, being sure to put it in the form requested.**

Tips and tricks when multiple-choice answers are provided

- Remember that easy problems often have easy answers.
- Eliminate illogical answer choices.
- Don't choose a "close enough" answer.
- Don't be afraid to skip.
- Give your pencil a workout. Plug in numbers, write down formulas, and draw pictures.

General Math Tips

- Bring a calculator.
- Keep in mind that the SAT doesn't test calculus or trigonometry.
- Remember that formulas are given at the end of the directions.

by Suzee Vlk
Author of *The ACT For Dummies, The GRE For Dummies, The GMAT For Dummies*

Wiley Publishing, Inc.

The SAT* I For Dummies®, 5th Edition

Published by
Wiley Publishing, Inc.
909 Third Avenue
New York, NY 10022
www.wiley.com

Published by Wiley Publishing, Inc., Indianapolis, Indiana

Published simultaneously in Canada

For general information on our other products and services or to obtain technical support, please contact our Customer Care Department within the U.S. at 800-762-2974, outside the U.S. at 317-572-3993, or fax 317-572-4002.

Wiley also publishes its books in a variety of electronic formats. Some content that appears in print may not be available in electronic books.

Library of Congress Control Number: 2002106032

ISBN: 0-7645-5472-7

Manufactured in the United States of America

10 9 8 7 6 5 4 3 2 1

5B/QZ/QY/QS/IN

About the Author

Suzee Vlk

"I'm not a complete idiot. Parts of me are missing."

Although more likely to admit to being a mortician, used-car salesperson, or guinea pig for Army experiments, Suzee Vlk has been a test prep specialist since 1975, working her way through law school and graduate business school teaching courses in SAT, ACT, LSAT, GRE, GMAT, and TOEFL preparation. She found the paranoia and take-no-prisoners mind-set required for doing well on the SAT a big help in developing cut-throat tactics to use in the courtroom or boardroom.

Today Suzee is president of Suzee Vlk Test Prep (no ego involved in *that* company name!) and has taught thousands of students in dozens of courses at universities and private corporations. (All victims have, so far, survived.) She has written materials used in SAT preparation software and videos (starring in one set of videos when she was younger and blonder) and had a test prep column that ran in several California high school newspapers. Her prep books for the SAT and other standardized exams have been published worldwide.

Suzee currently specializes in one-on-one tutorials and teaches SAT prep tricks and traps to all levels of students, from those who are overjoyed to be able to walk upright ("My knuckles don't bleed anymore!") to whiz kids who will probably be her bosses one day. Her students have not only been accepted at colleges and universities worldwide, including such dream schools as Harvard, Yale, Stanford, and the Naval Academy, but have done well enough on their SATs to be awarded scholarships (to the unbounded joy of their parents, who can now spend their kids' college funds on sailboats and other midlife-crisis toys).

One of Suzee's students, Craig Kessler, had the following to say about his tutoring sessions: "With Suzee's help (and despite her horrible jokes), I raised my score over 300 points!"

Suzee lives by the following motto, which she is delighted to share with you.

"Madness takes its toll. Please have exact change ready."

Dedication

This book is dedicated to Fran, George, and Ron Vlk, my family, who have made me what I am today (and yet somehow escaped being locked up). My friends also deserve much of the blame for the warped outlook I have developed and that comes through in these pages: Marcy Stras, Kim Buchanan, Gwen Morgan, Jane Kinoshita, Janet and Marshall Thompson, Lael Kovtun (*and* Jay), and everyone else who can't wait to tell me the latest jokes but skates away when I say *I've* heard a good one.

Author's Acknowledgments

After years of having California students groan at my puns (they frequently remind me of the Fred Allen joke that "hanging is too good for a person who makes puns; he should be drawn and quoted"), make rude hand gestures in response to my scintillatingly clever quips, and threaten to storm out of the room if I tell my geometry jokes one more time, it's wonderful to get the chance to inflict my dysfunctional sense of humor on a worldwide, unsuspecting audience. The decline of civilization begins here.

Thanks to my agent, Bill Gladstone of Waterside Productions in Cardiff, California, for getting me this opportunity. A thousand thanks to Dani Grubbs for her quick response to my many desperate pleas for help, and for all her input. Special thanks to Tere Drenth, Milissa Koloski, Kathy Welton, Sarah Kennedy, Diane Steele, Kristin Cocks, and Mary Corder. Kudos and plaudits to my ever-diplomatic series editor, Colleen Rainsberger, for her professionalism, punctiliousness, and extreme patience. Many thanks also go to this book's cast of long-suffering editors: Suzanne Thomas, Diana Conover, Pam Mourouzis, Bill Barton, Corbin Collins, and Kathy Cox. Thanks to Matt McMillion, Dr. Della Bell, Dr. Margaret Benedict, Elsa Bethanis, Marcy D. Manning, Richard Menke, Colin Rizzio, and Dr. Cary Wintz, who reviewed the manuscript for technical accuracy. The comedy panel and test testers, Nick Bednarek, Joe Bednarek, Shane Brown, Wendy Carmichael, Josh Horrigan, Hiley Smallwood, Kalleen Steele, and Drew Steele, made sure that my humor didn't go overboard and my examples were hip.

It's important for me to acknowledge one of the most underused and underappreciated resources today's students have: high school counselors. Thanks to all of you who go out of your way to help students to do their best to prepare for that rite of passage known as the SAT. Special thanks also to independent college counselor Jill Q. Porter, of La Jolla, California, for her insights on what colleges are looking for and how they use the SAT scores.

And finally, thanks go to my students over the years, those wonderful kids and adults who have had enough faith in me to use my tricks and tips . . . and enough kindness to let me share their joy in the good scores that result. (Michael Jensen of Stanford University — this means you!) You all keep this fun.

Publisher's Acknowledgments

We're proud of this book; please send us your comments through our Dummies online registration form located at `www.dummies.com/register/`.

Some of the people who helped bring this book to market include the following:

Acquisitions, Editorial, and Media Development

Project Editor: Tere Drenth

(Previous Editions: Ryan Rader, Barb Terry)

Acquisitions Editor: Kathy M. Cox

Technical Editor: Matthew McMillion

Editorial Supervisor: Michelle Hacker

Editorial Assistant: Carol Strickland

Production

Project Coordinator: Dale White

Layout and Graphics: Joyce Haughey, Jacque Schneider, Betty Schulte, Rashell Smith, Erin Zeltner

Proofreaders: Laura Albert, Dave Faust, Andy Hollandbeck, Arielle Carole Mennelle, Susan Moritz, Angel Perez, Carl Pierce, Dwight Ramsey, Charles Spencer

Indexer: Johnna VanHoose

Publishing and Editorial for Consumer Dummies

Diane Graves Steele, Vice President and Publisher, Consumer Dummies

Joyce Pepple, Acquisitions Director, Consumer Dummies

Kristin A. Cocks, Product Development Director, Consumer Dummies

Michael Spring, Vice President and Publisher, Travel

Brice Gosnell, Publishing Director, Travel

Suzanne Jannetta, Editorial Director, Travel

Publishing for Technology Dummies

Andy Cummings, Vice President and Publisher

Composition Services

Gerry Fahey, Vice President of Production Services

Debbie Stailey, Director of Composition Services

Contents at a Glance

Cartoons at a Glance

By Rich Tennant

"I wish you'd practice for the math section of the SATs on your own time and not when you're calculating the tip on three cheeseburger specials with Cokes all around."

page 93

"If it's okay for them to ask experimental questions, I figure it should be okay for me to give some experimental answers."

page 193

Darryl makes a big mistake during the break in his SAT exam.

page 331

"That 'Analogies' section was a snap. It was like taking candy from a fish."

page 35

"You're a stand-up guy, Jimmy. You made your hits, did your time and never ratted on nobody. And I would like to promote you in this organization, but OH-look at these SAT scores you made! I mean, c'mon-this is embarrassin'."

page 7

Cartoon Information:
Fax: 978-546-7747
E-Mail: richtennant@the5thwave.com
World Wide Web: www.the5thwave.com

Table of Contents

Introduction

Welcome to *The SAT I For Dummies,* 5th Edition. Don't take the title personally. You're no dummy; you're just normal. Unfortunately, the SAT is anything *but* normal. As I've learned in more than two decades of fighting the SAT wars, the SAT has no connection to the Real World. No matter how great your high school teachers are (or were), many of them aren't prepared to equip you for this battle. High school teachers can give you good math and verbal backgrounds, but the particular weapons (skills) you need for the SAT are best provided by a specialist. Think of this book as a SWAT team you can call in when the situation gets desperate.

Like a SWAT team, this book aims to deal with the crisis efficiently, do the job, save the day, and get you out as quickly as possible. I know that you have a life you'd like to get back to. The goal of this book is to help you learn what you need and can use on the SAT — period. No extra garbage is thrown in to impress you; no filler is added to make this book the fattest one on the market. If you need a doorstop, go pick up the New York City telephone directory. If you need a quick 'n' easy guide to surviving the SAT, you're in the right place.

In one way, this book beats even a SWAT team: It can make you laugh. I believe in humor as a learning tool. Too many test prep books are dull, dull, dull. Hey, the SAT is dull and boring enough; there's no need to add insult to injury by going through a prep program that bores you to tears. In *The SAT I For Dummies,* 5th Edition, you'll laugh while you learn. For example, if you're suffering through geometry, why not lighten up with a joke like this:

What did Humphrey Bogart say to his geometry teacher?

"Here's looking at Euclid!"

I got a million of 'em, but they're sprinkled throughout. You'll have to read the entire book to get to all the jokes.

About This Book

It's You versus Them. Who are They? Sadists Against Teenagers, the creators of the SAT. You can't avoid them if you intend to go to college. More and more colleges are emphasizing SAT scores to compensate for the grade inflation that skews GPAs (grade point averages). Because an A from Whiz Kid Central is not the same as an A from Merely Mediocre High, colleges need a standardized mode for comparing students. Believe it or not, that's good news for you. By doing well on this test, you can overcome years of goofing off in school. A dynamite SAT score can get you into a college or university that may not even look at you and your C+ (or lower) GPA otherwise.

In *The SAT I For Dummies,* 5th Edition, you discover how to approach each type of question, recognize the traps that are built in to the questions, and master the tricks that help you to avoid those traps. The book is full of gotchas that I (a test prep tutor since the Dawn of Time) have seen students fall for repeatedly. In this book, you begin to think the SAT way, identifying the point behind the various styles and types of questions and what each is trying to test. This book also gives you a review of the basics (math formulas and roots, prefixes and suffixes useful for improving your vocabulary) along with a laugh or two to make digesting the material as painless as possible. (Only the lame humor itself will hurt. . . .)

Note to nontraditional students: Not everyone reading this book is 16 or 17. Maybe you took a few years off after high school before deciding to head for college and are just now getting back into math and verbal stuff that you had in what seems like another lifetime. I sympathize with you; it's tough to deal with nonagons, quadratic equations, and analogies again. Don't despair; you can get outside help, especially in math, which is one of the first things to go for most people when they get away from school. Call a high school or community college for help finding a tutor or for suggestions on finding a quick review course in your area. You can also call your local library for assistance. Just please, please don't give in to despair and give up too quickly. As after-dinner speakers are fond of saying, "After the Middle Ages comes the Renaissance. . . ."

Pardon Me for Having a Life: Who Has Time for This?

You have school or work, sports or other after-school activities, family responsibilities, and, when your parents lighten up, a social life. How on earth are you going to fit in studying for the SAT?

Time required to go through the SAT "lecture" chapters

Buying this book was brilliant. (Okay, so your dad bought it and threw it at you with the demand that you study *or else.* He — or whomever — was brilliant for buying these pearls of wisdom.) How much time should you take to go through it? I suggest 23 hours.

Each subject (Analogies, Sentence Completions, Critical Reading, Quantitative Comparisons, and Problem Solving) includes a chapter that discusses the format, approach, and tricks and traps for that particular type of question. A quiz chapter, featuring questions that test what you learn in the discussion chapter, follows each discussion chapter. The detailed answer explanations point out the traps you may have fallen for and the tips you *should* have used to avoid the traps. You find out which questions to skip (as either too hard or too time-consuming) and which to double-check. Each section, including the quiz, should take you about two hours. The book also includes a three-part math review in Part III; each section (geometry, algebra, and arithmetic) should take roughly one hour, for a total of three hours.

Time required to go through the practice SATs

At the end of the book are two full-length SATs. (I left out the experimental sections; no need to make you suffer any more than you absolutely have to.) Each test takes 2½ hours (not including the 10-minute breaks you can give yourself at the end of each hour of testing) and about another hour or hour and a half to review. My thinking that you should take an hour and a half to review the test is not a slam. I'm not saying that you're such a loser that you're going to miss a ton of questions. My suggestion is that you review *all* the answer explanations, even for the questions you answer correctly. You'll learn some good stuff there, review formulas, find shortcuts, and see even more tricks and traps. So, I'll exaggerate and say that the whole test and review should take you five hours. The following table gives you (what I think is) a reasonable timetable.

Activity	*Time*
5 verbal review chapters at 2 hours per chapter	10 hours
3 math review chapters at 1 hour per chapter	3 hours
2 tests at 5 hours per test	10 hours
Time spent laughing hysterically at author's jokes	5 minutes
Time spent composing letter complaining about author's lame jokes	5 minutes
Total	**23 hours, 10 minutes**

No one expects you to do these 23 hours all at once. Each chapter is self-contained. The answer explanations may remind you of information from other chapters because repetition aids learning and memorizing, but you can do each chapter separately from the others.

Are you ready? Stupid question. Are you resigned? Have you accepted your fate that you're going to take the SAT no matter what and you may as well have fun studying for it? Take a deep breath and go for it. Good luck. Here's hoping that, for you, SAT comes to stand for Success And Triumph!

How This Book Is Organized

The SAT I For Dummies, 5th Edition, is organized into five parts to help you quickly get right to the chapters you need.

Part I: An Aerial View: Putting the SAT into Perspective

Part I is an overview of the exam, explaining what it tests, how the scoring works, and so on.

Part II: A Word to the Wise: Verbal Questions

This part covers the verbal (sometimes called qualitative) portion of the SAT: the Analogies, Sentence Completion, and Critical Reading questions.

Part III: Two Years of Math in Three Hours: The Dreaded Math Reviews and Mini-Tests

Part III takes you into the thrilling world of math, including Quantitative Comparisons, Problem Solving questions with multiple choice answers, and grid-in questions. As a "gift with purchase," you even get three math reviews: geometry, algebra, and miscellaneous math.

Part IV: It All Comes Down to This: Full-Length Practice SATs

This is the part you've either been waiting for or dreading. Here, you find two full-length SATs that look similar to the real deal. Although these questions are not identical to what you'll see on the SAT, they're close enough for good practice.

Part V: The Part of Tens

Assuming you've survived all that excitement, the book finishes up with the good stuff, The Part of Tens. There's much important stuff in this part, and it's also a lot of fun to read.

Icons Used in This Book

To help you get through this book more quickly, I include some icons that flag the particularly important information. If you need to work on your vocabulary, for example, flip through the book to find the Vocabulary icons and make a list of the accompanying words and their meanings. The icons look like this:

Be wary of the important warnings that this icon points out. If you skip these paragraphs, I claim no responsibility for what may happen to you.

The test makers throw in some nasty traps that may "get" you if you don't think about the questions carefully. Learn the tricks marked by this icon, and you'll be amazed at how easily you can outsmart the SAT.

This icon directs you to tips that can make taking the SAT go much more smoothly.

This icon marks sample problems that appear in the chapter discussion.

This icon points out words that you may not know. Memorizing these words and their definitions may help you on the SAT. The words themselves are in a special typeface — ***like this*** — and their meanings appear next to them.

This icon points out information pertaining to international students and suggestions that can make life easier if English is your second or third language. It notes instances in which English words are similar to those in your native tongue, such as *diabolical* (which means evil, like the devil) from the Spanish *diablo, devil.*

Where to Go from Here

If you use this book just to prop open a door or as a booster step so that you can sneak out of the bathroom window when you're grounded, you won't get the best out of it. I suggest two alternatives:

- **Fine-tune your skills.** Turn to specific sections for specific information and help. The organization of the book makes it very easy to find the type of math question you always have trouble with, suggestions for answering reading questions without having finished the passage, and tricks for guessing. If you're nearly perfect and need just a nudge in one or two areas, you can work through only those sections.
- **Start from scratch.** Read through the whole book. Actually, this approach is the one I'd like you to do. No matter how well you do on a section, you can improve. It's a common mistake to believe that you should work on your weakest sections only. The 50 points you gain in your mediocre section by skimming through the suggestions are just as worthwhile as the 50 points you get by grunting and groaning and sweating and fretting through the most difficult portions. If you have the time, do yourself a favor and read the book from cover to cover.

The SAT I For Dummies, 5th Edition, is simple and straightforward, so if you're a first-time SAT victim, er, taker, you can understand the whole test and do well right out of the starting gate. But it's also detailed and sophisticated enough so that if you're a veteran — if you've taken the test once or twice before but aren't resting on your laurels (sounds painful, anyway) — you can get the more complicated information that you need to achieve those truly excellent scores.

Part I

An Aerial View: Putting the SAT into Perspective

"You're a stand-up guy, Jimmy. You made your hits, did your time and never ratted on nobody. And I would like to promote you in this organization, but OH—look at these SAT scores you made! I mean, c'mon—this is embarrassin'."

In this part . . .

I know, I know — the only aerial view you'd like to have of the SAT is the one you see from 20,000 feet up as a jet takes you far, far away from this test. Use the info in this book correctly, and you can ace the SAT, go to a top college, and get a great job — and then buy your own private jet and buzz the high schools when the SAT is being given. Hey, it's something to aim for.

You're probably eager to get right into studying for the SAT (or maybe not), but take a few minutes to go through this part, which in addition to giving you a bird's-eye view of the test, also shares tips and tricks for succeeding on the SAT and for being the type of applicant that colleges want.

Chapter 1

Knowing Your Enemy: The SAT Up Close

In This Chapter

- Putting it all in perspective: number and types of questions
- Clocking in: timing it right
- Doing the backpack boogie: what to take to the test with you
- Dealing with unusual circumstances
- Scoring the exam (and canceling scores)
- Avoiding the serial guesser syndrome
- Repeating the test

Need to get some sense of perspective regarding the SAT? Table 1-1 provides a quick overview of what the SAT is all about, how many questions there are, and how much time you have. The sections of the test may be arranged in any order.

Table 1-1 SAT Breakdown by Section

Section	*Number of Questions*	*Time Allotted*
Verbal	30	30 minutes
Math	25	30 minutes
Verbal	35	30 minutes
Math	25	30 minutes
Verbal	11–13 (it varies)	15 minutes
Math	10	15 minutes
Experimental	25–35	30 minutes (This section is called the *equating* section and may be verbal or math)

Table 1-2 shows another way to look at the SAT: by the number of each type of question.

Table 1-2 SAT Breakdown by Question Style (excluding the experimental questions, which don't count toward your score)

Question Type	*Number of Questions*
Analogies	19
Sentence Completions	19
Critical Reading	40
Total verbal questions	**78**
Quantitative Comparisons	15
Problem Solving with multiple-choice answers	35
Problem Solving without multiple-choice answers	10
Total math questions	**60**
Total SAT questions (verbal and math)	**138**

Want it spelled out? You have three verbal sections and three math sections. Two verbal sections are 30 minutes each; one verbal section is 15 minutes. Two math sections are 30 minutes each; one math section is 15 minutes. You also have a 30-minute experimental section (discussed in the following section), which may be verbal or math.

Add it all up, and you find that the test itself takes three hours (not including the bladder breaks discussed in the "Gimme a Break! The SAT Intermission" section). Keep in mind, though, that you'll probably be at the test site for at least four hours (the test is officially scheduled from 8:30 to 12:30), including the time before the test when the proctors give out the papers and go through directions. In other words, kiss the whole morning good-bye.

Eighteen Hundred Totally Wasted Seconds: The Experimental (Equating) Section

The SAT has seven sections. Six of the sections count; one is a complete waste of your valuable time and limited brainpower. Called an "equating" section, this section is usually referred to by students and tutors as an *experimental section* because you're being used in an experiment by the SAT question writers. You are the guinea pig on whom questions are tested that may be used on future tests.

You will not, repeat, will *not,* know which section is experimental. It could be either a verbal or a math section. If you get four verbal sections, you'll know that one of them is experimental . . . but which one? If you get four math sections, you'll know that one of them is experimental . . . but which one? Don't try to outfox the test makers. What if you think you know which section is experimental? Then you'll probably kick back and veg out for a half hour and not do any questions. But what if (gasp!) you're wrong? If you guessed wrongly, you just blew one entire section of the SAT. (Don't laugh; I've had students do that before.) In short, don't try to guess which section is experimental; just do your best on every section.

A student's not-so-serious take on the SAT

Maybe preparing for the SAT has you feeling ***irritated, exasperated, incensed***, or other SAT-type vocabulary terms for *ticked off*. If so, you may enjoy reading the following tongue-in-cheek essay submitted by one of my students:

> Surely the most wonderful, exciting, thrill-a-minute thing that all teenagers get to do during their high school careers is to take the Scholastic Assessment Test, more commonly known as the SAT.
>
> Because I personally have had *soooo* much fun preparing for this excellent test, I've decided to prepare a short guide to taking the SAT. I hope this guide will be helpful for those students who have to — I mean, have the great privilege of being allowed to — go through what I'm going through now.
>
> First, you should start studying early. I made a late start, not opening an SAT prep guide until I was in fifth grade. I would advise you to begin in kindergarten, in order to get an extra edge over your peers. One of my friend's parents played SAT verbal tapes to her while she was in the womb. The tapes paid off when my friend got a perfect 800 on the verbal portion of the test.
>
> Point two: My suggestion is that you skip doing any homework whatsoever during high school in order to focus all of your free time on studying for the SAT. You know free time: what you have left over after you've won the Olympics, toured the world with the Prague Symphony Orchestra, joined 80 different school clubs, started your own business, saved the world. . . and of course got the 30 minutes of sleep you require nightly. So what if your high school grades are terrible? When you get a 1600 on your SAT, do you think colleges will really care about your grades?
>
> My third piece of advice is that you forget about having a social life. It's imperative that you spend every waking moment cramming for the SAT. At 16, when I began to drive, I found it helpful to listen to SAT tapes in the car going to and from school. Otherwise I would have wasted 30 valuable minutes doing nothing but driving or chatting with my friends. I also brought the tapes along on my dates, sharing them with my boyfriend. (I'm sure he appreciated my help. I'll get his new girlfriend to ask him whether he did.)
>
> Naturally, it's very important that you spend all of your parents' hard-earned money on several expensive SAT prep courses. Spend your weekends listening to a teacher drone on about how "critical reading can be fun!" and how "getting the answer right is important." (Duh!) Focus strongly on the verbal portion of the exam, as you will, of course, need to use such big words as "pulchritudinous," "avuncular," "spoonerism," "pusillanimous," and "sartorial" on a daily basis in the real world. This doesn't mean, however, that you can ignore the math portions of the test. Even if you have been a math whiz since the second grade, you can fall for some of the tricks built into the exam. Now, wouldn't you be embarrassed at missing something easy like "If $n * m = n$ multiplied by 3! squared divided by the fifth root of x times m, what is 5 * 8?"
>
> That brings me to my suggestions for the day before the SAT. Why not skip school in order to cram for this life-determining exam? Make sure to get plenty of sleep that night, as well. If you don't go to bed before 5 p.m., you might not be able to perform your best and have tons of fun taking the exam. No exam proctor likes a cranky student! Be sure to follow a low-fat, high-protein, low soy-product, high-lactose diet for at least a year before the exam!
>
> On the day of the big event, it's best to wear your most comfortable outfit — I showed up to take my exam in my underwear! Have a good breakfast and arrive at the testing center at least three hours early to be sure you're on time. Recently, kids interviewed after the test said that the best way to enjoy the testing experience was to be very, very nervous and hyperventilate throughout the entire exam while contemplating how these 138 problems would determine the rest of their lives. Be sure to make friends with your proctor, so she can read out the directions in an even more monotonous voice than usual. Also, I suggest bringing an alarm clock into the exam and setting it for five minutes before each section is to end. This not only alerts you that time is running out, but breaks the concentration of all the others in the room, meaning that they will score worse than you will.
>
> Well, I hope my little guide has helped you to feel more prepared for studying for the SAT. Good luck studying and remember — have fun! Don't worry at all about the pressure to do well in these three most important hours of your life!
>
> — by Michelle Marco, of San Diego, California (accepted to Stanford University)

Gimme a Break! The SAT Intermission

Yes, you get a break at the end of each hour of testing. Depending on whether your bladder is the size of Rhode Island or Texas, you'll probably spend most of it in the bathroom. Do yourself a favor: Don't drink more than a mouthful or eat much during the break. There's nothing worse than sitting there crossing and uncrossing your legs during the test, feeling your eyeballs slowly turn yellow.

You may want to take some munchies to eat at the breaks, but make sure that they're nutritious and low in sugar. Sugar makes you high for a few minutes and then brings you way down. You don't need to crash right in the middle of a quadratic equation ("Twinkie Trauma: Film at 11 . . ."). Take a handful of peanuts, some trail mix, or anything that won't send all the blood from your brain down to your stomach for digestion. Life's hard enough without trying to figure out how to find the interior angles of a nonagon by using your stomach instead of your brain.

Beating the Clock: Timing Tips

As you go through the chapters in this book that show you how to approach each question style (on your knees, humbly and submissively acknowledging the awesome power of the SAT), you'll find out how much time to allot to each style of question. In general, questions go from easier to harder. The last two or three questions in each section are incredibly difficult — so hard that only those students with brains oozing out their ears get them right. If you're an oozer, go for it. But if you're like most people, you may want to skip those super-hard ones at the end. Doing so frees up more time for the easy- and medium-level ones in the rest of the section. In other words, don't worry about finishing every single question. You can get a terrific SAT score even with quite a bit of skipping. (See the "Number of correct answers needed for specific scores" section, later in this chapter.)

One last point: Don't take a watch that beeps on the hour. Proctors get ticked off (ticked off — get it? Oh, lighten up!) if they think your watch is disturbing others. They're likely to take it away. (I did have one particularly quick-witted student who told the proctor that the noise she heard was his stomach growling. The proctor bought it, even though she must have wondered why the kid's stomach gurgled only at three minutes before the hour, every hour.)

Fun fact: Do you suffer from borborygmus? Probably; most people do. ***Borborygmus*** is the name for tummy rumbling. (Don't panic! This is not an SAT word, just something fun to spring on your parents at the dinner table to impress them with your brilliance.)

Six things not to do during the SAT

Be sure to avoid the following:

- Trying to get the telephone number of the stud/babe sitting next to you.
- Picturing the proctor naked.
- Clipping your toenails and arranging them on your desk to try to determine the number of degrees in the arc of a circle.
- Swapping underwear with your best friend during the break "for luck."
- Making rude noises, hoping to distract the other students and make your score look better in comparison to theirs.
- Trying to impress the babe/stud next to you by answering your cellular telephone with, "Yes, Mr. President? A matter of national security? I'll be right there, Mr. President!"

What's the difference between the SAT I, SAT II, and ACT?

Many people confuse the SAT I with the SAT II, and the ACT with the old ACH (achievement tests). The following points can help you to keep these three very different exams clear.

- **Who requires the tests?**

  The SAT I, the basic SAT, is required by nearly all colleges and universities.

  The SAT II, the Single Subject Tests (these used to be called the Achievement Tests; some college materials still call them that), are not required by most universities (except in California).

  The ACT is not required by a lot of schools but is accepted by many as an alternative to the SAT I. In other words, you can take both the SAT I and the ACT. Usually, the school will use whichever score is higher.

  Find out from your specific schools which exams are required. This information is given in the school application form and bulletins.

- **What's tested by these exams?**

  The SAT I tests verbal skills (primarily vocabulary and reading) and math skills (arithmetic, basic geometry, and algebra).

  The SAT II tests individual subjects, ranging from literature to biology to U.S. history to Japanese. Seventeen subject tests are available.

  The ACT tests reading comprehension, English grammar, science reasoning, and math (arithmetic, algebra, geometry, and a little trigonometry).

- **Which test is the easiest?**

  The SAT I is easiest if your vocabulary is good, but your grammar is bad (because it has no grammar on it). Some students also think the math on the SAT I is easier than the math on either the SAT II or the ACT, mostly because the SAT I has quantitative comparisons, which you can ace after you know the tricks; the SAT II and ACT have only basic multiple-choice math.

  The SAT II grammar and math are about the same level of difficulty as the ACT grammar and math. Other individual subjects, such as the chemistry test, can be quite challenging.

  The ACT is easier than the SAT I in the reading comprehension (I'm told by my students) but harder in the math. The good news is that the ACT has no vocabulary (no analogies or sentence completions like the SAT I) and so is good if you have a weak vocabulary.

- **How are the tests scored?**

  The SAT I has a verbal score of 200 to 800 and a math score of 200 to 800. Each correct question counts one point; each omitted question counts zero points. A wrong answer can have no penalty (grid-in math questions) or cost you a third of a point (Quantitative Comparisons) or a quarter of a point (all the multiple-choice questions).

  The SAT II scores also go from 200 to 800. You get a point for every right answer and zero points for every omitted answer. You lose ¼ point for every wrong answer.

  The ACT scores range from 1 to 36 (don't ask; the scoring system is definitely weird. You can read more about it in *The ACT For Dummies,* 3rd Edition, written by me and published by Wiley Publishing, Inc.). The ACT doesn't subtract points for wrong answers (unlike the SAT I and SAT II), so even wild guessing can help you.

- **How long does each test take?**

  The SAT takes 3 hours. You have five 30-minute sections (two verbal, two math, one experimental) and two 15-minute sections (one verbal and one math).

  The SAT II takes one hour for each subject test.

  The ACT takes 2 hours and 55 minutes (45 minutes for the English test; 60 minutes for the math test; 35 minutes for the science test; 35 minutes for the reading test).

- **When are the tests given?**

  The SAT I is given seven times a year, usually in October, November, December, January, March, May, and June.

  The SAT II is given six times a year, usually in October, November, December, January, May, and June. The SAT I and SAT II are given on the same day at the same time; you can't take both exams on the same administration date.

  The ACT is given five times a year, usually in October, December, February, April, and June. Often, the ACT is given one week after the SAT I.

Have you taken the ACT (an alternate entrance test accepted by many colleges)? If so, you know that on the ACT you should guess at every question because you don't lose points for wrong answers. Alas, the SAT isn't so nice. On the SAT, there is a *penalty* for a wrong answer. Every answer you miss counts $-\frac{1}{4}$ point (that's MINUS one-quarter point), or $-\frac{1}{3}$ point, depending on the type of question. Therefore, random guessing can seriously hurt you. Don't just wildly fill in all the ovals when the proctor calls time. (Scoring is discussed in excruciating detail in the "Everyone Wants to Score" section later in this chapter. Please try to restrain your thirst for knowledge until then.)

Your Brain — Don't Leave Home without It (and Other Things to Take to the SAT)

Take your brain down from the shelf, dust it off, and take it to the test with you. In addition, you'll want to jam a couple more items in your backpack or purse.

- **Admission ticket:** Your admission ticket should come in the mail a week or two before the actual test. If you haven't gotten it by one week before the test, call the College Board at 609-771-7600. If your dog ate your ticket or you lost the ticket, call the same number. Face it: There's no way you're going to get out of it. They have your number (and now you have theirs).

- **Photo ID:** You have to take a picture ID with you. You can't, however, use that great snapshot of you from last year's Halloween party when you looked so hot in your caveman/cavewoman leopard skin; you must use a current, recognizable photo (shoulders drooping, eyes glazed over from studying for this test). You can use your driver's license, a passport, or a school ID. If you don't have any of these, you can bring in a piece of school stationery with a description of yourself signed by the school principal or guidance counselor. Some forms of identification are not acceptable, including a library card, social security card, birth certificate, or a credit card (even if it does have your photo on it).
- **Map or directions:** Be sure you know how to get to the test center. Drive there a few days before the SAT and check out how long the drive takes you, where to park, and so on. The last thing you need the morning of the test is more stress.
- **Pencils:** Take two, three, or a dozen sharpened number two pencils with you. Take a small pencil sharpener and a good eraser as well (for the *remote* chance that you're not perfect after all).
- **Watch:** The clock in the test room may not work, or it may be in some corner of the room way behind your seat such that you have to keep twisting and turning to see the time. It's easier to take a watch with you. Just be sure that it doesn't have a beeper. Proctors often confiscate watches that beep and disturb other test takers.
- **Calculator:** Since March 1994, you've been allowed to use a calculator on the SAT. Let the rejoicing begin! Don't go out and buy a new calculator for the test; use the one you've been comfortable using every day.

  You won't even use your calculator for most problems. Forget dishing out fifty bucks for a calculator with a zillion functions; save the money for the celebration party when you get your SAT scores back.

- **Clothes:** You signed up for the special Nude SAT, you say? Well, everybody else should remember to take a few extra layers. Classrooms are notorious for being either freezing cold or boiling hot. You don't want to sit in a room for three hours shivering because you've been cold or sweating all over your answer grid from the heat.

The watch game: Using your watch to simplify taking the test

Here's the deal: The proctor — whom you're pretty sure you saw on America's Most Wanted last week — tells you at 8:47 that you may begin. You have 35 questions. The time is now 9:09, and you're on question 17. How are you doing for time? Can you relax and slow down, or is it Panic City?

Who needs this kind of stress? It's like adding on another whole math problem. Don't strain your brain; make life easier by resetting your watch. What's your lucky number? Three? Then when the proctor tells you to begin, set your watch for 2:30. That way, you're counting down the minutes to your lucky number. A glance at your watch tells you how many minutes you have left. Who cares what the time is outside in the Real World. You want to use your watch as a stopwatch for the SAT, not as a clock.

Question: What's the best time to see your dentist?

Answer: Two-thirty (Get it? Say it aloud.)

Knowing What Not to Take to the Test with You

You may as well leave the following items at home or in your car because you won't be allowed to take them into the test room with you:

- **Books and notes:** Forget about last-minute studying. If you don't know the material by then, you never will.
- **Scratch paper:** You're not allowed to bring scratch paper. The good news is that the test booklet has plenty of empty space on which to do your calculations and scribbling. I understand, however, that Educational Testing Service (ETS) owns the copyright to all Last Wills and Testaments written during the test. . . .
- **Testing aids:** You may not take in highlighters (which would be useful with the Critical Reading passages), rulers, compasses, protractors, or personal CD players, like a Walkman (so much for listening to that stress-reduction CD).

Everyone Wants to Score

You don't have the Ferrari yet. You don't have the six-digit paycheck yet. It's rough being 16 (or 18, or 25, or whatever). You need *something* to boast about. How about your SAT score? SAT scores are to high school students what salaries are to adults. Students brag about them, exaggerate them, or try to impress others with them. How does ETS figure out the scores?

How scores are determined

There are two separate scores: verbal and math. The combined score is what most people mean when they say "my SAT score." If your buddy tells you that he got a 1200 on the SAT, he's referring to the sum of his verbal and math scores.

Most colleges and universities look primarily at the combined scores. They may care about the individual math and verbal scores if you apply for some special scholarship or program; for example, if you're trying for admission to a math program, your math score is obviously considered more important than your verbal score.

I wish it were all Greek to me: A welcome to international students

Students all around the world take the SAT to attend schools in the U.S. I've taught SAT-prep courses that included students from Canada, the U.K., Mexico, Egypt, the Ivory Coast, Holland, India, Japan, Hong Kong, Israel, Brazil, China, Saudi Arabia — you name it. All over the globe, students have fretted and sweated over this test. If you're a reader from around the world who is trying to survive the SAT and come to school in America, welcome!

Because you grew up speaking a different language, living in a different culture, and attending a different educational system, your strengths and weaknesses are different from those of kids in the U.S. Therefore, the focus of your study should be different as well. In this book, I use an icon like the one in the upper-left corner of this text box to make comments directly to you. I point out questions that are so ridiculously hard, you may as well skip them, along with questions in which (believe it or not!) you have an advantage over the American kids. Look for those icons and pay special attention to them.

In addition, here are some suggestions to help you get the most from this book and do your absolute best on the SAT.

- **Concentrate on the analogies.** You probably have an advantage over American students in this section — especially if your native tongue is a Romance language, such as Spanish or French. Romance languages are Latin-based and commonly use words that are uncommon in English (and, naturally, show up on the SAT!). Take, for example, bibliophile. A Spanish speaker knows biblio means book (*biblioteca* means library) and can figure out this "hard" word pretty easily, especially if he or she has learned the roots in this book (phil = love). (A ***bibliophile*** is a book-lover.)

  One more thing: Because you've studied English, you're used to memorizing vocabulary tests (unlike American students who haven't taken vocabulary tests since junior high). Although you probably can't dramatically change your basic reading skills (for the Critical Reading passages) in a few hours, you can dramatically add to your vocabulary. You, more than American students, need to make lists of all the new words you encounter in this book and start learning them. (P.S. Go back and harass your English teacher with them. So many of the words in this book are super-hard that I bet even he or she won't know them. It'll be fun to show your teacher just how great your English has become!)

- **Don't stress out over Critical Reading.** The SAT's reading passages are long, hard, and boooooring. They are difficult enough to understand for people who grew up speaking and reading English, but are totally demoralizing for people who didn't. My suggestion is that you not take Critical Reading portions too seriously. Take your time, read one of the passages (there are two in most sections) very slowly and carefully, and try to answer the questions regarding just that passage. It's better to do fewer questions and get them right than to try to do all the questions and miss them. Remember, the SAT subtracts a quarter point off your raw score, and more off your converted (final) score, for each question you miss. It's better to skip, therefore, than to miss.

- **Concentrate on the math, especially geometry.** Although you do get separate verbal and math scores, many colleges focus on your overall or combined score. Doing extremely well on math can compensate for weaker verbal skills. I suggest that you pay particular attention to the geometry problems. They rarely are "word problems" — questions that require a lot of reading. Geometry problems usually feature figures that you can easily understand and use to answer the questions even if English is not your strong suit.

- **Avoid random, desperate guessing.** I've said it before, and I'll say it again: Wild guesses can hurt you. The SAT penalizes you for each wrong answer: You get 1 point for every correct answer, 0 points for every omitted answer, and minus either $\frac{1}{3}$ or $\frac{1}{4}$ point for every wrong answer, depending on the type of question. (Only one type of question, the math grid-ins, has no penalty for wrong answers.) It's better to skip than to miss a question. Keep in mind that you can skip a huge number of questions and still get a respectable score. For example, suppose you want a 500 in verbal, a score that's in the middle and is good enough for admission to quite a few colleges. You can get as low as 34 out of 78 questions right. That means you can skip 44 questions! You can skip more questions than you answer and still get a respectable score. However, if you answer all 78 questions, get 34 right, and 44 wrong, your score is only 420. You can raise your score 80 points by not making wild guesses.

How are scores determined? Well, ETS takes all the test booklets to the top of a very high tower and tosses them down. The ones that land on the top step get 800s, the ones that land on the middle steps get 400s . . . nah, just kidding. Sort of.

In general, it makes no difference whether you get a 1200 by getting a 600 verbal and a 600 math or by getting a 400 verbal and an 800 math. Your overall score is what counts. But I'll talk about those scores separately because you see them that way on the score report.

- **The verbal score:** The verbal score ranges from 200 to 800. The good news is that you don't have to be perfect to get a perfect score. On some editions of the SAT, you can get as low as a 75 out of 78 for your raw score and still get the perfect 800. If you sign your name but don't get any questions correct, your raw score is 0, but your scaled score is 230. To get down to a 200, you need a *negative* two (–2) for your raw score.
- **The math score:** The math score also ranges from 200 to 800. Fittingly enough, the math scores are more precise than the verbal scores; to get a perfect 800, you usually have to get a perfect 60 out of 60 questions correct. But you still get a 230 for signing your name (if your raw score is 0, you get 230), and you still can't get a 200 unless your raw score is negative (–2 gets you 200).

Many international students do better on the math than on the verbal. It's hard to know all the English vocabulary and very hard to get through those long and boring reading passages when English is your second language. But numbers are numbers. You can do an algebra problem just as quickly and as well as a student who grew up speaking English. Keep reminding yourself as you read through this book that most colleges care only about the combined score, so that every extra point you get in math is another point you can afford to lose in verbal.

You may get a chuckle from a joke my Japanese teacher told me: A mother mouse was taking her babies out for a walk when they encountered a huge, ferocious cat, eyeing them hungrily. The baby mice were terrified, but the mother mouse looked the cat right in the eye and yelled, "WOOF! WOOF!" The cat jumped and ran away. The mother mouse turned to her babies and said, "See? Didn't I tell you speaking a second language would be useful?"

How you win — and lose — points

You get one point for every answer you get correct.

You get zero points for every question you don't answer. Omitting an answer doesn't help you or hurt you (although leaving too many blank, of course, hurts in the long run).

You lose ⅓ point — the warped minds responsible for this test *subtract* a third of a point — for every Quantitative Comparison question (a strange type of math discussed in Chapter 13) you miss.

You lose ¼ point — the test makers subtract a fourth of a point — for every multiple-choice question you miss (math or verbal, it doesn't make a difference).

There is no penalty for a wrong answer on the ten grid-in math questions. These are the only questions on the entire test that can't hurt you. Be sure to fill in something, anything (your age; the number of points your football team scored last weekend; the number of pounds you want to lose before the prom), in case you get amazingly lucky and hit on the right answer.

All your pluses and minuses are added together, a magic wand is waved, three virgins are sacrificed, and somehow the scores are ***transmogrified*** (changed) into that 200-to-800 scale. Isn't modern science wonderful?

The whine cellar: What is a good score?

Your individual goals should depend on which colleges you are applying to and what GPA (grade point average) you have. There's no such thing as a passing or failing score — only what you need to get accepted to the college you have your heart set on.

However, college-planning books such as *Peterson's Guide to Four-Year Colleges, The College Blue Book,* and *College Planning For Dummies* (published by Wiley Publishing, Inc.) can help you figure out how your scores match up to the requirements of colleges.

Use the chart shown in Figure 1-1 to get a general idea of the relationship between SAT scores and levels of college admissions standards. Obviously, getting into the most difficult colleges requires the highest SAT scores, but take heart — no matter what your score, a college out there somewhere will be delighted to have you.

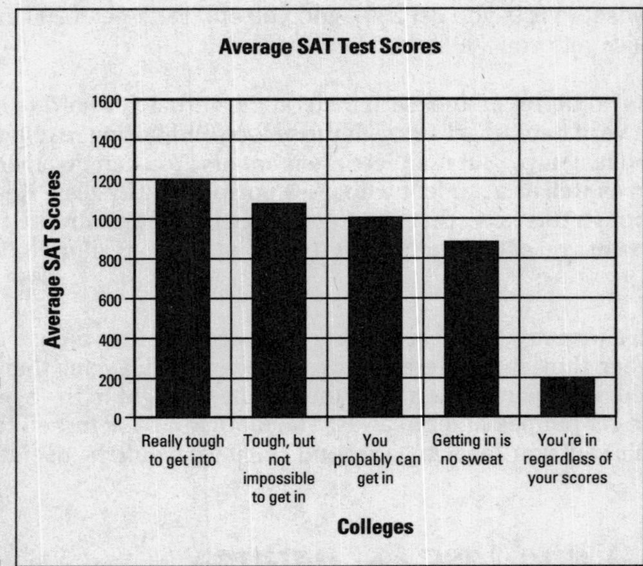

Figure 1-1: So what's the big deal about SAT scores?

Canceling scores and Score Choice

Suppose that you (heaven forbid!) get into a fender bender on the way to the test and are so shaken up during the test that you can't concentrate. You know as you're taking the test that you're blowing it. What can you do? You have the option of canceling your scores. If you decide right then and there to cancel, ask the proctor for a Request to Cancel Test Scores Form and fill it out. Or you can go home, calm down, and think about whether you really want to cancel your scores. You have until the Wednesday after the test to inform ETS in writing of your desire to cancel.

People have a lot of misconceptions about something called Score Choice. Score Choice applies to the SAT II: Subject Tests only, not to the regular ol' SAT I, the one for which you are preparing now (and Score Choice is being phased out soon, so that both the SAT I and SAT II will be the same.) Score Choice allows you to release to colleges only those SAT II scores you like. Colleges will never know all the exams you took, only those ones whose scores you send. Again, this option is *not* available for the SAT I. For the SAT I (the regular SAT), you can't send only your highest scores, or only your most recent scores, or only your math scores, or only your verbal scores. Everything goes. Every score you get goes on the score reports sent to the colleges. Some colleges may use only your highest scores or mix and match the highest verbal and the highest math (even from two different exams), but you have no say in the matter. All SAT I scores are sent to all colleges you designate.

Number of correct answers needed for specific scores

Here are rough estimates of how many questions you must answer correctly to get certain scores on each section. Keep in mind that these tallies are very rough and don't count penalty points. That is, I'm assuming that you don't actually miss any questions but just skip the ones you're not sure of.

Verbal scores

To get a 400, you need 18 out of 78 questions correct (about 23 percent).

To get a 500, you need 34 out of 78 questions correct (about 44 percent).

To get a 600, you need 52 out of 78 questions correct (about 67 percent).

To get a 700, you need 66 out of 78 questions correct (about 85 percent).

Math scores

To get a 400, you need 14 out of 60 questions correct (about 23 percent).

To get a 500, you need 29 out of 60 questions correct (about 48 percent).

To get a 600, you need 42 or 43 out of 60 questions correct (about 70 to 72 percent).

To get a 700, you need 54 out of 60 questions correct (about 90 percent).

Stop me before I guess again: Serial guessers

Given all these penalty points, should you guess? Yes and no. Random guessing can hurt you. If the proctor calls time (have you ever noticed how close the words *proctor* and *proctologist* are? Just a thought . . .), don't just start filling in all the As or all the Bs. It's better to leave the answers blank.

Statistically, you should guess if you can eliminate at least one answer. However, be forewarned that questions often have trap answers. If you aren't sure of your answer, you may want to skip the question unless you can narrow down the answers to two. Don't worry about it for now. As you go through each type of question in this book, you get suggestions on when to guess and when not to guess. Just remember: Guessing wildly is like trying to kiss someone in a dark room. You may get lucky and score the way you want — or you may end up kissing your fat Uncle Buford.

Déjà Vu All Over Again: Repeating the Test

Can repeating the test hurt you? Not really. Most schools look only at your highest score. (Find out from the individual schools whether this is their policy; not all schools do so.) If you're borderline or several students are vying for one spot, sometimes having taken the test repeatedly can hurt you (especially if your most recent score took a nose-dive). On the other hand, a college admissions counselor who sees several tests with ascending scores may be impressed that you stuck to it and kept trying, even if your score went up only a little bit. In general, if you're willing to take the time to study and take the repeat test seriously, go for it.

If you decide to retake the test, it's helpful to know exactly what you missed on the first one. Two options are available to you.

- **Question and Answer Service:** This service costs $10 (the price may go up soon) but is worth its weight in gold. If you send for this service (you can opt for it when you sign up for the test or get it as late as five months after the test), you get the actual questions from the test (except for the experimental questions, which don't count anyway), a copy of your answer grid, a copy of the correct answers, and the level of difficulty of each question. That way you can go over every single question and see exactly what you did right and wrong. This is a wonderful service. Unfortunately, it is often available for only two administrations a year, usually November and May. (Check your Registration Bulletin for the test dates that include this service.)
- **Student Answer Service:** For the other test administrations, you can pay $5 (price subject to change, of course) and get the Student Answer Service. You don't get a copy of the actual questions but a printout telling you, for example, that of 19 Analogy questions, you got 11 right, missed 4, and skipped 4. You'll see exactly how many of each type of question you got right, got wrong, or omitted, and the difficulty level of each question. Even though this doesn't provide as much info as the Question and Answer Service, it's still definitely worth getting.

Chapter 2

Succeeding on the SAT

In This Chapter

- Mellowing, chilling, and relaxing before and during the SAT
- Giving careless mistakes the raspberry by knowing ten critical points to double-check
- Identifying and sidestepping ten easy ways to mess up your score

On the wall of my office, I have a padded cushion that is imprinted with the words, "BANG HEAD HERE!" I've found that most of my students use it either to reduce stress (I guess one headache can replace another!) or — much more commonly — to express their exasperation over unnecessary, careless (I'm trying not to say it, but okay — dumb!) mistakes. Going through the material in this chapter about how to relax and how to recognize and avoid common mistakes can prevent your having to be a head-banger later.

Ten Relaxation Techniques You Can Try Before and During the SAT

Question: What sits at the bottom of the sea and shivers? ***Answer:*** A nervous wreck!

If you're too hyper and anxious to laugh at my lame jokes, you *really* need this section. Most people are tense before the test and have butterflies doing hip-hop in their stomachs. The key is to use relaxation techniques that keep your mind on your test and not on your tummy.

Breathe deeply

Breathing is grossly underrated. Breathing is good. Take a deep breath until your belly expands, hold your breath for a few counts, then expel the air through your nose. Try not to take short, shallow breaths, which could cause you to become even more anxious as your body becomes deprived of oxygen.

Rotate your head

Try to see behind your head. Move your head as far as possible to the right until you feel a tug on the skin on the left side of your neck. Then reverse it and move your head all the way to the left until you feel a tug on the skin on the right. Move your head back, as if you're looking at the ceiling, and then down, as if looking at your feet. You'll be surprised how much tension drains out of you after you do this a few times.

Note: Be careful that you perform this exercise with your eyes closed and make what you're doing obvious. You don't want a suspicious proctor to think that you're craning your neck to look at someone else's answer grid.

Hunch and roll your shoulders

While breathing in, scrunch up your shoulders as if you're trying to touch them to your ears. Then roll them back and down, breathing out. Arch your back, sitting up super-straight, as if a string is attached to the top of your head and is being pulled toward the ceiling. Then slump and round out your lower back, pushing it out toward the back of your chair. These exercises relax your upper and lower back. They are especially useful if you develop a kink in your spine.

Cross and roll your eyes

Cross your eyes and then look down as far as you can into your lower eyelids. Look to the right and then up into your eyelids, and then look to the left. After you repeat this sequence a few times, your eyes should be refreshed. Look down at your desk as you're doing this one so that people don't think that you're even stranger than they already know you are.

Shake out your hands

You probably do this automatically to try to get rid of writer's cramp. Do it more consciously and more frequently. Put your hands down at your sides, hanging them below your chair seat, and shake them vigorously. Imagine all the tension and stress going out through your fingers and dropping onto the floor.

Extend and push your legs

While you're sitting at your desk, straighten your legs out in front of you; think of pushing something away with your heels. Point the toes back toward your knees. You feel a stretch on the backs of your legs. Hold for a count of three and then relax.

Cup your eyes

Cup your hands and fingers together. Put them over your closed eyes, blocking out all the light. You're now in a world of velvety-smooth darkness, which is very soothing. Try not to let your hands actually touch your eyes. (If you see stars or flashes of light, your hands are pushing down on your eyes.)

Rotate your scalp

Put your open hand palm-down on your scalp. Move your hand in small circles. You feel your scalp rotate. Lift your hand and put it down somewhere else on your scalp. Repeat the circular motions. You're giving yourself a very relaxing scalp massage.

Curtail negative thoughts

Any time you feel yourself starting to panic or thinking negative thoughts, make a conscious effort to say to yourself, *"Stop!"* Don't dwell on anything negative; switch over to a positive track. Suppose that you catch yourself thinking, "Why didn't I study this vocabulary more?

I saw that word a hundred times but can't remember it now!" Change the script to "I got most of this vocabulary right; if I let my subconscious work on that word, maybe I'll get it, too. No sense worrying now. Overall, I think I'm doing great."

(And no fair asking yourself hypothetical questions, either. Wondering, "Why are they doing this to me?" is useless. You may as well ponder my favorite hypothetical question, "Why do feet smell and noses run?")

Visualize before the test or during a break

Don't do this *during* the test; you just waste time and lose concentration. Before the exam, however, or at the break, practice visualization. Close your eyes and imagine yourself in the test room, seeing questions that you know the answers to, cheerfully filling in the bubble grids, happily finishing early, and double-checking your work. Picture yourself leaving the test room uplifted and then, five weeks later, getting your scores and rejoicing. Think of how proud your parents are of you. Imagine the acceptance letter you get from your college. Picture yourself driving a red Ferrari 20 years from now, telling the *Time* magazine reporter in the passenger seat that your success started with your excellent SAT scores. The goal is to associate the SAT with good feelings.

Ten Points Always to Double-Check

My father's favorite thing to say to me before I take a test is, "Always double-check! If your mother and I had double-checked before we left the hospital with you, we might have brought home a *normal* child. . . ."

Mental and emotional harassment aside, Dad has a point. Double-checking is integral to getting what you want. The test-makers know what types of careless mistakes students make, and so they build these mistakes into the test. The following are some of the most common areas in which people get sloppy.

Exponents

Make sure that as you multiplied like bases you added the exponents ($x^3 \cdot x^3 = x^6$) and that as you divided like bases, you subtracted the exponents ($x^9/x^3 = x^6$). A common — yet incorrect — method is just multiplying ($x^3 \cdot x^3 = x^9$) or dividing ($x^9/x^3 = x^3$) instead of adding or subtracting.

Sentence Completion questions

With a Sentence Completion question, you can easily predict what type of words complete the sentence, find something you think looks right, choose it, and then go on. But doing that and not double-checking can lead you right into careless mistakes, creating awkward sentences that don't quite scan with the new words inserted. Double-check your work by putting the answer into the sentence and *rereading the entire sentence*, checking it for logic and flow.

Commonsense connections

Think about what a math question is asking. If you are asked to find the weight of a (human) child and your answer is 400 pounds, something went haywire somewhere. If Paul is bicycling, and you deduce that he bikes at a rate of 80 mph, sign that man up for the Olympics!

Decimal places

If a question has two or more answer choices with the same digits, you know that the decimal point is being tested. If the choices are .05, .5, 5, 50, and 500, double-check to make sure that your decimal point is in the right place.

Political correctness

The verbal portion of the SAT contains very few correct negative answers. If a passage talks about people, especially those in a minority group, it never says nasty things about them. The entire SAT is sweetness and light; if your answer is petty and mean-spirited, it is probably wrong.

Roots, prefixes, and suffixes

Any time you see a root, suffix, or prefix, double-check to make sure that it doesn't change the meaning of the question. The analogy INSOLVENT: MONEY is very different from SOLVENT: MONEY.

Note: Did you know these words? *In-* means not. ***Insolvent*** means not having money, or bankrupt. ***Solvent*** means having money — that is, able to pay your bills.

Commonsense relationships in analogies

The relationship between two words in an Analogy question must have some logic. If the question is COW: FRIGHTEN, your common sense should tell you that the subject is not quaking quadrupeds. Double-checking helps you decide to change your definition of COW to make the word a verb, *to* cow, meaning to intimidate or to frighten.

Order of relationships in analogies

If the question features, for example, the part:whole relationship, one answer choice is almost always the whole:part relationship. Look for this choice and eliminate it, and then you can thumb your nose at the test-makers. (No, that's not being juvenile. As I always say, I'm not childish; I'm maturity-impaired!)

Grid-in bubbles

As you solve one of the ten grid-in math questions, write the answer in the blank spaces provided and grid-in the answers on the bubbles. Check to make certain that you perform that last step. Many people write down the answer in the boxes but forget to fill in the bubbles. ***Remember:*** Only the bubbles are scored. You receive no credit for an answer that's written down — only for one that's been filled in on the grid.

Scale in quantitative comparisons

QCs may display figures that have written below them: "Note: Figure not drawn to scale." This information makes all the difference in the world. In the discussion of math tricks in

Chapter 10, you learn that a figure not drawn to scale often indicates a D answer. If a figure is not drawn to scale, you can't just "eyeball" it and base your answer on what the picture looks like.

Ten Dumb Things You Can Do to Mess Up Your SAT

Throughout this book, you discover techniques for doing your best on the SAT. I'm sorry to say, however, that there are just as many techniques for messing up big time on this test. Take a few minutes to read through them now to see what dumb things people do to blow the exam totally. By being aware of these catastrophes, you may prevent their happening to you.

And, no — no booby prize is awarded to the student who makes the most of these mistakes.

Losing concentration

When you're in the middle of an excruciatingly boring critical reading passage, the worst thing you can do is let your mind drift off to a more pleasant time (last night's date, last weekend's soccer game, the time you convinced your parents that your *brother* put the bag of garbage in the fridge and the bag of groceries in the trash). Although visualization (picturing yourself doing something relaxing or fun) is a good stress-reduction technique, it stinks when it comes to helping your SAT score. Even if you need to pinch yourself to keep from falling asleep or flaking out, stay focused. The SAT is only three hours of your life. You've had horrible blind dates that lasted longer than that, and you managed to survive them. This, too, shall pass.

Panicking over time

Every section on the SAT is either 30 minutes or 15 minutes long. You know going into the test exactly how many questions are in each section and, therefore, how many minutes you have per question. It's not as if this is some big mystery. You can waste a lot of time and drive yourself crazy if you keep flipping pages ahead, counting up how many more questions you have to do. Because questions go from easier to harder and you're probably going to skip some of the super-hard ones at the end anyway, why fuss? You can do what you can do; that's all. Looking ahead and panicking only wastes time and is counterproductive.

Messing up numbering on the answer grid

Suppose that you decide to skip question 11. Good for you — skipping on this test is very smart. You're so busy patting yourself on the back, however, that you accidentally put the answer to question 12 in question 11's blank . . . and mess up all the numbers from that point on. After you answer question 25, you suddenly realize that you just filled in bubble number 24 and have one bubble left — *aaargh!* Stroke City! It's easy for me to say, "Don't panic," but the chances are that your blood pressure will go sky high, especially after you eyeball the clock and see that only one minute is left.

If you have a good eraser with you (one of the things I suggest in Chapter 1 that you bring with you), the wrong answers on the grid should take only a few seconds to erase. But how on earth are you going to resolve all those problems and reread and reanswer all the questions? You're not. You're going to thank your lucky stars that you bought this book and took the following advice: After you choose an answer, *circle that answer in your test booklet first* and *then* darken in the answer on the answer grid. Doing so takes you a mere nanosecond and helps you not only in this panic situation but also as you go back and double-check your work.

Rubbernecking

Rubbernecking is craning your neck around to see how everyone else is doing. Forget those bozos. You have too much to do on your own to waste precious seconds checking out anyone else. You don't want to psych yourself out by noticing that the guy in front of you is completely done with his section and is leaning back whistling while you're still sweating away. Maybe the guy in front of you is a complete moron and didn't notice that the section has yet another page of problems — so he did only half the section. After the exam booklet is put in front of you, don't look at anything but it and your watch until time is called.

Try not to sit by the clock in the classroom. Because everyone looks at the clock constantly, you may become self-conscious, thinking that *you're* being checked out. People staring at you every few seconds can be quite distracting (especially if they're cute). You need to keep your mind entirely on what you're doing, not continually looking up and catching someone's eye.

Cheating

Dumb, dumb, *dumb!* Cheating on the SAT is a loser's game — it's just plain stupid. Apart from the legal, moral, and ethical questions, let's talk practicality: You don't know what the exact vocabulary is on the test before you take it, so what are you going to do — copy a dictionary onto the palm of your hand? Many of the math formulas appear in the directions; those that don't can't all fit onto the bottom of your shoe. Copying everything that you *think* you may need would take more time than just learning it. Besides, the SAT tries very hard to test critical reasoning skills, not just rote memorization. The test never asks a question as straightforward as "How many degrees in a triangle?" The questions require thinking and reasoning, not just copying down a formula.

Worrying about the previous sections

Think of the SAT as seven separate lifetimes. You are reborn six times and so get six more chances to "do it right." Every time the proctor says, "Your time is up; please turn to the next section and begin," you get a fresh start. The SAT rules are very strict: You can't go back to a previous section and finish work there or change some of your answers. If you try to do so, the proctor is sure to catch you, and you'll be in a world of hurt. But suppose that you're too ethical even to consider going back to earlier material. There's still the problem of *worrying* about the previous section. If you're now in section five, working on math, you shouldn't be wracking your brain, trying desperately to remember what that frustrating "It's-on-the-tip-of-my-tongue" vocabulary word in section four meant. Forget one section as soon as you enter the next.

Worrying about the hard problems

As you see throughout this book, the SAT includes some incredibly hard problems and questions. Forget about 'em. Almost no one gets them right anyway. (A ridiculously few 1600s are scored every year, and if you score in the 1500s or even the 1400s, you are in a super-elite club of only a very small percentage of the three million or so kids who take the SAT annually.) Just accept the fact that you either won't get to or can't answer a few of the final questions and learn to live with your imperfection. If you do go fast enough to get to the hard questions, don't waste too much time on them. Scan them; if you can't think of how to begin, go back and double-check your easy questions. Keep reminding yourself that every question counts the same in a section, whether that question is a simple $1 + 1 = 2$ or some deadly word problem that may as well be written in Lithuanian.

Transferring information from problem to problem or section to section

Each question exists in its own little world. If $x = 17$ in question 15, it does not necessarily equal 17 in question 16 (unless a note says something like: "Questions 15 and 16 refer to the following information"). Now, that sounds incredibly simplistic, but you'd be surprised how many people transfer information from problem to problem. This practice is especially prevalent in dealing with symbolism questions. If you learn in a symbolism question in section one that $\overset{x}{\triangle} = 25$, it is highly unlikely to equal 25 in another triangle problem in section five.

Here's something else that can make your life totally miserable: Even vocabulary can change! Remember that words can have more than one meaning. *Check,* for example, can be used in section two to mean "to review for mistakes" (as in "James Michael decided to *check* his homework before turning it in, knowing that he often made careless mistakes"). But in section four, *check* may mean to stop or to hold back (as in "Frances wanted to tell her friend off but *checked* herself, deciding not to make a scene in public"). Erase everything from your mind as you move from one question to another.

Forgetting to double-check

If you finish a section early, go back and double-check the easy and medium-difficulty questions. Don't spend more time trying to do the hard questions. If a question was too hard for you five minutes ago, it's probably still too hard for you. Your brain capacity probably hasn't doubled in the last few minutes. If you made a totally careless or dumb mistake on an easy question, however, going back over the problem gives you a chance to catch and correct your error. You're more likely to gain points by double-checking easy questions than by staring open-mouthed at the hard ones. ***Remember:*** Every question counts the same. A point you save by catching a careless mistake is just as valuable as a point you earn, grunting and sweating, by solving a mondo-hard problem.

Looking back and playing "coulda-shoulda"

Don't discuss the questions with your friends in the bathroom during break. They don't really know any more than you do. Your friends may all tell you that they got answer A for question five — but maybe answer A was the trap answer, and they all fell for it. If you get depressed because you chose answer B, you're hurting only yourself. Maybe B was right all along, and you alone brilliantly recognized and circumnavigated the trap. Why put yourself through this grief? The same is true after the exam. Forget the postmortem. You did what you did; no sense biting your nails and fretting about it until you get back your scores.

Bonus! Do you suffer from onychophagia? I'd be willing to bet you have, at some time in your life, had this condition and that taking the SAT ***exacerbates*** it (makes it worse). ***Onychophagia*** is the technical term for biting your nails. I used to use this term on my parents when I didn't feel like going to school: "Mom, I can't face classes today. My onychophagia is acting up." It worked . . . until Mom bought a bigger dictionary.

Chapter 3

Reading the Admissions Committee's Mind: What Colleges Want

In This Chapter

- Pinpointing what the colleges *really* want from you
- Masterminding the right mix of academics, sports, and extra-curricular activities
- Preparing for the all-important essay and interview
- Eliminating the biggest mistake most anxious applicants make

The number one question that I'm asked by my students is, "What do the colleges want outta me?" I took that question to an expert, Jill Q. Porter, M.S., of La Jolla, California. An independent college counselor, Jill has helped thousands of students get into the schools that best meet their needs and fulfill their dreams. She visits dozens of colleges every year, talks with the admissions officers, and knows what's important to them. She's great at debunking some of the rumors that make the rounds. Here are her answers to 12 of the most important questions a student recently posed in an interview.

What's the Number One Thing Colleges Look For?

"Grades and the level of coursework. If you get straight A's but you take basket weaving and lint picking, the schools aren't going to be impressed. If you take five solids, like physics, calculus, Spanish, history, and English lit, and get a few A's and a few B's, schools are going to be very impressed. It's not just the grades, but the difficulty level of the classes that's important."

How Important Is the SAT I, Really?

"The SAT I is crucial. Do you think the colleges would spend so much time and money separating students by their SAT I scores if the schools didn't consider the scores important? The colleges need to have some universal measure of skills, something that can put all students on an equal footing. Some kids don't have the chance to take calculus in their high schools, or they go to schools that just plain don't offer AP (Advanced Placement) classes. By having everyone take the same test, schools have a more fair and equitable frame of reference."

Do Schools Care Whether I Repeat the SAT I?

"The answer to this depends on the college. The very top-tier colleges don't expect you to take the SAT I six or seven times and may be dubious if you do so. Twice is enough for the top schools. The second-rung schools don't mind if you take the SAT I three or four times. Check directly with each individual school to find out its policy."

Can I Take the ACT Instead of the SAT I?

"Many schools in the Midwest accept ACT scores in lieu of SAT I scores. Other schools let you take both exams and will evaluate both scores. My suggestion is that you plan to take both exams. You want to keep your options open. What if you suddenly decide you want to go to a different college, one you hadn't considered before? By the time you realize you need an ACT score, it may be too late to take the test. Automatically plan on taking both tests, if possible."

It just so happens that your friendly neighborhood bookstore has copies of *The ACT For Dummies,* written by Yours Truly (and published by Hungry Minds, Inc.) ready to help you prepare for that exam. Could life *get* any better?

If I Mess Up Big Time on the SAT I, What Can I Do to Compensate?

"Adjust your expectations. Reality is the name of the game when it comes to college planning. While we'd all love to go to Status U., most will have to settle for less. If you do very badly on the SAT I and don't have time to take it again, there's nothing you can do but look at another school. You always have the option of transferring after your first or second year.

"Keep in mind that schools do get last-minute openings. Even if you think your SAT I score absolutely disqualifies you from your Dream School, send in the application and try to get on a waiting list. You never know how lucky you can get."

What Classes Do You Recommend That I Take As a Senior? Junior? Sophomore?

"In general, the more challenging and complete your course load, the more likely you are to get accepted by a good college. And let me warn you: You can't slack off your senior year. Many students tell me that they work super-hard their junior year and then take easy classes their senior year because it's too late for the colleges to get those grades. Wrong. Some schools don't send out confirmation notices until the end of March of the senior year. That means they get the first semester grades and know whether you've signed up for and then dropped classes your senior year. Remember, the application form is a legal contract. If you write that you're taking a bunch of hard classes that you actually stayed in for a day and then dropped, you're lying to the college, and that's called fraud.

"Enough of scaring you. Here's what most colleges are looking for: three years of math (four is even better); four years of English; two to three years of language (any language is fine; you won't get extra points for taking a 'classy' language like Latin); two to three years of science; and two years of social studies. As far as the math goes, you don't have to take calculus unless you are trying to get into a math, engineering, or architecture program. And physics isn't required by all colleges, either."

How Helpful Are Charity Work and Sports?

"The colleges *expect* you to have some sort of community involvement. The key is doing something you enjoy. Don't sign up to work at a preschool if you don't have patience with small children, for example. The newspaper is always full of organizations requesting volunteers; somewhere, there's a perfect match for you. In my opinion, it's more important to be very involved with one charity than to sign up for ten different charities just to have them on your application form. The schools aren't dumb; they'll know what you're doing.

"As for sports, they show you're well rounded. You don't have to play varsity sports, just be involved in something, even intramurals. A word of caution: Sports are *not* more important than grades. Don't let your athletics stand in the way of your academics."

What Should I Say on the College Essay?

"I stress individuality. Show the colleges who you really are. College admissions officers read hundreds, maybe even thousands, of essays every year. They don't award points when you say what you obviously think the college wants to hear. They're impressed when you let your personality shine through. If you are archconservative and take pride in campaigning for right-wing candidates, mention your experiences. If you are really into pyramid power, channeling, and New Age stuff, talk about that. The key is to write about something you enjoy.

"And it goes without saying that your writing should be well organized and grammatically correct. With spell checkers (both mechanical and that type called 'parents'), there's no excuse to turn in a sloppy essay."

What Will They Ask Me in the Interview, and What Should I Say?

"Colleges have two basic types of interviews, those done by alumni and those done by college staff. The alumni interviews tend to be a little less formal, but that doesn't mean you don't have to take them seriously.

"In both types of interviews, the most important thing is to show you are seriously interested in *this* school. Demonstrate that you've done your homework. By that, I don't mean bring in your algebra scratch paper, but indicate that you've done your background reading on the college. Mention some programs you find impressive or something about the history of the school. Above all, be very careful not to annoy the interviewer by asking some trite question that's already been answered in the promotional literature. For example, asking 'How many students are on campus?' is lame when that number is given in the school bulletin. Ask questions that relate to your personal goals in college."

How Can I Decide Which School Is Best for Me?

"This is the big question. First, be realistic. Everyone wants to go to the best schools in the country, but we can't all get accepted there. While you should have one Dream School just for fun, be prepared by having several more realistic schools as backups.

"Next, look at affordability. Be absolutely sure that you can afford a school before you go through all the visitations and applications (which cost money). You may think you'll get a scholarship and financial aid, but they are getting harder and harder to acquire and rarely cover all the costs. Figure out just exactly how much you have to contribute, and then have a realistic talk with your parents about how much they can help. Yes, you can get a job during school as well, but that money usually goes toward daily expenses and fun, not tuition and books. You will be able to work only part time, remember.

"Of course, the physical comfort of a school is vital. By that I mean, would you enjoy living in that particular city and on the campus? If you are a Big-City sophisticate, you may not want to live in a small college town in the Midwest that has few of the extras you grew up with. If you are a laid-back, Small-Town type, life in the Big City may be so distracting that you don't concentrate on your studies. And you have to like the campus, too, because you'll probably live on it for at least a few years.

"And last, I always recommend thinking about long-range internships and job opportunities. If you want to be a schoolteacher, for example, does the college have a good student-teaching program? Are there jobs in the community for teachers after you graduate? Many students fall in love with the city in which their school is located and want to stay there after they graduate. You're only in high school now and may not be thinking as far ahead as graduation and job hunting, but they should be a vital part of your decision on colleges."

What's the Biggest Mistake Most Students Make in College Planning?

"Relying on misinformation. The school grapevine and rumor mill are always working. I have students come to me who are convinced that they can have a mediocre SAT I score and still get into their Dream School 'because a friend of a friend at school, this guy who plays water polo, did it.' Check your facts. You may want to believe what you hear, but trust me, much of it will be wrong. Read the school bulletin. Talk to the admissions office or to an alumnus of the school. Talk to your high school guidance counselor or get help from an independent counselor.

"The second biggest mistake is choosing a college based solely on how much money it will give you in scholarships or financial aid. While money is critical, it should not be your *only* reason for attending a school. Somewhere out there, you can find a school you love, one that fits you to a T. You don't have to settle for the first school that offers you money, thinking that you won't find anything better. Your college experience is something you'll remember forever. It will affect your friendships, your career, and the rest of your life. Don't just settle for 'good enough'; look for 'just right.'"

Anything Else I Should Know?

"Colleges are getting more and more competitive. The proportion of children who are reaching college age is always growing, yet relatively few new colleges and universities are being built. Simple logic tells you that the current schools are getting more and more selective. Do everything you can to do well in your classes and absolutely everything you can to get a great SAT I score. It may be annoying now to give up your afternoons and weekends to study, but you'll greatly increase your options by doing so. The higher your grades and SAT I scores, the more colleges will want you. Good luck!"

Part II

A Word to the Wise: Verbal Questions

"That 'Analogies' section was a snap. It was like taking candy from a fish."

In this part . . .

Three of the six sections on the SAT are verbal. Altogether, the SAT has 78 verbal questions in three styles: analogies (far and away the easiest for most people), sentence completions (good ol' fill-in-the-blanks, the same stuff you've been doing since kindergarten), and critical reading (the new and improved reading comprehension). Each question style has a chapter of its own in this part.

You look at the format of the question (what it looks like), an approach to the question (where to begin, how to develop an organized plan of attack), and the various tricks and traps built into the question (with, of course, suggestions for recognizing and avoiding such traps). Vocabulary-building material features roots, prefixes, and suffixes. After each discussion chapter is a chapter that includes a dozen particularly wicked practice questions, followed by detailed answer explanations that show you what you should have done, what you should have skipped, and how to make the best use of your time. And, of course, doses of sick jokes are sprinkled throughout. (Is it any wonder my friends have nicknamed me "Joko Ono"?!)

Chapter 4

Starting with the Easy Stuff: Analogies

In This Chapter

- Understanding the format of an Analogy
- Building your vocabulary with prefixes and suffixes
- Answering an Analogy question with the correct two-step approach
- Recognizing the nasty, naughty, and nefarious traps built into analogies
- Spotting and avoiding tricks and traps

The answer: The shiny red bike you got for your tenth birthday. Your first kiss from someone who wasn't related to you. Analogies.

The question: Name three of the best gifts you've ever received.

Analogies are a gift. Manna from heaven. Freebies. For most students, the analogies are the place to scarf up the points — big time. The SAT has 19 Analogy questions. On the current scoring table, if you get all the Analogy questions right and absolutely nothing else, you already have a 410. That's right. Analogies alone give you a 410 on the verbal section. Each verbal question after that is icing on the cake. Verbal questions count about eight points each; get a 410 with analogies and figure out how many more questions you need to reach your goal score.

The great thing about Analogy questions is that they're do-able. Some Critical Reading questions can seem so hard that you're not sure whether the passages are printed in English or Pig Latin. Some of the Sentence Completion questions are so long that you may be tempted to take a snooze in the middle of them. But Analogies are great. You read 12 words, apply a few tricks, and you're outta there. Here's how it's done.

If Only All Relationships Were This Easy: The Format

Some people look at the Analogy questions and wonder "Where's the question?" Even though the Analogy questions are quite simple (with practice), the format is bizarre. Here's an example of what you see:

PIG: STY::

(A) teenager: rubble

(B) sister: bathroom

(C) bird: nest

(D) swine: bathtub

(E) barnacle: barn

You see two words in uppercase letters. The five answer choices consist of two words in lowercase letters. Not a lot of reading here. When you get good at Analogy questions, you can zoom through them faster than you can finish a pint of Häagen-Dazs. And remember: Every minute you save in the Analogy questions is another minute you can use for the Critical Reading questions (where you need all the time you can get).

Your job is to identify the *relationship* between the question words and then choose a pair of answer words that expresses the *same* relationship.

Understanding the Approach

When you see an Analogy question, take the following straightforward two-step approach:

1. **Use both words in a descriptive sentence.**

   Make a sentence using the words. Avoid something vague and useless, such as "has." For example, do *not* say, "A pig *has* a sty." That tells me nothing. From the sentence, I have no idea what the relationship between a pig and a sty is. Pretend that I'm a Bulgarian exchange student. I come up to you and say, "Excuse me, please. What is this pig: sty?" If you tell me that a pig *has* a sty, I may go away thinking that a sty is a curly tail, a snout, or a big stink. But if you say to me, "A pig *lives in* a sty," I now understand the relationship. A good sentence paints a mental picture; you can actually see the scene in your mind.

2. **Apply the *exact* same sentence to each answer choice.**

   Go through each of the answer choices using your sentence.

   A. *A teenager lives in rubble.*

   Well, maybe in *your* case, but this is the SAT, and the writers assume that all of you are sweet students who obey your parents, respect traffic signals, and don't ever use the middle finger of your hand for pointing or otherwise gesticulating. By the way, ***rubble*** is the ruined remains of a building, such as knocked-down bricks and junk. If you forget this word, think of Barney Rubble from the Flintstones. He's short, like a knocked-down pile.

   B. *A sister lives in the bathroom.*

   It may seem like it sometimes, but it ain't so. Any answer that is funny, witty, or charming is almost certainly the wrong answer. (The SAT has noooooo sense of humor; count on it.) If you think that the answer is funny — or desperately *trying* to be funny — you can be sure that it's wrong.

   C. *A bird lives in a nest.*

   Sounds pretty good, but you have to go through all the answer choices, just in case. You wouldn't marry the first person you kiss, so don't immediately choose the first answer that looks good. Something later may make you happier.

   D. *A swine lives in a bathtub.*

   If you choose this answer, remind me not to come to your house! The trap here is that a pig (from the question) and a swine are much the same. Be careful: Just because a word in the answer choice is connected in *meaning* to a word in the question does not mean that the answer is right. The *relationship* between the words is being tested. For example, the question may be about perfume, and the correct answer may involve sweaty socks. No connection.

   E. *A barnacle lives in a barn.*

   If you don't know what a barnacle is, you may be tempted to choose E, but C is the right answer. A ***barnacle*** is a creature that lives in the water (not in a barn) and often attaches itself to the bottoms of ships. You scrape the barnacles off the ship periodically to clean the ship's hull.

Ten words to cheer you up

bliss
dynamic
ebullient
effervescent
exultation
felicity
jubilant
rapture
serendipity
vivacious

Just Because You're Paranoid Doesn't Mean They're Not Out to Get You: Traps, Tricks, and Tips

Admit it — this is why you really bought this book. You want to know those little traps that are built into the questions, sitting there waiting to pounce on unsuspecting victims. What time bombs have the test makers created, ready to go off in your face? Here are suggestions for how to deal with a few traps.

Turn a verb into an infinitive

No, an infinitive is not the latest Japanese import car. An infinitive is the "to" form of any verb: to burp, to hiccup, to disgust, to party. When an Analogy question features a verb, turn it into an infinitive and the sentence practically writes itself.

GIGGLE: LAUGH::

To giggle is *to laugh* a little bit.

YELL: TALK::

To *yell* is to *talk* loudly.

RUN: WALK::

To run is *to walk* rapidly.

Notice that I'm adding another word on the end, an adverb to answer the "How?" question. How do you laugh when you giggle? A little bit. How do you talk when you yell? Loudly. How do you walk when you run? Rapidly. It's not enough to say, "To giggle is to laugh." You want to fine-tune the sentence, tweak it a little bit to clarify the relationship between the words. Remember: That Bulgarian exchange student is counting on you.

Identify which part of speech the question word is

Sometimes your sentence is easier to write if you know which part of speech — noun, verb, or adjective — a difficult word is. You find out by looking at its counterparts in the answer choices. That is, if you want to know which part of speech the first word in the question is, look at the first words in the answer choices. If you want to know which part of speech the second word in the question is, look at the second words in the answer choices.

DASHIKI: TAILOR::

(A) shovel: teacher

(B) table: singer

(C) garment: jock

(D) cake: baker

(E) moon: actor

Don't know what the word *dashiki* means? You're not alone; it's a pretty hard word. Not to worry. You know by looking at the first words in the answer choices — shovel, table, garment, cake, and moon — that dashiki must be a noun and is a thing. (Remember that nouns are persons, places, or things.) Your simple sentence should be: "A dashiki is a thing of a tailor." That's all you can do for now. The next step is to go through each answer choice.

(A) shovel: teacher

Although it can get deep in the classroom sometimes, a shovel is not standard equipment for a teacher.

(B) table: singer

A singer may stretch herself out on a table during a Las Vegas lounge act, doing a sexy, sultry number, but a table is not normally associated with a singer.

(C) garment: jock

This is a trap answer. You may be tempted to choose it because a tailor (from the question) deals with garments. However, you've already learned that the meanings of the question words are not necessarily related to the answer; the *relationship* between the pairs of words is important. Had the question said GARMENT: SEAMSTRESS or even GARMENT: MODEL, it would have been a good choice. But a garment is not necessarily a thing of a jock.

(D) cake: baker

A cake is a thing of a baker. Yeah, this answer sounds pretty good. There is a logical connection. Try the next one to be sure, but D is probably right.

(E) moon: actor

What on earth does a moon have to do with an actor? There seems to be no relationship here at all. (I have seen a few actors become famous by mooning the camera, but that's an entirely different thing.)

The right answer is D. A ***dashiki,*** by the way, is a type of shirt: A tailor creates a dashiki just as a baker creates a cake. You can get the question right without knowing what the word means.

Backing into it

Question: Is it okay to make the sentence by using the words backward?

Answer: Sure, as long as you remember to use the answer choices backward, as well. Don't say, "A tailor makes a dashiki," and then say, "A moon makes an actor."

Assume that unknown words are synonyms

This great tip is worth the price of the book alone (tax included). The Analogy questions include a lot of words that you don't know (and I don't mean you *personally;* no one knows them). Assume that the words are synonyms and simply put an "is" between them.

BEAUTY QUEEN: PULCHRITUDINOUS::

Very few normal people know the word *pulchritudinous.* (Sounds like something you'd scrape off the bottom of your shoes, doesn't it?) Assume that it's the same as beauty queen and make the sentence, "A beauty queen *is* pulchritudinous." Now use your common sense. What is a beauty queen? Purple? Hunch-backed? No, she is beautiful . . . which just happens to be what ***pulchritudinous*** means. Try a few more.

COWARD: PUSILLANIMOUS::

Who has a clue what *pusillanimous* means? Not I. Assume that it's synonymous with coward, and say, "A coward *is* pusillanimous." What is a coward? Cowardly, afraid, fearful. ***Pusillanimous,*** in fact, does mean cowardly, afraid, fearful.

CHEAPSKATE: PARSIMONIOUS::

What is it with all these *P* words? No clue on *parsimonious*? Don't head for the fridge to drown your sorrows in Sara Lee just yet. Create the *is* sentence: A cheapskate *is* parsimonious. What is a cheapskate, in your own words? He or she is someone cheap, stingy with money, and tightfisted. ***Parsimonious*** — you guessed it — means cheap and stingy.

Notice that the grammar doesn't always work in these sentences. You may sound clunky and funky at times, but who cares? No one is going to hear the sentences you make. (I'm assuming that you don't sit in a corner of the SAT testing room drooling over your paper and muttering the sentences aloud. Have a little class.)

Keep in mind that these tips are just that: *tips,* not rules. That means that they work most of the time, but not always. Suppose the question is

PHILANTHROPIST: PARSIMONIOUS::

If you use the handy-dandy tip to assume that the words are synonyms and say, "A *philanthropist is* parsimonious," you miss the question. A ***philanthropist*** is a generous person who, therefore, is *not* parsimonious, or cheap and stingy. How do you know which questions the tip works on and which ones it fails on? You don't. Sorry 'bout that. Hey, it's not a perfect world. But for a tip to make the cut in this book, it has to be true most of the time. The odds are greatly in your favor if you assume that the words are synonyms. If you miss one, you just have to suck up the pain and live with it.

Why, you ask, doesn't the tip work all the time? Because the test makers don't want you to get a perfect score just by using tips and tricks. They have to find some way of rewarding those Walking Websters, the students who have swallowed the dictionary and know every word from *aah* to *zymosan*. Therefore, although you can get a *great* score without knowing what you're doing, you can't get a *perfect* score. So just settle for great and let it go already.

Use roots, prefixes, and suffixes

These are my favorite words. Other women like "I love you," but I live for "roots, prefixes, and suffixes." Roots, prefixes, and suffixes can bump up your score significantly. If you know just a few basic roots, prefixes, and suffixes, you can write magnificent analogy sentences and prevent yourself from falling into traps.

Songs as the SAT would sing them

Scintillate, scintillate, little star
How I cogitate on what you are

Rock-a-bye progeny, on the tree apogee
When the bough fractures, the cradle will plummet

The minuscule arachnid ascended the water spout
Down came the precipitation and decimated the arachnid

How desiccated I am, how inundated I'll be
If I can't find the lavatory key

I'm a diminutive teapot, short and corpulent . . .

Oh pulchritudinous for spacious skies . . .

Home, home for deranged
Where never is heard, a disparaging word . . .

For example, suppose the question is

IMPECUNIOUS: MONEY::

If you don't know *impecunious,* you may be tempted to make the words synonyms and simply say, "Impecunious *is* money." A tempting and logical answer may be, for example, reservoir: water. Sorry, MegaBrain, not this time.

Suppose that you know that *-ous* means full of and *im-* means not. Now you can make a good sentence: "***Impecunious*** is *not full of* money." That changes the whole picture. Now the right answer may be, for example, vacuum: air. A *vacuum* is *not full of* air. Note that a *reservoir* in fact *is* full of water, just the opposite of what you want to say.

Although you can learn hundreds of prefixes and suffixes, I realize that you have a limited number of brain cells you are willing to devote to this subject. Therefore, here is a list of some of the most commonly used prefixes and suffixes, with examples of each. Memorize them. Burn them in your brain. I'll get to some of the most common roots in Chapter 6. I don't want you to get overexcited all at once.

Prefixes

a- **= not or without:** Someone *a*moral is without any morals, like the sadist who designed this test. Someone *a*typical is not typical, like the pocket protector-wearing students who love to take tests. Someone *a*pathetic is without feeling, or uncaring, which is like most students by the time they have finished the test and are leaving the test room. ("The world is going to end tomorrow? Fine; that means I can get some sleep tonight.")

ab- **= away from:** Your parents ask you to *ab*stain from drinking and driving (stay away from it). What does a queen do when she *ab*dicates the throne? She goes away from it. When a thief *ab*sconds with your valuables, she takes them away from you.

ad- **= toward, addition:** When you *ad*vocate a point of view, you go toward it. Because you are hopelessly *ad*dicted to the SAT, you are drawn toward it.

an- **= not or without:** An *an*aerobic environment is without oxygen (like the test room feels when a killer question leaves you gasping for air). *An*archy is without rule or government, like your classroom when a substitute teacher is in for the day.

ante- **= before:** When the clock tells you that it's 5 a.m., the a.m. stands for *ante* meridian, which means before the middle, or the first half of the day. *Ante*bellum means before the war.

Tara in *Gone with the Wind* was an antebellum mansion, built before the Civil War. *Ante*diluvian literally means before the flood, before Noah's deluge. Figuratively, it means very old; if you call your mother antediluvian, you mean that she's been around since before the flood. It's a great word to use as an insult because almost no one knows what it means and you can get away with it.

***ben-/bon-* = good:** A *bene*fit is something that has a good result, an advantage. Someone *bene*volent is good and kind; a benevolent father lets you take his new car on a date rather than your old junker. *Bon* voyage means have a good voyage; a *bon* vivant is a person who lives the good life.

***caco-* = bad:** Something *caco*phonous is bad-sounding, such as nails scratching on a chalkboard.

***de-* = down from, away from (to put down):** To *de*scend or *de*part is to go down from or away from. To *de*nounce is to put down or to speak badly of, as in *de*nouncing those hogs who chow down all the pizza before you get to the party.

Many unknown words on the SAT that start with *de* mean to put down in the sense of to criticize or bad-mouth. Here are just a few: ***defame, demean, denounce, denigrate, derogate, deprecate, decry.***

Guess? Yes!

Question: Should I skip an Analogy question if I don't know the words?

Answer: Noooo! That's what these tips and tricks are all about. If you know the words, you can make a sentence and be done with it. But even if you don't know the words, you rarely have to skip the question. Look for a root, prefix, or suffix. If you can't find one you know, try making the words synonyms (like, "A beauty queen is pulchritudinous"). If that doesn't work, then and only then should you skip the question. You can make at least a logical guess most of the time.

Here's an example of a *rare* time when a question would be good to skip.

TALON: HAWK::

(A) den: bear

(B) feather: bird

(C) claw: tiger

(D) joey: kangaroo

(E) beak: chicken

Suppose that you don't know what a talon is. There's no known root, prefix, or suffix to help you. You try making the *is* sentence: A talon *is* a hawk. That doesn't help. A den is a place where a bear lives; maybe a talon is a place where a hawk lives. Feathers cover a bird; maybe talons cover a hawk. A claw is the hand and nails of a tiger; maybe a talon is the hand and nails of an eagle. A joey is a baby kangaroo (interesting word, no?); maybe a talon is a baby hawk. A beak is the bill of a chicken; maybe a talon is the bill of a hawk.

All the answers look good. Because using the tricks hasn't helped you at all, skip this question entirely. Don't make a wild guess; there's no way to narrow down the answers.

By the way, the correct answer is C. A ***talon*** is the claw of a hawk. To help you remember this word, look at your zipper on your jacket or pants. There is a zipper company called Talon. It makes sense when you think about it; a zipper is rather like a little claw going up and down.

Bonus: You've seen the car called Tercel, but did you ever wonder how it got its name? What is a tercel? A tercel (sometimes spelled tiercel) is a small male hawk. I suppose the car-namers hoped the car would make you feel as if you are flying and soaring free.

Ten words that Sarah Michelle Geller never hears

corpulent
drab
flaccid
fleshy
frowzy
homely
obese
rotund
slovenly
unkempt

***eu-* = good:** A *eu*logy is a good speech, usually given for the dearly departed at a funeral. A *eu*phemism is a polite expression, like saying that someone has passed away instead of calling him worm meat.

ex-* = out of, away from:** An *ex*it is literally out of or away from it — *ex*-it. (Exit is probably one of the most logical words around.) To *ex*tricate is to get out of something. You can *ex*tricate yourself from an argument by pretending to faint, basking in all the sympathy as you're carried away. To *ex*culpate is to get off the hook — literally to make away from guilt. (Culp*** means guilt.) If the dean of students wants to know who egged his house last weekend, you can claim that you and your friends are not *culpable*.

***im-* = not:** Something *im*possible is not possible. Someone *im*mortal is not going to die but will live forever. Someone *im*placable is not able to be calmed down, stubborn. Notice that *im-* can also mean inside (*im*merse means to put into), but that meaning is not as common on the SAT. First think of *im-* as meaning not; if that doesn't seem appropriate, switch to Plan B and see whether it can mean inside in the context of the question.

***in-* = not:** Something *in*appropriate is not appropriate. Someone *in*ept is not adept, not skillful. Someone *in*solvent has no money, is bankrupt, like most students after the prom. *In-* can also mean inside (*in*nate means something born inside of you) or beginning (the *in*itial letters of your name are the beginning letters). However, its most common meaning is *not.* Think of that one first; if it doesn't seem to work, try the others.

***ne-/mal-* = bad:** Something *ne*gative is bad, like a negative attitude. Someone *ne*farious is "full of bad," or wicked and evil, like a nefarious wizard in a science fiction novel. Something *mal*icious also is "full of bad," or wicked and harmful, like a malicious rumor that you are really a 30-year-old narc in disguise. A *mal*apropism is a ridiculous use of words. I heard my favorite *malapropism* on a television show: "Lincoln freed the slaves with the Emasculation Proclamation." Ouch.

***post-* = after:** When the clock tells you that it's 5 p.m., the p.m. stands for *post* meridian. It means after the middle, or the second half of the day. Something *post*mortem occurs after death. A postmortem exam is an autopsy.

pro-* = big, much:** *Pro*fuse apologies are big, much — in essence, a *lot* of apologies. A *pro*lific writer produces a great deal of written material. ***Note: *Pro* has two additional meanings less commonly used on the SAT. It can mean *before,* as in "A *pro*logue comes before a play." Similarly, to *pro*gnosticate is to make known before or to predict. A *pro*gnosticator is a fortune teller. *Pro* can also mean *for.* Someone who is *pro* freedom of speech is in favor of freedom of speech. Someone with a *pro*clivity toward a certain activity is for that activity or has a natural tendency toward it.

Suffixes

***-ate* = to make:** To duplic*ate* is to make double. To renov*ate* is to make new again (*nov-* means new). To plac*ate* is to make peaceful or calm (*plac-* means peace or calm).

***-ette* = little:** A cigar*ette* is a little cigar. A din*ette* table is a little dining table. A coqu*ette* is a little flirt (literally, a little chicken).

***-ify (-efy)* = to make:** To beaut*ify* is to make beautiful. To oss*ify* is to make bone. (If you break your wrist, it takes weeks to oss*ify* again, or for the bone to regenerate.) To de*ify* is to make into a deity, a god.

***-illo* = little:** An armad*illo* is a little armored animal. A peccad*illo* is a little sin. (Do you speak Spanish? *Pecar* is to sin.)

***-ist* = a person:** A typ*ist* is a person who types. A pugil*ist* is a person who fights (*pug-* means war or fight), or is a boxer. A pacif*ist* is a person who believes in peace, or is a noncombatant (*pac-* means peace or calm).

***-ity* = noun suffix that doesn't actually mean anything; it just turns a word into a noun:** Joll*ity* is the noun form of jolly. Seren*ity* is the noun form of serene. Timid*ity* is the noun form of timid.

***-ize* = to make:** To alphabet*ize* is to make alphabetical. To immun*ize* is to make immune. To ostrac*ize* is to make separate from the group, to shun.

***-ous* = full of (very):** Someone joy*ous* is full of joy. Someone amor*ous* is full of *amor,* or love, and is very loving. Someone pulchritudin*ous* is full of beauty, beautiful.

See Chapter 6 for plenty of examples of roots.

A flash of brilliance: How to use flash cards

Go out and buy the largest index cards you can find. Get them in white and two other colors. Put all the roots, prefixes, and suffixes you learn that have negative connotations on one color. For example, *ne-* means bad or not; put it on a pukey green card. *ben-* means good; put it on a pink card. *-ous* means full of. It doesn't "feel" good or bad; it's neutral. Put it on a white card.

When you get to the exam, you may encounter the word nefarious. You know you've seen it before, but you can't for the life of you remember what it means. Then a little picture unfolds in front of your eyes: You see *ne-* on a pukey green card. Aha! If it's on a pukey green card, it must be something negative. Just knowing that much often helps you to get the right answer.

Say the analogy is: NEFARIOUS: SAINT:: Normally, you assume that the words are synonyms and say, "A saint is nefarious." However, remembering that *ne-* is on a pukey green card, which means that it is negative, makes you change the sentence to "A saint is not nefarious," because saints are generally considered good.

There is no right or wrong way to classify the roots. If you think that a root is positive, fine, it's positive. If you think that a root is negative, fine, it's negative. The whole purpose of flash cards is to help you associate the words. Go with whatever works for you.

Bonus! When you come across a word that incorporates the root, put that word on the card as an example. That way, you learn both the root and the vocabulary word: two for the price of one. If you're reading a newspaper article about a program that will have a salubrious effect on the economy, you should note that *sal-* means health and *-ous* means full of. You know immediately that the word means healthful. Put it on both the *sal-* card and the *-ous* card. You'll learn the vocabulary without realizing it.

Look for the salient features of a word

The *salient feature* is what makes something stand out. The salient feature of a basketball player is his or her height. The salient feature of a genius is his or her intelligence.

MINNOW: FISH::

(A) elephant: animal

(B) amphibian: tadpole

(C) gnat: insect

(D) giraffe: quadruped

(E) student: befuddled

The salient feature of a minnow is that it is a *small* fish. Although all the answers are synonyms (an elephant *is* an animal; a student *is* befuddled), only C gives the salient or outstanding feature. A gnat is a *small* insect. In choice B, an amphibian is an animal that lives on both land and water, like a frog (not a tadpole, although a tadpole grows into a frog). I had a high school swim coach who always bellowed at us, "Are you amphibian or just a tad uncomfortable in water?"

Identify common relationships

Certain standard relationships are often found in the analogies. There is a ***plethora*** (a lot) of them; here are ten of the most useful ones.

1. **Cause and effect**

   TICKLE: LAUGHTER

   OSSIFY: BONE

2. **Characteristic**

   BLEAT: SHEEP (a ***bleat*** is the sound a sheep makes)

   POD: WHALES (a ***pod*** is a group of whales)

3. **Greater to lesser**

   OVERJOYED: HAPPY

   OBESE: PLUMP

4. **Location**

   PIG: STY

   WARREN: RABBIT

5. **Member to group (or specific to general)**

   FORK: UTENSIL

   ISLANDS: ARCHIPELAGO (an ***archipelago*** is a group of islands)

6. **Opposites**

   BIG: LITTLE

   PULCHRITUDINOUS: UGLY

7. **Part to whole**

   TOES: FOOT

   TALON: EAGLE

8. **Position**

   FRAME: PICTURE (a frame goes around a picture)

   SHOULDER: ROAD (a shoulder is to the side of a road)

9. **Purpose or function**

   PILOT: FLY

   PUGILIST: BOX

10. **Synonyms**

    HAPPY: GLAD

    PUSILLANIMOUS: COWARDLY

Eliminate trap answers

The first answer to eliminate is the one that is backward. Putting answers in reverse order is a common trap. If the question goes from greater to lesser (OVERJOYED: CONTENT), there is almost certainly a trap answer that goes from lesser to greater (DISPLEASED: FURIOUS). Look for it.

Another good answer to eliminate is one that duplicates the *meaning* rather than the relationship between the words. The question may be PROFESSOR: EDUCATED. The words are synonyms. A good answer to eliminate is teacher: moronic. Even though a professor is a teacher and those words have the same meaning, the *relationship* between the trap answer words is antonymous, not synonymous.

Cross off any words that are too hard or too easy. If you are working on question 1, the correct answer is not going to feature the word *lachrymose;* any word that can bring you to tears (inside joke if you know the meaning of lachrymose) is just too hard for the first question. If you have narrowed down the answers for the *last* question to two, go with the harder of the two.

Finally, forget about humor. Anything funny or trying to be funny is outta here. Correct answers are almost always dull and boring.

Money makes the world go 'round . . . or not

Use these words when you're ***flush*** (rich) or flat broke:

affluent	mercenary	pelf
fiscal	miserly	penurious
impecunious	opulent	prosperity
indigent	parsimonious	solvent
mendicant	pecuniary	

Déjà vu: Analogy Question review

The approach:

- Use both words in a descriptive sentence.
- Use the exact same sentence on each answer choice.

Tips and tricks:

- Turn a verb into an infinitive.
- Identify which part of speech (noun, verb, or adjective) the question word is by looking at its answer choice counterpart.
- Assume that unknown words are synonyms.
- Use roots, prefixes, and suffixes.
- Identify the salient feature of a word; that is, what makes it stand out.
- Remember the common relationships: cause and effect, characteristics, greater to lesser, location, member to group (or specific to general), opposites, part to whole, position, purpose or function, and synonyms.
- Eliminate trap answers.

Chapter 5

The Dirty Dozen: Practice Analogy Questions

In This Chapter

- Strutting your stuff: showing off what you know
- Relating to the test: identifying analogy relationships
- Downloading a dozen: answering a sample dozen questions

Ready to practice what I've been preaching? Here are the dirty dozen Analogy Questions to get you into the swing of things. This chapter is loaded with good vocabulary words to put on your list for study. Don't forget to pay extra-careful attention to the words that look like this: ***vocabulary word.***

Bonus! At the end of every answer explanation, you are told which tip (from Chapter 4) you could have and should have used to answer the question correctly. If you missed the question, be sure to go and look at that specific tip again:

- Tip 1: Turn a verb into an infinitive
- Tip 2: Identify which part of speech the question word is
- Tip 3: Assume that unknown words are synonyms
- Tip 4: Use roots, prefixes, and suffixes
- Tip 5: Look for the salient features of a word
- Tip 6: Identify common relationships
- Tip 7: Eliminate trap answers

1. PILOT: FLY::

   (A) carpenter: draw

   (B) seagull: squawk

   (C) editor: create

   (D) clown: amuse

   (E) pessimist: hope

Your sentence should be: "The purpose of a pilot is to fly." The purpose of a clown is to amuse. The correct answer is D. Although a carpenter may draw, a seagull may squawk, and an editor may create (a ***pessimist,*** a person who always looks on the gloomy side of things, does not hope), those are not their primary tasks. Tip: 6

And here's a quick joke to make you squawk:

Question: Why do seagulls fly by the sea?

Answer: If they flew by the bay, they'd be bay gulls (bagels)!

2. WHISPER: QUIETLY::
   (A) mumble: indistinctly
   (B) screech: gently
   (C) mutter: loudly
   (D) scream: miserably
   (E) shout: clearly

Use the tip about turning a verb into an infinitive, and your sentence should be: "To whisper is to speak quietly." To ***mumble*** is to speak indistinctly. The correct answer is A. To ***screech*** is to speak loudly and shrilly, not gently. To ***mutter*** is to speak softly, not loudly. To ***scream*** may be to speak miserably (when you think of having to study for the SAT on the weekend) or to speak joyously (when you see your new and improved SAT score). To ***shout*** may or may not be to speak clearly. Tip: 1

3. EMPHASIZE: SAY::
   (A) inquire: ask
   (B) compliment: glorify
   (C) implore: request
   (D) state: specify
   (E) admire: disdain

Because emphasize is a verb, turn it into an infinitive: "To emphasize is to say strongly" (or insistently, powerfully, demandingly; any word like that will work). To ***implore*** is to request strongly. You emphasize that you will not go out on a blind date; you implore that you meet the victim before the event. The correct answer is C.

Choice E is exactly wrong. To ***admire*** is not to disdain strongly, but the opposite of disdain (to disdain is to dislike). Often, one of the answer choices will be the 180-degree opposite of the correct answer.

Did you notice that choice D is backward? To specify is to state strongly, or at least in detail. Choice B is backward, too. To ***glorify*** is to compliment highly, to praise greatly, to butter up. Tip: 1

Question: Why were the cannibals thrown out of school?

Answer: They were caught buttering up the teacher!

4. GASOLINE: AUTOMOBILE::
   (A) canoe: paddle
   (B) telephone: number
   (C) table: polish
   (D) wood: pencil
   (E) batteries: toy

Your sentence should be: "Gasoline makes an automobile go." Batteries make a toy go. The correct answer is E. (When I was a little girl, my smartaleck brother gave me batteries for my birthday with a card that said, "Toys not included.") Choice A is backward. Tip: 1

5. INNOCUOUS: POISON::

(A) wealthy: money

(B) elegiac: sadness

(C) boring: ennui

(D) insipid: flavor

(E) wanton: weight

Use your roots, prefixes, and suffixes to define the relatively difficult word, innocuous. *In-* = not; *noc* = poison; *-ous* = full of, very. Your sentence should be: "Innocuous is not full of poison." Insipid is not full of flavor. The correct answer is D.

What if you don't know the word *insipid?* Because *in* = usually means not (remember, it has three meanings: not, inside, and beginning), you can make a good guess that it means the opposite of the word next to it: not flavor, or not full of flavor. ***Insipid*** means bland, dull, tasteless.

Elegiac means sad. An ***elegy*** is a sad poem. ***Ennui*** is boredom. Unless you have a super crazy accent, wanton has nothing to do with weight. (Get it: one ton?) And no, it's not a soup, either. ***Wanton*** means reckless. Speeding drivers often get tickets for "wanton disregard for human safety." Tip: 4

6. SENTRY: GUARD::

(A) clairvoyant: ignore

(B) geologist: mine

(C) entrepreneur: conserve

(D) sycophant: insult

(E) pugilist: box

A ***clairvoyant*** is a fortune teller, a soothsayer. Do you speak French? This word comes from the French words, *clair,* meaning clear, and *voyant,* a form of the verb *voir,* meaning to see. Literally, the word refers to someone who can see things clearly.

Using the root *pug* (fight) and the suffix *-ist* (a person), you know that a ***pugilist*** is a person who fights, or a boxer. The purpose of a pugilist is to box. The correct answer is E. You could get this answer even without knowing the rest of the words. Ignorance is no excuse in the analogies portion of the SAT.

A ***sycophant*** is a brownnoser, a yes-man, a kiss up, one who flatters to excess. His job is not to insult, but to praise. A ***geologist*** works with rocks, but doesn't necessarily mine them himself. (Granite that I'm a geology buff myself, but I thought this answer was especially gneiss.) An ***entrepreneur*** often starts a new business but is not especially noted for conserving things. Tips: 3, 4

7. BOMBASTIC: GRANDILOQUENT::

(A) immodest: humble

(B) carping: piscine

(C) gentle: irreligious

(D) halcyon: inclement

(E) indecorous: improper

You can figure out grandiloquent from the roots: *grand* (I didn't specifically give you this one, but you know *grand* means big) and *loq* = speech or talk. Someone ***grandiloquent*** is a big talker, like an agent who promises, "Stick with me baby, and I'll make you a star." The problem now is that you probably don't know what bombastic means. Not to worry. Assume that unknown words are synonyms and simply say, "***Bombastic*** is grandiloquent" (which, son of a gun, it is!).

You get this question right by process of elimination. *Im-* means not, such that ***immodest*** means not modest and is the opposite of humble. Choice B is a joke. A carp is a fish, yes, and ***piscine*** means like a fish (*-ine* = like, similar to), but the two words aren't the same. To remember piscine, think of the fish sign of the zodiac, Pisces. To ***carp*** is to nit-pick, to criticize, to complain. To remember carp, think of a fish-faced grouch, complaining all the time.

In- means not, so indecorous means not decorous. ***Decorous*** means proper, having good taste. ***Indecorous*** would therefore mean improper. The correct answer is E.

In D, ***halcyon*** means calm, peaceful, idyllic. I once heard a halcyon day described as "being faxed from Heaven." ***Inclement*** means stormy (*in-* = not; *clem* = mild). An inclement day is not halcyon. Tips: 3, 4, 7

8. PROGNOSTICATION: SOOTHSAYER::

(A) tumult: arbitrator

(B) duplicity: idiot

(C) fanaticism: zealot

(D) adulation: adult

(E) retrospection: prophet

If you simply say, "Prognostication is soothsayer," you can get the right answer, assuming that you also know what all the answer choices mean!

Tumult is turbulence, violence (you may be more familiar with this word in another form, ***tumultuous***). An ***arbitrator*** is a mediator, a go-between in a fight or controversy. Her job is to stop the tumult, to calm things down and bring about a rational discussion. The words are closer to antonyms than synonyms.

An SAT trap is to give you a common word (tumultuous) in an uncommon form (tumult). My favorite example of this is *ruth*. If someone says you are ***ruth,*** do you kiss or clobber that person? No idea, right? Ah, but I bet you know the more common form of the word, ruthless. If you are ruth*less* you are without mercy, so when you are ruth, you must be merciful, kind. (In your grandmother's day, a lot of girls were named Ruth.)

In choice B, ***duplicity*** is duality (*dup-* = double), the state of being deceptive. A spy, not an idiot, is noted for his duplicity. However, just to confuse matters, a ***dupe*** is a person who has been tricked, or, in other words, an idiot.

Choice C is correct. ***Fanaticism*** is the state of being a fanatic, being really into something (the word ***fans***, like a rock star's groupies, comes from the word *fanatic*). A ***zealot*** is very into something, enthusiastic, involved (a more common form of this word is ***zealous***).

Choice D is a little trap. Adulation has nothing to do with being an adult. ***Adulation*** is hero worship, extreme admiration. You have adulation for a war hero or the person who develops the cure for AIDS.

Choice E is also closer to antonyms than synonyms. ***Retrospection*** is a look back (*retro-* = back; *spect* = look). At my sixteenth birthday party, my parents showed home movies of my baby pictures, me naked in the bathtub at six months, me crawling around on a rug at seven months, and so on. They called it the "Suzee Retrospective." I called it "Death by Embarrassment." A prophet predicts the future and does not look back at the past. It doesn't take a prophet to predict that all my friends who were at my sixteenth birthday party would remind me of that Moment of Mortification every birthday since. Tips: 3, 4

9. METEOROLOGY: WEATHER::

(A) fruit: bananas

(B) linguistics: language

(C) sociology: socks

(D) phrenology: friends

(E) pedantry: feet

Meteorology is the study of weather. The TV forecaster is a meteorologist. If you chose E, I gotcha! Yes, *ped* is a root meaning foot, but pedantry is not the study of feet. A ***pedant*** is a teacher; ***pedantry*** is excessive concern for learning. And choice D is a trap, too. Just because phrenology sounds kind of like friend-ology does not mean that it is the study of friends. Cheap trick. ***Phrenology*** is the study of the bumps on your head! Some people believe that you can tell a person's character by the shape of his head, just as others believe that you can tell a person's future by the lines in his palm.

Sociology is the study of human society, not the study of socks. (Is there, in fact, a word for the study of socks? If you know one, please send it to me; I'd love to know.) Bananas are a type of fruit; fruit is not the study of bananas. (A very Southern California joke: How do you prevent a banana from peeling? SPF 100!) Only choice B is left. ***Linguistics*** is the study of language. Tip: 4

You may be getting depressed right about now by these big words, but don't worry: The American students don't know them either. In fact, you have an advantage in certain situations over kids who grew up speaking only English. If you speak Spanish or French or Italian or Romanian, your language is very close to Latin, from which many of the hard words are derived. If you don't know a word in English, pronounce it as if it were in your own language. You may find that the similarity is just enough for you to get the answer right (for example, *lingua* in Latin is *lengua* in Spanish).

10. BLUNDERBUSS: WEAPON::

(A) spaceship: vehicle

(B) archipelago: island

(C) cauldron: pot

(D) minnow: fish

(E) corset: garment

On the real SAT, you would skip this question. In this rare instance, all of the tips let you down. First, there are no known roots, prefixes, or suffixes to help you. Second, if you're normal, you don't know the meaning of blunderbuss, so your sentence should be: "A blunderbuss is a weapon." So far so good, but now what? If a blunderbuss is a futuristic weapon, then A looks good. In B, an ***archipelago*** is a group of islands. If a blunderbuss is a group of weapons, B is right. In C, a ***cauldron*** is a big pot. If a blunderbuss is a big weapon, C is right. In D, a ***minnow*** is a little fish. ***Bonus:*** Here's a fascinating fact. Do you ever watch the old sitcoms on Nick at Nite? (You do? Hey, you should be studying, not watching TV!) Ever see *Gilligan's Island*? The ship on that show is called *The Minnow*. How did it get its name? No, it's not named after the fish, but after a lawyer, Newton Minow. He was chairman of the Federal Communications Commission in the 1960s and is noted for calling television "a vast wasteland." In E, a ***corset*** is an old-fashioned garment. If a blunderbuss is an old-fashioned weapon, E is right.

The only way to get this question right (besides sheer luck) is to know what a blunderbuss is. The correct answer is E. A ***blunderbuss*** is an old-fashioned weapon. Think back to the pictures of the Pilgrims that decorated your elementary school classroom every Thanksgiving. The long rifles the Pilgrims carried were called blunderbusses. The word is pretty interesting. It's Dutch for "thunder box," which is a logical way of describing a noisy rifle.

11. IMPECCABLE: FAULT::

(A) inconsistent: error

(B) inept: ability

(C) indecent: descent

(D) ineligible: legibility

(E) insalubrious: disrespect

If you don't know the meaning of impeccable, use the prefix *im-*, which usually means not, in the sentence, "Impeccable is not fault." (Sure, the grammar stinks, but who cares? No one is going to hear these sentences besides you. Don't get fancy.) Now you can use the process of elimination to choose B as the correct answer. ***Inept*** means having no skill or ability, clumsy, incapable.

If you chose C or D, you should be feeling pretty foolish right about now. Go back and look at those answers; you probably misread them. In C, ***indecent*** is a lack of decency — not a lack of *descent.* (And no, that is not a typo. The SAT has no typos.) In D, ***ineligible*** means not eligible; it does not mean "not legible." Be careful to read the words that are printed and not automatically supply your own words.

Use roots to figure out choice E. *In-* = not; *sal* = health; *-ous* = full of, very. ***Insalubrious*** means not full of health, unhealthy. It has nothing to do with saluting someone out of respect and, therefore, is not the opposite of disrespect. Tip: 4

12. PRECIPICE: STEEP::

(A) bridge: immutable

(B) garden: sere

(C) lecture: soporific

(D) maelstrom: turbulent

(E) theory: ubiquitous

If you don't know precipice, your sentence should be: "A precipice is steep." (You know that precipice is a noun because the first words of the answer choices are all nouns as well.) In fact, a ***precipice*** is a steep cliff. Now it's all a matter of elimination.

Why would a bridge be immutable, or unchangeable (*im-* = not; *mut* = change)? That answer makes no sense at all. If you don't know sere, in B, leave that as a "maybe" for the moment. In C, a lecture should not be ***soporific,*** or sleep-inducing (*sop* = sleep).

A ***maelstrom,*** in fact, is turbulent. A maelstrom is a whirlpool. Have you ever been to EPCOT Center in Disney World? There's a (supposedly) wild water ride in one exhibit, called the Maelstrom. Choice D is the correct answer.

In B, ***sere*** means dry. (I always remember this by thinking that when the sun sears me, I am sere, or dry.) In E, ***ubiquitous*** means everywhere at once. Reminders about the SAT are ubiquitous; there's nowhere to hide.

Don't confuse ubiquitous (a common SAT word) with ubiety (a less common, but fun, word). ***Ubiety*** is the quality of being in one particular place at one particular time. For example, the planets have ubiety. You can count on them to be at one site in the sky at a specific time. Tips: 1, 5

Trivia: Did you know that the planet Saturn is so light it could float in your bathtub? (Yeah, but it would leave a ring. . . .)

Chapter 6

Finishing What You Start: Sentence Completions

In This Chapter

- Recognizing Sentence Completion questions
- Dissecting and simplifying the sentences
- Eliminating wrong answers

Sentence completions are the blind dates of the SAT. What you see is not necessarily what you get . . . or what you want. Looks can be deceiving. Don't judge a book by its cover. Beauty is only skin deep. Let's see, have I left out any other trite, banal, hackneyed clichés? The point of all this babbling is that sentence completions can be sneaky, tricky, duplicitous, and worse than they look. Fortunately, there are ways to beat the sentence completions at their own game.

What Sentence Completion Questions Look Like: The Format

A Sentence Completion question consists of one sentence with one or two blanks. Your mission, should you choose to accept it, is to fill in the blanks. Usually only one word goes in each blank; occasionally, however, the blank requires a few words or a short phrase instead. Here is an example:

Sick and tired of studying for the SAT, Faye - - - - her book across the yard with such - - - - that it soared high into the sky, causing three of her neighbors to call the UFO hot line.

(A) tossed .. gentleness
(B) hurled .. ferocity
(C) pitched .. sluggishness
(D) carried .. gloom
(E) conveyed .. reluctance

Look at the second blank first. If the book went high into the sky, the toss was huge. Eliminate choices A and C. She eagerly threw the book, eliminating choice E. Your answers are narrowed down to B or D. If Faye carried her book (choice D), it wouldn't go high into the sky unless Faye flew too. By process of elimination, choice B is correct.

Understanding the Approach

Do you look at Sentence Completion questions and draw a blank? (Sorry, I couldn't resist.) Knowing where to start is a great confidence builder and time-saver. Try the following steps.

1. **Read the entire sentence for its gist.**

   Although this may seem obvious, many people read until they get to the first blank and then head for the answers. The problem is that the sentence may change in midstream, messing everything up. Note, for example, the big difference between

   > Talked into going on a blind date, Mitzi was ---- *because* Marty turned out to be ----.
   >
   > — and —
   >
   > Talked into going on a blind date, Mitzi was ---- *although* Marty turned out to be ----.

   In the first example, you may want to say something like this:

   > Talked into going on a blind date, Mitzi was *ecstatic* because Marty turned out to be *gorgeous*.

   In the second example, you could say the following:

   > Talked into going on a blind date, Mitzi was *content* although Marty turned out to be *mediocre*.

   How you fill in the blanks depends on the middle term — in this case the conjunction *because* or *although*.

2. **If possible, predict words to fit into the blanks.**

   Notice the careful hedge, "if possible." You can't *always* predict words. But it's amazing how often you can get close. Consider the following:

   > Hal was ---- when his new computer arrived because he realized he'd have no excuse for not finishing his homework.

   You can predict that the word should be something negative, such as *depressed, sad,* or *unhappy*. Did you predict something positive, such *happy* or *glad*? If you did, you probably headed for the answers before you read the entire sentence. What did I just tell you in the preceding section? Tsk, tsk. Try another.

   > Kelly was nearly deafened by the ---- of the crows landing in the cornfield, completely ---- the scarecrow that the farmer had placed there.

   Because Kelly was "nearly deafened," predict that the crows were making a lot of noise. If this question were near the beginning of the section, an easy word such as *noise* or *sound* may be the correct answer. Because questions become progressively more difficult, this question at the end of a section may feature more challenging vocab, such as *clamor* or *cacophony*.

   Quickly eliminate answer choices with first words that don't fit. For example, if a choice is *silence .. unaware of,* you know that *silence* doesn't make sense, and you can dump the whole answer. You don't have to strain the brain considering the second blank.

   For the second blank, deduce that the crows were ignoring the scarecrow. Answer choices might be *unaware of, unfazed by,* or *oblivious to.*

3. **Insert every answer choice into the blanks and reread the sentence.**

   Sentence completions are not a place to try to save time. You just need to plug and chug. Plug in every answer choice and chug through the whole darn sentence again.

Occasionally, you can eliminate answers because you know the word *must* be positive, but that particular answer choice is negative. After you eliminate everything you can, you must insert the remaining answers into the blanks and read through the finished sentences. Try the following example:

As a public relations specialist, Susan realizes the importance of treating someone with ---- and ---- when dealing with even the most exasperating tourists.

(A) dignity .. etiquette

(B) fantasy .. realism

(C) kindness .. patience

(D) courtesy .. compassion

(E) truth .. honesty

Because the two blanks are connected by the word *and,* the words in those blanks should be synonyms (or almost synonyms). They may not need to mean exactly the same thing, but they certainly should not be opposites. They should be on the same wavelength. That means that you can eliminate choice B because *fantasy* and *realism* are opposites. That's the only answer, however, that you can eliminate immediately. The others are all close enough in meaning to fit together.

This leaves you with no choice but to plug and chug. Insert every answer and see which one makes the most sense. The right answer here is choice C. Choice A looks pretty good, but you don't "treat someone with etiquette." *Etiquette* is a system of rules for manners. Choice D also looks pretty good, but treating an exasperating person with compassion is not as logical as treating the person with patience. Choice E is very tempting until you plug it into the sentence. *Truth* and *honesty* are synonyms, but they don't fit as well in the context of the sentence as *kindness* and *patience*.

Forget about taking a lot of shortcuts. After you eliminate the obviously incorrect answers, take your sweet time going back and inserting every remaining answer into the sentence. Sentence Completion answers aren't right/wrong so much as good/better/best. Sometimes all the answers seem to "sorta fit." Your job is to choose the one that fits best, just like the right piece in a puzzle.

Question: Why was Suzee thrilled when she finished the jigsaw puzzle in six months?

Answer: Because the box said, "Two to four years."

SAT words "in store" for you

So you think you'll take a break from studying and head for the market to get some brain food (like chocolate!)? Ha! There's no escaping the SAT, even in the stores. Here are some SAT words (or close facsimiles thereof) that you're likely to encounter as you do your shopping.

Adorn hair spray

Alleve pain reliever (like ***alleviate***)

Arid deodorant

Bounty paper towels

Brawny paper towels

Efferdent (like ***effervescence***)

Hefty trash bags

Imperial margarine (like ***imperious***)

Sominex sleep aid (like ***somnolent*** or ***somniferous***)

Stridex acne medication (like ***strident***)

Surge energy drink

TNT: Tips 'n' Traps

Let me introduce you to the nasty little gremlins lurking in the Sentence Completion questions and give you some dynamite suggestions for dealing with them.

Look for key connecting words that may change the meaning of the sentence

Changing an *and* to an *or* or a *because* to a *however* can change everything, as the following shows:

> Buzz was content to ---- *and* ---- on his weekend, answering to no one but himself, doing exactly as he liked.

Perhaps you would fill the blanks with *rest .. relax*. Now check out this sentence:

> Buzz was content to ---- *or* ---- on his weekend, answering to no one but himself, doing exactly as he liked.

The *or* changes everything. You may fill the blanks with *sleep .. party* or perhaps *work .. play*. You know that the concepts must be opposites here.

Here's a brief list of some of the most common connecting words:

although	despite	moreover
and	either/or	nonetheless
because	however	or
but	in spite of	therefore
but for		

Whenever you see the preceding words, your antennae should go up, putting you on the alert for a plot twist — a trap of some sort.

Predict positive or negative words to fit in the blanks

Sometimes the sentences are so long and ***convoluted*** (twisting or turning) that you can't make heads or tails of them. In that case, dissect the sentence. Isolate just a bit of the sentence around the blank and try to predict whether that blank requires a positive or negative word. Consider the following:

> "Blah blah blah blah blah blah blah blah blah blah blah," Frances cursed ----.

Because people rarely curse or swear nicely, you can predict that the blank must be filled with a negative word. Maybe Frances curses *harshly, rudely,* or *viciously.* You can eliminate answer choices such as *sweetly, kindly,* or *courteously.*

A fun word: antepenultimate

You probably know that *ultimate* means *the last,* just as Z is the ultimate letter of the alphabet. But which letter is the antepenultimate? Give up? It's X. The *ultimate* is the last; the *penultimate* is the second to last; the *antepenultimate* is the third to last (literally *before the second to last*). If you have three younger brothers, therefore, you can introduce them as your antepenultimate, penultimate, and ultimate siblings.

Skip questions with answers that depend entirely on unknown vocabulary words

Many times you can get the right answer in Sentence Completion questions by process of elimination. You may have a hazy idea what type of word (positive or negative) or words (antonyms, synonyms) go into the blank or blanks. But what happens if you can't eliminate any answers because you don't know what any of the words mean? Hit the road, Jack. Skip that sucker. Get outta there fast. Unless you're a Walking Webster's, you may want to skip a question like the following:

Although usually of a cheerful nature, Putty was ---- after she learned that the history teacher insisted that she work with her ex-boyfriend as her partner on the semester project.

(A) lugubrious

(B) ebullient

(C) indolent

(D) supercilious

(E) gelatinous

Okay. You know that the blank needs to be filled with a word that means sad, gloomy, or glum. So far so good. But then you get to the answer choices, and life as you know it ceases to exist. You don't know *any* of those words. Because everything depends on vocabulary words you don't know, skip the question. You can't get this one right except by randomly guessing. Why take a chance on losing the points and chew up your precious time in doing so? Blow it off and go on to the next question.

Leaving you hanging on this question would be too vicious. The correct answer is A. ***Lugubrious*** means sad. As for the other words, ***ebullient*** means happy, overjoyed. ***Indolent*** means lazy, laid back. ***Supercilious*** means stuck-up, conceited. ***Gelatinous*** is just what it looks like, the consistency of gelatin, jelly-like.

Trivia: I absolutely love Jello, but even I wasn't surprised to hear that these five Jello flavors flopped: (1) apple; (2) celery; (3) cola; (4) salad; (5) mixed vegetables.

Rely on roots

In Chapter 4, you learn basic prefixes and suffixes. In this chapter, you can increase your vast storehouse of knowledge by adding some of the important roots. The following is just a short list, but it is representative of what can greatly help you figure out SAT words.

A vocabulary helper bonus

You'll be delighted to know that roots, prefixes, and suffixes (RPS) help you immensely on the Sentence Completion vocabulary, just as they do on the Analogies. If you don't know what the words mean, use your RPS to figure them out (see Chapter 4 for more on RPS). For example, consider the following sentence:

Jane refused to eulogize Donald, saying that she thought he was a ---- fellow.

Obviously, the entire sentence depends on the meaning of ***eulogize.*** If it means something bad, Jane refused to bad-mouth Donald and thought that he was a swell fellow. If it means something good, Jane refused to say anything good about Donald, thinking he was a bad fellow. Which is it? As you may have seen in Chapter 4, *eu-* (along with *ben* and *bon*) means good. That Chapter also tells you that the suffix *-ize*, means to make. You can figure out that to *eulogize* means to make good. If she refused "to make good" about Donald, she didn't like him. You'll have five answer choices. Narrow them down to the one that is a bad word, such as *rotten, terrible,* or *disgusting.*

Try this one:

Ashamed of his obvious trembling and - - - - when confronted by the farmer's wife, Blind Mickey told his two good friends, "I thought I was a man, but I'm just a mouse."

You need a word here that means fear. Among the five answer choices may be ***trepidation,*** which would be correct. You can figure out the word if you know that the root *trep* means fear.

***ambu* = walk, move:** In a hospital, patients are either bedridden (they can't move) or *ambu*latory (they can walk and move about). A somn*ambu*list is a sleepwalker. *Som-* means sleep; *-ist* is a person; *ambu* is to walk or move. A *somnambulist,* therefore, is a person who walks or moves in his or her sleep.

***andro* = man:** Commander Data on *Star Trek: The Next Generation* is an *andro*id; he's a robot shaped like a man. Someone *andro*gynous exhibits both male (*andro*) and female (*gyn*) characteristics (literally, he/she is full of man and woman) — for example, the character Pat on the TV show *Saturday Night Live* was androgynous.

***anthro* = human or mankind:** *Anthro*pology is the study of humans (not just men and not just women but humans in general). A mis*anthro*pe hates humans (an equal-opportunity hater: He or she hates both men and women).

***bellu, belli* = war, fight:** If you're *belli*gerent, you're ready to fight — in fact, you're downright hostile. An ante*bellu*m mansion is one that was created before the Civil War. (Remember that *ante-* means *before*. See Chapter 4.)

***cred* = trust or belief:** Something in*cred*ible is unbelievable, such as the excuse: "I was abducted by aliens over the weekend and didn't have time to finish my homework." If you are *cred*ulous, you are trusting and naive (literally, full of trust). In fact, if you're credulous, you probably actually *believe* I was beamed up to a flying saucer.

Be careful not to confuse the words *credible* and *credulous*. Something *credible* is trustable or believable. A credible excuse can get you out of trouble if you come home late for curfew. *Credulous*, on the other hand, means full of trust, naive, or gullible. The more credulous your parents are, the less credible that excuse needs to be.

***gnos* = knowledge:** A doctor shows his or her knowledge by making a dia*gnos*is (analysis of the situation) or a pro*gnos*is (prediction about the future of the illness). An a*gnos*tic is a person who doesn't know whether a god exists. Differentiate an *agnostic* from an *atheist.* An *atheist* is literally without God, a person who believes that there is no god. An *agnostic* is without knowledge, believing that a god may or may not exist.

greg* = group, herd:** A con*greg*ation is a group or herd of people. A *greg*arious person likes to be part of a group — is sociable. To se*greg*ate is literally to make away from the group. *Se-* means apart or away from, as in ***separate, sever, sequester, and ***seclusion.***

***gyn* = woman:** A *gyn*ecologist is a physician who treats women. A miso*gyn*ist is a person who hates women.

***loq, log, loc, lix* = speech or talk:** Someone *loq*uacious talks a lot. (That person is literally full of talk.) A dia*log*ue is talk or conversation between two people. E*loc*ution is proper speech. A pro*lix* person is very talkative. (*Pro-* means big or much. Literally, he or she engages in big, or much, talk.)

***luc, lum, lus* = light, clear:** Something *lum*inous is shiny and full of light. Ask the teacher to e*luc*idate something you don't understand (literally, to make clear). *Lus*trous hair reflects the light and is sleek and glossy.

***meta* = change, transformation:** A *meta*morphosis is a change of shape.

***morph* = shape:** Something a*morph*ous is without shape. *Morph*ology is the study of shape. ("Hey, Mom, I'm going to the beach to work on morphology . . . .")

***mut* = change:** The Teenage *Mut*ant Ninja Turtles *mut*ated, or changed, from mild-mannered turtles to pizza-gobbling crime fighters. Something im*mut*able is not changeable but remains constant.

Don't confuse *mut* (change) with *mute* (silent).

***pac* = peace, calm:** Why do you give a baby a *pac*ifier? To calm him or her down. To get its name, the *Pac*ific Ocean must have appeared calm at the time it was discovered.

***path* = feeling:** Something *path*etic arouses sympathy or a feeling of pity. To sym*path*ize is to share the feelings (literally, to make the same feeling). Anti*path*y is a dislike — literally, a feeling against, as in: No matter how much the moron apologizes, you still may harbor *antipathy* toward the jerk who backed his car into yours, denting the fender and getting you grounded for two weeks.

***phon* = sound:** *Phon*ics helps you to sound out words. Caco*phon*y is bad sound; eu*phon*y is good sound. Homo*phon*es are words that sound the same, such as *red* and *read.*

***plac* = peace, calm:** To *plac*ate someone is to calm him or her down or to make peace with that person. You *placate* your irate sweetheart, for example, by sending a dozen roses (hint, hint). Someone im*plac*able is someone you are not able to calm down — or someone really stubborn. If those roses don't do the trick, for example, your sweetheart is too *implacable* to placate.

***pug* = war, fight:** Someone *pug*nacious is ready to fight. A *pug*ilist is a person who likes to fight — such as a professional boxer. (Did you ever see those big sticks that the American Gladiators use — the ones that look like Q-Tips with a thyroid condition? Those are called *pug*il sticks.)

scien = knowledge: A *scien*tist is a person with knowledge. Someone pre*scien*t has forethought or knowledge ahead of time — for example, a ***prognosticator*** (a fortune teller). After you learn these roots, you'll be closer to being omni*scien*t — all-knowing.

som = sleep: Take *Som*inex to get to sleep. If you have in*som*nia, you can't sleep. (The prefix *in-* means not.)

son = sound: A *son*ic boom breaks the sound barrier. Dis*son*ance is clashing sounds. (My singing, quite frankly, is so bad that the governor declared my last opera a disaster aria!)

sop = sleep: A glass of warm milk is a *sop*orific. So is a boring teacher.

Enough for now. You'll find no ***paucity*** (lack or scarcity) of roots to learn, but these should provide you with a good foundation.

Say it again: Sentence Completion review

The approach:

- Read the entire sentence for its gist.
- If possible, predict words to fit into the blanks.
- Insert *every* answer choice into the blanks and reread the sentence.

Tips and tricks:

- Look for key connecting words that may change the meaning of the sentence.
- Predict positive or negative words to fit in the blanks.
- Skip questions with answers that depend *entirely* on unknown vocabulary.
- Use a few basic RPS (roots, prefixes, and suffixes) to figure out the killer vocabulary.

Chapter 7

Taking Time Out for a Reality Check: Sentence Completion Practice Exam

In This Chapter

- Serving your sentence: practice Sentence Completion questions
- Making the connection: recognizing the key connector words that change everything
- Giving yourself a chance: checking *all* the answer choices

It's that time — when you use it or lose it. Answering the following dozen questions should reinforce the lessons in Chapter 6 about Sentence Completion questions. Also, don't forget to add the vocabulary words that ***burgeon*** (blossom, grow, spring up) all over this chapter to any vocabulary list you may be keeping.

Try to identify each question as one of the types of Sentence Completions described in Chapter 6 and use the tips I give you in the last section of that chapter for reading that type of passage:

- Tip 1: Look for key connecting words that may change the meaning of the sentence
- Tip 2: Predict positive or negative words to fit in the blanks
- Tip 3: Skip questions with answers that depend entirely on unknown vocabulary words
- Tip 4: Rely on roots

1. ---- by her accomplice Ron, Kathy wrapped the tuba-playing Neighbor-from-Hell's house in toilet paper, ---- a feud that dragged on for the next ten years.

   (A) Hampered .. instigating

   (B) Aided .. ending

   (C) Impeded .. starting

   (D) Assisted .. triggering

   (E) Hindered .. terminating

   Because an ***accomplice*** is a person who helps you do something, predict that the first word means "helped." That narrows the answers down to B or D. (To ***impede, hamper,*** or ***hinder*** is to obstruct or block.) If the feud dragged on for the next ten years, the toilet paper didn't end the feud but *triggered,* or started, it. The correct answer is D. Tip: 2

2. Even though he was aware of the ---- he was causing, the speaker droned on and on, determined to ignore the snores of his audience and get to the end of his presentation.

(A) hope

(B) excitement

(C) ennui

(D) paranoia

(E) happiness

If the audience was snoring, everyone was probably pretty bored. Even though you may not know that ***ennui*** means boredom, you can eliminate the rest of the answers. Choice C is correct.

Paranoia is a feeling of persecution, being convinced everyone is out to get you. As I often say, "Sure, I'm paranoid, but am I paranoid *enough?*" Tip: 2

3. Although not unaware of her ----, Connie the contortionist always bent over backward to do her most flashy work whenever the ---- critic from the *Circus Times* was in the audience.

(A) limitations .. renowned

(B) proclivities .. headstrong

(C) vanity .. pitiable

(D) pretentiousness .. unimportant

(E) artistry .. disreputable

In this example, look at the second blank first. Sometimes, it is the key to a Sentence Completion question. An artist would want to impress someone she considers important, eliminating choices C, D, and E. As quickly as that, you've narrowed your choices down to two. If you're in a rush, a 50-50 guess is worth making (although you, of course, remember that a wrong answer costs you points).

The first blank may be a little confusing because of the double negative (a favorite SAT trap). "Not unaware" means Connie is aware. She knows her ***limitations,*** or the extent of her abilities. ***Renowned*** means famous and well known. Choice A is the correct answer. ***Proclivities*** are tendencies, inclinations toward something. A proclivity to choose the hardest word automatically, even though you don't know what it means, can get you into trouble on this test. Tip: 1

4. Many surfers feel the perfect wave is ----, a mere pipe dream, so to speak.

(A) unattainable

(B) gratuitous

(C) cacophonous

(D) abstemious

(E) translucent

If you groaned when you got the pun, my work here has not been in vain. A ***pipe dream*** is something that is sheer fantasy, a dream that most likely won't come true. For most of us, having a date with a rock star or a model is a pipe dream. Surfers know that a pipeline is a type of wave that most riders seek.

Even if you didn't get the pun, even if you don't know exactly what a pipe dream is, you can ignore the "pipe" and focus on just the dream. Something that is a mere dream is probably ***unattainable,*** not able to be achieved or obtained. The correct answer is A.

You can use roots to eliminate many of the answers. ***Cacophonous*** means unpleasant-sounding (*caco* = bad, not; *phon* = sound; *-ous* = full of, very). ***Abstemious*** means doing without (*ab* = away from; *-ous* = full of, very). This is another form of the more common word, abstain. When you ***abstain*** from drinking, you are abstemious. ***Translucent*** means letting the light through, clear (*luc* = light, clear). Choice B was the only one you couldn't get with roots. ***Gratuitous*** means free, costing nothing, or unnecessary. For example, if you suddenly turn to me and say, "What's up, codfish breath?" I'll ask what prompted the gratuitous insult (it cost you nothing and was totally unnecessary). Tip: 4

5. Pulling from her locker a string of frog guts wired into the shape of a heart, Marcella remarked that her boyfriend (who just finished Biology lab) had a unique way of showing his ----.

(A) consternation

(B) trepidation

(C) empathy

(D) lassitude

(E) ardor

Use roots to eliminate choices B and C. ***Trepidation*** is fear (*trep* = fear). The only trepidation here is what the boyfriend has when he thinks about Marcella's revenge. ***Empathy*** is relating to, putting yourself in another's shoes, having the same feelings (*em-* = inside; *path* = feeling).

When you are left with three choices, should you guess? Statistically, yes. Practically, no. The odds are technically in your favor because you lose only ¼ point; look at this as your having the odds 2 to 1 against you. Personally, I don't guess unless I get the odds down to 50-50, but you have to make your own decision. I suggest that as you go through this book, you guess at absolutely everything. Put a big G by each guess. Then go back and count up the Gs. Are you a lucky guesser or an unlucky guesser?

Consternation is concern, upset. ***Lassitude*** is weariness, fatigue. ***Ardor*** means passion, desire. The correct answer is E. Tip: 4

6. Perhaps because she sensed the ---- in Bruno's tone when he called her SuperBrain, Liz redoubled her studies, ---- to get a perfect score on the test.

(A) apathy .. refusing

(B) bafflement .. aspiring

(C) glee .. hoping

(D) cheer .. determined

(E) derision .. resolved

Here's another time when you can look at the second blank first. Liz most likely wanted to get a perfect score on the test. Eliminate choice A. ***Apathy*** is indifference, a lack of feeling or emotion. (When someone is frustrated with you and asks whether you're stupid or just apathetic, you can really push his buttons by responding, "I don't know and I don't care!") The sentence sounds as if Bruno is making fun of Liz and has little respect for her brainpower. Predict that the first blank is a negative answer, eliminating choices C (***glee*** is joy) and D. At this stage, even a wild guess would be worth making. ***Bafflement*** means confusion. There's no reason to think that Bruno was confused. Instead, he was disrespectful and treated Liz with ***derision*** (contempt). The correct answer is E. Tip: 2

Many words beginning with *de* mean to put down, in the sense of to criticize or insult: ***decry, defame, deride, denounce, demean, denigrate, deprecate,*** and so on.

7. Describing Lefty as clumsy is inaccurate, for although his ---- did destroy four aisles' worth of delicate glassware at Tiffany's, he used his ---- fingers to repair most of the damage.

(A) prudence .. atrophied

(B) bungling .. deft

(C) actions .. muscular

(D) peregrinations .. awkward

(E) juggling .. unskilled

Focus on the second blank first. If Lefty repaired most of the damage, his fingers could not be unskilled, or awkward, and probably not muscular (it doesn't take muscles to repair glassware, but skill and finesse). As quickly as that, you've narrowed the answers down to two, making even a quick guess worthwhile.

Don't skip a question just because you don't know the words. By the process of elimination, you can often narrow the answers down to two or three very quickly. If you don't know a word, don't automatically choose it ("Big hard word, it must be right!") or eliminate it; leave it as a "maybe."

Predict that the first word must be similar to clumsiness. ***Prudence*** means caution, just the opposite of what you want. Therefore, the correct answer is B. ***Bungling*** means clumsiness. ***Deft*** means skillful, adept, dexterous. Tip: 1, 2

Have you been noticing how I give two or three synonyms whenever I define a word? That's not just my natural ***garrulousness*** (talkativeness, loquacity, prolixity), but a cunning plan to expand your vocabulary painlessly. Whenever you learn a new word, try to learn as many synonyms for it as possible. When you get to the exam, you may not exactly remember deft, but you connect it in your mind to ***dexterous,*** which you know means skillful. The subconscious is a powerful tool.

8. Highly offended at being addressed as Dumpy instead of Dopey, the ---- dwarf hastened to inform Ms. White about the ---- .

(A) exasperated .. gibberish

(B) short .. intrigue

(C) incensed .. misnomer

(D) affable .. mistake

(E) amiable .. error

If the dwarf was highly offended, he was upset or annoyed. Eliminate ***affable*** (friendly; I remember this word by thinking that someone affable is a-friend-able) and ***amiable*** (friendly; in Spain, your amigo is your friend; in France, your amí is your friend). Also eliminate B; a dwarf by definition is short.

Exasperated means annoyed, irritated. It works, but the second blank does not. ***Gibberish*** means nonsense talk, babble. Calling poor Dopey Dumpy is not right, but it is not nonsense; it is perfectly lucid or clear. ***Incensed*** means angry, burning mad (think of burning incense). A ***misnomer*** is the wrong name. *Mis* = not, wrong, bad (like a mistake or a mishap); *nom* = name (like nombre in Spanish, or nom in French). The correct answer is C. Tip: 2

9. So ---- as to be nearly comatose, the students in Dr. Ennui's class blame their sluggishness on the professor's ---- lectures.

(A) energetic .. boring

(B) effervescent .. vivacious

(C) resourceful .. exciting

(D) vibrant .. prosaic

(E) lethargic .. soporific

If the students are nearly ***comatose*** (appear to be in a coma), they must not be too energetic. Eliminate ***vibrant*** (lively; *vi* = life) and ***effervescent*** (lively; think of Efferdent tablets that bubble when they hit the water. Someone effervescent is bubbly, like a hyper talk show host). If the students are nearly in a coma, the lectures must be pretty dull. Eliminate ***vivacious*** (lively, animated; *vi* = life) and exciting. Now it's all a matter of vocabulary.

Sop is a root meaning sleep. ***Soporific*** means causing sleep as well and this time correctly refers to the lectures. ***Lethargic*** means lazy, indifferent. Choice E is the correct answer.

Prosaic means dull, humdrum, common. I remember this word by associating prosaic with prose. Prose is everyday, common writing. Poetry is fancy writing, such that something poetical is more flowery and fancy. Saying, "Hi, how ya doin'?" is prosaic; saying, "Salutations to you on this ***matinal*** (early) occasion" is poetical. Tip: 2

Did you catch the joke in the professor's ***moniker*** (name)? ***Ennui*** means boredom.

10. ---- in its approach but ---- in its conclusions, the research paper titillated and impressed its sophisticated, highly educated audience.

(A) Notorious .. hackneyed

(B) Nefarious .. irksome

(C) Unconventional .. sound

(D) Fresh .. provincial

(E) Perfunctory .. mendacious

If the paper impressed the sophisticated audience, it must be pretty good. Predict that the second word is positive and eliminate ***irksome*** (annoying), which eliminates choice B. You may not know the other words, so you have to leave them as "maybes" for now.

Because of the "but" connecting the two blanks, you know that the first word must be negative, and somewhat the opposite of the second word. Eliminate D. In case you haven't eliminated choice B by ruling out *irksome,* use roots to figure out that ***nefarious*** (*ne* = bad, not; *-ous* = full of, very) means very bad and eliminate it (because it is not the opposite of irksome).

Now it's all a matter of vocabulary. ***Notorious*** means famous for bad or wicked deeds. ***Hackneyed*** means not fresh, unoriginal, trite. "Have a happy day!" is a hackneyed saying. ***Provincial*** means unsophisticated. Someone from a small province or town is presumed to be much less sophisticated than someone from a large city. ***Perfunctory*** means automatic, dutiful, mechanical, a no-brainer. When someone asks how you are, your perfunctory response is, "Fine, how are you?" ***Mendacious*** means dishonest, lying.

The correct answer is C. ***Unconventional*** means not normal, unusual. That fits here because the report ***titillates*** (excites, stimulates pleasurably). ***Sound*** means accurate, reliable, valid. Tip: 2

11. Such a ---- job deserves a grade no higher than a C, as the student obviously just walked through the project.

    (A) pedestrian

    (B) puerile

    (C) profane

    (D) pithy

    (E) pejorative

Skip questions that depend entirely on unknown vocabulary. You can probably predict that the job is mediocre, because it gets a C or average grade. But which of those words means mediocre? Pedestrian. The correct answer is A. You are probably more familiar with pedestrian as a noun, a person who walks. (I put the "walked through it" part into the question as an inside joke, in case you know that *ped* means foot.) ***Pedestrian*** as an adjective means common, everyday. *Pedestrian* chitchat includes discussions of clothes, CDs, and homework. A *pedestrian* job on a paper didn't involve much effort.

On to the other words. ***Puerile*** means childish, immature. ***Hint:*** I think of this word as "pure child." If you do something puerile, you are acting like a child. Profane is more familiar to you in its noun form, profanity. ***Profane*** means unholy, obscene. ***Pithy*** means short and to the point. I once asked a student what he thought of the SAT. He made a thumbs-down gesture. That was a pithy comment; I got his meaning immediately. And finally, ***pejorative*** means critical, belittling. Many of my students make pejorative comments about the SAT words they have to learn. (The most common is "As if I have to know this for real life!") Tip: 3

12. Although Mr. Kummert is a ---- ice dancer, noted for his precise artistic footwork, his friend Ms. Clinton gathers ---- for her grace and artistry.

    (A) painstaking .. scorn

    (B) meticulous .. kudos

    (C) slovenly .. plaudits

    (D) haphazard .. infamy

    (E) zealous .. diatribes

Predict that both words will be positive because Mr. Kummert is precise and Ms. Clinton is graceful. Eliminate any answer with negative words. You probably know scorn. The other words are somewhat difficult: ***Slovenly*** means sloppy, ***haphazard*** means not methodical, unplanned; ***infamy*** is fame for evil deeds; ***diatribes*** are bitter and abusive speeches, tirades. Only the correct answer, choice B, has two positive words. ***Meticulous*** means painstaking, careful. ***Kudos*** are praises (you sing the praises of Kudos candy bars). ***Plaudits*** are also praises (just like *applaud*). Tip: 2

Chapter 8

Everyone's a Critic: Critical Reading

In This Chapter

- Discovering five commonly tested reading passage styles
- Ducking for cover: avoiding killer questions
- Speeding through reading while avoiding the traps

My students often ask me, "Why do they call it 'reading comprehension' if I don't understand a thing I've read?" Good question. And the answer is . . . they don't. At least, not any more. The test makers finally wised up and figured out that no one comprehended much of the SAT's so-called reading comprehension. They had two choices: Make the existing reading comprehension passages easier to understand or change the name of the section. Heaven forbid that they should do anything to make your life easier; therefore, they just changed the name of the section. The erstwhile reading comprehension section is now called (drum roll, please) *Critical Reading.*

Feared by more students than Monday's mystery meat in the high school cafeteria, Critical Reading questions compose just over half the SAT verbal sections (40 of 78 questions). One verbal section is exclusively Critical Reading, without Analogy or Sentence Completion questions. If you're sitting there scowling now, thinking, "I never finish reading; there's just not enough time," you're not alone. This chapter shows you how to develop a game plan so that you're way ahead at that two-minute warning.

Read 'Em and Weep: The Format

In the Critical Reading sections, you're given a passage to read and several questions to answer based on that passage. The topics for the passages can concern science, humanities, fiction, or opinions, or you may find paired passages that are related by topic. Each Critical Reading question is a basic multiple-choice question, such as the following:

According to the passage, what contributed to the difficulties the Apollo 13 voyage encountered?

(A) The astronauts were ill-prepared.

(B) The equipment was operated incorrectly.

(C) The ground control personnel were unqualified.

(D) The equipment had mechanical failure.

(E) The funding for Apollo 13 was inadequate.

All questions may be answered from information stated or implied in the passage. You aren't expected to answer questions based on your own knowledge, and you don't need to know anything special about science or humanities to answer these questions (unlike the SAT II: Single Subject Tests, formerly known as the Achievements, which test what you know already).

A touch of humor: Do you know why the astronauts of Apollo 13 really never made it to the moon? They refused to ask the Apollo 12 crew for directions.

The Five Commonly Tested Reading Passages*

**Caution:* May cause drowsiness in some people.

In their torture chambers over the years, the test makers have developed five basic types of passages. This section offers a preview of the passages to help you separate the devastating from the merely intolerable.

If you're a slow reader and usually have trouble finishing all the reading, pay special attention to the following material. Here you will find out how to identify the various types of passages and how well you do on each. Obviously, if you find that you always ace a science passage but don't understand a word of a humanities passage, you know where to focus your energies on the actual SAT.

Beam me up, Scotty! Science passages

A *science passage* is straightforward, giving you information on how laser beams work, how to build a suspension bridge, how molecular theory applies, and so on. Although the passage itself is often very booooooring to read (because it is full of facts, facts, and more facts), this type of passage is often the best passage to tackle first because it has so few tricks and traps.

Reading suggestion: Read the passage *quickly* — more for format than for content.

Let's talk reality here: You're not going to remember — and maybe not even understand — what you read in a science passage. It's all just statistics and dry details. No matter how carefully and slowly you read through it the first time, you're almost certain to need to go back through the passage a second time to find specific facts. You end up reading the passage twice. Why waste time? Zip through the passage, just to get a general idea of what it's about and where the information is. (Paragraph one tells how molecules combine; paragraph two tells how scientists are working to split the atom; paragraph three tells . . . .) You may want to jot down a one- or two-word note in the margin next to each paragraph: *Molecules. Atoms. Research.* No need to waste time understanding every nuance if you can get the answer right by going back and finding the specific fact quickly. Because science passages are so quick to do, work on them first.

Questions: Science questions can often be answered directly from the facts provided in the passage itself. They are rarely the "inference" type that require you to read between the lines and really *think* about what the author is saying, what point she is trying to make, how she feels about the subject, and so on. Here's an example:

The author states that spices were used in Chicago in the 1800s

I. to improve the taste of food

II. for medicinal purposes

III. to preserve food before refrigeration

(A) I only

(B) II only

(C) III only

(D) I and III only

(E) I, II, and III

Two-hundred-year-old SAT words

So you think all these vocabulary words are pretty useless, found only on the SAT? Although it's true that you and your friends don't sit around using words like ersatz and pusillanimous, the words haven't been made up just to torture you — really. Check out these SAT words found in such historical documents as the Declaration of Independence, the Preamble to the Constitution, the Gettysburg Address, and even Richard Nixon's resignation speech:

abdicated	arbitrary	denounce	invective	perfidy	resolve	tyranny
abhorrent	belaboring	hallow	magnanimity	persevere	tranquility	vindication
adversary	consecrate	heed	ordain	posterity	transient	

To answer the question, return to the passage and look for the specific answers — which should be easy to locate if you made those handy little marginal notes during your first run-through (in this case, the notation may be *Purposes*).

The human touch: People passages

The test usually includes at least one humanities passage. *Humanities* passages may be about literature, art, and philosophy, but they are usually about humans (well, duh!) and often about minority groups. Keep in mind that the test makers are not going to say anything bad about African-Americans, Asians, or women. In these politically correct times, everyone is wonderful, marvelous, a true pioneer, salt of the earth, *et cetera, et cetera, et cetera.* Even if the passage were related to a serial killer ("Wheaties wipe-out — Police fear cereal killer on the loose! Film at 11."), it would probably try to find something positive to say. Keep such thoughts in mind as you read through the passage. Sweetness and light.

Reading suggestion: Slow down — waaaaaay down.

In many ways, humanities passages are nearly the opposite of science passages. The questions here deal more with inference and less with explicitly stated facts. You must read the passages slowly and carefully, therefore, trying to understand not only what is said, but also what is implied. Take your time. Underline key concepts. Circle important words. Think about what you are reading.

Questions: The questions that follow humanities passages may not be as straightforward as those for a science passage. You may not be able to go back to a specific line and pick out a specific fact. Instead, you're asked to understand the big picture, to comprehend what the author meant but didn't come right out and say. In other words, you're expected to be a mind-reader. For example:

The author's primary motive in mentioning Ms. Buttinski's skill on the ukulele was to

(A) impress the reader with Ms. Buttinski's importance

(B) show that Ms. Buttinski overcame great odds to become a musician

(C) ridicule Ms. Buttinski's adversaries, who were unable to accomplish as much as she did

(D) predict great things for Ms. Buttinski's future

(E) evaluate the effect Ms. Buttinski's music has had on our everyday lives

Determining the author's motive involves reasoning as much as reading. No sentence specifically says: "Okay, listen up, troops. I'm going to tell you something, and my motive for doing so is *blah, blah, blah*." You need to read the passage slowly enough to develop an idea of why the author is telling you something and what exactly he wants you to take from this passage. Going back and rereading the passage doesn't do you much good; thinking about what you read does.

By the way, in the sample question provided here, every answer given probably would be true in the context of the passage itself. That is, the author probably thought Ms. Buttinski was important, probably believed that Ms. Buttinski had to overcome great odds to be a musician, and so on. Keep in mind, however, what the question is asking: Why did the author mention this specific thing? You must probe the author's mind.

Trivia: *Ukulele* comes from the Hawaiian word for "leaping flea." Now that's something you can bring up the next time your parents ask you what you learned in school.

Fiction is stranger than truth: Fiction passages

One passage may be a fiction passage, taken from a novel. The novel could be a best-seller from just a year ago or a hoary favorite from 400 years ago. (***Hoary*** simply means old, so get your mind out of the gutter — the SAT contains no X-rated passages.)

Reading Suggestion: Sit back and enjoy the ride.

The good news is that the fiction passages are usually a lot of fun to read — something that can't be said about the other types of passages. You read these normally, just as you would a regular book that you read for pleasure. You don't skim them, as you do the science passages. You don't read them slowly and carefully for knowledge and understanding, as you do the humanities passages. You just read.

The bad news is that fiction passages follow none of the tips that other types of passages follow. Just remember that fiction passages are the rebels, the outlaws of the Critical Reading family. They follow no rules. (Yeah, you pay a price for everything. You *finally* get a passage that's fun and often easy to read, and they mess you up on the questions. It figures.)

Questions: You can't really pinpoint any "typical" fiction question because the passages are all so different. The following example, however, is representative of the type of question you may see:

The author feels which of the following about her husband?

(A) She is dismayed by his flamboyant attitude, which embarrasses her.

(B) She is impressed by his wide range of knowledge.

(C) She is intimidated by him, concerned for her physical well-being.

(D) She is bored with him and looking for companionship outside the marriage.

(E) She thinks he has a really hot bod.

(Whaaaaaat? Choice E would never appear on the test, of course; I'm just checking to see whether you're paying attention.)

Fiction passages have become rare lately. Although you are virtually certain to get a science passage and a humanities passage, don't be unduly surprised if you don't get a fiction passage at all. I put the info here just in case. You know Murphy's Law ("anything that can go wrong, will"): If you didn't prepare for fiction passages, they'd be everywhere.

That's your opinion: Theory passages

Theory passages give an author's opinion and may seem more like editorials than reading passages. Sometimes, the opinion is well-reasoned and logical, substantiated with facts and examples. Other times, the "opinion" is nothing more than ranting and raving, similar to what you may hear on a radio call-in show.

These passages can cover a wide range of topics, such as the pros and cons of capital punishment, whether to participate in a war, or how to rear children. They may discuss overwhelmingly important topics (such as religion or the meaning of life) or ridiculous trivia (for example, whether to have your nose pierced). The topics of theory passages can be popular (such as the importance of recycling) or horrendous (like ethnic cleansing). They can, in short, deal with just about anything. They are, however, almost always easy to read and at least somewhat interesting. You may disagree with the opinions expressed in a passage, but you usually can understand them.

Reading suggestion: Go slowly. Again, you must read between the lines to comprehend what the author is implying instead of what he or she is coming right out and saying. You're not skimming for facts; you're reading for comprehension.

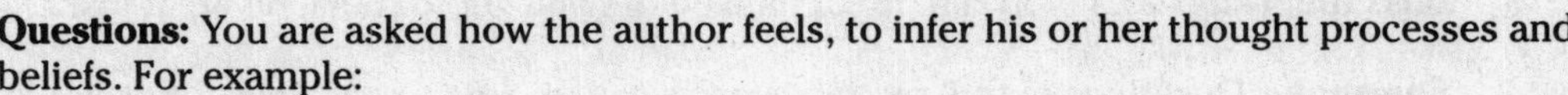

Questions: You are asked how the author feels, to infer his or her thought processes and beliefs. For example:

With which of the following would the author most likely *disagree*?

(A) Legal cases are necessary for economic stimulation.

(B) The cycles of laws are relatively predictable.

(C) Jurisprudence offers advantages that most people don't realize.

(D) Law-abiding civilizations are an aberration in history; lawlessness is the norm.

(E) Not having laws is more expensive in the long run than having and enforcing laws is in the short term.

Nowhere in the passage does the author directly say, for example, "I think that the cycles of laws are not predictable." You must infer from the overall tone of the passage that the author is trying to make this point. You need to understand the author's thought processes to answer this sort of question. You do, therefore, want to take the time to read the passage carefully.

Double trouble: Paired passages

One of the verbal sections consists of reading, reading — nothing but reading. This section is only 15 minutes long (as opposed to 30 minutes for each of the other verbal sections) and contains 11 to 13 questions based on two relatively long passages. The passages usually are related by topic and sometimes feature different points of view or different perspectives on that topic. Passage one, for example, may discuss recycling — how important recycling is for the environment, how we should spend more money encouraging recycling programs, and so on. Passage two may take the view that preventing the unnecessary use of resources is more important than recycling and that monies should be directed toward reducing excess packaging in the first place.

Reading suggestion: Divide and conquer.

Do not dive right in, read both passages (two full pages, usually), and then try to remember everything. Your best course is to read passage one and answer only those questions that pertain to that passage — usually the first five or six questions. After you finish those questions, read passage two and answer the questions that pertain to it — generally the next six questions. After you've read both passages and answered the individual questions about each passage, you're ready for the last two (or maybe three) questions, which compare or contrast the two passages.

Because the questions are grouped by passage, you can easily treat this section as two separate passages. The point at which you finish with the questions for passage one and must go on to passage two should be quite obvious. Question five, for example, may begin as follows:

In the last paragraph of passage one, the author . . .

Then question six may say:

The author of passage two believes . . .

You don't have to be a brain surgeon to figure out that after you answer question five, it's time to go back and read passage two.

The last two (or maybe three) questions are usually based on both passages. But keep in mind that these last two or three questions are usually killer questions and that many people miss them anyway. If you run out of time before you get to them, no great loss.

Questions: Questions in this section run the gamut. Some questions, for example, ask about specific facts and details; others require more abstract reasoning, reading between the lines, and inference. You get hit with a little of everything. The only new questions — which you don't encounter in the other styles of passages — are those last few, asking you to compare and contrast the two passages. For example:

Which of the following is most likely, given the authors' opinions of school curricula?

(A) The author of passage one favors complete revision at the state level; the author of passage two believes that the current curricula are excellent.

(B) The author of passage one believes that the current curricula are good and could serve with only a few minor revisions; the author of passage two wants to throw out the curricula and begin again from scratch.

(C) The author of passage two basically agrees with the author of passage one but adds a few more practical suggestions on curricula revision.

(D) The author of passage two based her theories on those of the author of passage one and offers very little new information.

(E) The author of passage one does not directly discuss the matter of curricula revision but merely mentions the potential for doing so; the author of passage two provides a plan and suggestions for its implementation.

Notice how long and confusing this question is. Because this is the last question (or is close to the end), it's usually hard, time-consuming, tricky . . . and worth skipping if you don't have a clue.

Trivia: Did you know that *clue* originally meant a ball of yarn? You may have read the legend of the Minotaur, a monster that was half man and half bull. It lived in a maze and ate youths who were sent as sacrifices. Our hero, Theseus, went to slay the monster. A local princess fell in love with Theseus and gave him a ball of yarn — known as a *clew* — to help him find his way out of the maze and to return to safety. While *clew* is still used to refer to a ball of yarn, the spelling and meaning have also changed to the word *clue*.

Ten pretentious words to weasel into your college essay

Try these on your college application essay:

- abstruse
- chimerical
- ephemeral
- evanescent
- iconoclastic
- innocuous
- laconic
- overweening
- stymie
- verisimilitude*

*What's special about this word? It's one of just a few long words that alternate consonant-vowel-consonant-vowel throughout.

Last Things First: Reading the Questions Before You Read the Passages

Question: Should I read the questions before I read the passage?

Answer: Try working the passages both ways in the practice exam, one time reading the questions first, and a second time saving them until after the passage. My anything-but-humble opinion, however, is that reading the questions first doesn't do you much good. You have sooooooo much information floating around in that brain of yours; are you *really* going to remember the questions while reading the passage? If you can do so, bully for you; go join the CIA! If you're normal, however, you just waste time reading the questions, reading the passage, reading the questions a second time, going back to the passage again to look for the answers . . . . You get the idea.

All or Nothing: Questions You Should Always Do; Questions You Should Never Do

Knowing how to approach the passages on your SAT is extremely important. Even more important than the passages themselves, however, are the questions you must answer for each passage. After all, the admissions officer at Harvard isn't going to say to you: "Hey, tell me about that SAT passage you read on the curative properties of heavy metal music." The admissions officer is far more likely to ask: "How many reading questions did you answer correctly on the SAT?" No matter how carefully you read the passage, no matter how well you understand it, you must be able to put that knowledge to work to answer the questions that follow those passages. (***Bonus:*** Did you hear about the two musicians who walked into a heavy metal bar? The third one ducked.)

So just what kind of questions are you are most likely to encounter in the Critical Reading sections of the test? The following sections describe the basic question types that you may face in the dark alleys of the SAT.

It's the attitude, dude!

The author's opinion may be described as . . .

The tone of the passage is . . .

These two questions are variations on a single theme: What is the *tone* of the passage or the *attitude* of the author? Nothing in the passage answers this type of question directly. You can't find any one line reading: "In my opinion, which, by the way, is sardonic, the importance of . . . ." You simply must reason this one out.

The tone or attitude (found after the type of each passage in the following paragraphs) usually depends on the type of passage in question.

Science: Neutral or positive. A science passage gives you just the facts. The author rarely evaluates the facts one way or the other and rarely expresses an opinion. After all, how opinionated can someone be about how a camera works, for example? (***Bonus joke:*** Why was Cinderella hanging around outside the camera shop? She was waiting for her prints to come.)

Humanities: Positive or neutral. These passages are PC to the max — totally politically correct. No minority group gets trashed on the SAT. If the passage is about Miss Sklodowska, the passage tells you all the wonderful things about Miss Sklodowska (and only the wonderful things): her accomplishments despite great odds, her determination and tenacity, her charm and beauty, blah, blah, blah. Once in a while, such a passage may be neutral, giving you just the facts about someone, but you are extremely unlikely to encounter a humanities passage that is negative in tone.

Question: Just who was Miss Sklodowska (I couldn't make up a name like that!)? ***Answer:*** You know her better as Madam Curie.

Fiction: Who knows? Your guess is as good as mine. Remember that fiction passages follow no rules. The attitude or tone of a fiction passage could be negative, positive, or neutral. Everything just depends on the passage itself.

Theories: Most theory passages are positive in tone. The author is trying to make a point about his or her beliefs on a topic — something that he or she strongly feels should be done or changed. If, however, the first sentence of the passage reads something like "The educational system in this country stinks and should be completely abandoned," well then, you have a pretty good idea that the passage is negative.

Double or paired passages: Most paired passages are either neutral or positive. You are very unlikely to find any that are negative overall. Even if the two passages contradict each other, each individual passage presents its point.

Because so many of the tones or attitudes of the various passages are positive or neutral, certain words are often good to choose as answers to attitude or tone questions. The following table offers several positive words that you may want to consider choosing should any appear as potential answers to this kind of question:

Common Positive-Attitude Word	*More Difficult Word with the Same Meaning*
admiring	reverential
optimistic	sanguine
praising	laudatory

You get the idea. Wrong answers — that is, negative answers — may include the following words:

Common Negative-Attitude Word	*More Difficult Word with the Same Meaning*
belittling	denigrating
ridiculing	lampooning
sarcastic	sardonic

Because so many passages are neutral, the term *objective* (which means neutral, not taking one side or the other, not subjective or opinionated) is often a correct answer. Don't simply turn off your own brain and choose *objective* automatically . . . but it's a good guess if you're stumped for an answer. Think of it as guilty until proven innocent.

An attitude or tone question is a good one to take a stab at, even if you didn't read the entire passage or you read it but couldn't make heads or tails out of it. Because most correct answers to these questions are either neutral or positive, you can eliminate negative answer choices and at least make a pretty good guess.

If you don't recognize *any* of the words among the answer choices, your best bet is to skip this question. For example:

Which of the following best describes the author's attitude about his faux pas in attending the formal ceremony in a denim vest and jeans?

(A) craven

(B) impenitent

(C) lachrymose

(D) ebullient

(E) sanguinary

If you don't know what any of these words mean, all you're doing is making a random guess, with the odds against you. Skip it.

Trivia: Know the history of the words *denim* and *jeans*? They both derive from the place of origin of the fabric. *Denim* comes from the French *de Nimes,* meaning "of Nimes," the place the cloth was manufactured. *Jeans* is a corruption of *Genes,* which was French for the Italian city Genoa, where jeans were made.

What's the main idea or best title?

You can bet the farm (but, of course, only in states with legalized gambling) that you'll see a few *main idea* or *best title* questions; each passage usually has one. This type of question can assume any of the following forms:

The main idea of the passage is . . .

The best title for the passage is . . .

The primary purpose of Descartes's example is . . .

(Inside joke if you've studied philosophy: Descartes, the philosopher, strolled into his favorite restaurant one day, and the waiter asked him whether he'd like some soup. "I think not," murmured Descartes, and poof! He vanished.)

Words to describe Arnold, Sly, and Bruce . . . or not

- audacious
- cowering
- craven
- dastard*
- dauntless
- doughty
- intrepid
- mettlesome
- poltroon
- pusillanimous
- resolute
- timorous
- valiant

*It doesn't mean what you think!

The best place to find the main idea of the passage is in its topic sentence, which is usually the first or second sentence of the first paragraph. The topic sentence *may* be the last sentence of the passage, but such a structure is definitely rare. Your game plan upon encountering one of these questions should be to head right back to the first sentence to locate a main idea.

After you've read the entire passage, all the darn answers in a main idea question may look pretty good. That's because all of them usually consist of facts stated in the passage. Just because something is true and just because it is discussed in the passage doesn't mean that it's necessarily the *main* idea.

A main idea or best title question is one you should always answer. This type of question is pretty easy if you remember to go back and read the first few sentences. Even if you don't have time to read the entire passage — or even get started on it — you can nearly always hustle up an answer to this question by glancing at one sentence. It's worth a shot.

Hint: Because passages are almost always positive or neutral, the main idea/best title is almost always positive or neutral, too. Eliminate any negative answer choices right away. For example:

The main idea of this passage is

(A) the submission and shame of the Native Americans

(B) the unfair treatment of Native Americans

(C) how Native Americans are taking charge of their own destinies

(D) the prodigious difficulties facing Native Americans

(E) the causes behind Native American problems

Because all the answers but C are negative, choose C. ***Remember:*** Humanities passages are often about people who have beaten the odds: inspirational pioneers and leaders. The passage is certain to be very admiring of those people.

Did you know the word ***prodigious?*** It means huge. I'm always repeating my favorite Mark Twain quote: "I must have a prodigious quantity of mind. It takes me as long as a week to make it up."

What do you call the class kiss-up?

- deferential
- fawning
- obsequious
- servile
- slavish
- soft-soaper
- sycophant
- toady
- truckler

Consider the vocabulary in context

A vocabulary-in-context question merely asks you to define a term *as it is used in the passage*. The word is not some big, hairy old thing, but a normal, everyday word. You are lulled into a false sense of security as you say to yourself, "Well, I certainly know what *that* word means; why should I go back and look at the passage?" Uh-oh! Is that the theme from *Jaws* I hear? Dum dum, *dum dum,* DUM DUM . . . you are headed for a trap.

The reading passages tend to use somewhat, well . . . bizarre meanings of otherwise quite common words. Suppose that I ask you to define the word *cow*. You would probably start mooing and tell me the question is udderly ridiculous. (Did you think I had more pride than to sink so low? I didn't think so.) The reading passage, however, uses *cow* as a verb: "Refusing to let the prejudiced official *cow* her into waiving her rights, Janine demanded that her attorney be called immediately." *Cow* obviously has a different meaning in this context. Here, it means to intimidate or frighten.

If you didn't return to the passage, you would be content with your definition, which probably appears as one of the answer choices, just to trap unsuspecting fools — er, that is, victims — such as yourself. Always go back to the passage to see how the word is used in context. The vocabulary-in-context question actually can turn out to be one of the very easy ones — a real freebie for you — but only if you invest a few seconds going back to look for the word as it's used in the passage. The question bends over backward to help you, usually going so far as to give you the number of the line in which the word in question can be found! ("In line 41, *cow* means . . .") Go back and look! Get the point?

The vocabulary-in-context question is another good one to answer, no matter what. If you haven't time to answer all the questions about a passage, make sure that you at least try to answer this one. Even if you read the passage and don't understand it, you can still answer this question. In fact, even if you don't get to the passage at all and are almost out of time, you can still answer this question in only a few seconds by going back to the indicated line and seeing how the word is used.

The detail or fact question

If a question begins with the phrase "According to the passage . . ." you've hit a *detail* or *fact* question — which is usually a very easy question to answer correctly. All you need to do is identify the key words in the question, return to the reading passage, and skim for those words. The answer is usually within a few sentences of those key words. For example:

> According to the passage, what two elements make up Compound Q?

The key words here are *Compound Q*. Go back to the passage and find the exact answer.

According to the passage, why did Mr. Sanchez call his brother, "The Mad Hatter"?

The key words in this question are *Mr. Sanchez, brother,* and *Mad Hatter.* Go back to the passage and find the exact answer.

Trivia: Where did we get the expression "mad as a hatter" or the nickname "the Mad Hatter?" The term came from Victorian times. Hat makers used mercury to make a glossy finish on the top hats. The hatters breathed the mercury fumes and absorbed them through the skin. The fumes were toxic and caused madness.

"According to the author" is not the same thing as "According to the passage." The two phrases may look the same, but author questions are often more difficult than passage questions and are not as straightforward. A question that asks you about the author may be more of a read-between-the-lines question than one about the passage — something you can answer only if you truly understand what you read. An "according to the passage" question, on the other hand, can often be answered even without reading the whole passage, by skimming for the key words.

Negative or exception questions

One type of question is a trained killer and should often be skipped: the *negative* or *exception* question. These questions usually take one of the following forms:

Which of the following is *not* true?

The *least* likely situation is . . .

With which of the following would the author *disagree?*

All the following are true, *except:*

These questions are phrased in the negative. They are very tricky questions. You're actually looking for four correct answers and then, by the process of elimination, choosing the one that is not correct. Getting confused is easy; wasting too much time on these questions is even easier. This type of question is a good one to save for last — or avoid entirely.

Toga! toga! toga! The Roman numeral question

Roman numeral questions (which are becoming rare) can scar you for life. Here's an example of a Roman numeral question:

The author mentions which of the following as support for her argument that depression is an underdiagnosed disease in our society?

I. low productivity rates

II. high divorce rates

III. governmental cut backs in mental health programs

(A) I only

(B) II only

(C) III only

(D) I and II only

(E) I, II, and III

Roman numeral questions are usually time-wasters. In effect, you must reread almost the entire passage to determine whether I, II, or III is mentioned anywhere. A common trap is to mention I and II close together and then mention III much farther down within the passage. Most people find I and II and then, if III doesn't appear to be hanging around, choose I and II only, missing the question and sending their scores down the tubes. (Hey, maybe the test makers get *bonus points* for every student they snare with such a trick — kind of like a cop writing speeding tickets to meet his quota in a speed trap! Just a thought.) To answer a Roman numeral question, you must reread most of the passage, just in case one of the concepts is floating around where you least expect it. If you aren't willing (or able) to commit enough time to do so, you'd better just forget about answering this question.

Defeating Reading: Tricks for Making Life a Little Easier

Now you know about the five types of passages and the six primary types of questions associated with these passages. Time now for the fun stuff — the *tricks*.

Be positive or neutral, not negative

I intend to say this over and over until you're exasperated enough to cut off my air supply. Because most of the reading passages are positive or neutral, most of the correct answers also are positive or neutral. Because test makers don't want to get sued for saying mean and vicious things about anyone, they are sweet and charming when choosing the passages and creating the questions (and they probably snarl at the dog when they get home to get the excess saccharine out of their systems after being so nice at work all day long). Be sweet and charming right back at 'em: Choose positive, goody-goody answers.

Choose answers containing key words

The key words, found in the topic sentence, are what the whole passage is all about. The correct answers usually feature those words as well. If the passage is about Chicano history, the right answer often contains the words *Chicano history* in it. Don't choose an answer only because it contains the key words, but if you can narrow the answers down to two, choose the one with the key words.

Passages that you'll never see on the SAT

If I ruled the world, all passages would be interesting and fun. Here are a few of the passages I'd like to see on the test.

- **Science:** "Cannibalism and You: The Science of Pigging Out at a Barbecue."
- **Humanities:** "The End of Political Correctness: An Analysis of the Philosophies of Howard Stern and Rush Limbaugh."
- **Fiction:** An excerpt from *Confessions from the Funny Farm*, Chapter Two: "How the SAT Pushed Me over the Edge."
- **Theories:** "Difficult Choices: Lobotomy or SAT. Which Messes You Up Less? The Insider's View."
- **Paired passages:** "Brain Cell Extinction: A Debate between *Mad Magazine* and *The National Enquirer*."

Be wishy-washy, not dramatic

The test makers realize that people have different points of view. They don't want to be dogmatic or doctrinaire, saying that this is the right way, the only way, so zip your lip and don't argue. They want to hedge their bets by leaving some space for personal interpretation. And, of course, they don't want to get sued. If you're down to a choice of two answers, choose the more moderate or wishy-washy of the two. Wimp out big time.

Suppose you manage to narrow the answer choices down to the following two:

(A) The author hates discrimination.

(B) The author is saddened by the discrimination and tries to understand its causes.

Answer B is the kinder, gentler, more wimpy answer — and is probably the correct one.

Correct answers are usually above or below the key words or indicated line numbers

This can get nasty. The question asks you about something and sends you to a particular line number. But either you don't find an answer in that line or you find the trap answer. Expand your horizons. Read a few sentences above the indicated line and a few sentences below the line. The correct answer is usually somewhere in the vicinity. If you just keep looking where the question sends you, it's like looking for your house keys where they're normally kept and where you've searched a thousand times already to no avail. You need to branch out.

A Final Review

Wow. You've had a lot of information thrown at you in this chapter. You've discovered the types of passages, the types of questions, and the tricks and traps built into both. Are you having trouble keeping everything straight? Here is a short-and-sweet summary.

An overview of the types of passages and reading suggestions for each passage

You're likely to encounter five types of passages on the SAT, as described in the following sections.

Science

Keep the following in mind when you see science passages:

- They are neutral or positive.
- The passages may be hard to understand, but their questions are easy and straightforward.

Read science passages quickly, just to get an overview of what they cover; don't try to understand everything you read.

Humanities

Humanities passages have the following in common:

- They are often about minority groups.
- They are usually positive or neutral, often focusing on a pioneer in a field or someone who overcame great obstacles.
- They are all sweetness and light and rarely say anything even remotely critical about their subjects.

Read the passage slowly and carefully; questions usually require an understanding of between-the-lines concepts and can't be answered merely by going back and skimming for a fact.

Fiction

The following describe fiction passages:

- They are excerpts from novels or short stories, which could be recent or very old.
- Fiction passages follow no rules! Ignore all the tips and traps you were given for the other passages; you're on your own here.

Read fiction passages "normally." Don't skim them, as you would a science passage, or go very slowly, as you would in a humanities passage. Read for fun, as you would read a pleasure book.

Theories

Theories passages normally display the following traits:

- They express personal opinion, which may or may not be correct.
- They can be either positive or neutral, rarely negative.
- You must answer the questions based on the author's opinions (not yours!), even if you think the writer is delusional.

Read these passages slowly and carefully. Try to understand where the author is coming from and how he or she thinks.

Double or paired

Double, or paired, passages have the following characteristics:

- They are two separate passages that cover related topics; the two passages may present similar or opposing views of the topic.
- The last few questions about these passages ask you to compare or contrast the passages; these questions are often both difficult and time-consuming. Skip them unless you're absolutely sure of your answer.

Treat these passages as if they were two separate entities: Read passage one and answer the questions about it. Then read passage two and answer the questions on it.

An overview of the types of questions and the traps hidden in each one

As you take the SAT, you'll encounter the following types of questions. When you do, remember the traps and tricks for handling them.

Attitude or tone

Attitude or tone questions have the following characteristics:

- The correct answers are usually neutral or positive; they are rarely negative.
- This type of question is easy to answer, even without reading the passage; make sure that you eliminate negative answers first.

Main idea/best title

The following is true of a main idea or best title question:

- You can frequently find the answer in the topic sentence, which is usually the first sentence of the passage.
- The correct answer often contains certain key words that usually come from the first sentence of the passage.
- The correct answer is usually positive or neutral, rarely negative.
- This type is a good question to try to answer, even without reading (or understanding) the entire passage.

The end is near: The Critical Reading question review

Tips and tricks:

- Be positive or neutral, not negative.
- Choose answers containing key words.
- Be wishy-washy, not dramatic.
- Look for answers above or below the key words or indicated line numbers.

Chapter 9

Practicing What I Preach: Critical Reading Practice Exam

In This Chapter

- Looking at two incredibly soporific and typically boring full-length reading passages and one abbreviated passage
- Examining tricky, tacky, and traumatic questions
- Rubbing your nose in what you *should* have done through detailed answer explanations

No, don't panic; this section isn't *War and Peace, The Sequel.* It just features a dozen questions based on two full-length passages and one abbreviated one. For now, don't worry about timing yourself. Try to identify each selection as one of the types of reading passages described in Chapter 8 (science, humanities, fiction, and so on) and use the tips I give you in the second-to-last section of that chapter for reading that type of passage:

- Tip 1: Be positive or neutral, not negative
- Tip 2: Choose answers containing key words
- Tip 3: Be wishy-washy, not dramatic
- Tip 4: Correct answers are usually above or below the key words or indicated line numbers

As you answer the questions, try to identify which type each question is (attitude/tone, main idea/best title, Roman numeral, and so on) and to recall any traps inherent in that type of question.

Look for words in ***this special type*** throughout the answer sections of this chapter for more additions to your vocabulary lists. Each answer explanation is followed by the number of a tip that you can use to determine the answer choice.

Passage 1

The following is adapted from a paper by Geological Survey Professionals, 1981.

Microbiological activity clearly affects the mechanical strength of leaves. Although it cannot be denied that with most species the loss of mechanical strength is the result of both invertebrate feeding and microbiological breakdown, the example of *Fagus sylvatica* illustrates loss without any sign of invertebrate attack being evident. *Fagus* shows little sign of invertebrate attack even after being exposed for eight months in either lake or stream environment, but results of the rolling fragmentation experiment show that loss of mechanical strength, even in this apparently resistant species, is considerable.

Most species appear to exhibit a higher rate of degradation in the stream environment than in the lake. This is perhaps most clearly shown in the case of *Alnus*. Examination of the type of destruction suggests that the cause for the greater loss of material in the stream-processed leaves is a combination of both biological and mechanical degradation. The leaves exhibit an angular fragmentation, which is characteristic of mechanical damage, rather than the rounded holes typical of the attack by large particle feeders or the skeletal vein pattern produced by microbial degradation and small particle feeders. As the leaves become less strong, the fluid forces acting on the stream nylon cages caused successively greater fragmentation.

Mechanical fragmentation, like biological breakdown, is to some extent influenced by leaf structure and form. In some leaves with a strong midrib, the lamina break up, but the pieces remain attached by means of the midrib. One type of leaf may break clean while another tears off and is easily destroyed once the tissues are weakened by microbial attack.

In most species the mechanical breakdown will take the form of gradual attrition at the margins. If the energy of the environment is sufficiently high, brittle species may be broken across the midrib, something that rarely happens with more pliable leaves. The result of attrition is that, where the areas of the whole leaves follow a normal distribution, a bimodal distribution is produced, one peak composed mainly of the fragmented pieces, the other of the larger remains.

To test the theory that a thin leaf has only half the chance of a thick one for entering the fossil record, all other things being equal, Ferguson (1971) cut discs of fresh leaves from 11 species, which covered a range of different leaf thicknesses, and rotated them with sand and water in a revolving drum. Each run lasted 100 hours and was repeated three times, but even after this treatment, all species showed little sign of wear. It therefore seems unlikely that leaf thickness alone, without substantial microbial preconditioning, contributes much to the probability that a leaf will enter a depositional environment in a recognizable form. The results of experiments with whole fresh leaves show that they are more resistant to fragmentation than leaves exposed to microbiological attack. Unless the leaf is exceptionally large or small, leaf size and thickness are not likely to be as critical in determining the preservation potential of a leaf type as the rate of microbiological degradation.

1. Which of the following would be the best title for the passage?

   (A) Why Leaves Disintegrate

   (B) An Analysis of Leaf Structure and Composition

   (C) Comparing Lakes and Streams

   (D) The Purpose of Particle Feeders and Other Vegetarians

   (E) How Leaves' Mechanical Strength Is Affected by Microbiological Activity

The main idea, main purpose, or best title is found in the topic sentence, which is usually the first sentence of the passage. The correct answer here, choice E, is taken nearly word-for-word from the first sentence. Notice that, because the passage is talking primarily about leaves, the word *leaf,* or *leaves* needs to be in the title, which eliminates choices C and D right off. Choice A is too broad; there may be other causes of disintegration that the passage doesn't mention. Choice B is too specific. The passage mentions leaf structure but doesn't make that topic its primary focus. Choice D is a joke. Although the passage talks about particle feeders, it doesn't directly discuss vegetarians. Tip: 2

Trivia: Can you name five famous vegetarians (one of whom is indirectly connected to the SAT)?

Answer: Pythagoras, Leonardo da Vinci, Mahatma Gandhi, George Bernard Shaw, and Adolf Hitler (and it's Pythagoras, *not* Hitler, who's connected to this exam — you use the Pythagorean theorem).

2. Which of the following is mentioned as a reason for leaf degradation in streams?

I. mechanical damage

II. biological degradation

III. large particle feeders

(A) II only

(B) I and II only

(C) I and III only

(D) II and III only

(E) I, II, and III

Paragraph two of the passage tells you that ". . . loss of material in stream-processed leaves is a combination of biological and mechanical degradation." Reason III is incorrect because lines 12 and 13 specifically state that the pattern of holes is contrary to that of large particle feeders. The correct answer is B. Tip: 4

3. The conclusion the author reached from Ferguson's revolving drum experiment was that

(A) leaf thickness is only a contributing factor to leaf fragmentation

(B) leaves submersed in water degrade more rapidly than leaves deposited in mud or silt

(C) leaves with a strong midrib deteriorate less than leaves without such a midrib

(D) microbial attack is exacerbated by high temperatures

(E) bimodal distribution reduces leaf attrition

Lines 31–33 tell you that it is unlikely that leaf thickness *alone* affects the final form of the leaf. You probably need to reread that sentence a few times to understand it, but this is the type of question you should definitely attempt to answer — a detail or fact question. Choice A is the correct answer. Choice B introduces facts not discussed in the passage; there was no talk of leaves in mud or silt. Choice C is mentioned in the passage but not in Ferguson's experiments. Be careful to answer *only* what the question is asking; the mere fact that a statement is true or is mentioned in the passage means nothing if the question isn't asking about that point. Nothing appears in the passage about high temperatures, which eliminates choice D. (Did you know the word ***exacerbated***? It means made worse — like this reading passage probably exacerbated your headache.) Choice E sounds pretentious and pompous — and nice and scientific — but again has nothing to do with Ferguson. To answer this question correctly, you need to return to the passage to look up Ferguson specifically, not merely rely on your memory of the passage as a whole. Tip: 2

4. The tone of the passage is

(A) mesmerizing

(B) diffident

(C) objective

(D) bemused

(E) supercilious

You *had* to get this question correct. If you missed this question, please consider yourself totally humiliated. The correct answer is C. Most of the time, a science passage has a neutral, objective, unbiased tone. The author neither praises nor criticizes anything; he just gives the facts. Tip: 1

As for the other words, here's a quick vocabulary lesson: Choice A, ***mesmerizing,*** means hypnotic or captivating. You probably weren't held spellbound by this passage. If you were, do yourself a favor: Get a life! (By the way, do you know who Felix Mesmer was? He was called "the father of hypnotism." What we now know as hypnotism used to be called *mesmerism,* after Felix.) In choice B, ***diffident*** means unassertive, reserved, laid-back. You are diffident if you ask someone to the prom by digging your toes into the carpet and saying, "Uh, I don't suppose you'd want to go with me, would you?" Choice D, ***bemused,*** means confused. You are bemused by the information given to you and must read it over several times to comprehend it. ***Supercilious,*** in choice E, means arrogant, conceited, stuck-up.

5. The author most likely is addressing this passage to

(A) gardeners

(B) botanists

(C) hikers

(D) mechanical engineers

(E) Adam and Eve

The passage is talking about the microbiological activity affecting the strength of leaves. (You know this because you already answered a best title question on the topic — question number 1.) Although choosing D is tempting, given the topic of the passage, mechanical engineers are usually interested more in machines than in leaves. Botanists are the ones who would most likely read this passage. The correct answer is B. The advice is probably too technical for gardeners, choice A, and is waaaay too specific for hikers, choice C. Choice E was added for comic relief. (If anyone needed to know how and why leaves disintegrate, especially fig leaves, it would be Adam and Eve.)

Passage II

This passage is from the Robert Louis Stevenson novel, *Kidnapped,* 1886.

Meanwhile such of the wounded as could move came clambering out of the fore-scuttle and began to help; while the rest that lay helpless in their bunks harrowed me with screaming and begging to be saved.

The captain took no part. It seemed he was struck stupid. He stood holding by the shrouds, talking to himself and groaning out aloud whenever the ship hammered on the rock. His brig was like wife and child to him; he had looked on, day by day, at the mishandling of poor Ransome; but when it came to the brig, he seemed to suffer along with her.

All the time of our working at the boat, I remember only one other thing; that I asked Alan, looking across at the shore, what country it was; and he answered, it was the worst possible for him, for it was a land of the Campbells.

We had one of the wounded men told off to keep a watch upon the seas and cry us warning. Well, we had the boat about ready to be launched, when this man sang out pretty shrill: "For God's sake, hold on!" We knew by his tone that it was something more than ordinary; and sure enough; there followed a sea so huge that it lifted the brig right up and canted her over on her beam. Whether the cry came too late or my hold was too weak, I know not; but at the sudden tilting of the ship I was cast clean over the bulwarks into the sea.

I went down, and drank my fill; and then came up, and got a blink of the moon; and then down again. They say a man sinks the third time for good. I cannot be made like other folk, then; for I would not like to write how often I went down or how often I came up again. All the while, I was being hurled along, and beaten upon and choked, and then swallowed whole, and the thing was so distracting to my wits, that I was neither sorry nor afraid.

Presently, I found I was holding to a spar, which helped me somewhat. And then all of a sudden I was in quiet water, and began to come to myself.

It was the spare yard I had got hold of, and I was amazed to see how far I had traveled from the brig. I hailed her indeed; but it was plain she was already out of cry. She was still holding together; but whether or not they had yet launched the boat, I was too far off and too low down to see.

While I was hailing the brig, I spied a tract of water lying between us, where no great waves came, but which yet boiled white all over, and bristled in the moon with rings and bubbles. Sometimes the whole tract swung to one side, like the tail of a live serpent; sometimes, for a glimpse, it all would disappear and then boil up again. What it was I had no guess, which for the time increased my fear of it; but I now know it must have been the roost or tide race, which carried me away so fast and tumbled me about so cruelly, and at last, as if tired of that play, had flung me and spare yard upon its landward margin.

6. The author compares the ship to the captain's wife and child to

(A) lament the captain's long separation from his family

(B) demonstrate the difficulty the captain has keeping focused on his job

(C) predict the captain's future madness

(D) show the depth of the connection the captain has to his ship

(E) enlist the reader's sympathy for the captain's plight

The focus of the second paragraph is on how the captain is very upset by the condition of his ship. To compare his ship to his wife and child is to show how much he loves the ship and thus to emphasize the deep attachment he has to the vessel. The correct answer is D. Tip: 2

7. Which of the following may you infer from the passage?

(A) Alan and the Campbells are enemies.

(B) The ship had been attacked by another ship.

(C) The narrator was on his first sea voyage.

(D) Alan and the author are brothers.

(E) The ship's crew was in the process of a mutiny.

This is a pretty simple question. In lines 8-10, you read that Alan felt the land was the worst possible for him because it was a land of the Campbells. From this, you may readily infer that he and the Campbells weren't about to sit down to soup together — that they were enemies. The correct answer is A. Tip: 1

8. By saying that he "got a blink at the moon" in line 17, the author means that

(A) he foresaw his own demise

(B) he saw the sky as he came up out of the water to get air

(C) he was hallucinating as he was drowning

(D) he was able to see the ship as it sailed away

(E) he saw the captain with his pants down

The fifth paragraph, in which this statement is found, describes the author's dunking and near-drowning. He was bobbing up and down in the water, going under the sea and then coming up for air, at which point he saw the moon. The correct answer is B. Make sure that you answer the question in the context in which you find the statement; don't use your own common sense. And if you chose E — man, you're having altogether too much fun for the SAT. Tip: 4

9. The purpose of the passage is

   (A) to portray a mood of terror

   (B) to urge others not to go to sea

   (C) to contrast lifestyles of sailors from different countries

   (D) to describe an event

   (E) to praise the camaraderie between shipmates

The passage merely tells of something that happened to the author. (Choices using the words *describe, discuss,* and *explain* are often excellent answers to a "What is the purpose?" question.) Choice A is tempting, but surprisingly, the passage is not all that terrifying. You read in line 21 that the author was so distracted that he was "neither sorry nor afraid." The correct answer is D.

10. The author was saved from drowning

   (A) by the efforts of his captain

   (B) by holding onto floating debris

   (C) by his excellent swimming ability

   (D) after the tide carried him back to the ship

   (E) after his crewmates launched a lifeboat and went out to him

Line 22 tells you that the author "was holding to a spar." Even if you don't know what a spar is (it's a mast, a pole, a boom), you can infer that it is something that was floating in the water. The correct answer is B. As for choice A, the captain didn't seem to be doing anything but grieving over his ship — forget the men. Choice C is definitely out; the author practically drowned, bobbing up and down, before finding something to hold onto. Choice D also is out. This excerpt doesn't tell whether the narrator *ever* gets back to the ship. Choice E is a trap answer. Lines 26 and 27 tell you that the writer couldn't see whether his shipmates had, in fact, launched a boat. This question requires careful reading of the passage and the questions to answer correctly.

Passage III

This passage is from a narrative on explorations by individuals in the West.

Line Gustave Eisen was a cosmopolitan, world-traveling, many-sided scientist who was drawn in the spring of 1898 to a study of ancient civilizations and turquoise mining in a far corner of San Bernardino County.

He was born in Stockholm, Sweden, on August 2, 1847. He came to America in October 1872, after earning a Ph.D. degree at Upsala University earlier that same year. He apparently headed straight for California, settling in Fresno, which at the time was a pioneer community. There he became interested in horticulture. By pamphleteering and by lectures, he urged the introduction into California of the Symrna fig and the avocado. He joined the California Academy of Sciences in 1871, serving as curator from 1892 to 1900. Eisen helped to create the Sequoia National Park; as a result Mount Eisen, elevation 12,000 feet, was named in his honor. He led academy expeditions to Baja, California, in 1892, 1893, and 1894. In these years, Eisen's interests broadened to include geology, archaeology, and helminthology.

Therefore, when in March of 1898 the San Francisco *Call,* as a circulation stunt, decided to send an expedition into the deserts of San Bernardino County to verify the prospectors' tales of long-lost Aztec turquoise mines, the newspaper asked Dr. Eisen, as perhaps California's leading scientist, to accompany its expedition. In early March 1898, the *Call*'s party left for the desert.

The expedition began in comfortable luxury aboard a Santa Fe train, which it rode to Blake, a small station 25 miles west of Needles. From Blake, a spur line led to Manvel, a supply point in the eastern California mountains. It took 44 hours to get that far from San Francisco. From there, the group proceeded by wagon and team over a rough trail of 60 miles to the site of the rumored mines, under the guidance of veteran desert traveler J.W. Stine.

When the expedition reached the mines in northeastern San Bernardino County, it found them in the center of an extinct volcanic crater. This spot was almost where Arizona, California, and Nevada met just west of the Colorado River. The principal turquoise mines in the area were fifteen miles long by three or four miles wide. Delighted with the find, Eisen told the other expedition members that he had heard of and believed a Piute legend stating that some Mayans had taught the Mojaves to mine. Then, out of jealousy, the Piutes had killed most of the Mojaves and had driven out the rest.

11. In line 1, "drawn" means

(A) pictured

(B) attracted to

(C) expanded

(D) diagrammed

(E) forced by

From line 2, you may infer that Eisen was attracted to his studies. This is a typical vocabulary-in-context question. If you answered it based on your own commonsense definition of *drawn* instead of going back to the passage (trap!), you probably chose A or D. Make sure, if faced with this type of question, that you always go back to see how the word is used in the passage. The correct answer is B. Tip: 4

12. The passage answers all of the following questions, except:

I. Why was Dr. Eisen asked to participate in the search for turquoise mines?

II. Why were turquoise mines located in a volcanic crater?

III. Why did Dr. Eisen believe the Piute legend of killing the Mojaves that the Mayans had taught to mine?

(A) I only

(B) I and II only

(C) I and III only

(D) II and III only

(E) I, II, and III

The first question is answered in lines 15–16, which tells, you that Dr. Eisen was asked to go along "as perhaps California's leading scientist." Eliminate all answer choices with I in them. Hey! The answer must be D! You don't really have to go through the rest of the question, but I'll do so here just to prove the answer to you skeptics. (If you eliminate answers as you go, you are often rewarded by not having to do so much work.) Answer II is tricky. You are told in line 24 that the mines were *in* a volcanic crater but not *why* they were there. As for answer III, line 28 tells you only that the Piutes killed the Mojaves "out of jealousy" and doesn't tell why Dr. Eisen believed the legend. Tip: 4

Part III

Two Years of Math in Three Hours: The Dreaded Math Reviews and Mini-Tests

"I wish you'd practice for the math section of the SATs on your own time and not when you're calculating the tip on three cheeseburger specials with Cokes all around."

In this part . . .

No, no, please don't go get your pillow and PJs. I promise that *this* math review won't put you to sleep. I'm not going to start at 1 + 1 = 2 and take you through every math concept you've learned since kindergarten; I have more respect for you than that. This math review neither insults you nor wastes your time. Instead, I keep the instruction down to what you *really* need for the SAT. For example, because ratios are often on the test, I cover them in detail. Because calculus is not on the SAT, I don't even mention it.

Even if you're a math whiz, humor me and go through all the reviews. I guarantee that somewhere, hidden in a nook or cranny of one of the reviews is some esoteric formula that either you never knew or you forgot because you use it so rarely. Naturally, that's just the type of thing the SAT would test. And do all the example problems yourself; don't just look at the answers. If you fall for a trap ("How many three-cent stamps in a dozen?" Think about it . . .), you're more likely to remember it on the SAT than if you just read about the trap.

Chapter 10

Ogling More Figures Than a Beauty Pageant Judge: Geometry Review

In This Chapter

- Getting to the point with angles
- Taming triangles
- Matchmaking similar figures
- Presenting polygons
- Running in circles

Angles are a big part of the SAT geometry problems. Fortunately, understanding angles is easy when you memorize a few basic concepts. And keep in mind the best news: You don't have to do proofs. Finding an angle is usually a matter of simple addition or subtraction.

You Gotta Have an Angle

These three rules generally apply to the SAT:

- There are no negative angles.
- There are no zero angles.
- It is extremely unlikely that you'll see any *fractional angles.* (For example, an angle won't measure 45½ degrees or 32¾ degrees.)

1. **Angles greater than zero but less than 90 degrees are called *acute.*** Think of an acute angle as being a *cute* little angle.

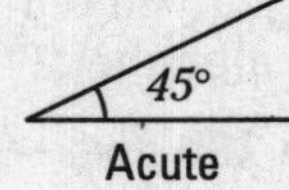

2. **Angles equal to 90 degrees are called *right angles.*** They are formed by perpendicular lines and are indicated by a box in the corner of the two intersecting lines.

A common SAT trap is to have two lines appear to be perpendicular and look as if they form a right angle. Do not assume this to be true. An angle is a right angle *only* if (A) you're expressly told, "This is a right angle"; (B) you see the perpendicular symbol (⊥) indicating that the lines form a 90-degree angle; or (C) you see the box in the angle. Otherwise, you may be headed for a trap!

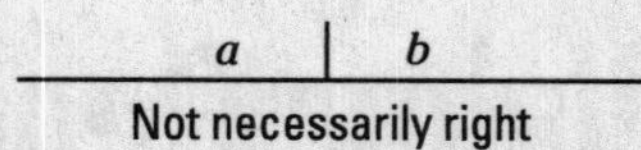

Not necessarily right

3. **Angles that sum up to 90 degrees are called *complementary angles.*** Think of C for corner (the lines form a 90-degree corner angle) and C for complementary.

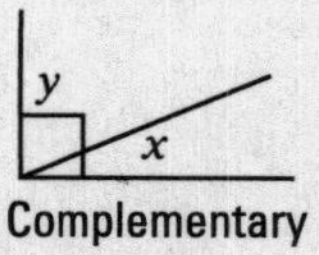

Complementary

4. **An angle that is greater than 90 degrees but less than 180 degrees is called *obtuse.*** Think of obtuse as *obese* — an obese (or fat) angle is an obtuse angle.

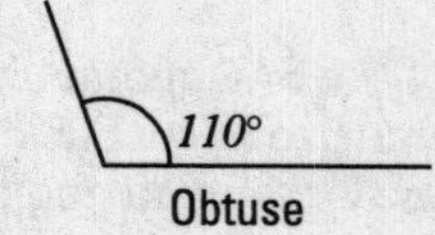

Obtuse

5. **An angle that measures exactly 180 degrees is called a *straight angle.***

Straight

6. **Angles that sum up to 180 degrees are called *supplementary angles.***

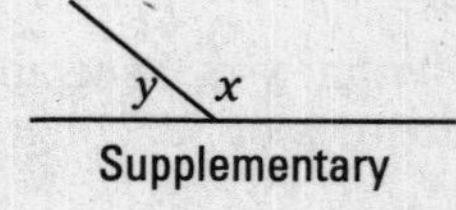

Supplementary

Think of S for straight angles and S for supplementary angles. Be careful not to confuse complementary angles (C for complementary; C for corner) with supplementary angles (S for supplementary; S for straight). If you're likely to get these confused, just think alphabetically. C comes before S in the alphabet; 90 comes before 180 when you count.

7. **An angle that is greater than 180 degrees but less than 360 degrees is called a *reflex angle.***

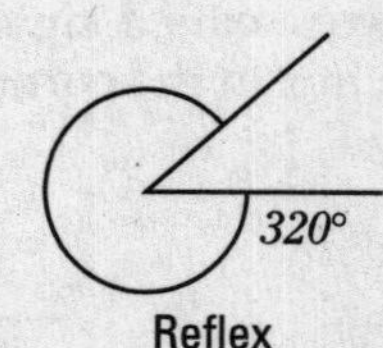

Reflex

Think of a reflex angle as a reflection or mirror image of an acute angle. It makes up the rest of the angle when there's an acute angle.

Reflex angles are rarely tested on the SAT.

8. Angles around a point sum up to 360 degrees.

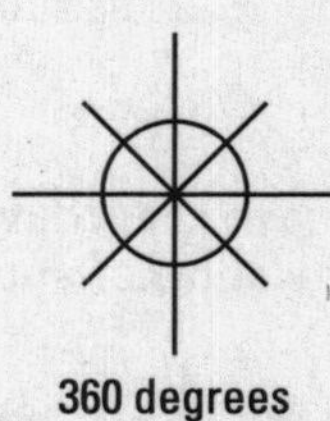

9. Angles that are opposite each other have equal measures and are called *vertical angles.*

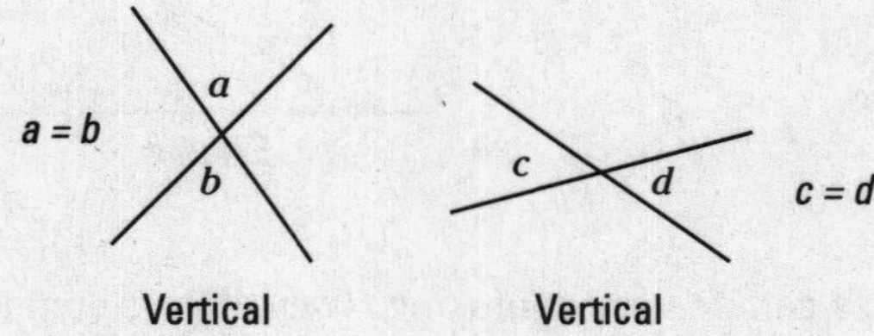

Note that vertical angles may actually be horizontal. Just remember that vertical angles are across from each other, whether they are up and down (vertical) or side by side (horizontal).

10. Angles in the same position — *corresponding angles* — around two parallel lines and a transversal have the same measures.

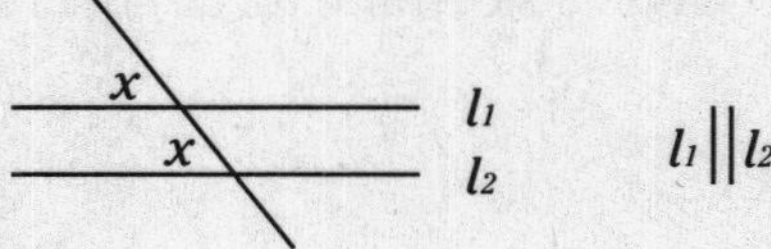

When you see two parallel lines and a transversal, number the angles. Start in the upper right corner with 1 and go clockwise. For the second batch of angles, start in the upper right corner with 5 and go clockwise:

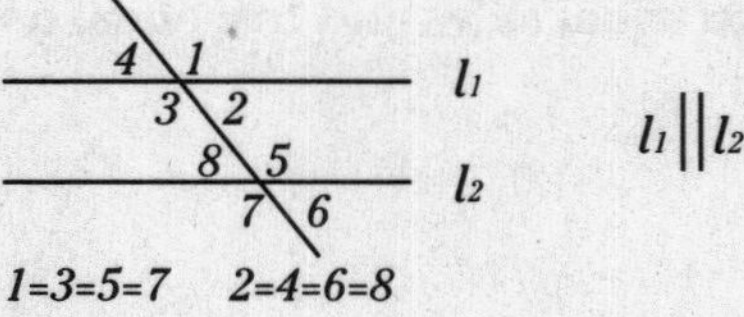

Note that all the odd-numbered angles are equal and all the even-numbered angles are equal.

Be careful not to zigzag back and forth when numbering, like this:

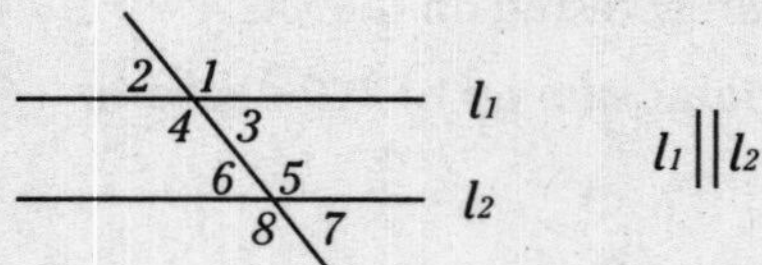

If you zig when you should have zagged, you can no longer use the tip that all even-numbered angles are equal to one another and all odd-numbered angles are equal to one another.

11. **The *exterior angles* of any figure are supplementary to the interior angles and sum up to 360 degrees.**

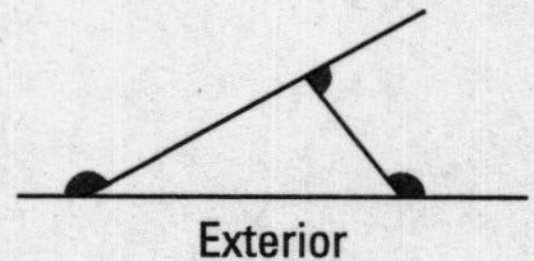
Exterior

Exterior angles can be very confusing. They always sum up to 360 degrees, no matter what type of figure you have. Many people think that angles are exterior angles when they aren't. ***Remember:*** To be called an exterior angle, an angle must be supplementary to an interior angle.

Triangle Trauma

1. **A triangle with three equal sides and three equal angles is called *equilateral.***

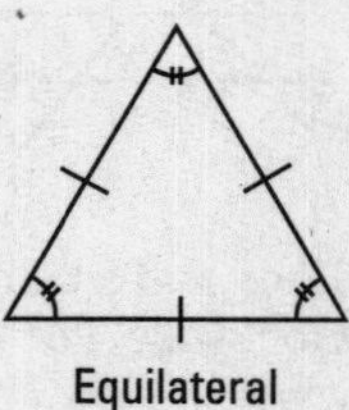
Equilateral

2. **A triangle with two equal sides and two equal angles is called *isosceles.***

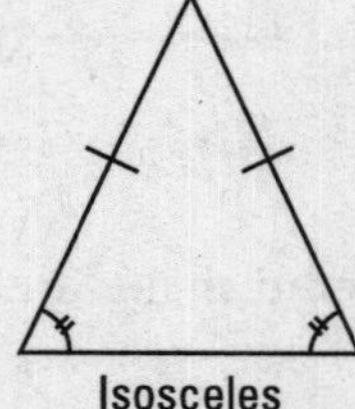
Isosceles

3. Angles opposite equal sides in an isosceles triangle are also equal.

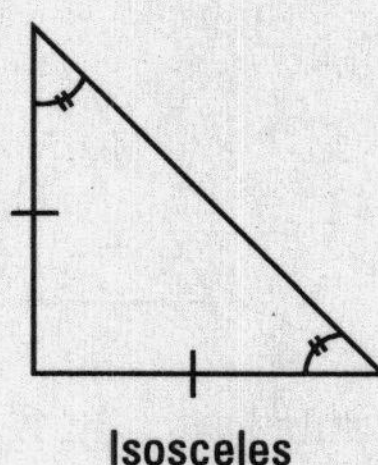

Isosceles

4. A triangle with no equal sides and no equal angles is called *scalene.*

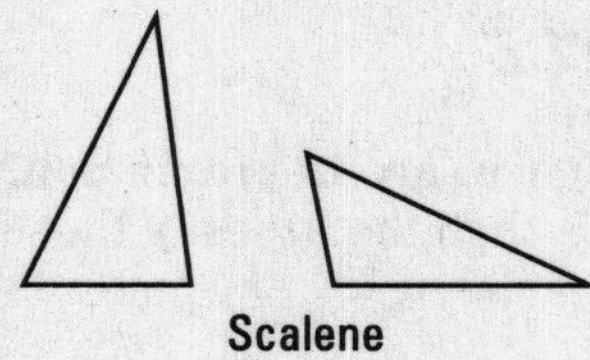

Scalene

5. In any triangle, the largest angle is opposite the longest side.

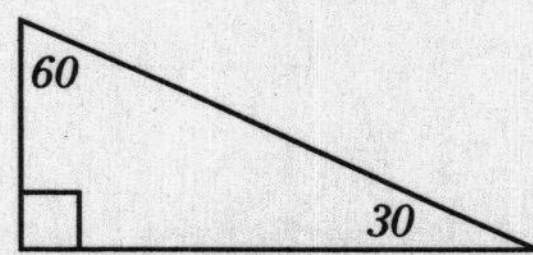

6. In any triangle, the sum of the lengths of two sides must be greater than the length of the third side. This is often written as $a + b > c$, where a, b, and c are the sides of the triangle.

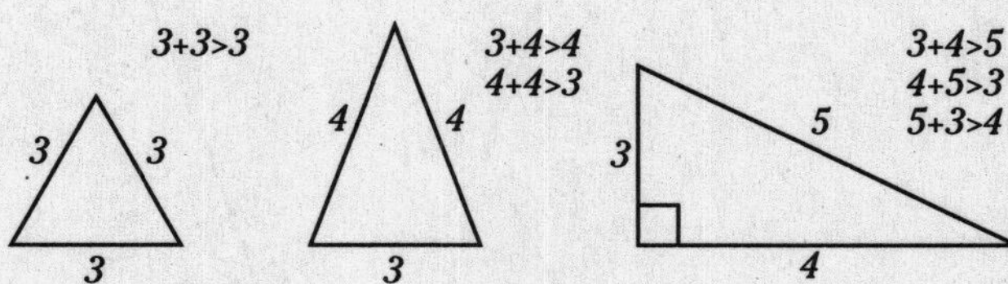

7. In any type of triangle, the sum of the interior angles is 180 degrees.

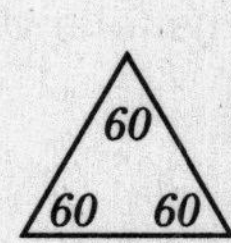

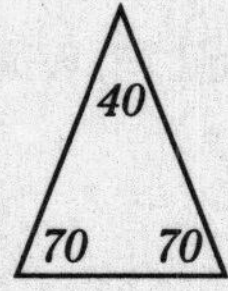

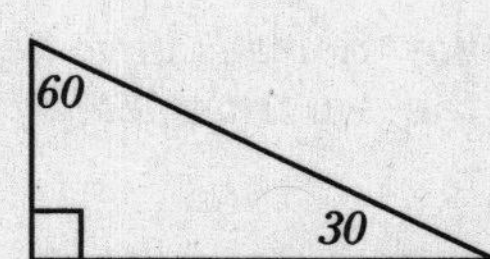

Often, a trap question wants you to assume that different-sized triangles have different angle measures. Wrong! A triangle can be seven stories high and have 180 degrees or be microscopic and have 180 degrees. The size of the triangle is irrelevant; every triangle's internal angles sum up to 180 degrees.

8. The measure of an exterior angle of a triangle is equal to the sum of the two remote interior angles.

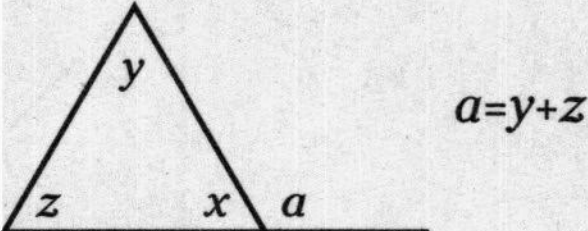

When you think about this rule logically, it makes sense. The sum of supplementary angles is 180. The sum of the angles in a triangle is 180. Therefore, angle $x = 180 - (y + z)$ or angle $x = 180 - a$. That must mean that $a = y + z$.

Similar figures

1. **The sides of similar figures are in proportion.** For example, if the heights of two similar triangles are in a ratio 2:3, then the bases of those triangles are in a ratio of 2:3, as well.

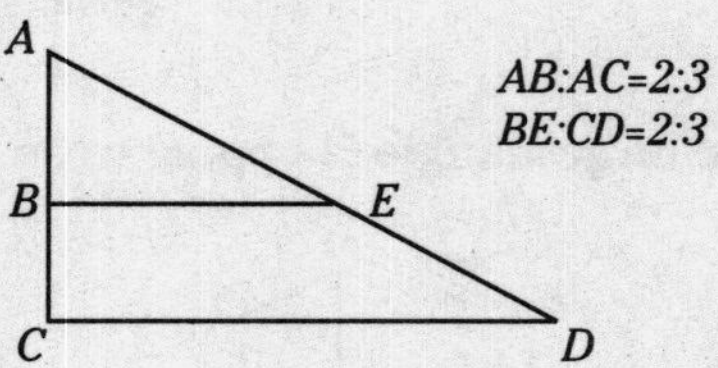

2. **The ratio of the areas of similar figures is equal to the square of the ratio of their sides.** For example, if each side of Figure A is ⅓ the length of each side of similar Figure B, then the area of Figure A is ⅑ (which is $[\frac{1}{3}]^2$) the area of Figure B.

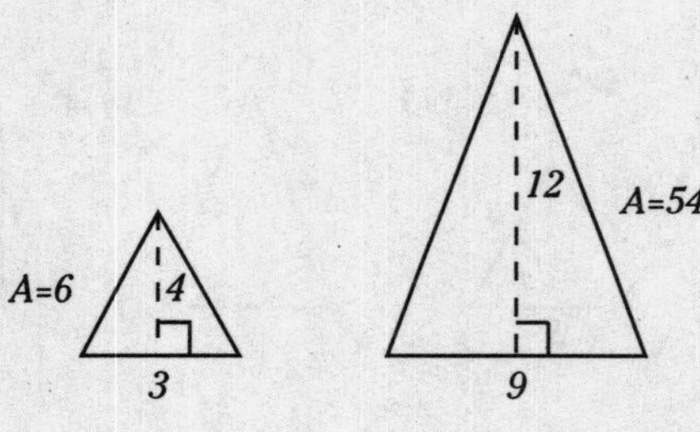

Two similar triangles have bases 5 and 25. Which of the following expresses the ratio of the areas of the two triangles?

(A) 1:5

(B) 1:15

(C) 1:25

(D) 2:15

(E) It cannot be determined from the information given.

The ratio of the sides is ⅕. The ratio of the areas is the *square* of the ratio of the sides: ⅕ × ⅕ = 1/25. The correct answer is C. Note that answer E is a trap for the unwary. You can't figure out the exact area of either figure because you don't know the height (the area of a triangle is ½ base × height). However, you aren't asked for an area, only for the ratio of the areas, which you can deduce from the formula discussed.

Bonus: What do you suppose the ratio of the *volumes* of two similar figures is? Because volume is found in cubic units, the ratio of the volumes of two similar figures is the *cube* of the ratio of their sides. If Figure A has a base of 5 and similar Figure B has a base of 10, then the ratio of their volumes is 1:8 ($(\frac{1}{2})^3$, which is ½ × ½ × ½ = ⅛).

Don't assume that figures are similar; you must be told that they are.

Area

1. **The area of a triangle is ½ *base* × *height*.** The height is always a line perpendicular to the base. The height may be a side of the triangle, as in a right triangle.

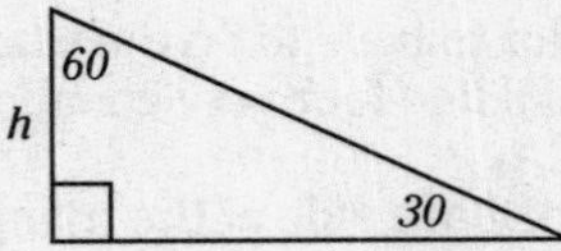

The height may be inside the triangle. It is often represented by a dashed line and a small 90-degree box.

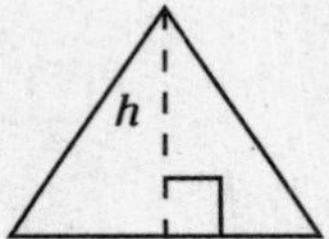

The height may be outside the triangle. This is very confusing and can be found in trick questions. ***Remember:*** You can always drop an altitude. That is, put your pencil on the tallest point of the triangle and draw a line straight from that point to the base. The line can be outside the triangle, as follows.

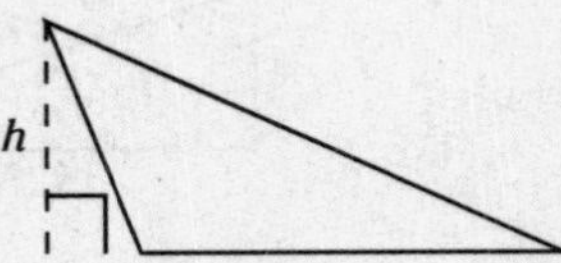

2. **The perimeter of a triangle is the sum of the lengths of the sides.**

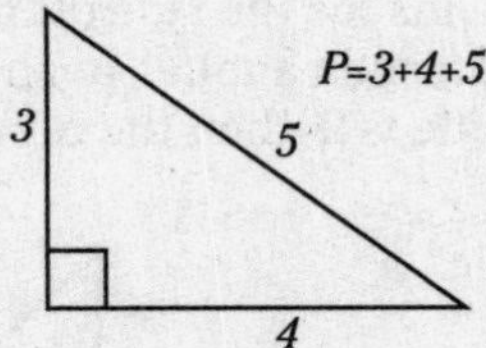

Pythagorean theorem

You have probably studied the Pythagorean theorem (known colloquially as PT). Keep in mind that it works only on *right* triangles. If a triangle doesn't have a right or 90-degree angle, you can't use any of the following information.

In any right triangle, you can find the lengths of the sides with the formula:

$$a^2 + b^2 = c^2$$

where a and b are the sides of the triangle and c is the hypotenuse. The hypotenuse is always opposite the 90-degree angle and is always the longest side of the triangle. Why? Because if one angle in a triangle is 90 degrees, no other angle can be more than 90 degrees. All the angles must sum up to 180 degrees, and there are no negative or 0 angles. Because the longest side is opposite the largest angle, the hypotenuse is the longest side.

Pythagorean triples

It's a pain in the posterior to have to do the whole PT formula every time you want to find the length of a side. You'll find four very common PT ratios in triangles.

1. **Ratio 3:4:5.** In this ratio, if one side of the triangle is 3, the other side is 4 and the hypotenuse is 5.

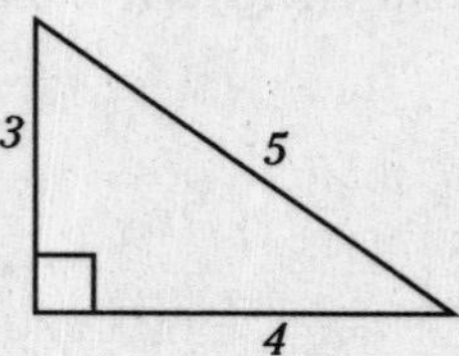

Because this is a ratio, the sides can be in any multiple of these numbers, such as 6:8:10 (twice 3:4:5), 9:12:15 (three times 3:4:5), or 27:36:45 (nine times 3:4:5).

2. **Ratio 5:12:13.** In this ratio, if one side of the triangle is 5, the other side is 12 and the hypotenuse is 13.

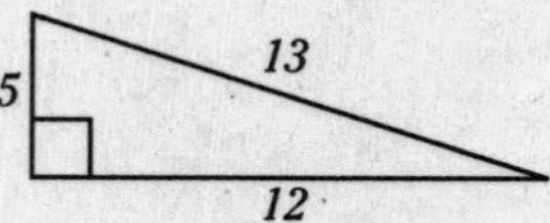

Because this is a ratio, the sides can be in any multiple of these numbers, such as 10:24:26 (twice 5:12:13), 15:36:39 (three times 5:12:13), or 50:120:130 (ten times 5:12:13).

3. **Ratio s:s:$s\sqrt{2}$,** where s stands for the side of the figure. Because two sides are alike, or two sides are the same, this formula applies to an isosceles right triangle, also known as a 45:45:90 triangle. If one side is 2, then the other side is also 2, and the hypotenuse is $2\sqrt{2}$.

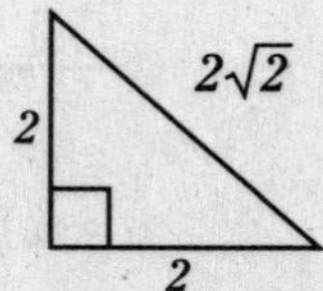

This formula is great to know for squares. If a question tells you that the side of a square is 5 and wants to know the diagonal of the square, you know immediately that it is $5\sqrt{2}$. Why? A square's diagonal cuts the square into two isosceles right triangles (*isosceles* because all sides of the square are equal; *right* because all angles in a square are right angles). What is the diagonal of a square of side 64? $64\sqrt{2}$. What is the diagonal of a square of side 12,984? $12,984\sqrt{2}$.

There's another way to write this ratio. Instead of $s{:}s{:}s\sqrt{2}$, you can write it as $\frac{s}{\sqrt{2}}{:}\frac{s}{\sqrt{2}}{:}s$. So, *s* still stands for the side of the triangle, but now you've divided everything through by $\sqrt{2}$. Why do you need this complicated formula? Suppose you're told that the diagonal of a square is 5. What is the area of the square? What is the perimeter of the square?

If you know this formula, $\frac{s}{\sqrt{2}}{:}\frac{s}{\sqrt{2}}{:}s$, you know that *s* stands for the hypotenuse of the triangle, which is the same as the diagonal of the square. If $s = 5$, then the side of the square is $5/\sqrt{2}$ and you can figure out the area or the perimeter. After you know the side of a square, you can figure out just about anything.

4. **Ratio $s{:}s\sqrt{3}{:}2s$** is a special formula for the sides of a 30:60:90 triangle.

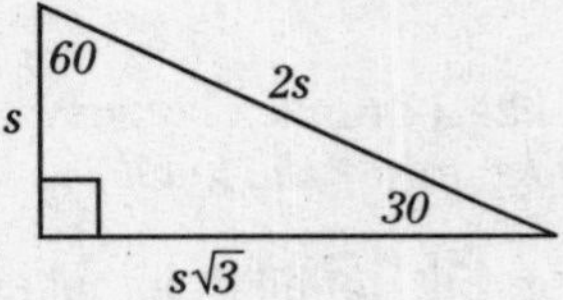

This type of triangle is a favorite of the test makers. The important thing to keep in mind here is that the hypotenuse is twice the length of the side opposite the 30-degree angle. If you get a word problem saying, "Given a 30:60:90 triangle of hypotenuse 20, find the area" or "Given a 30:60:90 triangle of hypotenuse 100, find the perimeter," you can do so because you can find the lengths of the other sides.

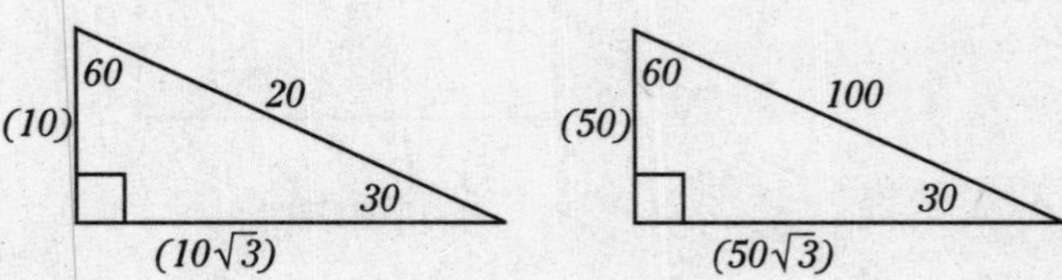

Thanks 4 Nothing: Quadrilaterals

1. **Any four-sided figure is called a *quadrilateral*.**

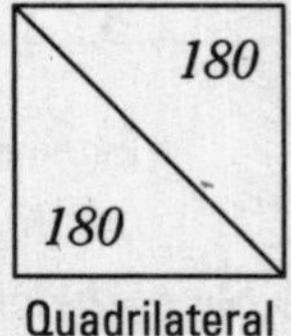

Quadrilateral

The interior angles of any quadrilateral sum up to 360 degrees. Any quadrilateral can be cut into two 180-degree triangles.

2. **A *square* is a quadrilateral with four equal sides and four right angles.**

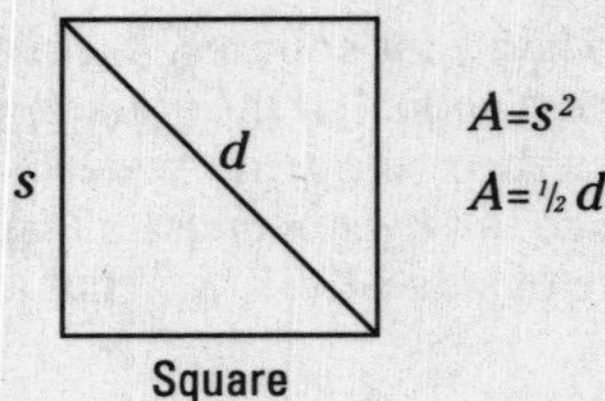

Square

The area of a square is $side^2$ (also called *base* × *height*), or ½ $diagonal^2$.

3. **A *rhombus* is a quadrilateral with four equal sides and four angles that are not necessarily right angles.**

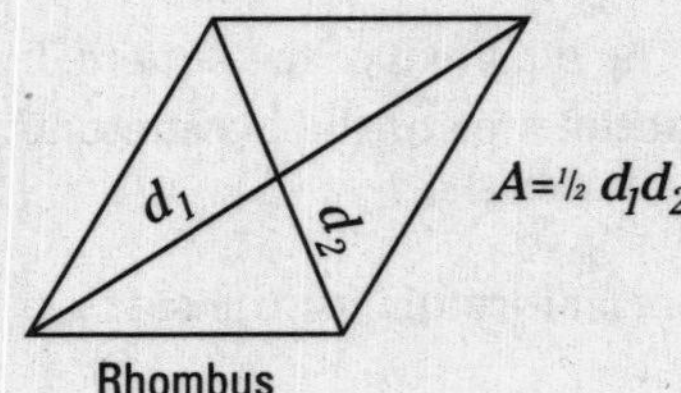

Rhombus

A rhombus often looks like a drunken square, tipsy on its side and wobbly. The area of a rhombus is ½d_1d_2 (½ *diagonal* 1 × *diagonal* 2).

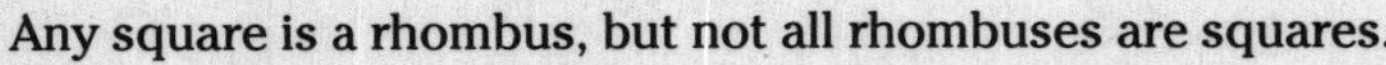

Any square is a rhombus, but not all rhombuses are squares.

4. **A *rectangle* is a quadrilateral with two opposite and equal pairs of sides.** That is, the top and bottom sides are equal, and the right and left sides are equal. All angles in a rectangle are right angles (rectangle means right angle). The area of a rectangle is *length* × *width* (which is the same as *base* × *height*).

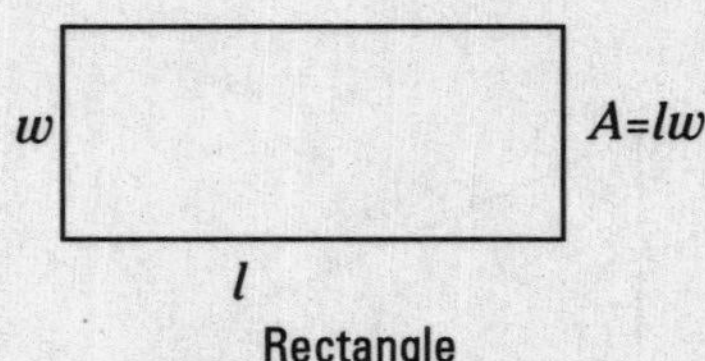

Rectangle

5. **A *parallelogram* is a quadrilateral with two opposite and equal pairs of sides.** The top and bottom sides are equal, and the right and left sides are equal. Opposite angles are equal but not necessarily right (or 90 degrees).

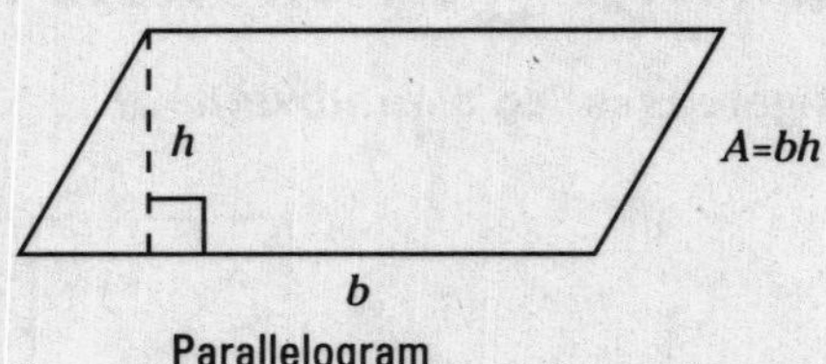

Parallelogram

The area of a parallelogram is *base* × *height*. Remember that the height always is a perpendicular line from the tallest point of the figure down to the base. Diagonals of a parallelogram bisect each other.

All rectangles are parallelograms, but not all parallelograms are rectangles.

6. A *trapezoid* is a quadrilateral with two parallel sides and two nonparallel sides.

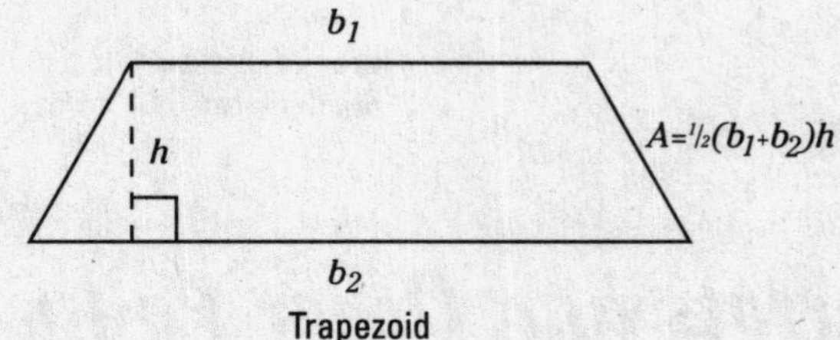

Trapezoid

The area of a trapezoid is ½ (*base* 1 + *base* 2) × *height*. It makes no difference which base you label *base* 1 and which you label *base* 2, because you're adding them together anyway. Just be sure to add them before you multiply by ½.

Quaint quads: Bizarre quadrilaterals

Some quadrilaterals don't have nice, neat shapes or special names.

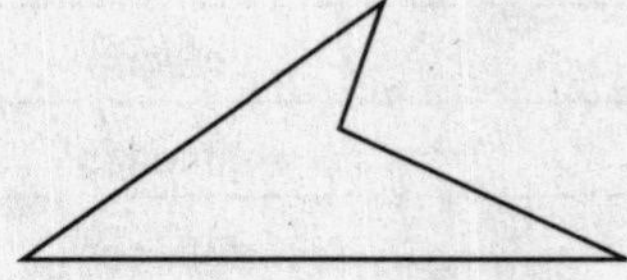

Don't immediately see a strange shape and say that you have no way to find the area of it. You may be able to divide the quadrilateral into two triangles and find the area of each triangle. You may also see a strange quadrilateral in a shaded-area problem.

Leftovers again: Shaded-area problems

Think of a shaded area as a *leftover.* It is "left over" after you subtract the unshaded area from the total area.

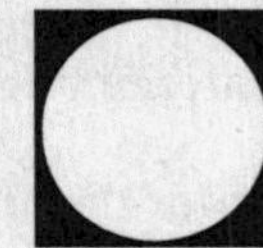

Shaded areas are often unusual shapes. Your first reaction may be that you can't possibly find the area of that shape. Generally, you're right, but you don't have to find the area directly. Instead, be sly, devious, and sneaky; in other words, think the SAT way! Find the area of the total figure, find the area of the unshaded portion, and subtract.

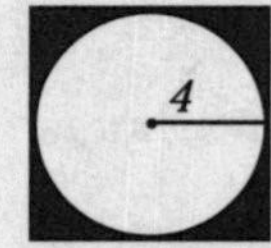

1. $s = 8$
   Area of square = 64
2. $r = 4$
   Area of circle = 16π
3. Shaded area = $64 - 16\pi$

Missing Parrots and Other Polly-Gones: More Polygons

Triangles and quadrilaterals are probably the most common polygons tested on this exam. Here are a few other polygons you may see:

Number of Sides	Name
5	pentagon
6	hexagon (think of *x* in six and *x* in hex)
7	heptagon
8	octagon
9	nonagon
10	decagon

1. **A polygon with all equal sides and all equal angles is called *regular*.** For example, an equilateral triangle is a regular triangle, and a square is a regular quadrilateral.

You will not be asked to find the areas of any of these polygons. You may be asked to find the *perimeter*, which is just the sum of the lengths of all the sides. You also may be asked to find the *exterior* angle measure, which is always 360.

2. **The exterior angle measure of *any* polygon is 360.**

Total interior angle measure

You may also have to find the interior angle measure. Use this formula:

$(n - 2)180°$, where n stands for the number of sides.

For example, the interior angles of the following polygons are

- **Triangle:** $(3 - 2)180 = 1 \times 180 = 180°$
- **Quadrilateral:** $(4 - 2)180 = 2 \times 180 = 360°$
- **Pentagon:** $(5 - 2)180 = 3 \times 180 = 540°$

- **Hexagon:** $(6 - 2)180 = 4 \times 180 = 720°$
- **Heptagon:** $(7 - 2)180 = 5 \times 180 = 900°$
- **Octagon:** $(8 - 2)180 = 6 \times 180 = 1{,}080°$
- **Nonagon:** $(9 - 2)180 = 7 \times 180 = 1{,}260°$
- **Decagon:** $(10 - 2)180 = 8 \times 180 = 1{,}440°$

Have you learned that proportional multiplication is a great time-saving trick? Numbers are in proportion, and you can fiddle with them to make multiplication easier. For example, suppose you're going to multiply 5×180. Most people have to write down the problem and then work through it. But because the numbers are in proportion, you can double one and halve the other: double 5 to make it 10. Halve 180 to make it 90. Now your problem is 10×90, which you can multiply to 900 in your head.

Try another one: $3 \times 180 = ?$ Double the first number: $3 \times 2 = 6$. Halve the second number: $^{180}/_{2} = 90$. $6 \times 90 = 540$. You can do this shortcut multiplication in your head very quickly and impress your friends.

One interior angle

If you are asked to find the average measure of one angle in a figure, the formula is

$$\frac{(n-2)180^{0}}{n}$$

where n stands for the number of sides (which is the same as the number of angles).

$$\text{Pentagon: } \frac{(5-2)\times 180}{5} = \frac{(3\times 180)}{5} = \frac{540}{5} = 108$$

Because all angles are equal in a regular polygon, the same formula applies to one angle in a regular polygon.

If you're given a polygon and are *not* told that it's regular, you can't solve for just one angle.

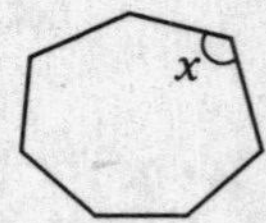

What's the measure of angle x? It cannot be determined. You can't assume that it is $\frac{(7-2)180}{7} = \frac{900}{7} = 128.57$.

Be sure to divide through by n, the number of sides (angles), not by $(n - 2)$. If you divide through by $(n - 2)$, you always get 180 ($^{900}/_{5} = 180$). Knowing this, triple-check your work if you come up with 180 for an answer to this type of problem in case you made this (very typical) careless error.

Volume

1. **The volume of any polygon is *(area of the base)* × *height.*** If you remember this formula, you don't have to memorize any of the following more specific formulas.

2. Volume of a cube: e^3

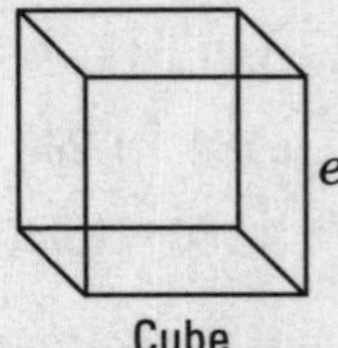

Cube

A cube is a three-dimensional square. Think of a die (one of a pair of dice). All of a cube's dimensions are the same; that is, *length* = *width* = *height.* In a cube, these dimensions are called *edges.* The volume of a cube is *edge* × *edge* × *edge* = *edge*^{3} = e^3.

3. Volume of a rectangular solid: $l \times w \times h$

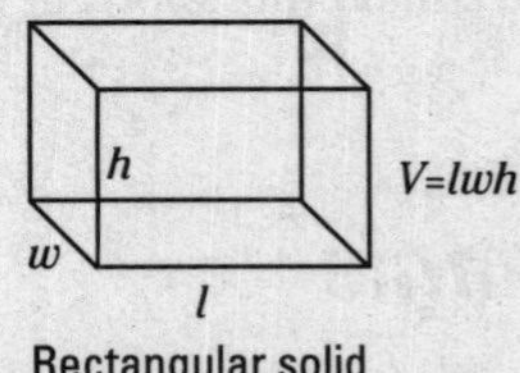

Rectangular solid

A rectangular solid is a box. The base of a box is a rectangle, which has an area of *length* × *width.* Multiply that by *height* to fit the original formula: Volume = *(area of base)* × *height*, or V = $l \times w \times h$.

4. Volume of a cylinder: (πr^2)*height*

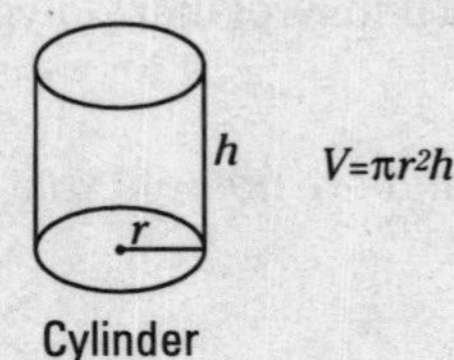

Cylinder

Think of a cylinder as a can of soup. The base of a cylinder is a circle. The area of a circle is πr^2. Multiply that by the height of the cylinder to get *(area of base)* × *height* = πr^2 × *height.* Note that the top and bottom of a cylinder are identical circles. If you know the radius of either the top base or the bottom base, you can find the area of the circle.

Total surface area

1. **The total surface area (TSA), logically enough, is the sum of the areas of all the surfaces of the figure.**
2. **TSA of a cube: $6e^2$**

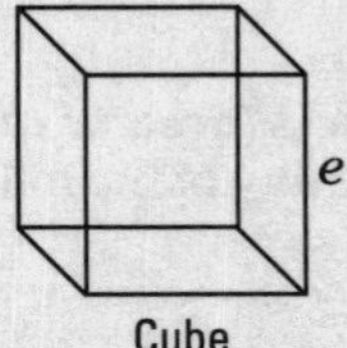

Cube

A cube has six identical faces, and each face is a square. The area of a square is *side*^{2}. Here, that is called *edge*^{2}. If one face is *edge*^{2}, then the total surface area is $6 \times edge^2$, or $6e^2$.

3. TSA of a rectangular solid: $2(lw) + 2(hw) + 2(lh)$

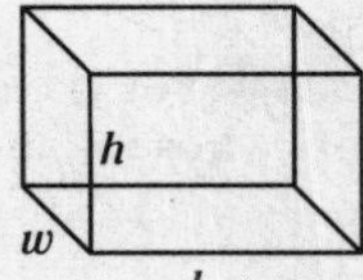

Rectangular solid

A rectangular solid is a box. You need to find the area of each of the six surfaces. The bottom and top have the area of *length* × *width.* The left side and right side have the area of *width* × *height.* The front side and the back side have the area of *height* × *length.* Together, they sum up to $2(lw) + 2(wh) + 2(hl)$ or $2(lw + wh + hl)$.

4. TSA of a cylinder: (*circumference* × *height*) + $2(\pi r^2)$

Cylinder

This is definitely the most difficult TSA to figure out. Think of it as pulling the label off the can, flattening it out, finding its area, and then adding that to the area of the top and bottom lids.

The label is a rectangle. Its length is the length of the circumference of the circle.

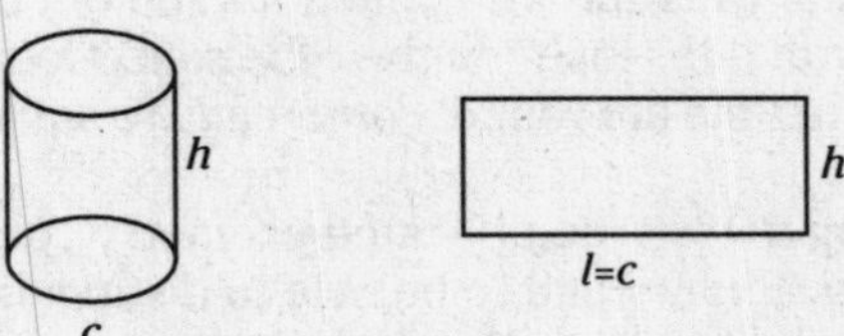

Its height is the height of the cylinder. Multiply *length (circumference)* × *height* to find the area of the label.

You also need to find the area of the top and bottom of the cylinder. Because each is a circle, the TSA of the top and bottom is $2(\pi r^2)$. Add everything together.

I'm Too Much of a Klutz for Coordinate Geometry

1. **The horizontal axis is the *x*-axis.** The vertical axis is the *y*-axis. Points are labeled (*x*,*y*) with the first number in the parentheses indicating how far to the right or left of the vertical line the point is and the second number indicating how far above or below the horizontal line the point is.

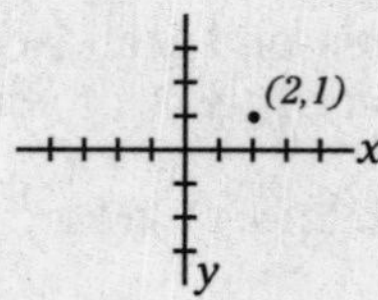

2. The intersection of the *x*- and *y*-axes is called the *point of origin,* and its coordinates are (0,0). A line connecting points whose *x*- and *y*-coordinates are the same forms a 45-degree angle.

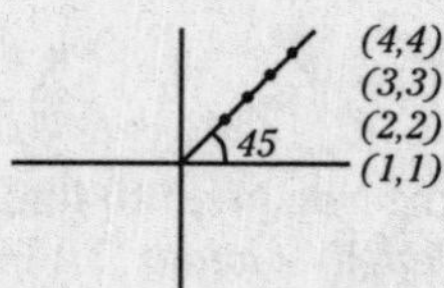

3. If you're asked to find the distance between two points, you can use the distance formula:

$$\sqrt{(x_2-x_1)^2+(y_2-y_1)^2}$$

Find the distance from (9,4) to (8,6).

$9 = x_1$	$4 = y_1$	$1 + 4 = 5$
$8 = x_2$	$6 = y_2$	$\sqrt{5}$ is the distance between the two points
$(8-9)^2 = -1^2 = 1$	$(6-4)^2 = 2^2 = 4$	

Running Around in Circles

Did you hear about the rube who pulled his son out of college, claiming that the school was filling his head with nonsense? As the rube said, "Joe Bob told me that he learned πr^2. But any fool knows that pie are round; *cornbread* are square!"

Circles are among the less-complicated geometry concepts. The most important things are to remember the vocabulary and to be able to distinguish an arc from a sector and an inscribed angle from an intercepted arc. Here's a quick review of the basics.

If you get desperate on the actual exam, you can always look back to the directions to the math section; many of the simple geometry formulas (such as the area or circumference of a circle) are given there. If, in the stress of the test, you think that you may be confusing two formulas ("Isn't the area of a circle $2\pi^2$, or is that $2d^2$?"), double-check.

1. A *radius* goes from the center of a circle to its circumference (perimeter).

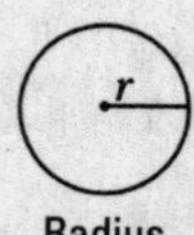

Radius

2. A circle is named by its center.

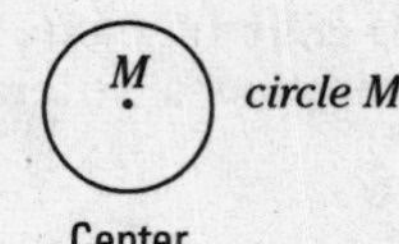

3. A *diameter* connects two points on the circumference of the circle, going through the center. A diameter is equal to two radii.

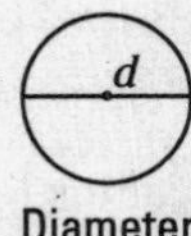

4. A *chord* connects any two points on a circle. The longest chord in a circle is the diameter.

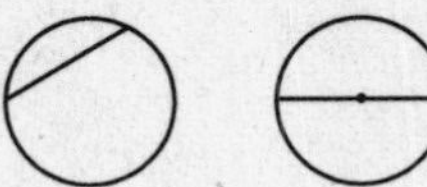

Here's a lovely question you may see on the test, and here are the QC (Quantitative Comparison) answer choices (see Chapter 13):

- A if the quantity in Column A is greater
- B if the quantity in Column B is greater
- C if the two quantities are equal
- Choose D if the relationship cannot be determined from the information given
- An E response will not be scored

EXAMPLE

Column A	***Column B***
Area of a circle of radius 6	Area of a circle of longest chord 12

Many people choose D for this question. Although it's usually true that in QCs a geometry question with no figure is D because it *depends* on how you draw the picture, a circle is frequently an exception to this tip. A circle is a circle is a circle; it rarely depends on how you draw it. The key here is knowing that the *longest chord* is a fancy-schmancy way of saying the *diameter.* Because the diameter is twice the radius, a circle of diameter (or longest chord) 12 has a radius of 6. Two circles with radii of 6 have the same area (don't waste even a nanosecond figuring out what that area actually is; it's irrelevant to comparing the quantities in the two columns). The correct answer is C.

Column A	***Column B***
Area of a circle of radius 10	Area of a circle of chord 20

If you chose C, you fell for the trap. A chord connects any two points on a circle. The *longest* chord is the diameter, but a chord can be any ol' thing. The correct answer is D.

5. **The perimeter of a circle is called the *circumference*.** The formula for the length of a circumference is $2\pi r$ or πd (logical because 2 radii = 1 diameter).

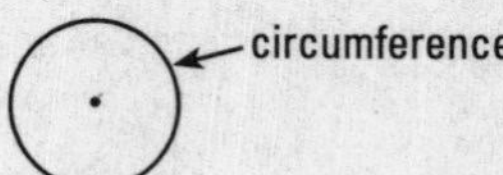

Bonus: You may encounter a wheel question in which you're asked how much distance a wheel covers or how many times a wheel revolves. The key to solving this type of question is knowing that one rotation of a wheel equals one circumference of that wheel.

A child's wagon has a wheel of radius 6 inches. If the wagon wheel travels 100 revolutions, approximately how many feet has the wagon rolled?

(A) 325

(B) 314

(C) 255

(D) 201

(E) 200

One revolution is equal to one circumference: $C = 2\pi r = 2\pi 6 = 12\pi$ = approximately 37.68 inches. Multiply that by 100 = 3,768 inches ≈ 314 feet. The correct answer is B.

6. **The area of a circle is π radius^2.**

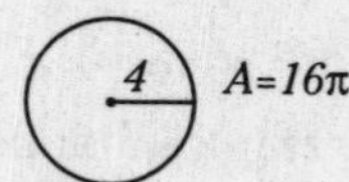

7. **A central angle has its endpoints on the circumference of the circle and its center at the center of the circle.** The degree measure of a central angle is the same as the degree measure of its intercepted arc.

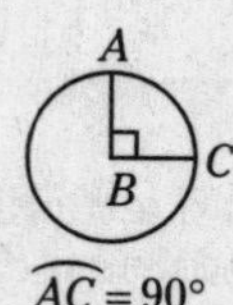

8. **An inscribed angle has both its endpoints and its center on the circumference of the circle.** The degree measure of an inscribed angle is half the degree measure of its intercepted arc.

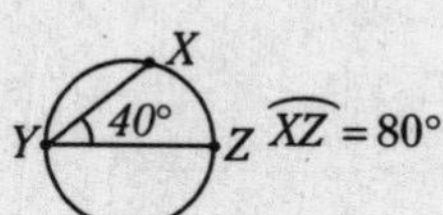

You may see a figure that looks like a string picture you made at summer camp, with all sorts of lines running every which way. Take the time to identify the endpoints of the angles and the center point. You may be surprised at how easy the question suddenly becomes.

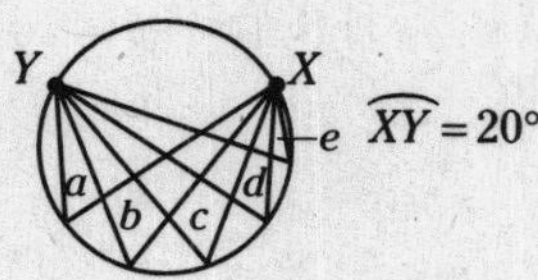

Note: Figure not drawn to scale

In this figure, find the sum of the degree measures of angles $a + b + c + d + e$.

(A) 65

(B) 60

(C) 55

(D) 50

(E) 45

Each angle is an inscribed angle. That means it has half the degree measure of the central angle, or half the degree measure of its intercepted arc. If you look carefully at the endpoints of these angles, they're all the same. They are along arc *XY*, which has a measure of 20°. Therefore, each angle is 10°, for a total of 50. The correct answer is D.

9. When a central angle and an inscribed angle have the same endpoints, the degree measure of the central angle is twice that of the inscribed angle.

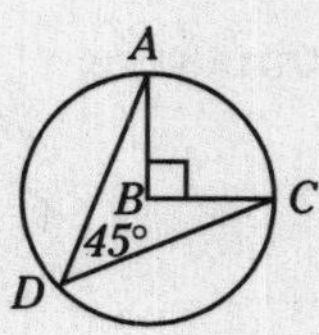

10. The degree measure of a circle is 360.

11. An *arc* is a portion of the circumference of a circle. The degree measure of an arc is the same as its central angle and twice its inscribed angle.

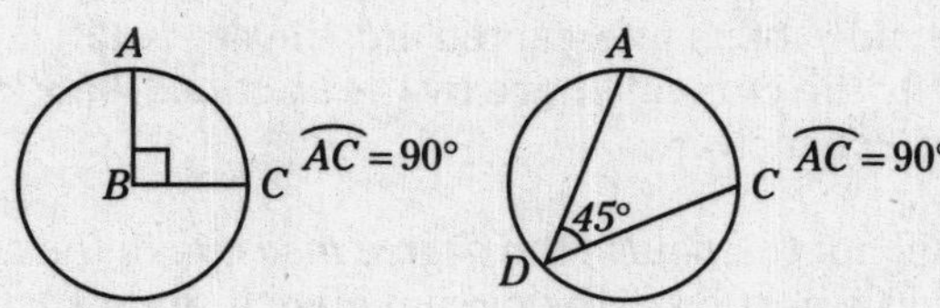

To find the length of an arc, follow these steps:

1. **Find the circumference of the entire circle.**
2. **Put the degree measure of the arc over 360 and reduce the fraction.**
3. **Multiply the circumference by the fraction.**

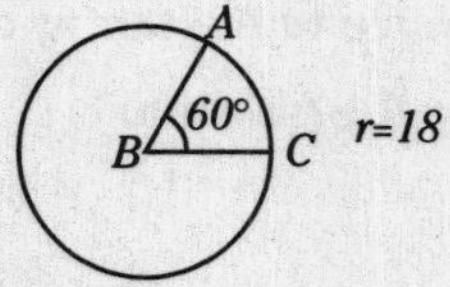

Find the length of arc *AC*.

(A) 36π

(B) 27π

(C) 18π

(D) 12π

(E) 6π

Take the steps one at a time. First, find the circumference of the entire circle: $C = 2\pi r = 36\pi$. Don't multiply π out; problems usually leave it in that form. Next, put the degree measure of the arc over 360. The degree measure of the arc is the same as its central angle, $60° = \frac{60}{360} = \frac{1}{6}$. The arc is $\frac{1}{6}$ of the circumference of the circle. Multiply the circumference by the fraction: $36\pi \times \frac{1}{6} = 6\pi$. The correct answer is E.

Try another one. When you get the hang of these, they're kinda fun.

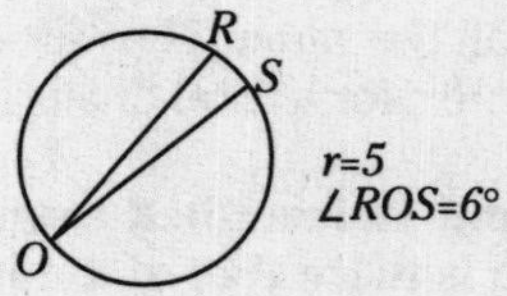

Find the length of arc *RS* in this figure.

(A) $\frac{1}{3}\pi$

(B) π

(C) 3π

(D) 4π

(E) 12

First, find the circumference of the entire circle. $C = 2\pi r = 10\pi$. Second, put the degree measure of the arc over 360. Here, the inscribed angle is 6°. Because an inscribed angle is $\frac{1}{2}$ of the central angle and $\frac{1}{2}$ of its intercepted arc, the arc is 12°. $\frac{12}{360} = \frac{1}{30}$. The arc is $\frac{1}{30}$ of the circle. Finally, multiply the circumference by the fraction: $10\pi \times \frac{1}{30} = \frac{10}{30}\pi = \frac{1}{3}\pi$. The length of the arc is $\frac{1}{3}\pi$. The correct answer is A.

Be very careful not to confuse the *degree measure* of the arc with the *length* of the arc. The length is always a portion of the circumference, always has a π in it, and always is in linear units. If you chose E in this example, you found the degree measure of the arc rather than its length.

12. A *sector* is a portion of the area of a circle. The degree measure of a sector is the same as its central angle and twice its inscribed angle.

To find the area of a sector, do the following:

1. **Find the area of the entire circle.**
2. **Put the degree measure of the sector over 360 and reduce the fraction.**
3. **Multiply the area by the fraction.**

Finding the area of a sector is very similar to finding the length of an arc. The only difference is in the first step. Whereas an arc is a part of the *circumference* of a circle, a sector is a part of the *area* of a circle. Try a few examples for sectors.

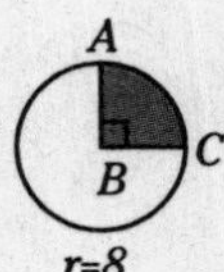

Find the area of sector *ABC*.

(A) 64π

(B) 36π

(C) 16π

(D) 12π

(E) 6π

First, find the area of the entire circle. $A = \pi r^2 = 64\pi$. Second, put the degree measure of the sector over 360. The sector is 90°, the same as its central angle. $\frac{90}{360} = \frac{1}{4}$. Third, multiply the area by the fraction: $64\pi \times \frac{1}{4} = 16\pi$. The correct answer is C.

Find the area of sector *XYZ* in the figure.

(A) 9.7π

(B) 8.1π

(C) 7.2π

(D) 6.3π

(E) 6π

First, find the area of the entire circle. $A = \pi r^2 = 81\pi$. Second, put the degree measure of the sector over 360. A sector has the same degree measure as its intercepted arc, here $36° = \frac{36}{360} = \frac{1}{10}$. Third, multiply the area by the fraction: $81\pi \times \frac{1}{10} = 8.1\pi$. The correct answer is B.

Chapter 11

Catching Some (Xs, Ys, and) Zs: Algebra and Other Sleeping Aids

In This Chapter

- Relating to each other: ratios
- Making life mysterious: symbolism
- Lining up: algebra, FOIL, roots, and radicals
- Taking your chances: probability

Trivia question: Where was algebra supposedly invented? ***Answer:*** Algebra was invented in Zabid, Yemen, by Muslim scholars. See — you can't blame the Greeks for everything!

The Powers That Be: Bases and Exponents

Many SAT questions require you to know how to work with bases and exponents. The following sections explain some of the most important concepts.

1. **The *base* is the big number (or letter) on the bottom. The *exponent* is the little number (or letter) in the upper right corner.**

   In x^5, x is the base; 5 is the exponent.

   In 3^y, 3 is the base; y is the exponent.

2. **A base to the zero power equals one.**

   $x^0 = 1$

   $5^0 = 1$

   $129^0 = 1$

I could give you a long, ***soporific*** (sleep-causing) explanation as to why a number to the zero power equals one, but you don't really care, do you? For now, just memorize the rule.

3. **A base to the second power is *base* × *base*.**

   This is pretty familiar stuff, right?

   $x^2 = x \times x$

   $5^2 = 5 \times 5$

   $129^2 = 129 \times 129$

The same is true for bigger exponents. The exponent tells you how many times the number repeats. For example, 5^6 means that you write down six 5s and then multiply them all together.

$$5^6 = 5 \times 5 \times 5 \times 5 \times 5 \times 5$$

4. **A base to a negative exponent is the reciprocal of itself.**

This one is a little more confusing. A *reciprocal* is the upside-down version of something. (Here's a ***conundrum,*** or riddle: Is the North Pole the reciprocal of the South Pole?) When you have a negative exponent, just put base and exponent under a 1 and make the exponent positive again.

$x^{-4} = 1/(x^4)$

$5^{-3} = 1/(5^3)$

$129^{-1} = 1/(129^1)$

The *number* is *not* negative. When you flip it, you get the reciprocal, and the negative just sort of fades away. *Don't* fall for the trap of saying that $5^{-3} = -1/(5)^3$ or $-1/125$.

When you take a base of 10 to some power, the number of the power equals the number of zeros in the number.

$10^1 = 10$ (one zero)

$10^4 = 10{,}000$ (four zeros)

$10^0 = 1$ (zero zeros)

5. **To multiply like bases, add the exponents.**

You can multiply two bases that are the same; just add the exponents.

$x^3 \times x^2 = x^{(3+2)} = x^5$

$5^4 \times 5^9 = 5^{(4+9)} = 5^{13}$

$129^3 \times 129^0 = 129^{(3+0)} = 129^3$

You cannot multiply *unlike* bases. Think of it as trying to make dogs and cats multiply — it doesn't work. All you end up with is a miffed meower and a damaged dog.

$x^2 \times y^3 = x^2 \times y^3$ (no shortcuts)

$5^2 \times 129^3 = 5^2 \times 129^3$ (you actually have to work it out)

6. **To divide like bases, subtract the exponents.**

You can divide two bases that are the same by subtracting the exponents.

$x^5 \div x^2 = x^{(5-2)} = x^3$

$5^9 \div 5^3 = 5^{(9-3)} = 5^6$

$129^4 \div 129^0 = 129^{(4-0)} = 129^4$

(Did I getcha on that last one? It should make sense. Any base to the zero power is 1. Any number divided by 1 is itself.)

Did you look at the second example, $5^9 \div 5^3$, and think that it was 5^3? It's easy to fall into the trap of dividing instead of subtracting, especially when you see numbers that just beg to be divided, like 9 and 3. Keep your guard up.

7. Multiply the exponents of a base inside and outside the parentheses.

That's quite a mouthful. Here's what it means:

$(x^2)^3 = x^{(2\times3)} = x^6$

$(5^3)^3 = 5^{(3\times3)} = 5^9$

$(129^0)^3 = 129^{(0\times3)} = 129^0$

Complaint department now open! I can hear your grumbling all the way down here in San Diego. "Why," you ask, "do I have to learn all this when I have a calculator and can just push a button or two?" Good question. You can figure out something when you have actual numbers, but what about when you have just the exponents? You're probably not going to use your calculator to solve something like the following example. (See Chapter 13 for more information on Quantitative Comparisons.)

Here are the QC answer choices:

- A if the quantity in Column A is greater
- B if the quantity in Column B is greater
- C if the two quantities are equal
- D if the relationship cannot be determined from the information given
- An E response will not be scored

Column A | **Column B**

$\frac{x^7}{x^4}$

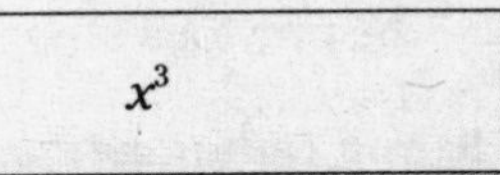

x^3

Because $x^{(7-4)} = x^3$, no matter what the value of x is, the correct answer is C.

Column A | **Column B**

$(x^3)^4$

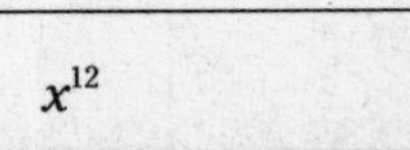

x^{12}

No matter what value x has, the two columns are the same: $x^{12} = x^{12}$. The correct answer is C.

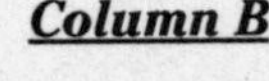

Column A | **Column B**

$(x^3)^4$ | 12

You're so busy thinking of $3 \times 4 = 12$ that you may be tempted to choose C. Boy, this trap is really easy to fall for. But the automatic shutdown valve in the back of your brain should alert you to the fact that *when two columns appear to be equal, it is usually a trap.* The correct answer is D. Everything *depends on* the value of *x*. (See Chapter 13 for more information on this QC trick.)

8. To add or subtract like bases to like powers, add or subtract the numerical coefficient of the bases.

The *numerical coefficient* (a great name for a rock band, don't you think?) is simply the number *in front of* the base. Notice that it is not the little exponent in the right-hand corner but the full-sized number to the left of the base.

$31x^3$: 31 is the numerical coefficient.

$-8y^2$: -8 is the numerical coefficient.

x^3: What is the numerical coefficient? 1, because any number is itself times 1; the 1 is not always written out. Good trap.

$37x^3 + 10x^3 = 47x^3$: Just add the numerical coefficients: $37 + 10 = 47$.

$15y^2 - 10y^2 = 5y^2$: Just subtract the numerical coefficients: $15 - 10 = 5$.

You cannot add or subtract terms with like bases with *different exponents.*

$13x^3 - 9x^2$ is *not* equal to $4x^3$ or $4x^2$ or $4x$. All it is equal to is $13x^3 - 9x^2$ The bases *and* exponents must be the same for you to add or subtract the terms.

Column A	***Column B***
$16x^4 - 4x^3$	$12x$

The answer *depends on* the value of x. If you chose C, you fell for the trap that I discussed in the previous step. The correct answer is D.

9. You cannot add or subtract the numerical coefficients of unlike bases.

$16x^2 - 4y^2 = 16x^2 - 4y^2$

It is *not* $12x^2$ or $12y^2$ or $12xy^2$.

Column A	***Column B***
$10x^3 - 2y^3$	$8xy$

It *depends on* the values of x and y. C is the trap answer. The correct answer is D.

Keep It in Proportion: Ratios

After you know the tricks, ratios are some of the easiest problems to answer quickly. I call them "heartbeat" problems because you can solve them in a heartbeat. Of course, if someone drop-dead gorgeous sits next to you and makes your heart beat faster, it may take you two heartbeats to solve a ratio problem. So sue me.

1. A ratio is written as $\frac{\text{of}}{\text{to}}$ or of:to.

The ratio *of* sunflowers *to* roses = $\frac{\text{sunflowers}}{\text{roses}}$.

The ratio *of* umbrellas *to* heads = umbrellas:heads.

2. A possible total is a multiple of the sum of the numbers in the ratio.

You may be given a problem like this:

> At a party, the ratio of blondes to redheads is 4:5. Which of the following can be the total number of blondes and redheads at the party?

Mega-easy. Add the numbers in the ratio: 4 + 5 = 9. The total must be a multiple of 9, like 9, 18, 27, 36, and so on. If this "multiple of" stuff is confusing, think of it another way: The sum must divide evenly into the total. That is, the total must be divisible by 9. Can the total, for example, be 54? Yes, 9 goes evenly into 54. Can it be 64? No, 9 does not go evenly into 64.

After a rough hockey game, Bernie checks his body and finds that he has three bruises for every five cuts. Which of the following can be the total number of bruises and cuts on poor ol' Bernie's body?

(A) 53

(B) 45

(C) 35

(D) 33

(E) 32

Add the numbers in the ratio: 3 + 5 = 8. The total must be a multiple of 8 (or, looking at it another way, the total must be evenly divisible by 8). Only E is a multiple of 8: 8 × 4 = 32.

Did you notice the trap answers? 53 is a good trap because it features both 5 and 3, the numbers in the ratio. 45 is a trap. If you multiply 3 × 5 = 15, you may think that the total has to be a multiple of 15. No, the total is a multiple of the *sum,* not of the product. *Add* the numbers in the ratio; don't multiply them. 35 again has both terms of the ratio. 33 is a multiple of 3. Only 32 is a multiple of the *sum* of the terms in the ratio.

One more, because you should always get this type of problem correct.

Trying to get Willie to turn down his stereo, his mother pounds on the ceiling and shouts up to his bedroom. If she pounds seven times for every five times she shouts, which of the following can be the total number of poundings and shouts?

(A) 75

(B) 57

(C) 48

(D) 35

(E) 30

Add the numbers in the ratio: 7 + 5 = 12. The total must be a multiple of 12. (It must be evenly divisible by 12.) Here, only 48 is evenly divisible by 12. The correct answer is C. Of course, 75 and 57 try to trick you by using the numbers 7 and 5 from the ratio. Choice D is the product of 7 × 5.

Notice how carefully I have been asking which *can be* the *possible* total. The total can be *any* multiple of the sum. If a question asks you which of the following *is* the total, you have to answer, "It cannot be determined." You only know which *can be* true.

Column A	***Column B***
Ratio of CDs to tapes = 2:9	
Total of CDs and tapes	11

You know the total must be a multiple of 11, but it can be an infinite number of terms: 11, 22, 33, 44, 55, and so on. The correct answer is D. This trap has destroyed a lot of overly confident students over the years.

When given a ratio and a total and asked to find a specific term, do the following, in order:

1. **Add the numbers in the ratio.**
2. **Divide that sum into the total.**
3. **Multiply that quotient by each term in the ratio.**
4. **Add the answers to double-check that they sum up to the total.**

Pretty confusing stuff. Take it one step at a time. Look at this problem:

> Yelling at the members of his team, which had just lost 21–0, the irate coach pointed his finger at each member of the squad, calling everyone either a wimp or a slacker. If he had 3 wimps for every 4 slackers, and every member of the 28-man squad was either a wimp or a slacker, how many wimps were there?

1. **Add the numbers in the ratio: $3 + 4 = 7$.**
2. **Divide that sum into the total: $^{28}/_{7} = 4$.**
3. **Multiply that quotient by each term in the ratio: $4 \times 3 = 12$; $4 \times 4 = 16$.**
4. **Add to double-check that the numbers sum up to the total: $12 + 16 = 28$.**

Now you have all the information you need to answer a variety of questions: How many wimps were there? Twelve. How many slackers were there? Sixteen. How many more slackers than wimps were there? Four. How many slackers would have to be kicked off the team for the number of wimps and slackers to be equal? Four. The SAT's Math Moguls can ask all sorts of things, but if you have this information, you're ready for anything they throw at you.

Be sure that you actually do Step 4, adding the terms to double-check that they sum up to the total again. Doing so will catch any careless mistakes you may have made. For example, suppose you divided 7 into 28 and got 3 instead of 4. Then you said that there were 3×3, or 9, wimps, and 3×4, or 12, slackers. That means that the total was $9 + 12 = 21$ — *ooooops!* You know the total has to be 28, so you can go back and try again. You'll also catch a careless mistake in your multiplication. Suppose you correctly divide 7 into 28 and get 4. But when you multiply 4×3, you get 43 instead of 12. (Hey, when the adrenaline's flowing during the exam, you'd be surprised at the kinds of mistakes you can make.) When you add the numbers, you get $43 + 16 = 59$ instead of the 28 you know is the total.

Things Aren't What They Seem: Symbolism

You may encounter two basic types of symbolism problems. If so, do one of the following:

- Substitute the number given for the variable in the explanation.
- Talk through the explanation to see which constraint fits and then do the indicated operations.

1. Substitute for the variable in the explanation.

You see a problem with a strange symbol. It may be a variable inside a circle, a triangle, a star, or a tic-tac-toe sign. That symbol has no connection to the real world at all. Don't panic, thinking that your teachers forgot to teach you something. Symbols are made up for each problem.

The symbol is included in a short explanation. It may look like this:

$$a \# b \# c = \frac{(a+b)^c}{(b+c)}$$

$$x * y * z = (z/x) + (y/z)x$$

$$m @ n @ o = mn + no - om$$

Again, the symbols don't have any meaning in the outside world; they mean only what the problem tells you they mean, and that meaning holds true only for this problem.

Below the explanation is the question itself:

$$3 \# 2 \# 1 =$$

$$4 * 6 * 8 =$$

$$2 @ 5 @ 10 =$$

Your job is one of substitution. Plug in a number for the variable in the equation. Which number do you plug in? The one that's in the same position as that variable. For example:

$$a \# b \# c = \frac{(a+b)^c}{(b+c)}$$

$$3 \# 2 \# 1 = 1 = \frac{(3+2)^1}{(2+1)} = \frac{5}{3}$$

Because *a* was in the first position and 3 was in the first position, substitute a 3 for an *a* throughout the equation. Because *b* was in the second position and 2 was in the second position, substitute a 2 for a *b* throughout the equation. Because *c* was in the third position and 1 was in the third position, substitute a 1 for a *c* throughout the equation.

Do the same for the other problems:

$$x * y * z = (z/x) + (y/z)^x$$

$$4 * 6 * 8 = (8/4) + (6/8)^4 = 2 + (6/8)^4 = 2 + .316 = 2.316$$

$$m @ n @ o = mn + no - om$$

$$2 @ 5 @ 10 = (2 \times 5) + (5 \times 10) - (10 \times 2) = 10 + 50 - 20 = 40$$

This is the simpler of the two types of symbolism problems. Just substitute the number for the variable and work through the equation.

2. Talk through the explanation and do the operations.

This type of symbolism problem may seem confusing until you've done a few. Then they become so easy that you wonder why you didn't see how to do them before. Here you see two possibilities.

> ⓧ = $3x$ if x is odd.
>
> ⓧ = $\frac{x}{2}$ if x is even.

Solve for ⑤ + ⑧

First, talk through the explanation. You have something in a circle. If that something in the circle is odd, you multiply it by 3. If that something in the circle is even, you divide it by 2.

In the question, you have a 5 in the circle. Because 5 is odd, you multiply it by 3 to get $5 \times 3 = 15$. In the second half of the question, you have an 8 in a circle. Because 8 is even, you divide it by 2. $8/2 = 4$. Now add: $15 + 4 = 19$.

Don't keep going. Do *not* say, "Well, 19 is odd, so I have to multiply it by 3, getting 57." You can bet that 57 is one of the trap multiple-choice answers.

You may still think of this second type of problem as a plug-in or substitution problem because you are plugging the number into the equation for x and working it through. However, you first have to figure out which equation to plug it into. That requires talking things through. You have to understand what you're doing in this type of problem. Try another:

> $\triangle x$ = $3x + \frac{1}{3}x$ if x is prime.
>
> $\triangle x$ = $x^2 + \sqrt{x}$ if x is composite.

$\triangle 16$ + $\triangle 3$ =

Ah ha! Now you need to know some math vocabulary. Prime numbers are not the numbers that have stars next to them in your little black book. *Prime numbers* are numbers that cannot be divided other than by 1 and themselves, like 2, 3, 5, 7, 11, and 13. *Composite numbers* are numbers that *can* be divided other than by just 1 and themselves, like 4, 6, 8, 9, 10, and 12. The first thing you do is decide whether the term in the triangle is a composite number or a prime number.

$\triangle 16$: Because 16 is a composite number, use the second equation. Square 16: $16 \times 16 = 256$. Take the square root of 16: $\sqrt{16} = 4$. Add them together: $256 + 4 = 260$.

$\triangle 3$: Because 3 is a prime number, use the first equation. $3(3) + \frac{1}{3}(3) = 9 + 1 = 10$. Add the two solutions: $260 + 10 = 270$.

Sometimes, the solutions have symbols in them as well. Here's an example:

> $\textcircled{x}$ = ½x if x is composite.
>
> $\textcircled{x}$ = 2x if x is prime.

Solve for $\textcircled{5} + \textcircled{10}$

(A) $\textcircled{15}$

(B) $\textcircled{25}$

(C) $\textcircled{50}$

(D) $\textcircled{100}$

(E) It cannot be determined from the information given.

First, you know to eliminate answer E. This is the sucker's answer, the one for people who have no idea what the cute little circle means and are clueless as to where to begin. You know by now that you *can* solve a symbolism problem — and pretty quickly, too.

Because 5 is prime, you multiply it by 2: 5 × 2 = 10.

Because 10 is composite, you multiply it by ½ : 10 × ½ = 5.

Multiply: 10 × 5 = 50.

Noooo! Don't choose answer C; that's the trap answer. Choice C doesn't say 50; it says $\textcircled{50}$. That means that you have to solve the answer choice to see what it really is. Because 50 is composite, you take half of it: 50 ÷ 2 = 25. That's not the answer you want. Now go through the rest of the choices:

$\textcircled{15}$: Because 15 is composite, multiply it by ½ : 15 × ½ = 7.5.

$\textcircled{25}$: Because 25 is composite, multiply it by ½ : 25 × ½ = 12.5.

$\textcircled{100}$: Because 100 is composite, multiply it by ½ : 100 × ½ = 50. You have a winner!

Whenever you see a symbol, get to work. That symbol may be in the question or in the answer choices. You still follow the explanation. But remember the trap I already discussed: Be super-careful not to keep on going. That is, when you come up with 50 as your answer, don't say, "Well, 50 is composite, so I have to multiply it by ½, getting 25." Stop when there are no more symbols.

Have you studied functions yet? Maybe not in school, but if you've read the preceding material on symbolism, you just studied functions. A function is very much like the symbolism you've just read about. You may see a problem like this:

$f(x) = (2x)^3$. Solve for $f(2)$.

The *f* stands for function. You do the same thing you did before: Talk through the problem. You say, "I have something in parentheses. My job is to multiply that something by 2 and then cube the whole disgusting mess." In other words, just plug in the 2 where you see an *x* in the explanation.

$f(2) = (2 \times 2)^3 = 4^3 = 64$

Try another one:

$f(x) = x + x^2 + x^3$. Solve for $f(10)$.

Just plug the 10 in for the x: $f(10) = 10 + 10^2 + 10^3 = 10 + 100 + 1{,}000 = 1{,}110$.

Now that you've acquired this skill, you can call yourself "fully functional."

Abracadabra: Algebra

You must be able to do three basic algebra concepts for the SAT.

- Solve for x in an equation.
- Use the FOIL method.
- Factor down a quadratic equation and take an algebraic expression from its final form back to its original form of two sets of parentheses.

Solving for x in an equation

To solve for x, follow these steps:

1. **Isolate the variable. This means getting all the x's on one side and all the non-x's on the other side.**
2. **Add all the x's on one side; add all the non-x's on the other side.**
3. **Divide both sides of the equation by the number in front of the x.**

Now you try it with this problem: $3x + 7 = 9x - 5$

1. **Isolate the variable. Move the $3x$ to the right, *changing the sign* to make it $-3x$.**

   Forgetting to change the sign is one of the most common careless mistakes students make. The test makers realize that and often include trap answer choices to catch this mistake.

   Move the -5 to the left, *changing the sign* to make it +5. You now have $7 + 5 = 9x - 3x$.

2. **Add the x's on one side; add the non-x's on the other side.**

   $12 = 6x$

3. **Divide both sides through by what is next to the x.**

   $\frac{12}{6} = \frac{6x}{6}$; $2 = x$

If you're weak on algebra or know that you often make careless mistakes, plug the 2 back into the equation and make sure that it works.

$3(2) + 7 = 9(2) - 5$

$6 + 7 = 18 - 5$

$13 = 13$

If you absolutely hate algebra, see whether you can simply plug in the answer choices. If this were a problem-solving question with multiple-choice answers, you could plug 'n' chug.

$3x + 7 = 9x - 5$. Solve for x.

(A) 5

(B) 3½

(C) 2

(D) 0

(E) –2

Don't ask for trouble. Keep life simple by starting with the simple answers first. That is, try plugging in 5. When it doesn't work, don't bother plugging in 3½. That's too much work. Go right down to 2. If all the easy answers don't work, you can go back to the hard answer of 3½, but why fuss with it unless you absolutely have to? Test makers often put mind-boggling choices at the beginning of the answers (or at the bottom, for those who like to work upside down); skip them.

Curses! FOILed again

The second thing you need to know to do algebra is how to use the FOIL method. FOIL stands for *First, Outer, Inner, Last* and refers to the order in which you multiply the variables in parentheses. With the equation $(a + b)(a - b) =$

1. **Multiply the *First* variables: $a \times a = a^2$.**
2. **Multiply the *Outer* variables: $a \times -b = -ab$.**
3. **Multiply the *Inner* variables: $b \times a = ba$ (which is the same as ab).**
4. **Multiply the *Last* variables: $b \times -b = -b^2$.**
5. **Solution: $a^2 - b^2$.**

Add like terms: $-ab + ab = 0ab$. (Remember that you can multiply numbers forward or backward, such that $ab = ba$.) The positive and negative ab cancel each other out. You're left with only $a^2 - b^2$.

Try another one: $(3a + b)(a - 2b) =$

1. **Multiply the *First* terms: $3a \times a = 3a^2$.**
2. **Multiply the *Outer* terms: $3a \times -2b = -6ab$.**
3. **Multiply the *Inner* terms: $b \times a = ba$ (which is the same as ab).**
4. **Multiply the *Last* terms: $b \times -2b = -2b^2$.**
5. **Combine like terms: $-6ab + ab = -5ab$.**
6. **Solution: $3a^2 - 5ab - 2b^2$.**

TIP

You should out-and-out memorize the following three FOIL problems. Don't bother to work them out every time; know them by heart.

1. **$(a + b)^2 = a^2 + 2ab + b^2$**

   You can prove this equation by using FOIL: $(a + b)(a + b)$

   a. Multiply the *First* terms: $a \times a = a^2$

   b. Multiply the *Outer* terms: $a \times b = ab$.

c. Multiply the *Inner* terms: $b \times a = ba$ (which is the same as ab).

d. Multiply the *Last* terms: $b \times b = b^2$.

e. Combine like terms: $ab + ab = 2ab$.

f. Solution: $a^2 + 2ab + b^2$.

2. $(a - b)^2 = a^2 - 2ab + b^2$

You can prove this equation by using FOIL: $(a - b)(a - b)$.

a. Multiply the *First* terms: $a \times a = a^2$.

b. Multiply the *Outer* terms: $a \times -b = -ab$.

c. Multiply the *Inner* terms: $-b \times a = -ba$ (which is the same as $-ab$).

d. Multiply the *Last* terms: $-b \times -b = +b^2$.

e. Combine like terms: $-ab + -ab = -2ab$.

f. Solution: $a^2 - 2ab + b^2$.

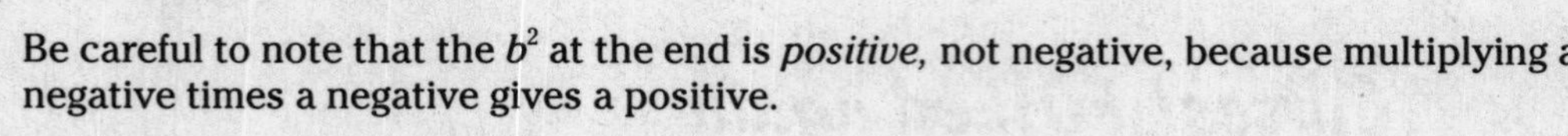
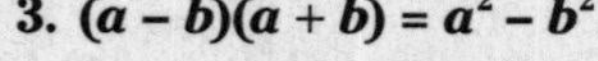

Be careful to note that the b^2 at the end is *positive*, not negative, because multiplying a negative times a negative gives a positive.

3. $(a - b)(a + b) = a^2 - b^2$

You can prove this equation by using FOIL: $(a - b)(a + b)$.

a. Multiply the *First* terms: $a \times a = a^2$.

b. Multiply the *Outer* terms: $a \times b = ab$.

c. Multiply the *Inner* terms: $-b \times a = -ba$ (which is the same as $-ab$).

d. Multiply the *Last* terms: $-b \times b = -b^2$.

e. Combine like terms: $ab + -ab = 0ab$.

f. Solution: $a^2 - b^2$. Note that the middle term drops out because $+ab$ cancels out $-ab$.

Memorize these three equations. Doing so saves you time, careless mistakes, and acute misery on the actual exam.

Fact-or fiction: Factoring

Now you know how to do algebra forward, are you ready to do it backward? You need to be able to factor down a quadratic equation and take an algebraic expression from its final form back to its original form of two sets of parentheses.

Given $x^2 + 13x + 42 = 0$, solve for x. Take this problem one step at a time.

1. Draw two sets of parentheses.

$()() = 0$.

2. To get x^2, the *First* terms have to be x and x. Fill those in.

$(x\ )(x\ ) = 0$.

3. Look now at the *Outer* terms.

You need two numbers that multiply together to be +42. Well, there are several possibilities: 42×1, 21×2, or 6×7. You can even have two negative numbers: -42×-1, -21×-2, or -6×-7. You aren't sure which one to choose yet. Go on to the next step.

4. **Look at the *Inner* terms.**

   You have to add two values to get +13. What's the first thing that springs to mind? 6 + 7, probably. Hey, that's one of the possibilities in the preceding step! Plug it in and try it.

   $(x+6)(x+7) = x^2 + 7x + 6x + 42 = x^2 + 13x + 42$.

Great, but you're not done yet. If the whole equation equals zero, either $(x+6) = 0$ or $(x+7) = 0$. That's because any number times zero equals zero. Therefore, x can equal –6 or –7.

Again, if you have a multiple-choice problem, you can simply try the answer choices. Never start doing a lot of work until you absolutely have to.

Too Hip to Be Square: Roots and Radicals

To simplify working with square roots (or cube roots or any radicals), think of them as variables. You work the same way with $\sqrt{7}$ as you do with x, y, or z.

Addition and subtraction

1. **To add or subtract *like* radicals, add or subtract the number in front of the radical (your old friend, the numerical coefficient).**

   $2\sqrt{7} + 5\sqrt{7} = 7\sqrt{7}$ $\quad 2x + 5x = 7x$

   $9\sqrt{13} - 4\sqrt{13} = 5\sqrt{13}$ $\quad 9x - 4x = 5x$

2. **You *cannot* add or subtract unlike radicals (just as you cannot add or subtract unlike variables).**

   $6\sqrt{5} + 4\sqrt{3} = 6\sqrt{5} + 4\sqrt{3}$. You cannot add the two and get $10\sqrt{8}$.

   $6x + 4y = 6x + 4y$. You cannot add the two and get $10xy$.

Don't glance at a problem, see that the radicals are not the same, and immediately assume that you cannot add the two terms. You may be able to simplify one radical to make it match the radical in the other term.

$\sqrt{52} + \sqrt{13} = 2\sqrt{13} + \sqrt{13} = 3\sqrt{13}$

To simplify: Take out a perfect square from the term. $\sqrt{52} = \sqrt{4} \times \sqrt{13}$. Because $\sqrt{4} = 2$, $\sqrt{52} = 2\sqrt{13}$.

$\sqrt{20} + \sqrt{45} = (\sqrt{4} \times \sqrt{5}) + (\sqrt{9} \times \sqrt{5}) = 2\sqrt{5} + 3\sqrt{5} = 5\sqrt{5}$

You must simplify *first.* You can't say that $\sqrt{20} + \sqrt{45} = \sqrt{65} = 8.06$. When you work out the correct answer, $5\sqrt{5}$, you see that it's not 8.06, but 11.18.

Multiplication and division

1. **When you multiply or divide radicals, you just multiply or divide the numbers and then pop the radical sign back onto the finished product.**

   $\sqrt{5} \times \sqrt{6} = \sqrt{30}$

   $\sqrt{15} \div \sqrt{5} = \sqrt{3}$

2. **If you have a number in front of the radical, multiply it as well. Let everyone in on the fun.**

   $6\sqrt{3} \times 4\sqrt{2} =$

   $6 \times 4 = 24$

   $\sqrt{3} \times \sqrt{2} = \sqrt{6}$

   $24\sqrt{6}$

Why do you have to know this when you have a calculator that can find an exact, precise, *bee-yoo-ti-ful* answer for you without going through all this garbage? Because the test wants to make sure that you know how to wade through all this garbage on your own.

Try this question:

$37\sqrt{5} \times 3\sqrt{6} =$

(A) $40\sqrt{11}$

(B) $40\sqrt{30}$

(C) $111\sqrt{11}$

(D) $111\sqrt{30}$

(E) 1,221

$37 \times 3 = 111$ and $\sqrt{5} \times \sqrt{6} = \sqrt{30}$, so $111\sqrt{30}$ Straightforward multiplication. The correct answer is D.

Sure, you can use your calculator for this problem, but why bother? You can find $37\sqrt{5}$ (82.73451516), find $3\sqrt{6}$ = (7.348469228), multiply them (607.9720388), and then go through and solve each answer choice to see which one comes out to 607.9720388. That's a lot more work than memorizing the rules to simple radical operations.

Inside out

When an operation is under the radical, do it first and then take the square root.

$$\sqrt{\frac{x^4}{40} + \frac{x^2}{9}}$$

First, solve for $x^2/40 + x^2/9$. You get the common denominator of 360 (40×9) and then find the numerators: $9x^2 + 40x^2 = 49x^2/360$. *Now* take the square roots: $\sqrt{49x^2} = 7x$ (because $7x \times 7x = 49x^2$). $\sqrt{360} = 18.97$. Gotcha, I bet! Did you say that $\sqrt{360} = 6$? Wrong! $\sqrt{36} = 6$, but $\sqrt{360}$ = approximately 18.97. Beware of assuming too much; you can be led down the path to temptation.

Your final answer is $7x/18.97$. Of course, you can bet that the answer choices will include $7x/6$.

Probably Probability

Probability questions are usually word problems. They may look intimidating, with a lot of words that make you lose sight of where to begin. Two simple rules can solve nearly every probability problem tossed at you on the SAT:

1. Create a fraction.

To find a probability, use this formula:

$$P = \frac{\text{Number of possible desired outcomes}}{\text{Number of total possible outcomes}}$$

Make a probability into a fraction. The denominator is the easier of the two parts to begin with. The denominator is the total possible number of outcomes. For example, when you're flipping a coin, two outcomes are possible, giving you a denominator of 2. When you're tossing a die (one of a pair of dice), six outcomes are possible, giving you a denominator of 6. When you're pulling a card out of a deck of cards, 52 outcomes are possible (52 cards in a deck), giving you a denominator of 52. When 25 marbles are in a jar and you're going to pull out one of them, you have 25 possibilities, giving you a denominator of 25. Very simply, the denominator is the whole shebang — everything possible.

The numerator is the total number of the things you want. If you want a head when you toss a coin, there is exactly one head, giving you a numerator of 1. The chances of tossing a head, therefore, are $\frac{1}{2}$, one possible head, two possible outcomes altogether. If you want to get a 5 when you toss a die, there is exactly one 5 on the die, giving you a numerator of 1. Notice that your numerator is *not* 5. The number you want happens to be a 5, but there is only *one* 5 on the die. The probability of tossing a 5 is $\frac{1}{6}$: There are one 5 and six possible outcomes altogether.

If you want to draw a Jack in a deck of cards, there are four Jacks: hearts, diamonds, clubs, and spades. Therefore, the numerator is 4. The probability of drawing a Jack out of a deck of cards is $\frac{4}{52}$ (which reduces to $\frac{1}{13}$). If you want to draw a Jack of Hearts, the probability is $\frac{1}{52}$ because there is only one Jack of Hearts.

> A jar of marbles has 8 yellow marbles, 6 black marbles, and 12 white marbles. What is the probability of drawing out a black marble?

Use the formula. Begin with the denominator, which is all the possible outcomes: $8 + 6 + 12 = 26$. The numerator is how many there are of what you want: six black marbles. The probability is $\frac{6}{26}$, which can be reduced or (as is more customary) changed to a percentage. The correct answer is $\frac{6}{26}$ or $\frac{3}{13}$ or approximately 23 percent. What's the probability of drawing out a yellow marble? $\frac{8}{26}$, or $\frac{4}{13}$. A white marble? $\frac{12}{26}$, or $\frac{6}{13}$.

> A drawer has 5 pairs of white socks, 8 pairs of black socks, and 12 pairs of brown socks. In a hurry to get to school, Austin pulls out a pair at a time and tosses them on the floor if they are not the color he wants. Looking for a brown pair, Austin pulls out and discards a white pair, a black pair, a black pair, and a white pair. What is the probability that on his next reach into the drawer he will pull out a brown pair of socks?

This problem is slightly more complicated than the preceding one, although it uses the same formula. You began with 25 pairs of socks. However, Austin, that slob, has thrown four pairs on the floor. That means that only 21 pairs are left. The probability of his pulling out a brown pair is $\frac{12}{21}$, or $\frac{4}{7}$, or about 57 percent.

> A cookie jar has chocolate, vanilla, and strawberry wafer cookies. The jar contains 30 of each type. Bess reaches in, pulls out a chocolate and eats it, and then in quick succession pulls out and eats a vanilla, chocolate, strawberry, strawberry, chocolate, and vanilla. Assuming that she doesn't get sick or get caught, what is the probability that the next cookie she pulls out will be a chocolate one?

Originally, the jar held 90 cookies. Bess has scarfed down 7 of them, leaving 83. Careful! If you're about to put $\frac{30}{83}$, you're headed for a trap. There are no longer 30 chocolate cookies; there are only 27, because Bess has eaten 3. The probability is now $\frac{27}{83}$, or about 33 percent.

Probability must always be between zero and one. You cannot have a negative probability, and you cannot have a probability greater than 1, or 100 percent.

2. Multiply consecutive probabilities.

What is the probability that you'll get two heads when you toss a coin twice? You find each probability separately and then *multiply* the two. The chance of tossing a coin the first time and getting a head is ½. The chance of tossing a coin the second time and getting a head is ½. Multiply those consecutive probabilities: $\frac{1}{2} \times \frac{1}{2} = \frac{1}{4}$. The chances of getting two heads is one out of four.

What is the probability of tossing a die twice and getting a 5 on the first toss and a 6 on the second toss? Treat each toss separately. The probability of getting a 5 is ⅙. The probability of getting a 6 is ⅙. Multiply consecutive probabilities: $\frac{1}{6} \times \frac{1}{6} = \frac{1}{36}$.

The following example is a good trick question. Here are the QC (Quantitative Comparison) answer choices:

- A if the quantity in Column A is greater
- B if the quantity in Column B is greater
- C if the two quantities are equal
- D if the relationship cannot be determined from the information given
- An E response will not be scored

Column A	***Column B***
A fair die is tossed twice.	
Chances of getting a 5 on the first toss and a 2 on the second toss	Chances of getting a 6 on both tosses

If you chose A, you fell for the trap. You may think that it's harder to roll the same number twice, but the probability is the same as rolling two different numbers. Treat each roll separately. The probability of rolling a 5 is ⅙. The probability of rolling a 2 is ⅙. Multiply consecutive probabilities: $\frac{1}{6} \times \frac{1}{6} = \frac{1}{36}$. For Column B, treat each toss separately. The probability of rolling a 6 is ⅙. The probability of rolling a second 6 is ⅙. Multiply consecutive probabilities: $\frac{1}{6} \times \frac{1}{6} = \frac{1}{36}$. The correct answer is C.

If you've had a course in statistics, you may have learned about independent events, mutually exclusive events, and interdependent events. Forget about them; they're not on the SAT. The material you just learned is about as complicated as probability gets.

Chapter 12

Reviewing Miscellaneous Math You Probably Already Know

In This Chapter

- Running in place: time, rate, and distance problems
- Averaging out
- Playing with percentages
- Identifying the players: number sets and prime and composite numbers
- Formulating a plan: additional formulas and terms you need to know

How many years' worth of math have you had? Ten? Eleven? Twelve? Think of how much you've learned in that time . . . and how much you've forgotten. The purpose of this chapter is to review those concepts that you knew once upon a time but haven't used in so long they've been shifted way, way, waaaaaay back in your brain. This chapter's job is to yank that information front and center, so you can use it on the test.

DIRTy Math: Time, Rate, and Distance

Let's dish the dirt here, shall we? D.I.R.T. Distance Is Rate × Time. $D = RT$. When you have a time, rate, and distance problem, use this formula. Make a chart with the formula across the top and fill in the spaces on the chart.

> Jennifer drives 40 miles an hour for 2½ hours. Her friend Ashley goes the same distance but drives at 1½ times Jennifer's speed. How many *minutes* longer does Jennifer drive than Ashley?

Do *not* start making big, hairy formulas with *x*'s and *y*'s. Make the DIRT chart.

Distance	=	***Rate***	×	***Time***

When you fill in the 40 mph and 2½ hours for Jennifer, you can calculate that she went 100 miles. Think of it this simple way: If she goes 40 mph for one hour, that's 40 miles. For a second hour, she goes another 40 miles. In a half hour, she goes ½ of 40, or 20 miles. (See? You don't have to write down 40 × 2½ and do all that pencil-pushing; use your brain, not your yellow #2 or your calculator.) Add them together: 40 + 40 + 20 = 100. Jennifer has gone 100 miles.

Distance	=	***Rate***	×	***Time***
100 (Jennifer)		40 mph		2½ hours

Because Ashley drives the same distance, fill in 100 under distance for her. She goes 1½ times as fast. Uh-uh, put down that calculator. Use your brain! 1 × 40 is 40; ½ × 40 is 20. Add 40 + 20 = 60. Ashley drives 60 mph. Now this gets really easy. If she drives at 60 mph, she drives one mile a minute. (60 minutes in an hour, 60 miles in an hour. You figure it out, Einstein.) Therefore, to go 100 miles takes her 100 minutes. Because your final answer is asked for in minutes, don't bother converting this to hours; leave it the way it is.

Distance	=	*Rate*	×	*Time*
100 (Ashley)		60 mph		100 minutes

Last step. Jennifer drives 2½ hours. How many minutes is that? Do it the easy way, in your brain. One hour is 60 minutes. A second hour is another 60 minutes. A half hour is 30 minutes. Add them together: 60 + 60 + 30 = 150 minutes. If Jennifer drives for 150 minutes and Ashley drives for 100 minutes, Jennifer drives 50 minutes more than Ashley. However, Ashley gets a speeding ticket, has her driving privileges taken away by an irate father, and doesn't get to go to this weekend's party. Jennifer goes and gets her pick of the hunks, ending up with Tyrone's ring and letterman's sweater. The moral of the story: Slow . . . but steady!

Distance	=	*Rate*	×	*Time*
100 (Jennifer)		40 mph		150 minutes
100 (Ashley)		60 mph		100 minutes

Be careful to note whether the people are traveling in the *same* direction or *opposite* directions. Suppose you're asked how far apart drivers are at the end of their trip. If you are told that Jordan travels 40 mph east for 2 hours and Connor travels 60 mph west for 3 hours, they are going in opposite directions. If they start from the same point at the same time, Jordan has gone 80 miles one way, and Connor has gone 180 miles the opposite way. They are 260 miles apart. The trap answer is 100, because careless people (not *you*!) simply subtract 180 – 80.

It All Averages Out

You can always do averages the way Ms. Jones taught you when you were in third grade: Add all the terms, and then divide by the number of terms.

5 + 11 + 17 + 23 + 29 = 85

$^{85}/_{5}$ = 17

Or you can save wear-and-tear on the brain cells and know the following rule:

1. **The average of evenly spaced terms is the middle term.**

   First, check that the terms are evenly spaced. That means that there is an equal number of units between each term. Here, the terms are six apart. Second, circle the middle term, which here is 17. Third, go home, make popcorn, and watch the late-night movie with all the time you've saved.

   Try another one. Find the average of these numbers:

   32, 41, 50, 59, 68, 77, 86, 95, 104

   Don't reach for your calculator. You look and see that the terms are all nine units apart. Because they are evenly spaced, the middle term is the average: 68.

Question: Why do this when it's so easy just to punch the buttons on the calculator?

Answer: Because it's so easy just to punch the *wrong* buttons on the calculator. Careless mistakes are rampant. When you punch in 9 or 15 or 21 numbers, your chances of making some slip of the tip are high.

This is an easy trick to love, but don't march down the aisle with it yet. The tip works only for *evenly spaced* terms. If you have just any old batch of numbers, such as 4, 21, 97, 98, 199, you can't look at the middle term for the average. You have to find the average of those numbers the old-fashioned way.

Find the average of these numbers:

3, 10, 17, 24, 31, 38, 45, 52

First, double-check that they are evenly spaced. Here, the numbers are spaced by sevens. Next you look for the middle number . . . and there isn't one. You can, of course, find the two central terms, 24 and 31, and find the middle between them. That works, but what a pain. Not only that, but suppose you have 38 numbers. It's very easy to make a mistake as to which terms are the central ones. If you're off just a little bit, you miss the question. Instead, use rule number two:

2. **The average of evenly spaced terms is $^{(\text{first + last})}/2$.**

   Just add the first and the last terms, which are obvious at a glance, and divide that sum by 2. Here, 3 + 52 = 55. $^{55}/_{2}$ = 27.5.

   Note: Double-check using your common sense. Suppose that you made a silly mistake and got 45 for your answer. A glance at the numbers tells you that 45 is not in the middle and therefore cannot be the average.

   This tip works for *all* evenly spaced terms. It doesn't matter whether there is a middle number, as in the first example, or no middle number, as in the second example. Go back to the first example:

   32, 41, 50, 59, 68, 77, 86, 95, 104

   Instead of finding the middle term, add the first and last terms and divide by 2, like this: 32 + 104 = 136. $^{136}/_{2}$ = 68. Either way works.

Missing term average problem

You are likely to find a problem like this:

> A student takes seven exams. Her scores on the first six are 91, 89, 85, 92, 90, and 88. If her average on all *seven* exams is 90, what did she get on the seventh exam?

This is called a *missing term average problem* because you are given an average and asked to find a missing term. Duh.

1. **You can do this the basic algebraic way.**

   $$\text{Average} = \frac{\text{Sum}}{\text{Number of Terms}}$$

   $$90 = \frac{\text{Sum}}{7}$$

   Because you don't know the seventh term, call it x. Add the first six terms (and get 535) and x.

$90 = \frac{(535 + x)}{7}$. Cross-multiply: $90 \times 7 = 535 + x$

$630 = 535 + x$

$95 = x$

The seventh exam score was 95.

There is another quick way to do this problem (as given in the following section). You've probably done it this way all your life without realizing what a genius you are.

2. **You can do these problems the commonsense way.**

   Suppose your dad tells you that if you average a 90 for the semester in advanced physics, he'll let you buy that motorcycle the two of you have been arguing about for months (he figures he's safe because there's no way you're going to get such a high grade in that incredibly difficult class). You take him at his word and begin working hard.

   On the first exam, you get 91 and you're +1 point. That is, you're one point above the ultimate score you want, a 90.

   On the second exam, you get 89 and you're –1. On that test, you're one point below the ultimate score you want, a 90.

   On the third exam, you get an 85, which is –5. You're five points below the ultimate score you want, a 90.

   Are you getting the hang of this? Here's how it looks (using the numbers from the previous example).

   91 = +1

   89 = –1

   85 = –5

   92 = +2

   90 = 0

   88 = –2

   The +1 and –1 cancel each other out, and the +2 and –2 cancel each other out. You're left with –5, meaning you're five points in the hole. You have to make up those five points on the last exam or get five points *above* what you want for your ultimate score. Because you want a 90, you need a 95 on the last test.

   Try another, using the no-brainer method.

   Ray takes seven exams. He gets an 88 average on all of them. His first six scores are 89, 98, 90, 82, 88, and 87. What does he get on the seventh exam?

   Average = 88

   89 = +1

   98 = +10

   90 = +2

   82 = –6

   88 = 0

   87 = –1

The +1 and –1 cancel. Then you have (10 + 2) = +12 and –6, for a total of +6. You are six points *above* what you need for the ultimate outcome. You can afford to lose six points on the final exam, or be six points *below* the average. That gives you an 82.

You may be given only five out of seven scores and asked for *the average of the missing two* terms. Do the same thing and then divide by 2.

Average of seven exams: 85

Scores of the first five exams: 86, 79, 82, 85, 84

Find: The average score of each of the remaining exams

Algebraic way: $85 = \frac{(86 + 79 + 82 + 85 + 84) + x + x}{7}$

Cross-multiply: $595 = 416 + 2x$

$595 - 416 = 2x$

$179 = 2x$

$89.5 = x$

Commonsense way:

Average = 85

86 = +1

79 = –6

82 = –3

85 = 0

84 = –1

The +1 and –1 cancel each other out. You are left with –9 for *two* exams or –4.5 per exam. If you are *down* 4½ points, you must *gain* those 4½ points on each of the two exams:

85 + 4.5 = 89.5

The shortcut, commonsense way is quick and easy, but don't forget to make the change at the end. That is, if you decide that you are *minus eight* points going into the final exam, you need to be *plus eight* points on that last exam to come out even. If you subtract eight points from the average rather than add them, you'll probably come up with one of the trap answers.

Weighted averages

In a *weighted average,* some scores count more than others.

Number of Students	Score
12	80
13	75
10	70

If you are asked to find the average score for the students in this class, you know that you can't simply add 80, 75, and 70 and divide by 3 because the scores weren't evenly distributed among the students. Because 12 students got an 80, multiply $12 \times 80 = 960$. Do the same with the other scores:

$13 \times 75 = 975$

$10 \times 70 = 700$

$960 + 975 + 700 = 2{,}635$

Divide *not by 3* but by the total number of students: 35 (12 + 13 + 10)

$\frac{2635}{35} = 75.29$

Percentage Panic

The mere mention of the word *percent* may strike terror in your heart. There's no reason to panic over percentages; there are ways of getting around them.

1. **Ignore their very existence.** You can express a percentage as a decimal, which is a lot less intimidating. You do so by putting a decimal point two places to the left of the percentage and dropping the % sign.

   35% = .35; 83% = .83; 50% = .50; 33.3% = .333; 66.6% = .666

   If you have a choice of working with percentages rather than decimals, it's better to choose decimals (in my humble opinion). You can use your calculator, so percentages are easier than ever. To find a percentage's decimal equivalent (that is, to convert a percent to a decimal), punch in the percentage on your calculator and then divide it by 100. The decimal shows up on the screen.

2. **Another way to ignore a percentage is to convert it to a fraction.** The word *percent* means *per cent,* or *per hundred.* Every percentage is that number over 100.

   $50\% = \frac{50}{100}$; $33\% = \frac{33}{100}$; $75\% = \frac{75}{100}$

   You can either work with the fraction (something you may not like too much) or punch the fraction into your calculator and make a decimal again. That is, for 22 percent, divide 22 by 100 to get .22.

   If you can't ignore the percentage, remember that a percent is

   $\frac{\text{Part}}{\text{Whole}} \times 100$, or $\frac{\text{is}}{\text{of}} \times 100$

   What percent *is* 45 *of* 90?

   Put the part, 45, over the whole, 90. Or put the *is,* 45, over the *of,* 90.

   $\frac{45}{90} \times 100 = \frac{1}{2} \times 100 = \frac{100}{2} = 50\%$

   42 *is* what percent *of* 126?

   Put the part, 42, over the whole, 126. Or put the *is,* 42, over the *of,* 126.

   $\frac{42}{126} \times 100 = \frac{1}{3} \times 100 = \frac{100}{3} = 33\frac{1}{3}\%$

Here's a slightly harder one: What is 40% of 80? You may be tempted to put the *is,* 40, over the *of,* 80, and get $\frac{40}{80} = \frac{1}{2} \times 100 = \frac{100}{2} = 50\%$. However, when the problem is worded this way ("what is . . ."), you don't know the *is.* Your equation must be $\frac{x}{80} = \frac{40}{100}$. Cross-multiply: $3200 = 100x$. $x = 32$. There's an easier way to do it: *of* means times, or multiply. Because 40% = .40, multiply that by 80 to get 32.

You may see a problem asking you what percent increase or decrease occurred in the number of games a team won or the amount of commission a person earned. To find a percent increase or decrease, use this formula:

$$\text{percent increase or decrease} = \frac{\text{number increase or decrease}}{\text{original whole}}$$

In basic English, to find the percent by which something has increased or decreased, you take two simple steps:

1. **Find the *number* (amount) by which the thing has increased or decreased.**

   For example, if a team won 25 games last year and 30 games this year, the number increase was 5. If a salesperson earned $10,000 last year and $8,000 this year, the number decrease was 2,000. Make that the numerator of the fraction.

2. **Find the original whole.**

   This figure is what you started out with before you increased or decreased. If a team won 25 games last year and won 30 games this year, the original number was 25. If the salesperson earned $10,000 last year and $8,000 this year, the original number was 10,000. Make that the denominator.

You now have a fraction. Because you have a calculator, you can punch in the fraction, make it a decimal, and multiply by 100 to make it a percentage.

In 1992, Coach Denges won 30 prizes at the county fair by tossing a basketball into a bushel basket. In 1993, he won 35 prizes. What was his percent increase?

(A) 100

(B) 30

(C) $16\frac{2}{3}$

(D) 14.28

(E) $.1\overline{66}$

The number by which his prizes increased, from 30 to 35, is 5. That is the numerator. The original whole, or what he began with, is 30. That is the denominator. $\frac{5}{30} = \frac{1}{6} = 16\frac{2}{3}\%$. The correct answer is C.

If you chose E, I fooled you. The question asks what *percent* increase there was. If you say E, you're saying that there was a $.1\overline{66}$ percent increase. Not so. The $.1\overline{66}$ increase *as a percentage* is $16\frac{2}{3}\%$. If you chose D, you fell for another trap. You put the 5 increase over the 35 instead of over the 30.

Two years ago, Haylie scored 22 goals at soccer. This year, she scored 16 goals. What was her approximate percentage decrease?

(A) 72

(B) 37.5

(C) 27

(D) 16

(E) .27

Find the number of the decrease: 22 – 16 = 6. That is the numerator. Find the original whole from which she is decreasing: 22. That is the denominator. $\frac{6}{22}$ = approximately .27. The correct answer is C.

If you chose A, you put 16 over 22 instead of putting the decrease over the original whole. If you chose E, you forgot the difference between .27 percent and 27 percent. If you chose B, you put the decrease of 6 over the new amount, 16, rather than over the original whole. Note how easy these traps are to fall for. My suggestion: Write down the actual formula before you plug in the numbers. Writing down the formula may be boring, but doing so takes only a few seconds and may save you ten points (the approximate value of each math question).

Here's a tricky question that many people do in their heads (instead of writing down the formula and plugging in numbers) and blow big time.

Carissa has three quarters. Her father gives her three more. Carissa's wealth has increased by what percent?

(A) 50

(B) 100

(C) 200

(D) 300

(E) 500

Did you fall for the trap answer, C? Her wealth has doubled, to be sure, but the percent increase is only 100. You can prove that with the formula: The number increase is 75 (she has three more quarters, or 75 cents). Her original whole was 75. $\frac{75}{75}$ = 1 = 100%. The correct answer is B.

When you double something, you increase by 100 percent because you have to subtract the original "one" you began with. When you triple something, you increase by 200 percent because you have to subtract the original you began with. For example, if you had three dollars and you now have nine dollars, you have tripled your money but increased by only 200 percent. Do the formula: number increase = 6 dollars. Original whole = 3 dollars. $\frac{6}{3}$ = 2 = 200 percent. Take a wild guess at what percent you increase when you quadruple your money? That's right, 300 percent. Just subtract the original 100 percent.

Ready, Sets, Go: Number Sets

There's no escaping vocabulary. Even on the math portion of the test, you need to know certain terms. How can you solve a problem that asks you to "state your answer in integral values only" if you don't know what integral values are? Here are the number sets with which you'll be working. (I once got a call from a *very* irate parent who misunderstood her child to say I was teaching "number sex." Life as an SAT tutor is never dull.)

- **Counting numbers:** 1, 2, 3. Note that 0 is *not* a counting number.
- **Whole numbers:** 0, 1, 2, 3. Note that 0 *is* a whole number.
- **Integers:** . . . –3, –2, –1, 0, 1, 2, 3 . . . When a question asks for *integral values,* it wants the answer in integers only. For example, you can't give an answer like 4.3 because that's not an integer. You need to round down to 4.
- **Rational numbers:** Rational numbers can be expressed as $\frac{a}{b}$, where *a* and *b* are integers.

  Examples: 1 (because 1 = $\frac{1}{1}$ and 1 is an integer), $\frac{1}{2}$ (because 1 and 2 are integers), $\frac{9}{2}$ (because 9 and 2 are integers), and $-\frac{4}{2}$ (because –4 and 2 are integers).

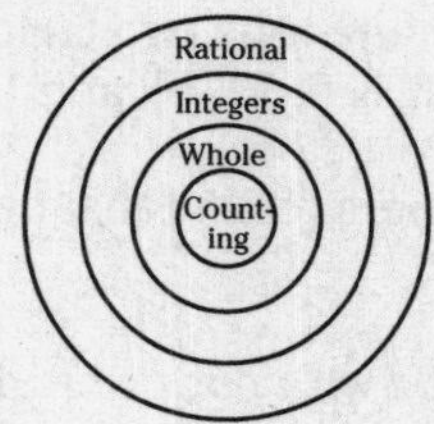

Notice that every number set so far has included the previous number sets. Whole numbers include counting numbers, integers include counting numbers and whole numbers, and rationals include counting numbers, whole numbers, and integers.

- **Irrational numbers:** The highly technical definition here is *anything not rational.* That is, an irrational number cannot be written as a/b, where a and b are integers and $b \neq 0$. Numbers that do not terminate and do not repeat can't be written as a fraction and, therefore, are irrational.

  Examples: π cannot be written *exactly* as 3.14; it is nonterminating and nonrepeating. $\sqrt{2}$ is approximately 1.4142 but is nonterminating and nonrepeating.

  Irrational numbers *do not* include the previous numbers sets. That is, irrational numbers don't include counting numbers, whole numbers, integers, and rational numbers.

- **Real numbers:** Briefly put, all of the above. Real numbers include counting numbers, whole numbers, integers, rationals, and irrationals. For all practical purposes, real numbers are everything you think of as numbers. When a question tells you to "express your answer in real numbers," don't sweat it. That's almost no constraint at all because nearly everything you see is a real number.

There are such critters as *imaginary* numbers, which are *not* on the SAT. (You will probably stop reading right there, figuring that you don't even want to hear about them if they're not going to be tested. I don't blame you.) Imaginary numbers are expressed with a lowercase i and are studied in upper-division math classes. I won't go into them here because, once again, *they are not tested on the SAT.* All numbers on the SAT are real numbers.

Prime and Composite Numbers

Prime numbers have exactly two factors; they cannot be divided evenly by numbers other than 1 and themselves. Examples include 2, 3, 5, 7, and 11.

There are a few lovely tricks to prime numbers.

- **Zero is *not* a prime number.** Why? Because it is evenly divisible by more than two factors. Zero can be divided by 1, 2, 3, and on to infinity. Although division by zero is undefined (and isn't tested on the SAT), you can divide zero by other numbers; the answer of course is always zero. $0 \div 1 = 0$; $0 \div 2 = 0$; $0 \div 412 = 0$.

- **One is *not* a prime number.** There are not two factors of 1. It cannot be divided only by 1 *and* itself. Confused? Don't worry about it. Just memorize the fact that 1 is not a prime number.

- **Two is the *only* even prime.** People tend to think that all prime numbers are odd. Well, almost. Two is prime because it has only two factors; it can be divided evenly only by 1 and itself.

- **Not all odd numbers are prime.** Think of 9 or 15; those numbers are odd but not prime because they have more than two factors and can be divided evenly by more than just 1 and themselves. $9 = (1 \times 9)$ *and* (3×3). $15 = (1 \times 15)$ *and* (3×5).

Composite numbers have more than two factors and can be divided by more than just 1 and themselves. Examples: 4, 6, 8, 9, 12, 14, and 15.

Note that composite numbers (called that because they are *composed* of more than two factors) can be even or odd.

Don't confuse *even* and *odd* with *positive* and *negative.* That's an easy mistake to make in the confusion of the exam. If a problem that you know should be easy is flustering you, stop and ask yourself whether you're making this common mistake.

I said that 0 and 1 are not prime. They are also not composite. What are they? Neither. You express this as "0 and 1 are neither prime nor composite." It's rather like wondering whether zero is positive or negative. You say, "Zero is neither positive nor negative." Why should you know this? Here's an example when the information can win you ten points (the approximate value of one correct math question).

Here are the QC (Quantitative Comparison) answer choices (see Chapter 13):

- A if the quantity in Column A is greater
- B if the quantity in Column B is greater
- C if the two quantities are equal
- D if the relationship cannot be determined from the information given
- An E response will not be scored

Column A	***Column B***
The number of prime numbers from 0 to 10 inclusive	The number of prime numbers from 11 to 20 inclusive

The prime numbers from 0 to 10 inclusive are 2, 3, 5, and 7. Note that 0 and 1 are *not* prime. If you count either or both as prime, you miss an otherwise very easy question. In Column B, the prime numbers from 11 to 20 inclusive are 11, 13, 17, and 19. Both columns have four prime numbers. The correct answer is C.

I'm All Mixed Up: Mixture Problems

A mixture problem is a word problem that looks much more confusing than it actually is. There are two types of mixtures: those in which the items remain separate (when you mix peanuts and raisins, you still have peanuts and raisins, not pearains or raispeans) and those in which the two elements blend (these are usually chemicals, like water and alcohol). Check out the separate mixture first.

Marshall wants to mix 40 pounds of beads selling for 30 cents a pound with a quantity of sequins selling for 80 cents a pound. He wants to pay 40 cents per pound for the final mix. How many pounds of sequins should he use?

The hardest part for most students is knowing where to begin. Make a chart.

	Pounds	Price	Total
Beads	40	$.30	$12.00
Sequins	x	$.80	$.80x$
Mixture	$40 + x$	$.40	$.40 (40 + x)$

Reason it out. The cost of the beads (1200) plus the cost of the sequins ($80x$) must equal the cost of the mixture ($1600 + 40x$). Note that you dump the decimal point (officially, you multiply by 100 to get rid of the decimal point, but really, you dump it). Now you have a workable equation:

$$1200 + 80x = 1600 + 40x$$

$$80x - 40x = 1600 - 1200$$

$$40x = 400$$

$$x = 10$$

Careful! Keep in mind what x stands for. It represents the number of pounds of sequins — what the question asks for.

Go back and double-check by plugging this value into the equation. You already know that Marshall spent $12 on beads. If he buys 10 pounds of sequins for 80 cents a pound, he spends $8, for a total of $20. He spends that $20 on 50 pounds: $2000 \div 50 = 40$. How about that, it works!

Greed Is Great: Interest Problems

This is a pretty problem: PRTI, to be exact. P = Principal, the amount of money you begin with, or the amount you invest. R = Rate, the interest rate you're earning on the money. T = Time, the amount of time you leave the money in the interest-bearing account. I = Interest, the amount of interest you earn on the investment. A problem usually asks you how much interest someone earned on his or her investment.

The formula is $PRT = I$. *Principal* $\times$ *Rate* $\times$ *Time* = *Interest.*

> Janet invested $1,000 at 5 percent annual interest for one year. How much interest did she earn?

This is the simplest type of problem. Plug the numbers into the formula.

$PRT = I$

$1{,}000 \times .05 \times 1 = 50$. She earned 50 dollars interest.

The answer choices may try to trap you with variations on a decimal place, making the answers 5, 50, 500, and so on. You know that $5\% = \frac{5}{100} = .05$; be careful how you multiply. (If you are percentage phobic or absolutely hate percentages, get a calculator with a percentage key. It does most of the work for you.)

These problems are not intentionally vicious (unlike 99 percent of the rest of the SAT, right?). You won't see something that gets crazy on interest rates, like "5 percent annual interest compounded quarterly for 3 months and 6 percent quarterly interest compounded daily, blah, blah, blah."

(Useless but fascinating trivia: In Bulgarian, the word for *thank you* is pronounced *blah-go-dah-ree-uh.* But a shortened form, like *thanks,* is simply *blah.* If your mother takes you to task for being a smart aleck and going "blah, blah, blah" when she talks, you can innocently claim that you're practicing your Bulgarian and are just thanking her for her wisdom.)

All Work and No Play: Work Problems

The formula most commonly used in a work problem is

$$\frac{\text{Time put in}}{\text{Capacity to do the whole job}}$$

Find each person's contribution. The denominator is the easy part; it represents how many hours (minutes, days, weeks, and so on) it would take the person to do the whole job, working alone. The numerator is how long the person has already worked. For example, if Janie can paint a house in four days and has been working for one day, she has done $\frac{1}{4}$ of the work. If Evelyn can paint a house in nine days and has been working for five, she has done $\frac{5}{9}$ of the project.

So far, so good. The problem comes when more than one person works at the task. What happens when Janie and Evelyn work together?

> Janie working alone can paint a house in six days. Evelyn working alone can paint it in eight days. Working together, how long will it take them to paint the house?

Find Janie's work: $\frac{x}{6}$. Find Evelyn's work: $\frac{x}{8}$. Together, the two fractions must add up to 1, the entire job.

$$\frac{x}{6} + \frac{x}{8} = 1$$

Multiply by the common denominator, 48, to eliminate the fractions.

$$\frac{48x}{6} + \frac{48x}{8} = 48$$

$$8x + 6x = 48$$

$$14x = 48$$

x = approximately 3.43. It would take the two women working together about 3.43 days to paint the house.

Double-check by using your common sense. If you get an answer of 10, for example, you know that you must have made a mistake because the two women working together should be able to do the job *more quickly* than either one working alone.

If you can't leave your calculator alone for a minute, here's how to use it for this problem. If Janie can paint the house in six days, in one day she can paint $\frac{1}{6}$ or approximately .167 of the house. If Evelyn can paint the house in eight days, in one day she can paint $\frac{1}{8}$ or .125 of the house. Working together, they can paint $.1\overline{66} + .125$ = approximately .292 of the house. Divide 1 (the whole paint job, the whole house) by .292 to get 3.43. If you have multiple-choice answers, you can choose one that's close enough to this value.

Smooth Operator: Order of Operations

When you have several operations (addition, subtraction, multiplication, division, squaring, and so on) in one problem, there is a definite order in which you must perform the operations:

1. **Parentheses: Do what's inside the parentheses first.**
2. **Power: Do the squaring or the cubing, whatever the exponent is.**
3. **Multiply or divide: Do these left to right. If multiplication is to the left of division, multiply first. If division is to the left of multiplication, divide first.**
4. **Add or subtract: Do these left to right. If addition is to the left of subtraction, add first. If subtraction is to the left of addition, subtract first.**

An easy ***mnemonic*** (memory) device for remembering these is *Please Praise My Daughter And Son* (PPMDAS): Parentheses, Power, Multiply, Divide, Add, Subtract.

$$10(3 - 5)^2 + (30/5)^0 =$$

First, do what's inside the parentheses: $3 - 5 = -2$. $30/5 = 6$. Next, do the power: $-2^2 = 4$. $6^0 = 1$. (Did you remember that any number to the zero power equals one?) Next, multiply: $10 \times 4 = 40$. Finally, add: $40 + 1 = 41$. *Correct Answer:* 41. Try another.

$$3 + (9 - 6)^2 - 5(8/2)^{-2} =$$

First, do what's inside the parentheses: $9 - 6 = 3$. $8/2 = 4$. Second, do the powers: $3^2 = 9$. $4^{-2} = 1/(4^2) = 1/16$. Multiply: $5 \times 1/16 = 5/16$. Finally, add and subtract left to right. $3 + 9 = 12$. $12 - 5/16 = 11\,11/16$. *Correct Answer:* $11\,11/16$.

Bonus: Speaking of mnemonics, here's my favorite. Can you tell me what it stands for? My Very Educated Mother Just Served Us Nine Pickles.

Give up? It's the mnemonic of the planets in our solar system: Mercury, Venus, Earth, Mars, Jupiter, Saturn, Uranus, Neptune, and Pluto.

Measuring Up: Units of Measurement

Joke: How many seconds are in a year? *Answer:* Exactly 12. January second, February second, March second. . .

Occasionally, you may be expected to know a unit of measurement that the test makers deem obvious but which you have forgotten. Take a few minutes to review this brief list.

International students, in particular — you need to memorize these because you may not have grown up using some of the same units of measurement (standard rather than metric) as those used in the United States (and on the SAT).

1. Time

60 seconds = 1 minute

60 minutes = 1 hour

24 hours = 1 day

7 days = 1 week

52 weeks = 1 year

365 days = 1 year

366 days = 1 leap year

Leap year is an interesting concept in terms of math problems. It comes around every four years. The extra day, February 29, makes 366 days in the year. Why do you need to know this? Suppose you see this problem:

Mr. Pellaton's neon sign flashes four hours a day, every day all year, for four years. If it costs him three cents a day for electricity, how much will he owe for electricity at the end of the fourth year?

You may be tempted to say that this problem is super easy — multiply 365 × 4 to find the number of days and then multiply that number by .03. Wrong-o! You forgot that extra day for leap year, and your answer is off by three cents. You *know* that the test makers will have that wrong answer lurking among the answer choices just to trap you. Whenever there is a four-year period, look out for the leap year with an extra day.

2. Quantities

2 cups = 1 pint

2 pints = 1 quart

4 quarts = 1 gallon

16 ounces = 1 pound

2,000 pounds = 1 ton

You can calculate that a gallon has 16 cups, or 8 pints. To help you remember, think of borrowing a cup of sugar. Sugar is sweet, and you have a Sweet 16 birthday party: 16 sweet cups of sugar in a gallon. It may be silly, but the best memory aids usually are.

3. Length

12 inches = 1 foot

3 feet (36 inches) = 1 yard

5,280 feet (1,760 yards) = 1 mile

Everyone knows that there are 12 inches in a foot. How many square inches are there in a square foot? If you say 12, you've fallen for the trap. 12 × 12 = 144 square inches are in a square foot.

Here's how you may fall for that trap in an otherwise easy problem.

Here are the QC (Quantitative Comparison) answer choices (see Chapter 13):

- A if the quantity in Column A is greater
- B if the quantity in Column B is greater

- C if the two quantities are equal
- D if the relationship cannot be determined from the information given
- An E response will not be scored

Column A	Column B
Number of square inches in 3 square feet	36

Your first reaction is to think that the columns are equal because there are 12 inches to a foot and $12 \times 3 = 36$. However, a square foot is $12 \times 12 = 144$ inches. Because 144×3 is definitely greater than 36 (don't waste any time doing the math), the answer is A.

Bonus: How many cubic inches are there in a cubic foot? Not 12, and not even 144. A cubic foot is $12 \times 12 \times 12 = 1{,}728$ cubic inches.

What's the Point: Decimals

Now that you're allowed to use a calculator on the SAT, working with decimals is easy; punch in the numbers and let the machine do the rest. However, a brief decimal review is helpful because you're almost certain to do a few "obviously easy" decimal problems in your head. As you know by now, when something is "obviously easy," it's a breeding ground for tricks and traps.

Adding and subtracting decimals

Line up the decimal points vertically and add or subtract the numbers.

$$\begin{array}{r} 3.09 \\ 4.72 \\ 31.9 \\ \underline{121.046} \\ 160.756 \end{array}$$

If you're rushed for time and don't want to do the whole problem, go to extremes. The extremes are the far-left and far-right columns. Often, calculating them alone gives you enough information to choose the right answer to a multiple-choice problem. In this case, you can look at the far right, which is the thousandths column, and know that it has to end in a 6. Suppose that the answer choices are

(A) 160.999

(B) 160.852

(C) 160.756

(D) 159.831

(E) 159.444

You know immediately that C has to be the correct choice.

Maybe more than one of the answer choices uses the correct digit for the far-right column. Okay, you're flexible; head for the far-left column, which here is the hundreds place. You know in this problem it has to be a 1. The answer choices are

(A) 160.756

(B) 201.706

(C) 209.045

(D) 210.006

(E) 301.786

Only choice A has the correct far-left number.

Multiplying decimals

1. **You're almost certain to want to use your calculator for these operations.**
2. **If you do the multiplication by hand, the biggest trap to beware of is keeping the number of decimal points correct.** The number of decimal places in the product (the number you get when you multiply the terms together) must be the same as the sum of the number of decimal places in all the terms.

   $5.06 \times 3.9 =$

   $$\begin{array}{r} 5.06 \\ \times\ \ 3.9 \\ \hline 19.734 \end{array}$$

   There are two decimal places in the first term and one in the second, for a total of three. Therefore, the final answer must have three decimal places.

The shortcut you learned for addition and subtraction works here, as well. Go to extremes. Look at the far-right and far-left terms. You know that $6 \times 9 = 54$, such that the last digit in the answer has to be a 4. You can eliminate wrong answers by using that information. You know that $5 \times 3 = 15$, but you may have to carry over some other numbers to make the far-left value greater than 15 (as it turns out here). At least you know that the far-left digits must be 15 *or more.* An answer choice starting with 14, 13, or anything less than 15 can be eliminated.

Dividing decimals

1. **The best thing to do is use your calculator.**
2. **If you decide to divide decimals by hand, turn them into integers by moving the decimal point the appropriate number of places to the right for both terms, the one you are dividing and the one you are dividing by.**

   $4.44 \div .06 = {}^{444}\!/_{6} = 74$

I won't spend much time on decimals because you almost certainly won't spend much time on them yourself. Just remember three things:

- Keep a wary eye on the decimal point; its placement is often a trap for the careless.
- Go to extremes: Determine the far-left or far-right digit and use that information to eliminate incorrect answer choices.
- Be a battery brain: If there is ever a place to use your calculator, this is it.

Broken Hearts, Broken Numbers: Fractions

Some calculators have a fraction function, a slash bar on the calculator keypad that lets you do fractions quickly and easily. I strongly suggest that you buy, borrow, or beg one of these calculators and get used to using it before you take the SAT.

$3/16 + 8/11 =$

(A) $106/299$

(B) $203/964$

(C) $301/669$

(D) $161/176$

(E) $102/103$

For now, I'm going to assume that you don't have a fraction key on your calculator. Enter $3/16$ to get .1875. Divide 8 by 11 to get .72. Add the two to get approximately .91.

Now look at the answer choices. You know that the answer, at .91 or 91 percent, is going to be very close to 1. Eliminate answer A because it is only about $1/3$. Eliminate answer B, which is about $2/9$, way less than 1. Eliminate C, which looks to be about $1/2$. Answer D is a possibility; skip it for the moment. Answer E is very, very, very close to 1, certainly more than .91. Enter $161/176$ on the calculator and see how it comes out: .91477, close enough. If you enter $102/103$, just to make sure, you get .99, which is more than you want. The correct answer is D.

In conclusion, you can always change a fraction into a decimal and work through the problem that way. True, it may take you a little while to do all the button-pushing, but you're almost certain to get the correct answer (barring careless mistakes or battery failure). You have to decide whether you have the time to do the problem this way.

Bonus joke: Did you hear about the town so small it had a fraction as a Zip Code?

Adding or subtracting

1. **You can add or subtract fractions only when they have the same denominator.**

   $$\frac{1}{3}+\frac{4}{3}=\frac{5}{3}$$

   $$\frac{3}{8}-\frac{2}{8}=\frac{1}{8}$$

2. **When fractions have the same denominator, add or subtract the numerators only.**

3. **When fractions don't have the same denominator, you have to find a common denominator.**

   You can, of course, multiply all the denominators, but that often doesn't give you the *lowest* common denominator. You end up with some humongous, overwhelming number that you'd rather not work with. Instead, use this little trick:

4. **To find the lowest common denominator, identify the highest denominator and count by it.**

   Find the lowest common denominator of 15 and 6. Sure, you can multiply $15 \times 6 = 90$, but that's not the *lowest* common denominator. Instead, count by 15s because it's the larger of the two. 15? No, 6 doesn't go into that. 30? Yes, both 15 and 6 go into 30. That's the *lowest* common denominator.

Try another one:

Find the lowest common denominator for 2, 4, and 5. Count by 5's: 5? No, 2 and 4 don't go into it. 10? No, 2 and 4 don't go into it. 15? No, 2 and 4 don't go into it. 20? Yes, all the numbers divide evenly into 20.

5. **In many problems, you don't even have to find the lowest common denominator. You can find any common denominator by multiplying the denominators.**

$$\frac{4}{15}+\frac{1}{6}=$$

The common denominator is 15 × 6 = 90. Cross-multiply: 4 × 6 = 24. The first fraction becomes $^{24}/_{90}$. Cross-multiply: 1 × 15 = 15. The second fraction becomes $^{15}/_{90}$. Now add the numerators: 24 + 15 = 39. Put the sum over the common denominator: $^{39}/_{90}$. Can you reduce? Yes, by 3: $^{13}/_{30}$.

Do the same thing when working with variables instead of numbers.

$$\frac{a}{b}-\frac{c}{d}=$$

Find the common denominator by multiplying the two denominators: $b \times d = bd$. Cross-multiply: $a \times d = ad$. Cross-multiply: $c \times b = cb$. Put the difference of the results of the cross-multiplication over the common denominator: $\frac{ad-cb}{bd}$

Multiplication

Multiply horizontally, multiplying the numerators and then multiplying the denominators.

$$\frac{3}{4}\times\frac{2}{5}\times=\frac{(3\times2)}{(4\times5)}=\frac{6}{20}=\frac{3}{10}$$

Always check whether you can cancel before you begin working to avoid having to deal with big, awkward numbers and to avoid having to reduce at the end. In the preceding example, you can cancel the 4 and the 2, leaving you with

$$\frac{3}{2\ \cancel{4}}\times\frac{\cancel{2}\ 1}{5}=\frac{(3\times1)}{(2\times5)}=\frac{3}{10}$$

You get to the right solution either way; canceling in advance just makes the numbers smaller and easier to work with.

Division

To divide by a fraction, invert it (turn it upside down) and multiply.

$$\frac{1}{3}\div\frac{2}{5}=\frac{1}{3}\times\frac{5}{2}=\frac{5}{6}$$

Mixed numbers

A *mixed number* is a whole number with a fraction tagging along behind it, like $2\frac{1}{3}$, $4\frac{2}{5}$, or $9\frac{1}{2}$. Again, it's usually easier to reach for your calculator, but if you're going to do this problem by hand, multiply the whole number by the denominator and add that to the numerator. Put the sum over the denominator.

$2\frac{1}{3} = (2 \times 3) + 1 = 7 \rightarrow \frac{7}{3}$

$4\frac{2}{5} = (4 \times 5) + 2 = 22 \rightarrow \frac{22}{5}$

$9\frac{1}{2} = (9 \times 2) + 1 = 19 \rightarrow \frac{19}{2}$

The Stats Don't Lie: Statistics

Don't panic; statistics are tested on the SAT only in the most rudimentary way. If you can master three basic concepts, you can do any statistics on this exam. Those concepts are median, mode, and range.

Median

Simply put, the *median* is the middle number when all the terms are arranged in order. Think of the median strip, which is the middle of the road. Median = middle. Be sure you arrange the numbers in order (increasing or decreasing, it makes no difference) before you find the median.

Find the median of –3, 18, –4, ½, 11.

(A) –3

(B) 18

(C) –4

(D) ½

(E) 11

Put the numbers in order: –4, –3, ½, 11, 18. The one in the middle, ½, is the median. It's as simple as that. The correct answer is D.

Mode

The *mode* is the most frequent number. I suggest you put the numbers in order again. Then look for the one that shows up the most often. It's the mode.

Find the mode of 11, 18, 29, 17, 18, –4, 0, 19, 0, 11, 18.

(A) 11

(B) 17

(C) 18

(D) 19

(E) 29

There are three 18s but no more than two of any other number. The correct answer is C.

Range

The *range* is the distance from the greatest to the smallest. In other words, you take the biggest term and subtract the smallest term, and that's the range.

Find the range of the numbers 11, 18, 29, 17, 18, –4, 0, 19, 0, 11, 18.

(A) 33

(B) 29

(C) 19

(D) 0

(E) –4

Ah, did this one getcha? True, 33 is not one of the numbers in the set. But to find the range, subtract the smallest from the largest number: 29 – (–4) = 29 + 4 = 33. The correct answer is A.

The only trap you are likely to see in the statistics questions is in the answer choices. The questions themselves are quite straightforward, but the answer choices may assume that some people don't know one term from another. For example, one answer choice to a median question may be the mean (the average). One answer choice to a range question may be the mode. Circle the word in the question that tells you what you are looking for to keep from falling for this trap.

A Picture Is Worth a Thousand Words: Graphs

Some of the math questions on the SAT are called Data Interpretation. That's a pompous name for reading a graph, something you've been doing for years. Don't let graph problems intimidate you. Here are the three most common types of graphs you're likely to see on the SAT.

- **Circle or pie graph:** The circle represents 100 percent. The key to this graph is noting of what total the percentages are part. Below the graph you may be told that in 1994, 5,000 students graduated with Ph.D.s If a 25 percent segment on the circle graph is labeled "Ph.D.s in history," you know to say that the number of history Ph.D.s is 25 percent of 5,000, or 1,250.
- **Two axes line graph:** A typical line graph has a bottom and a side axis. You plot a point or read a point from the two axes. This is probably the simplest type of graph you will encounter.
- **Bar graph:** A bar graph has vertical or horizontal bars. The bars may represent actual numbers or percentages. If the bar goes all the way from one side of the graph to the other, it represents 100 percent.

Some questions use two graphs in one problem. The following is such an example.

Two graphs on the following page must be read in conjunction. The bottom graph is a bar graph going from 0 to 100 percent. Read the graph by *subtracting* to find the appropriate percentage. For example, in 1990, job conflict begins at 20 and goes to 50, a difference of 30 percent. You'd be falling for a trap were you to say that job conflicts were 50 percent. In 1993, His Mother (as a cause of failed relationships) goes from 80 to 100, or 20 percent.

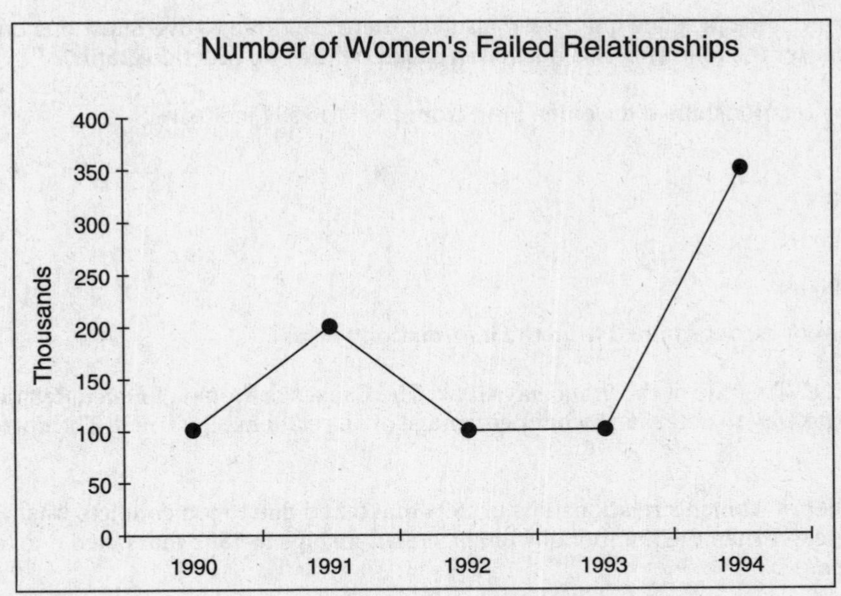

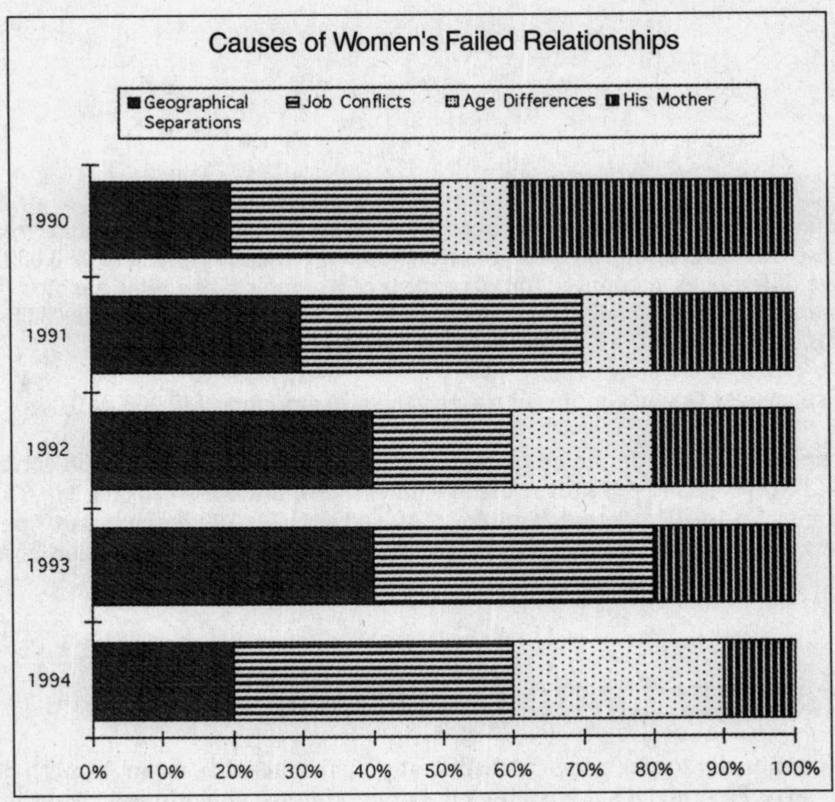

The top graph gives you the actual number of failed relationships in thousands. Be sure to look at the labels of the axes. For example, in 1990, there were not 100 failed relationships but 100,000. Use the graphs together to find out the number of relationships that failed because of a particular event or situation. For example, in 1991, there were 200,000 failed relationships. Also in 1991, age differences (from 70 to 80, or 10 percent) made up 10 percent. Multiply 10 percent or $.10 \times 200{,}000 = 20{,}000$ relationships.

Ready to try some practice questions? Usually, there are three to five questions below a graph. Answer the following two questions based on the two practice graphs.

How many relationships did women have from 1990 to 1994 inclusive?

(A) 850

(B) 8,500

(C) 85,000

(D) 850,000

(E) It cannot be determined from the information given.

Did I getcha? The title of the graph says it all: The Causes of Women's *Failed* Relationships. You have no way to determine what percentage of all relationships failed. The correct answer is E.

The number of women's relationships in 1994 that failed due to job conflicts was what percent greater than the number of women's relationships in 1992 that failed due to age differences?

(A) 700

(B) 600

(C) 500

(D) 120

(E) 7

In 1994, job conflicts accounted for 40 percent of women's failed relationships (from 20 to 60). Because there were 350,000 failed relationships in 1994, multiply $.40 \times 350{,}000 = 140{,}000$. In 1992, age differences accounted for 20 percent of women's failed relationships (60 to 80). In 1992, there were 100,000 failed relationships. Multiply $.20 \times 100{,}000 = 20{,}000$. The correct answer is B.

If you chose answer D, you simply subtracted the two amounts: $140{,}000 - 20{,}000 = 120{,}000$.

If you chose choice (E) 7, or choice (A) 700, you fell for the trap. Take the job conflicts number — 140,000 — and put it over the age differences number — 20,000. $140{,}000 \div 20{,}000 = 7$. The 7 translates to 700 percent. If you're confused why 7 is 700 percent, not 7 percent, or why 7 times is 600 percent greater, turn to the "Percentage Panic" section, earlier in this chapter.

Fun and Games: Logic Questions

The SAT occasionally tosses a logic question at you, disguised as a simple math question. It has two parts. First is the set of statements or conditions, sometimes called the *facts*. These statements describe the relationship between or among people, items, or events. You may, for example, be given statements about students at a school and asked which ones can be assigned to the same classes. You may be told facts about events that can happen on certain days of the week. A problem may tell you about possible different combinations of items. Here are examples of statements you may see in different games.

- Emily cannot join the same after-school group as Brittany.
- Girls basketball games take place on Mondays, Tuesdays and Wednesdays except when boys basketball games are held on the same day.
- Justine is taller than Kristi and weighs less than Marco.

Following the statements is one — possibly two — questions that test your understanding of how the statements work together. Here are a few samples of what these questions may look like.

- How many different after-school groups can Emily join?
- On which day of the week are no basketball games played at all?
- Which of the following represents the order of the students from tallest to shortest?

A logic question often takes a looooooong time. Make the decision whether you have the time — and the patience! — to invest that much time. If not, skip the question and come back to it later, if you can. Don't rush yourself.

The basic approach: Diagramming

Before you start doodling and diagramming, be sure you know all the parties involved. Make a "program" of the players by writing down the pool of people or events. For example, if the question talks about five teachers, Mahaffey, Negy, O'Leary, Plotnitz and Quivera, you jot down M, N, O, P and Q on the test booklet.

Next, use a diagram to show the relationship between people or events. Here are a few of the most common diagrams.

- **Calendar:** Draw a simple calendar and fill in the events that happen on particular days.
- **Ordering or sequencing:** You may have a relationship problem in which some people are taller or heavier than others. You would write a line of people, with A above B if A is taller than B, C at the bottom if she is the shortest, and so on.
- **Grouping or membership:** This problem asks you which items or people could belong to which group. For example, membership in a club may require four out of five characteristics. Often this type of question doesn't require a graph per se but a lot of "if then" statements, such as "If A is in the group, then B is not." You can also think of these as mathematical statements: $A \neq B$.
- **Personal characteristics:** In this type of problem, you are given information about people and asked what those people can or can't do based on their characteristics. For example, you may be told that Trent has a fear of heights and Lucilla has a fear of horses. If the question asks, "Which of the following could go on a horseback ride along a mountain crest?" eliminate Trent and Lucilla!

Looking at an example

Here's an example to help you use the tips in the preceding section:

Five spices — lemon pepper, marjoram, nutmeg, oregano, and paprika — are aligned next to one another between the left and right sides of a kitchen cabinet. Their arrangement must conform to the following conditions:

- The marjoram is to the right of the paprika.
- The oregano is first from the left or first from the right.
- The lemon pepper is to the left of the nutmeg.

Which of the following conditions would allow a determination of the order of all the spices?

(A) The paprika is first from the left.

(B) The oregano is first from the left.

(C) The paprika is second from the left.

(D) The lemon pepper is second from the left.

(E) The nutmeg is second from the left.

Answer: **E.** To help keep track of the information, write out initials for the roster of spices — L, M, N, O, and P — and make five simple dashes to represent the five positions of the spices:

__ __ __ __ __

The easiest condition to accommodate is the one that indicates that the oregano must be first from the left or first from the right. Draw these two possibilities:

O __ __ __ __

__ __ __ __ O

For the other conditions, there are too many possibilities to draw them all, but you can help yourself keep track of your rights and lefts by drawing the spices next to each other.

Quickly think through some of the overall arrangements to get your mind going in the right direction. For example, if O is on the far left, you know that P must be second, third, or fourth, with M in third, fourth, or fifth. If P is fourth, M has to be fifth, leaving L in second and N in third.

For the question at hand, run through the choices, trying each one. Choice A is not the answer, because putting P first would force O to be fifth, but there are still options with M, L, and N. For example, M could be second, with L and N third and fourth, respectively, or M could be third, with L second and N fourth.

Choice B is worse than choice A because it fixes only O in place.

Choice C is not helpful because P could be second from the left with O either first or fifth. For example, one order could be O P M L N, and another could be L P N M O.

Choice D is very similar to choice C. For example, the order could be O L N P M or P L M N O.

Choice E works because N in second forces L, which has to be to the left of N, to be first. Now, you must put O fifth, leaving only third and fourth for P and M. Because M must be to the right of P, P must be third and M fourth.

Ten math concepts you absolutely must know

If you got the news that the world would end in two hours, what would you do? Order a pizza? Go surfing or play hoops with your friends? Sneak into an R-rated movie?

Life has its priorities. If you were told that your SAT math study time was to end in two hours, what would be your priorities? This sidebar gives you my suggestions (although pizza doesn't sound half bad . . .). All of these concepts are discussed in detail in the math reviews, Chapters 10 (geometry), 11 (algebra), and this chapter.

- **Ratios:** The total possible is a multiple of the sum of the numbers in the ratio. A ratio is written as $^{OF}/_{TO}$ or OF:TO.
- **Common Pythagorean ratios:** In a right triangle, sides may be in the following ratios:

  3:4:5

  5:12:13

  7: 24: 25

  $s:s:s\sqrt{2}\left(or\ \frac{s}{\sqrt{2}}:\frac{s}{\sqrt{2}}:s\right)$

  $s:s\sqrt{3}:2s$
- **FOIL method of algebra:** To multiply algebraic expressions, use FOIL: First-Outer-Inner-Last. To reduce algebraic equations, use FOIL backward.
- **Linear algebraic equations:** Isolate the variable: Get the variables on one side of the equal sign and the nonvariables on the other side (remembering to change from a positive to a negative or vice versa when crossing over the equal sign). Add like terms. Divide both sides by what is next to the variable.
- **Symbolism:** The SAT tests two basic types of symbolism: Plug the numbers into the expression and talk through the symbolism explanation in English.
- **Exponents:** Know how to add, subtract, multiply, and divide like bases. Remember that a non-zero real number to the zero power equals one and that a non-zero real number to a negative power is the *reciprocal* (upside-down version) of that number.
- **Square roots:** Know how to multiply and divide like radicals and how to simplify radicals.
- **Plotting points on a graph:** Know how to find a point on a graph given its (x,y) coordinates. Remember that the point of origin is (0,0), and that points along a line with the same (x,y) coordinates form a 45-degree angle.
- **Angles:** Understand the various types of angles, especially how to identify exterior angles and how to solve for the sum of interior angles of any polygon.
- **Circles:** Be able to find circumference, area, sectors, arcs, and degree measures of central and inscribed angles.

Chapter 13

The Incomparable Quantitative Comparisons

In This Chapter

- Finding the elusive QC answer choices
- Performing a balancing act
- Recognizing and blowing past the built-in traps
- Working smarter, not harder

Quantitative Comparisons (QCs) consist of 15 questions with half a zillion traps. The QCs rarely require power math; they require paranoia (to recognize the traps) and finesse (to avoid the traps). Hmmm, "Paranoia & Finesse." Sounds like a firm of attorneys, doesn't it?

A riddle for you: What do quicksand and quantitative comparisons have in common?

Answer: They both can suck you in and pull you down before you realize what's happening.

Where Did All the Answers Go? The QC Format

A QC question lists a quantity in Column A and another quantity in Column B. The quantities can be numbers, variables, equations, words, figures, pictures of your Uncle Lance's prize cabbages — anything. Your job is to compare the quantity in Column A to the quantity in Column B. (Hence the title, "Quantitative Comparisons." I bet some rocket scientist got big bucks for thinking this one up!)

No answer choices are given below the quantities in QC questions. You are to compare the quantities and choose the following:

- A if the quantity in Column A is greater
- B if the quantity in Column B is greater
- C if the two quantities are equal
- D if the relationship cannot be determined from the information given
- An E response will not be scored

Got all that? Just choose A if A is bigger, B if B is bigger, C if they're the same (with C standing for *same,* if you spell as badly as I do), and D if you can't tell (as in D for *duuuuuh!*).

None of these questions has an E answer. If you fill in an E on your answer grid, it doesn't count for or against you. It's as if you skipped the question. Obviously, you're just wasting your time — and the potential for any Lucky Guess points — if you fill in an E oval.

As Easy as π: The Approach for QC Questions

The hardest part of a QC question is knowing where to begin. You can save considerable time — and frustration — if you develop good habits now that carry over to the test later. Follow this simple three-step approach:

1. **Solve for the quantity in Column A.** You might have to solve an equation, talk through a word problem, or do nothing but look at what's given. Here are some examples of what you may see in Column A:

Column A

x^2

40% of 340

The number of miles hiked by Ken, who hikes at 3 mph for 6½ hours

2. **Solve for the quantity in Column B.** Again, this can mean solving an equation, talking through a word problem, or just looking at the column. Here are some examples:

Column B

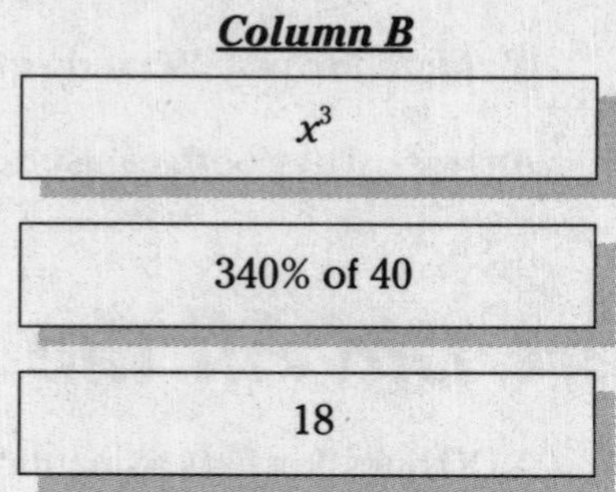

3. **Compare the two columns.** Sounds simple enough, right? Wait until you see some of the traps that they can build into the QCs.

Gotchas and Other Groaners: Tips, Traps, and Tricks

QCs have so many tricks and traps that I give you a separate section for each one, with a few examples to illustrate how easily you can fall for the traps.

If the columns look equal, it's a trap

If two columns appear at first glance to be equal, a trap is almost always involved. Suppose you see the following question:

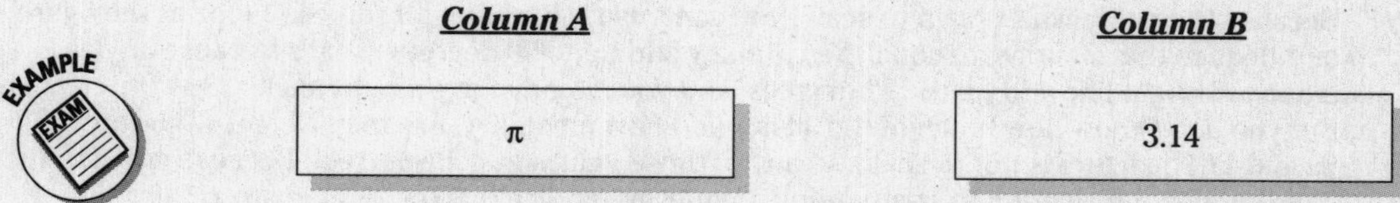

Your gut reaction may be to choose C because they are equal. At school, you've had 3.14 drilled into your head as π. But π is only *approximately* 3.14; it is actually larger. The correct answer to this problem is A. For convenience, π is rounded to two decimal places: 3.14. Actually, however, π continues as a nonrepeating, nonterminating decimal: 3.141592. . . .

Column A	Column B
$.0062 \times 3600$	$6200 \times .3600$

You probably checked that the number of digits and decimal places is the same and chose C. But the answer is B. When you multiply them out, Column A equals 22.32 and Column B equals 2,232. *Biiiiiig* difference. The moral of the story: If your first reaction is that the problem is a no-brainer — that the answer is obviously, clearly, undoubtedly C — slap yourself upside the head and work through the problem.

Problems go from easier to harder. The first five or six questions are probably just as easy as they look. Don't drive yourself crazy trying to find traps *early* in the section; more than enough rear their ugly heads later.

If a figure is not drawn to scale, the answer is often choice D

A problem may show a figure. Underneath the picture may appear the words: "Note: Figure not drawn to scale." This message should be a warning buzzer, alerting you to the presence of a built-in trap. If a figure is not drawn to scale, you can't rely on it. Because you can't just eyeball it to figure things out, you need solid information such as the lengths of lines or the measures of angles. If that information is not provided, you often can't determine the relationship between the columns and must choose D.

Column A **Column B**

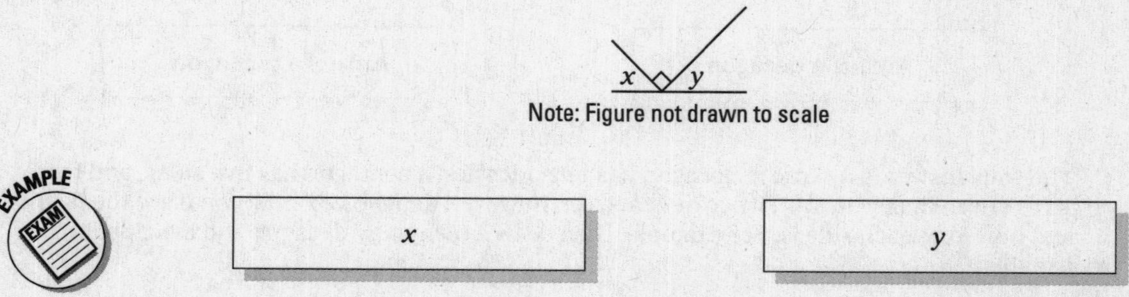

Note: Figure not drawn to scale

Sure, x and y each appear to be 45 degrees. Go ahead and choose C. You'll blow the SAT, never get into college, and end up walking some rich woman's poodles for a living, lamenting, "If only I had noticed that the figure wasn't drawn to scale!"

Because the figure isn't drawn to scale, you can't use it to estimate. You can't look at the figure and deduce that x and y are equal. Yes, x and y add up to 90 degrees. That's because angles along a straight line add up to 180 degrees, and you already have a right angle: $180 - 90 = 90$. But you *don't* know how much of the 90 is x and how much is y. Are they 45 and 45? 60 and 30? 89 and 1? The figure is not to scale, so any of those values may be correct. Because you don't have enough information to compare the quantities, choice D is the right answer.

Column A	Column B

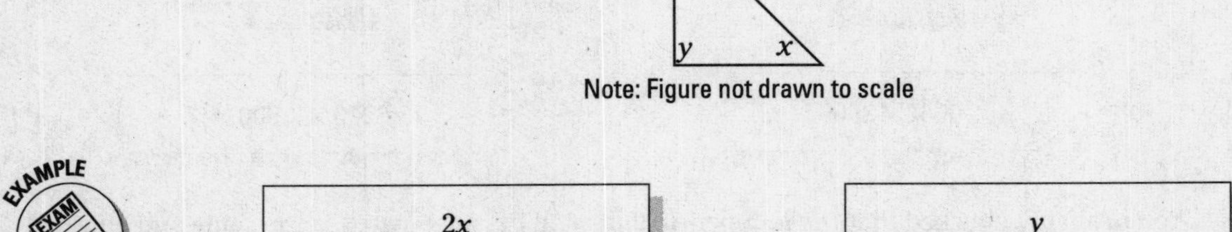

Note: Figure not drawn to scale

Column A	Column B
$2x$	y

If you fell for this one, you can kiss your 800 goodbye. This is a classic D. Yes, yes, the figure appears to be an isosceles right triangle. You know that the two x's are equal and that the angles in a triangle add up to 180 degrees. But no one said that angle y is 90 degrees. What's that you say? It *looks* like 90 degrees? Tooooo bad. You can't look at the figure if it's not drawn to scale. As far as you know, angle y may be 89 degrees, or 91 degrees, or all sorts of other possibilities. Maybe $x = 40$, so $2x = 80$ and $y = 100$. Maybe $x = 60$, so $2x = 120$ and $y = 60$. What? That can't be because it's obvious that this is not an equilateral triangle with all angles equal? Nothing is obvious; you can't use the figure if it's not drawn to scale. Because anything is possible, choose D.

If the answer depends on how you draw the figure, choose D

A third of SAT math is geometry. Some of the QC geometry problems are word problems that give no figures or diagrams. These questions often demand that you draw the figure yourself. In that case, the answer may depend on how you draw the figure.

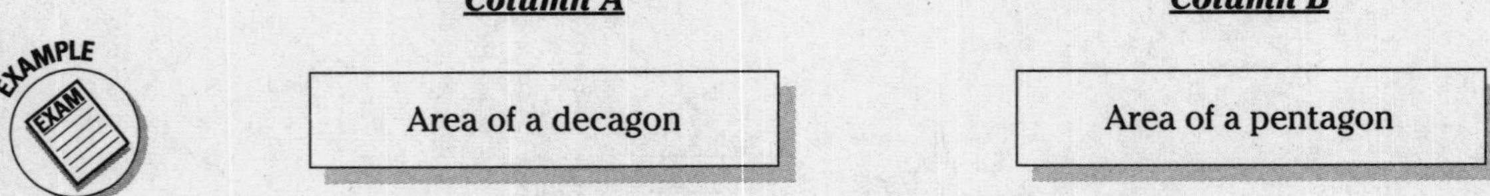

Column A	Column B
Area of a decagon	Area of a pentagon

The trap answer is A. True, a decagon has ten sides and a pentagon has five sides, and true, 10 > 5, even in new math. The correct answer, however, depends on how you draw the figures and how long each side is. For example, I can draw a teeny-tiny decagon and a big pentagon, like this:

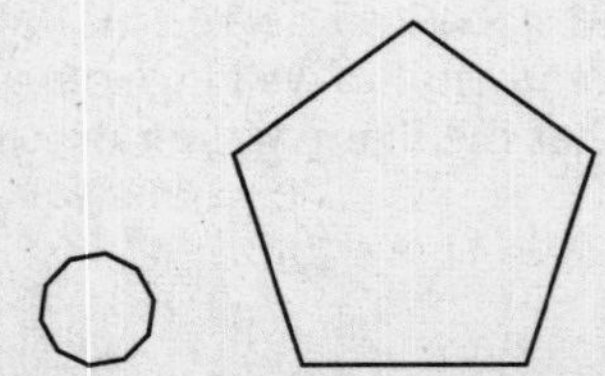

Or I could draw a big decagon and a small pentagon, like this:

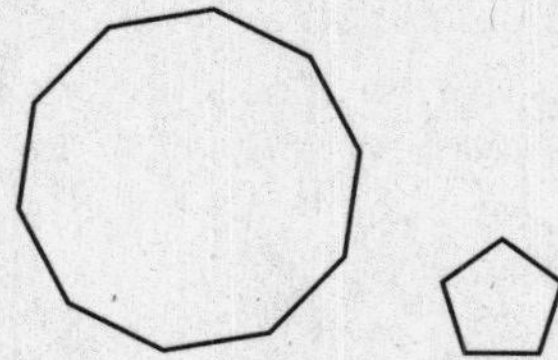

Or I can sketch in a decagon with exactly the same area as the pentagon, like this:

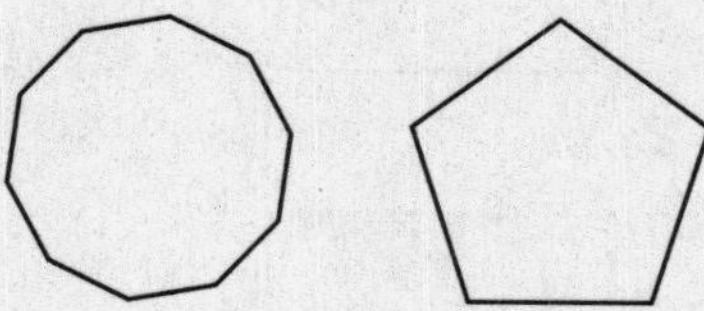

If everything *deeeeee*-pends on the *deeeeee*-rawing, choose D.

Column A	***Column B***
A skating rink is 5 miles from a nut store and 6 miles from a restaurant.	
Distance from the nut store to the restaurant	1 mile

Did you fall for the trap answer, C? Two tips come into play here: If the columns look equal, it's a trap, and if the answer depends on how you draw the figure, choose D.

Here are a couple ways of drawing the figure:

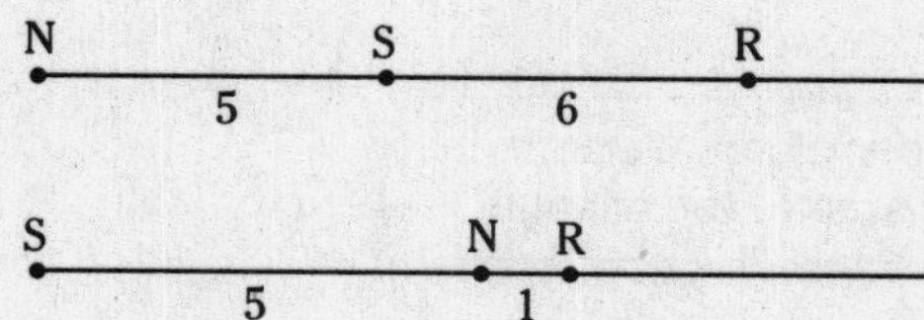

And speaking of nuts, here's a math riddle for you. If you have five piñon nuts in one hand, and six piñon nuts in the other hand, what do you have? A difference of a-pinion!

If a picture is drawn to scale, the answer is rarely D

This is the flipside of the preceding tip. If you have a pretty little picture, it *is* drawn to scale unless a note underneath it specifically tells you that it is *not* to scale. If a picture is to scale, you can use it in your estimates or calculations. The answer, therefore, is rarely D when a figure is given.

Keep in mind that these are just *tips,* not *rules*. That means that they work most of the time, but not always. Never shut off your own brain in favor of a tip. The purpose of a tip is just to make you think twice and avoid falling for a trap.

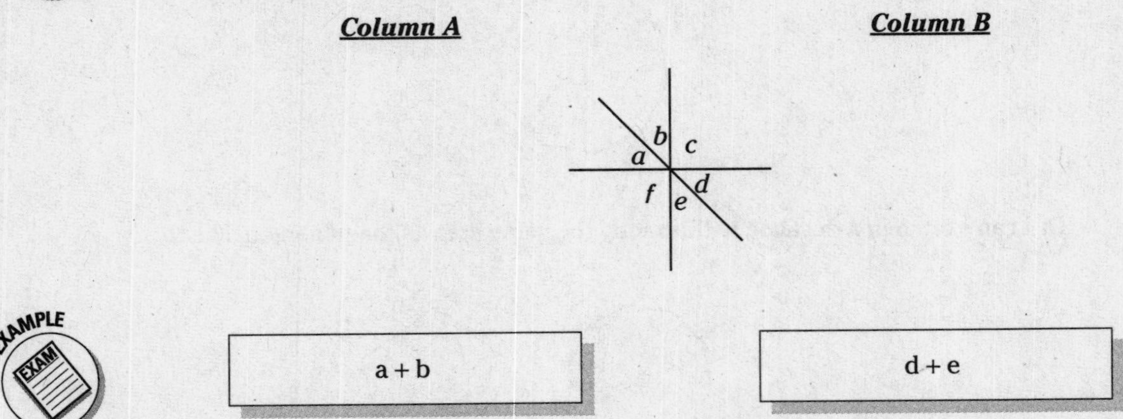

Angle *a* is a vertical angle to angle *d,* meaning that they are opposite and of equal measure and angle *b* is a vertical angle to angle *e,* meaning that they are opposite and of equal measure. Because each part of Column A is equal to its counterpart in Column B, both columns are equal. The right answer is C.

At first glance, you may be tempted to choose D for this problem because no numbers are given. It's true that you cannot solve for the exact measure of $a + b$ or the exact measure of $d + e$, but the question doesn't expect you to do so. This section is not about problem solving; it's quantitative comparisons — all you need to do is compare the quantities. You can compare them here (and see that they are equal), so D is wrong.

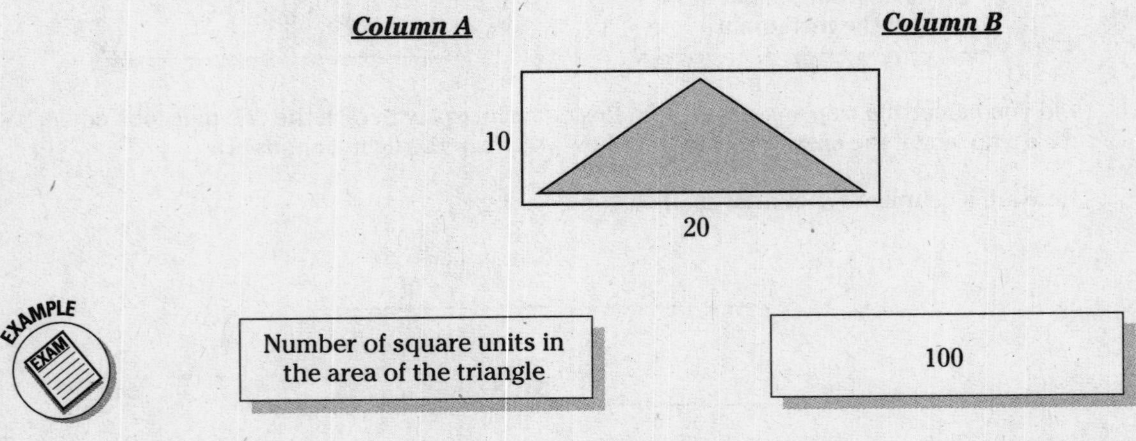

Fight the temptation to choose D automatically just because you don't have numbers for the lengths of the sides of the triangle. You know that the figure is drawn to scale; you can probably compare the quantities.

The formula for the area of a triangle is ½ *base* × *height.* What is the base? You don't know, but you *do* know that it is less than the base of the rectangle because the sides of the triangle don't extend all the way to the sides of the rectangle. Just call it *less than 20.* How much is the height? You don't know, but you *do* know that it is less than 10 because the top and bottom of the triangle don't touch the top and bottom of the rectangle. Call it *less than 10.* Multiply *less than 10* × *less than 20* = *less than 200.* Half of *less than 200* is *less than 100.* Because *less than 100* is smaller than 100, choose B.

Pretty cool. You don't do any Power Math; you just talk yourself through the formula and through the problem. Although D is a good trap answer, you're too smart to fall for that garbage. On the real SAT, it's fun to see a problem like this one. You recognize the trap, avoid the trap, and pat yourself on the back, while thumbing your nose at the test makers who didn't know just whom they were up against.

Cancel quantities that are identical in both columns

Think of this as clearing the decks or simplifying the picture. A QC problem is like a scale — a balance. If something is the same on one side as on the other, it doesn't affect the balance — you can ignore it. Be careful that you cancel only *identical* things; –5 does not cancel 5, for example.

Column A	Column B
$x^2 - 21$	$x^2 - 35$

Cancel the x^2 in both columns; just draw a big ol' line through them. That leaves you with –21 and –35. Caution! Remember that a *negative* 21 is greater than a *negative* 35. The answer is A.

$a > b > c > 2$

Column A	Column B
$(a + b)^2$	$(a - b)^2$

You can't cancel out the *a* and *b* on both sides and say that the columns are equal. $(a + b)^2$ is *not* the same as $(a - b)^2$.

You should memorize these two expressions (they are discussed in detail in Chapters 10, 11, and 12):

$$(a + b)^2 = a^2 + 2ab + b^2 \qquad (a - b)^2 = a^2 - 2ab + b^2$$

Now you can cancel identical terms: slash off the a^2 and the b^2 from both columns. You're left with $+2ab$ in Column A and $-2ab$ in Column B. Because both *a* and *b* are greater than 2, you don't need to worry about negatives or fractions or zero. A is greater.

Note: In the preceding problem, you don't need to do any work if you reason the answer out. Because *a* is greater than *b* and both *a* and *b* are positive numbers (greater than 2), you know that the sum $(a + b)$ must be greater than the sum $(a - b)$. Squaring a larger number gives you more than squaring a smaller number. You can deduce that Column A is bigger without doing any paperwork.

Lite math: reduced calories, no fat

You should be getting the picture by now that you don't need to do much pencil-pushing to answer QC problems. You can do many problems in a heartbeat just by knowing what the trap is and what to look for. The time you save on these questions is time you can use later in the "real math," or Problem Solving questions, for which you actually must come up with a solution.

Compare each part of Column A to its counterpart in Column B

Think of QCs as a scale. If both parts of Column A are greater, or "heavier," than both parts of Column B, A is greater.

Column A	Column B
$\frac{17}{21}+\frac{47}{80}$	$\frac{19}{81}+\frac{23}{97}$

Don't even *think* about reaching for your calculator. *Compare each part of Column A to its counterpart in Column B.* Which is greater: $17/21$ or $19/81$? Reason that 17 is more than half of 21, whereas 19 is much less than half of 81. The same is true for the second pair of numbers. You know that 47 is more than half of 80; 23 is less than half of 97. Because both parts of Column A are greater than both parts of Column B, A is the answer. No muss, no fuss.

Of course, some spoilsport always wants to know what happens if one part of Column A is greater than its counterpart in Column B, but the other part of Column A is less than its counterpart in Column B. Doesn't happen. Why? It ruins the trick that the test makers want you to recognize and use — you'd miss the entire point of the question. The question would reach back to a basic arithmetic, push-the-buttons-on-the-calculator problem. If lightning strikes and that problem does arise, well, you have no choice but to lift a finger. *Which* finger you lift is up to you.

When plugging in numbers, use 1, 2, 0, –1, –2, ½ — in that order

This is the best tip you're likely to get outside a racetrack. Whenever you have variables, *plug in numbers.* Instead of randomly choosing any old numbers, plug in these sacred six. You should memorize these numbers and throw them into a problem whenever possible. These numbers cover most of the contingencies: positive, negative, zero, odd, even, fraction, and 1, which has special properties.

Column A	Column B
 x^2	x^4

The *trap* answer is B. Everyone says that, *of course,* something to the fourth power is greater than the same number squared. (A variable must have the same value in Column A as in Column B *within any one problem.* That is, if x is 5 in Column A, it is also 5 in Column B. Always. No exceptions. A rose is a rose is a rose.)

Ah, but whenever you hear yourself saying "of course," you know that you're headed for a trap. Play the *what if* game: What if $x = 1$? Then the two columns are equal, and answer C prevails. What if $x = 2$? Then Column A = 4 and Column B = 16, and the answer is B. Therefore, the answer can be A or it can be B, depending on what you plug in. If an answer *de*pends on what you plug in, choose D.

Notice that you didn't have to go through all the sacred six numbers. As soon as you find that you get two different answers, you can stop. If plugging in 1 and 2 gives you the same answer, you should go on to 0, –1, –2, and ½, plugging in as many as necessary. You'll be pleasantly surprised, however, to find out how often 1 and 2 alone get the job done.

Column A	***Column B***
$x \neq 0$	
$\frac{1}{x}$	$\frac{x}{1}$

The trap answer is B. Most people think that Column A comes out to be a fraction of less than 1. It may . . . or it may not. And who's to say that x is more than 1 in the first place? Play the *what if* game again.

What if $x = 1$? Then the columns are equal, and choice C is correct. What if $x = 2$? Then Column B is greater. It depends on what you plug in, so choose D.

On the real test, you would stop here, but for now, plug in a few more numbers to see what else can happen. You can't plug in 0 because the problem tells you that x is not equal to 0 (division by 0 is undefined). What if $x = -1$? Then Column A is –1 and Column B is –1; they're equal. What if $x = -2$? Then Column A = –½, Column B = –2; now A is bigger. You've seen all the possibilities at this point: A can be bigger, B can be bigger, or the two columns can be the same. I haven't even gotten into fractions yet. And if it's all the same to you, I won't.

Plug in 100 for dollars and percentages

This is an exception to plugging in the sacred six (1, 2, 0, –1, –2, ½). If a question deals with dollars or percentages, plug in 100 to make it a nice round number. I'm all for an easy life here.

Column A	***Column B***
A book bag costs x dollars.	
Cost of the book bag on sale at 60% off	\$.6x

When pigs fly . . .

Question: Can you ever plug in all the sacred six and still fall for the trap?

Answer: Yeah, you can (although it's unlikely). Here's an example:

Column A		*Column B*
	$x \neq 0$	
$\frac{1}{x}$		3

Now you play the *what if* game. What if $x = 1$? Then Column B is larger. What if $x = 2$? Then Column B is larger. Because x is not equal to 0 (division by 0 is undefined), you skip to the next number in the sacred six. What if $x = -1$? Column B is still larger. What if $x = -2$? Yes, yes, Column B is still larger. Finally, what if $x = \frac{1}{2}$? Then Column A = 2 (to divide by a fraction, invert and multiply) and Column B is still larger. Now, 99 percent of the Thinking World would choose B at this point and feel very confident. And 99 percent of the Thinking World would go straight down the tubes. The answer, in fact, is D. What if $x = \frac{1}{3}$? Then Column A = 3, and the two columns are equal — choice C. If the answer could be B and could also be C, the answer depends and therefore is choice D.

A problem in which the sacred six don't do the job for you is incredibly rare, but it could happen. Sorry about that. This is a *tip*, not a rule. It's not perfect. Close, though . . . .

This type of problem is easy to miss because of carelessness. Many people choose C automatically. Of course, you know by now that *if the columns look equal, it's probably a trap*. You should slow down, plug in 100, and work out the problem. If you make the book bag cost \$100, you can easily determine that 60 percent of 100 is 60; subtract 100 – 60, and you get 40. In Column B, .6(100) = 60. The correct answer is B.

Column A	Column B
One year's interest on x dollars at 6% annual interest	\$12

Gotcha! I threw this one in to remind you once again that these are *tips,* not rules, and that you should never sacrifice common sense in favor of tips. Sure, if you plug in 100 for x dollars, you know that the interest is \$6 and B is the answer. But *what if* x = \$1,000,000? Then Column A is significantly larger. Here, the correct answer *depends* on which value you plug in for x. The correct answer is D. Although 100 often works, it is not infallible. Think!

Plug in consecutive terms first and then nonconsecutive terms

If you need to plug in numbers for two or three variables, first plug in the numbers all in a row: 1, 2, and 3. Then try it again, plugging in numbers that are not in a row: 1, 5, and 7. Sometimes the spacing between the numbers makes a difference.

Column A		Column B
	$a < b < c$	
$\frac{a+c}{2}$		b

The normal response is to plug in consecutive numbers: 1, 2, and 3. If you do that, Column A is $1 + 3 = 4 \div 2 = 2$. In Column B, b is 2. The columns are equal. *Uh-oh!* You know by now that *if the columns look equal, it's often a trap* and you should double-check your work.

Plug in some nonconsecutive numbers: 1, 5, and 7. Now Column A is $1 + 7 = 8 \div 2 = 4$. In Column B, b is 5. Now the answer is B. If the answer *de*pends on which values you plug in for the variables, choose D.

Column A		***Column B***
	$x > y > z$	
$y + z$		x

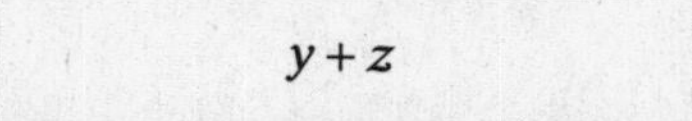

The trap answer is C. If you plug in 3, 2, and 1, $y + z = 2 + 1 = 3$. Because $x = 3$, the columns are equal. But plug in nonconsecutive numbers: 100, 2, and 1. Now $y + z = 2 + 1 = 3$. But $x = 100$; Column B is larger. The answer can be C or B — it *de*pends on what you plug in. Choose D.

Quantitative comparisons have no answer choice E. Do *not* fill in an answer E under any circumstances!

Familiarity breeds content(ment): The incomparable Quantitative Comparison question review

The approach:

1. Solve for the quantity in Column A.
2. Solve for the quantity in Column B.
3. Compare the two quantities.
4. Choose A if the quantity in Column A is greater

   B if the quantity in Column B is greater

   C if the two quantities are equal

   D if the relationship cannot be determined from the information given

Note: Quantitative comparisons have no answer choice E. Do not fill in an answer E under any circumstances.

Tips and tricks:

- If the columns look equal, it's usually a trap.
- If a figure is not drawn to scale, the answer is often choice D.
- If the answer depends on how you draw the figure, choose D.
- If a picture is drawn to scale, the answer is rarely D.
- Cancel quantities that are identical in both columns.
- Compare each part of Column A to its counterpart in Column B.
- When plugging in numbers, use 1, 2, 0, –1, –2, and ½ in that order.
- Plug in 100 for dollars and percentages.
- Plug in consecutive terms first and then nonconsecutive terms.

Chapter 14

Putting It All Together: Practice QC Questions

In This Chapter

- Surviving gruesome geometry problems
- Enduring annoying algebra problems
- Tolerating miserable math problems

If you're waiting until they make a movie of this stuff, forget it. You're outta luck. The information on quantitative comparisons (QCs) in Chapter 13 is all she wrote (so to speak . . .). If you didn't read it carefully, please do so now — before you humiliate yourself on the practice exam.

In Chapter 13, you'll find the following tips that will help you in this chapter:

- Tip 1: If the columns look equal, it's a trap
- Tip 2: If a figure is not drawn to scale, the answer is often choice D
- Tip 3: If the answer depends on how you draw the figure, choose D
- Tip 4: If a picture is drawn to scale, the answer is rarely D
- Tip 5: Cancel quantities that are identical in both columns
- Tip 6: Compare each part of Column A to its counterpart in Column B
- Tip 7: When plugging in numbers, use 1, 2, 0, –1, –2, ½ — in that order
- Tip 8: Plug in 100 for dollars and percentages
- Tip 9: Plug in consecutive terms first and then nonconsecutive terms

Along with the answers and explanations in this chapter, you'll find a reference to each of these tips.

All done? Good. Now, check your ego at the door or it may get trashed on this test. I've written a dozen problems that incorporate the meanest, the cruelest, the stupidest traps you're likely to see on the real SAT. How many are *you* going to fall for?

As a reminder, here are the QC answer choices:

- A if the quantity in Column A is greater
- B if the quantity in Column B is greater
- C if the two quantities are equal
- D if the relationship cannot be determined from the information given
- An E response will not be scored

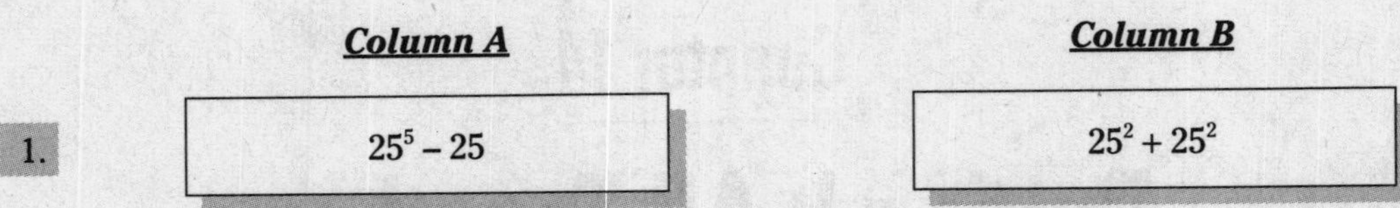

	Column A	Column B
1.	$25^5 - 25$	$25^2 + 25^2$

The trap answer is C; you didn't fall for it, did you? 25^5 is a huge number: 9,765,625 to be exact. You can always work it out on your calculator, although you don't need to. Subtracting 25 from it hardly makes a dent. $25^5 - 25$ does *not* equal 25^4; you simply can't subtract that way.

In Column B, $25^2 + 25^2$ does *not* equal 25^4; you can't add exponents that way. (Do you remember when you can add exponents? If you are *multiplying* like bases. For example, $x^3 \cdot x^5 = x^8$.) If you want to, you can figure out that 25^2 is 625 and add 625 + 625. However, you should be able to see that 25^5 is such a humongous number that the other column cannot compare. The correct answer is A. Tip: 1

If you've forgotten all this stuff (or blocked it out), head to the exponents section of Chapter 11.

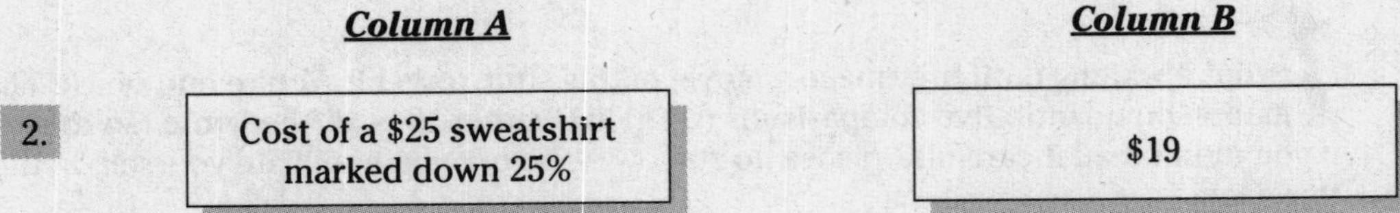

	Column A	Column B
2.	Cost of a $25 sweatshirt marked down 25%	$19

The long way to do this problem is to find 25 percent of $25 and then subtract it from $25. Multiply $.25 \times 25$ to get 6.25; $25 \times 6.25 = 18.75$.

There is a slightly shorter way to do this problem. You know that if something is marked down 25 percent, or ¼, the remaining price is 75 percent, or ¾, of the original price. In just one step, you can multiply $25 \times .75$ to get 18.75. The correct answer is B.

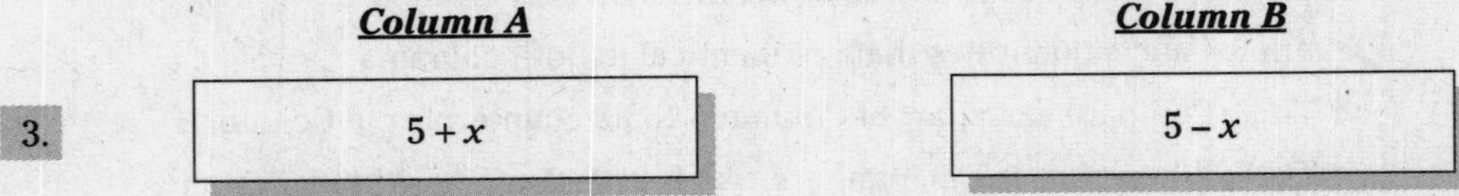

	Column A	Column B
3.	$5 + x$	$5 - x$

Uh-oh, did you fall for the trap and choose A? Logical, but wrong. The correct answer is D. Remembering two tricks, Tips 1 and 8, gets you the right answer here:

- **Cancel quantities that are identical in both columns.** Just slash off the 5 in each column. That leaves you with $+x$ and $-x$.
- **Plug in numbers.** *What if* $x = 1$? Then Column A is greater. *What if* $x = 2$? Column A is still greater. But *what if* $x = 0$? Then the columns are equal. If the answer *could be* A or *could be* C, it *depends on* what you plug in.

	Column A	Column B

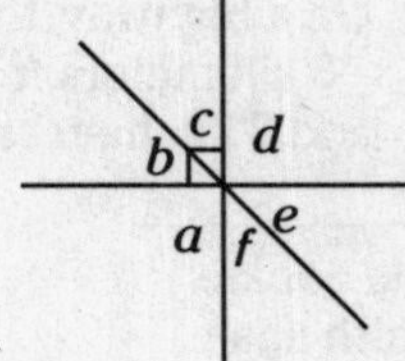

4.	$a + f$	$e + c$

First, scratch off f and c. Cancel quantities that are identical in both columns. Because f and c are opposite or vertical angles, they are equal. They don't affect the balance of the scales, so ignore them. Now you have to compare only a and e.

Next, you know that angle $a = 90$ degrees because it is supplementary to a 90-degree angle. (Angles along a straight line sum up to 180 degrees. You know that the box indicates a right or 90-degree angle, right?) Because both angles e and c sum up to 90 degrees (e is opposite and equal to b, and $b + c = 90$), e must be less than 90. You don't have any idea how much it actually measures — 45 degrees? 60 degrees? You have no way to tell — but as long as you know that it's less than 90 degrees, you can compare the columns. The correct answer is A. Tip: 1

If you chose D, you fell for a trap. Just because you have no numbers does not mean that you can't compare the quantities. Remember, too, that *if a figure is given, you should rarely choose D unless the figure is not to scale.* If you started to choose D here, you should have stopped and rethought your strategy. Tips can't always get you the right answer, but they do a great job of preventing you from choosing the wrong answer automatically.

	Column A	Column B

$a > b$
$a, b \neq 0$

5.	a/b	b/a

This is a very tricky question. You were probably tempted to choose A, reasoning that a bigger number over a smaller number is *obviously* larger. Oops! Any time you catch yourself thinking that something is *obvious,* back off and regroup. You're probably headed for a trap. The correct answer is D. Tip: 7

Plug in numbers. Play the *what if* game. *What if* $a = 2$ and $b = 1$? Then Column A is 2 and Column B is ½, and A is larger. But *what if* $a = -2$ and $b = -4$? (Remember: -2 *is greater than* -4.) Then Column A is $-2/-4$, which equals ½. Column B is $-4/-2$, which equals 2. Now Column B is larger. If the answer *depends* on which numbers you plug in, choose D.

	Column A	***Column B***
	On a highway, the ice cream parlor is 6 kilometers from the cookie shop and 8 kilometers from the health spa.	
6.	Distance from the cookie shop to the health spa	8 kilometers

If you chose C, you fell for the trap. Remember: If the columns look equal, it's a trap. You usually must do some sort of calculation to prove that the two columns are equal. As you can see from the following diagrams, the cookie shop *could be* 14 kilometers from the health spa, or it *could be* 2 kilometers. The answer *depends on* how you draw the picture. As you pick up your pencil and begin drawing, you should be thinking that the chances are very good that the answer will turn out to be D, which is the correct answer. Tip: 1

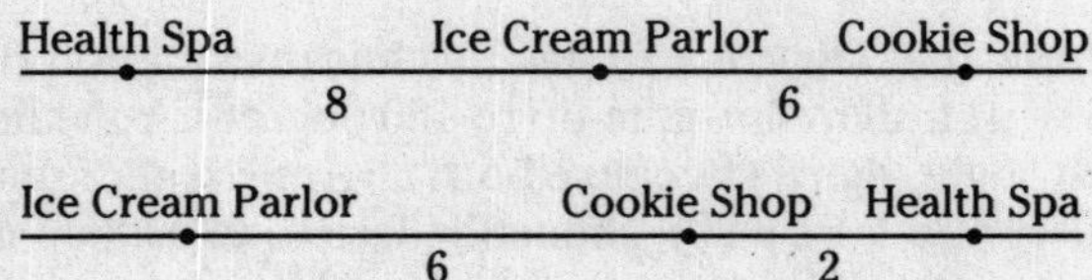

	Column A	***Column B***
	$x < y < z$	
7.	$x + y$	z

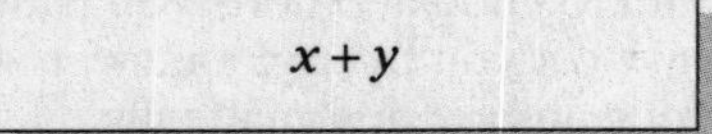

The answer *depends on* what numbers you plug in for *x, y,* and *z.* Suppose you make $x = 1$, $y = 2$, and $z = 3$; then the answer is C. But if you plug in $x = 1$, $y = 10$, and $z = 20$, Column B is larger. If you have variables, *plug in numbers.* And when you plug in numbers in a series, *plug in consecutive terms first and then plug in nonconsecutive terms.* The correct answer is D. Tips: 7, 9

Bonus! See whether I can double-cross you on the following bonus question.

Column A	***Column B***
$x < y < z < 0$	
$x + y$	z

Ah, you probably put D that time because I've brainwashed you into thinking that everything *depends* when it comes to variables. You must make sure that you don't *automatically* choose D whenever you see variables. Don't choose D until you have actually gone through all the work of plugging in different numbers and actually getting different answers.

Say that $x = -3$, $y = -2$, and $z = -1$. Then Column A is $-3 + -2$, which equals -5. That is definitely smaller than *z,* which is -1. Negative numbers are backward, inside out, upside down — a negative 1 is greater than a negative 2, 3, 4, 5, and so on.

Try plugging in nonconsecutive numbers. Maybe $x = -10$, $y = -3$, and $z = -\frac{1}{2}$. Now in Column A, $-10 + -3 = -13$, which is smaller than $-\frac{1}{2}$. By now it should be dawning on you that when you add two *negative* numbers, they get smaller. Because each number was less than z to begin with, their *smaller* sum must be less than z as well. The correct answer is B. The moral of the story: Automatically using the tricks without considering the individual situations is just as bad as not using the tricks at all. Tip: 9

Think about choosing D at three primary times:

- If no picture is given for a geometry problem.
- If a picture is given but it is not drawn to scale.
- If you have *actually* plugged in numbers, *actually* done the work, and *actually* gotten different answers to the question. Merely looking at an alphabet soup of variables and *assuming* that it makes answer D is incorrect.

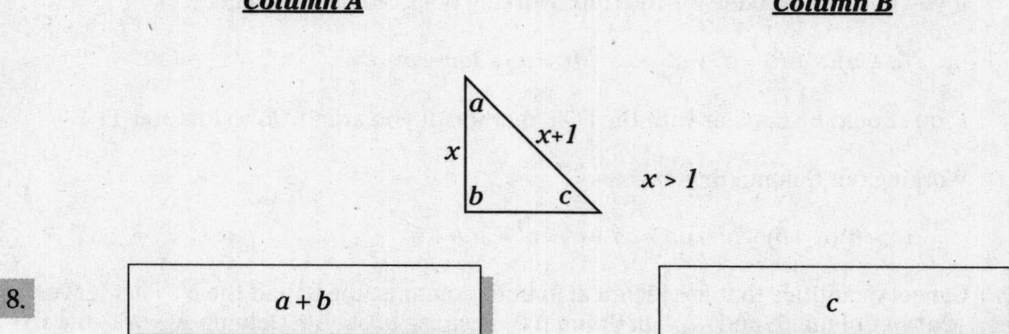

	Column A	Column B
8.	$a + b$	c

This question is easier than it looks, if you remember this math concept: A longer side is opposite a larger angle. You know that $x + 1$ is longer than x. That means that angle b is greater than angle c, *even before adding* a *to it.* The correct answer is A. Tip: 4

Column A | **Column B**

The average (arithmetic mean) of y and x is x.

	Column A	Column B
9.	y	0

If you chose C, you forgot that when the columns look equal, there's often a trap. Realize that y *could be* 0 if x is also zero because $^{(0+0)}/_2 = 0$. But y does not *have* to be 0; it may be something else. Say that $y = x = 1$. Then the average is $^{(1+1=2)}/_2 = 1$. As you plug in numbers, plug in more than one set to see whether the answer *depends on* what you plug in. And having two variables *doubles* the chances that the answer *depends on* what you plug in. The correct answer is D. Tip: 9

Column A | **Column B**

$$a \# b \# c = \frac{(a+b)^c}{c-a}$$

	Column A	Column B
10.	2 # 3 # 4	625

Substitute the 2, 3, and 4 for the *a, b,* and *c* in the equation. Wherever you see an *a,* put a 2. Wherever you see a *b,* put a 3. Wherever you see a *c,* put a 4. (How do you know which numbers should take the place of which letters? They are in the same position: *a* is first, so 2 is first; *b* is second, so 3 is second; *c* is third, so 4 is third.) That gives you $(2 + 3)^4$ or 5^4. Do it on your calculator; you get 625. If you divide that by 4 – 2, or 2, you get 312.5. The correct answer is B. If you chose C, you forgot to work the problem through to the end, dividing 625 by 2. Careless, careless.

	Column A	***Column B***
	$ab = -10$	
11.	$(a + b)^2$	$(a - b)^2$

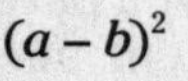

If you chose A, you fell for the trap. Working out Column A, you get

$$(a + b)(a + b) = a^2 + ab + ba + b^2 = a^2 + 2ab + b^2$$

(You should be familiar with the FOIL method. If you aren't, go to Chapter 11.)

Working out Column B, you get

$$(a - b)(a - b) = a^2 - ab - ba + b^2 = a^2 - 2ab + b^2$$

Cancel quantities that are identical in both columns: the a^2 and the b^2. That leaves you with $+2ab$ in Column A and $-2ab$ in Column B. Because ab is –10, Column A works out to –20 and Column B works out to +20. The correct answer is B. Tips: 5, 9

Did you see the shortcut way to do this problem? Plug in numbers. Because $ab = -10$, say that $a = 5$ and $b = -2$. Then $(a + b)^2 = (5 - 2)^2 = 3^2 = 9$. In Column B, $(5 + 2)^2 = 7^2 = 49$.

Of course, you plug in numbers more than once to be sure. Here, if you plugged in –1 and 10, or ½ and –20, or anything else such that $ab = -10$, you'd still get Column B.

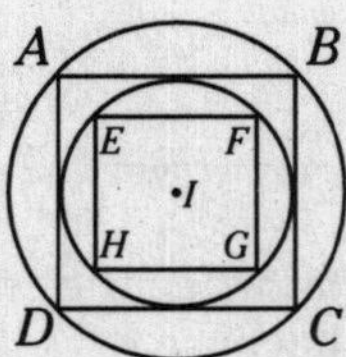

	Column A	***Column B***
	Area of square *EFGH* = 36. *ABCD* is a square.	
12.	Area of large Circle *I*	108 square units

This is a relatively difficult problem. If the area of square *EFGH* is 36, then each side is 6 (because the area of a square is *side*^{2}). That means that diagonal $EG = 6\sqrt{2}$. You can either find this by using the Pythagorean theorem ($6^2 + 6^2 = c^2$; $c^2 = 72$; $c = \sqrt{72} = 6\sqrt{2}$), or you can recall the special Pythagorean theorem for isosceles right triangles is side:side:side$\sqrt{2}$. (If all this is confusing to you, go to Chapter 10 and check out the section on the Pythagorean theorem.)

s d $d = 6\sqrt{2}$

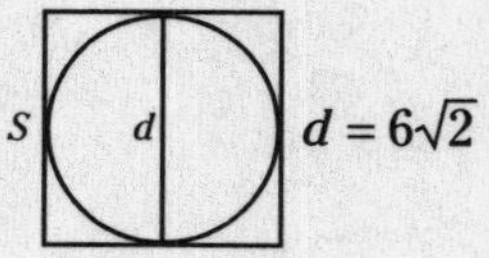

The diagonal *EG* is also the diameter of the small circle. The diameter of the small circle is the same as the length of a side of square *ABCD*, as shown here.

If the side of the square *ABCD* is $6\sqrt{2}$, the diagonal of the square is 12. Use the Pythagorean theorem:

$$(6\sqrt{2})^2 + (6\sqrt{2})^2 = c^2$$

$$72 + 72 = c^2$$

$$c^2 = 144$$

$$c = \sqrt{144} = 12$$

If diagonal *AC* is 12, the diameter of the large circle is 12, as well. That means that the radius (which is half the diameter) is 6. The area of a circle is πr^2, which is 36π. Because π is *slightly larger* than 3, the whole area must be larger than 108. The correct answer is A. Tip: 4

Whew! This is a *great* example of a problem to skip.

Chapter 15

Real Math at Last: Problem Solving

In This Chapter

- Developing a plan of attack for Problem Solving questions
- Avoiding grid grief
- Using time-saving techniques suggested by the Queen of Shortcuts
- Sidestepping snares and avoiding built-in traps

Problem solving is a rather ritzy name for "regular" math problems. A Problem Solving question, amazingly enough, actually expects you to solve a problem. This is different from the Quantitative Comparison questions (covered in Chapter 13), in which you often don't need to solve the problem through to the bitter end — you just compare the quantities. (Who thinks of these catchy names anyway? How much do they get paid and where can I apply for the job?)

The Answer: Einstein, Frasier, and SAT math.

The Question: Name a brain, a Crane, and a pain.

Form-al Introductions: The Format

The SAT contains two types of Problem Solving questions. One type features five multiple-choice answers. The other type is called *grid-ins* or *student-produced responses.* These questions give no multiple-choice answers; you have to come up with answers all by yourself. The techniques for mastering these two types of questions are slightly different, although the information tested is the same.

As discussed in Chapter 1, three of the six sections on the SAT are math. One of these sections features 25 Problem Solving questions with multiple-choice answers; you're given 30 minutes to complete the section. A second 30-minute section begins with 15 Quantitative Comparison questions and concludes with 10 grid-in questions. The third math section has only ten problems, which you are to do in 15 minutes — all Problem Solving questions with multiple-choice answers. Altogether, you have 35 Problem Solving questions with multiple-choice answers and 10 grid-in questions. The questions are approximately ⅓ algebra, ⅓ geometry (no proofs, thank goodness!), and ⅓ arithmetic (fractions, word problems, percentages, and so on).

Problem Solving with Multiple-Choice Answers: The Approach

Are you an Algebra Ace? Mathematics Master? Geometry Genius? Me neither. Isn't it lucky that you don't have to be any of those things to do well on the Problem Solving questions? All you need are the few basic strategies discussed here.

1. **Read the problem through carefully and circle what the question is asking for.**

   Your goal is to give 'em what they want. If the question asks for a circumference, circle the word *circumference* and don't solve for an area. If the question wants you to find the average number of fish per body of water, don't supply the total number.

   Of course, of course, *of course* the answer choices feature trap answers; this goes without saying on the SAT. The area of a figure will be a trap answer to a question that wants the perimeter. Just because the answer you got is staring you in the face doesn't mean that it's the correct answer. It may be . . . or it might be a trap. Circle what the question is asking for — what you are to solve for. Before you fill in a bubble on the answer grid, go back and look at this circle: Are you answering the right question?

2. **Predict how hard the problem is or how time-consuming solving it will be.**

   The difficulty level of questions goes from easiest to hardest. In most cases, you'll be able to answer the first third of the questions without much brain drain. The last third is very hard. The middle third is where most students have to make a conscious decision: Do you solve this problem or blow it off? Keeping in mind that there's a penalty for wrong answers, it's often wise to skip a hard problem or one that you could solve but wouldn't finish working on before a week from next Tuesday.

3. **Preview the answer choices; look to see how precise your answer has to be and how careful you have to be on the decimal points.**

   If the answer choices are 4, 5, 6, 7, and 8, you probably have to solve the problem to the bitter end, calculating rather than estimating. This type of problem may take a long time. However, if the answer choices are .05, .5, 5, 50, and 500, you know that the digit is definitely going to be a 5 and that you have to keep your decimal point straight. You may be able to use common sense on that problem and estimate the answer without working it out.

4. **Solve the problem forward and backward.**

   Work out the problem and get an answer; then plug that answer back into the problem to make sure that it makes sense. If you found the average of 4, 6, 7, 9, and 10 to be 36, you can look at the answer and reason that you made a mistake somewhere because the average can't be bigger than the biggest number.

Problem Solving with Grid-In Answers: The Approach

You increase your chances of getting correct answers to the grid-in questions by going through the following steps.

1. **Read the problem through carefully and circle what the question is asking for.**

   This is the same as the first step for Problem Solving questions that have multiple-choice answers. You always want to be sure that you're satisfying the audience and giving 'em what they want (even if you do think some of this math is about as useful as a solar-powered flashlight).

2. **Predict how hard the problem is or how time-consuming solving it will be.**

   Again, you need to make a decision about whether you want to do the problem now, postpone it for later (if you have time to come back to it), or forget you ever saw it.

3. **Solve the problem, double- and triple-checking your equations and calculations.**

   You have no safeguards here. When questions have multiple-choice answers, you at least know you're wrong when your answer isn't one of the choices. When it comes to the grid-ins, you have no help at all.

4. Darken in your answer, being sure to put it in the form requested.

If a problem asks you to express your answer as a decimal, do so. The question may ask you to put your answer in to the hundredths place, or to the thousandths place. Be sure to follow all directions.

Filling In the Grid

Because grid-in problems may be new to you, they're worth a separate section. If you're used to filling in Scan-trons or other bubble grids, just skim this part and go on to the next section.

Above the bubbles are white boxes. Write your solution in these boxes for your own convenience. The answer written in the white boxes will *not* be scored. If you forget to darken in the answer and have only the numerals written in the white boxes, tough luck. You get zip points for that one.

Your answer can be entered to the far left or the far right; the test makers will accept either.

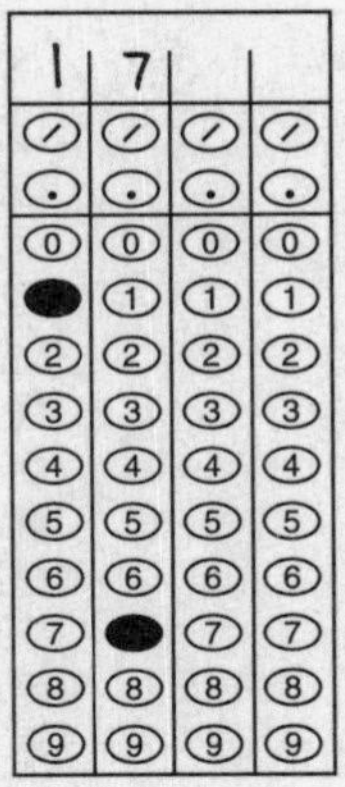

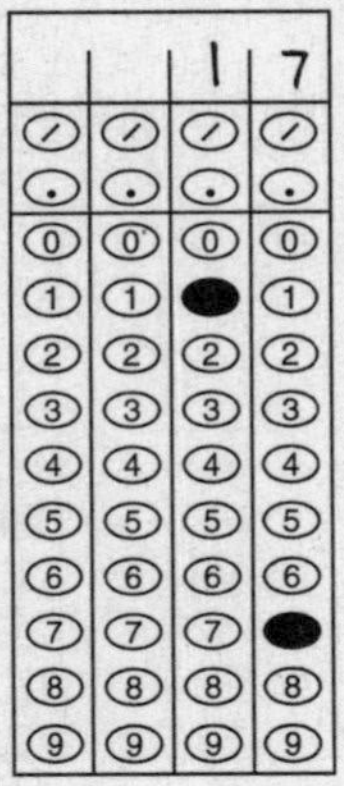

Work out a solution to as many number places as you have room for on the grid. For example, you know that $\frac{1}{3}$ is $.\overline{333}$. Do *not* put .33 on the answer grid and darken in just those two numerals. Put down .333 — as many 3s as you have spaces for. Do not, I repeat, *do not* round off a fraction unless the problem specifically tells you to do so. If the question says, "Solve for *x*, rounding off to the hundredths digit," then your answer can be .33.

Correct Wrong

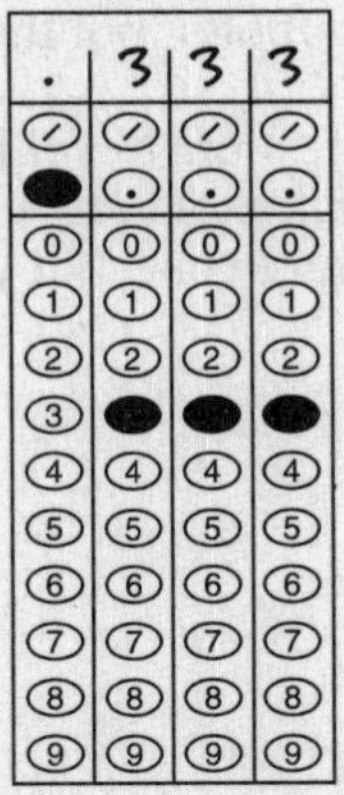

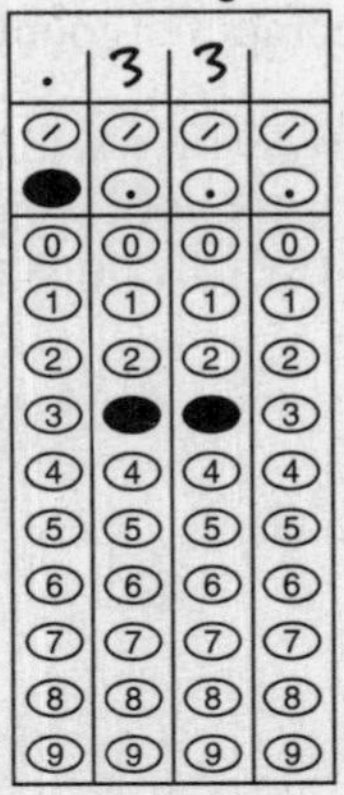

Notice that the slash mark and the decimal have bubbles of their own. Don't forget to fill them in. If your answer is .333 and you fill in the 333 bubbles but forget to fill in the decimal point, you just said that the answer is 333 and flubbed the question.

You do *not* have to insert a zero in front of a decimal. For example, .5 does not have to be written and darkened in as 0.5. If you want to do so to keep things straight in your own mind, that's fine. You'll get credit for either .5 or 0.5.

You can express an answer as either a fraction or a decimal unless the problem specifies which one it wants. For many students, using a calculator means that you're going to be dealing with decimals rather than fractions, and that's okay. But if you have a calculator that has a slash bar and does fractions, they're okay as well.

Don't enter a fraction as a mixed number. If your answer is $2\frac{1}{4}$, don't enter $2\frac{1}{4}$ or the computer will read it as $\frac{21}{4}$. Enter instead $\frac{9}{4}$ or 2.25.

You won't find any place to insert a dollar sign; just ignore it. Be careful, however, to include the decimal point when you're entering dollars and cents.

Correct: 5 . 4 4

Wrong: 5 4 4

After you've written down the numerals, fill in the appropriate bubbles underneath them. Shade in the whole bubble carefully; don't color like a 3-year-old and go outside the lines. The computer cuts you no slack.

Horror stories abound of students who first fill in the numerals for problems 16–25, meaning to go back and shade in the bubbles later. You guessed it — *later* never comes. The hapless students run out of time before they can return to their shady business. What happens? They get zero points for those ten questions (threats and pleading mean nothing to circuit boards). The computer counts *only* the bubbles, not the numerals.

There is *no penalty* for a wrong grid-in question. Never leave a grid-in blank. Fill in something, anything: your age? your weight? the number of brain cells destroyed by this problem? You may just get lucky (the odds are a gazillion to one, but you never know).

Use Your Powers for Good: Five Commonsense Suggestions

The Problem Solving questions are much more straightforward than the ***nefarious*** (wicked, evil) Quantitative Comparison problems (see Chapter 13). There aren't as many tricks or traps, but you can learn a few good, fairly commonsense techniques that can speed up your work or prevent your making careless mistakes.

Remember that easy problems often have easy answers

This tip is ridiculously simplistic, but it's true. If you're solving question number 5 out of 25, it's exceedingly unlikely that the correct answer will be

$$\sqrt{\frac{5ab^3}{3b-a}}$$

That's just too bizarre and too hard an answer for that early in the questions. That answer may (or may not) be correct for a super-hard problem near the end. The test makers know that you all have major insecurities and that you look at an answer and think the harder, the better. Don't immediately choose the easiest answer for an easy question and the hardest answer for a hard question, though; things don't usually work out that neatly. But if you have the answers narrowed down to two, go for the hard one at the end and the easy one at the beginning.

Eliminate illogical (dumb) answer choices

You know how some teachers always reassure students by saying, "Oh, there's no such thing as a dumb question or answer; just try!" Wrong. There *are* such things as dumb answers. If you're asked for the amount of time someone takes to stuff a hundred envelopes, don't choose an answer like 300 hours. If you're asked how fast a sheep can run, an answer like 100 mph is ridiculous. When you preview the answers, dump the ones that seem to make no sense. (Speaking of sheep, what do you call a chocolate-covered lamb? A candy baaaa.)

Don't choose a "close enough" answer

Suppose you do a ton of calculations and get the answer 36. One of the answer choices is 38. Don't shrug and say, "Ahh, close enough; I must have made a mistake somewhere." You sure did, and you're about to make a second mistake by being lazy and choosing an answer that's close.

Don't be afraid to skip

An intelligent skipper doesn't go down with the ship, if you'll forgive the pun. You'll know by the time you get through with this book which types of questions you ace and which ones drive you crazy. Feel free to skip around in the section, making sure that you get to the questions you're good at and ignoring for the time being those questions that would drive Mother Teresa to drink.

Questions progress from easiest to hardest in every section of the SAT. Don't be surprised if you can't answer any of the questions on the last page; that's normal. If you know that the questions are beyond you, forget about them and go back to double-check your work on earlier questions. ***Remember:*** You don't get points taken off for skipping questions, but you *do* lose points for missing questions (except the grid-in questions).

Give your pencil a workout

Although you get no scratch paper on the test, there is a lot of blank space on the test booklet — more than enough for you to draw and doodle as necessary. As you'll see when you go through the sample questions and practice exam, writing down formulas and plugging numbers into them or drawing pictures and putting numbers on the pictures is an excellent means of avoiding careless errors and clarifying and organizing thoughts. Don't think you're wasting time by using your pencil; you may actually be saving time by avoiding confusion.

I'm sure I know you from somewhere: The Problem Solving question review

The approach for Problem Solving questions with multiple-choice answers provided:

1. Read the problem through carefully and circle what the question is asking for.
2. Predict how hard the problem is or how time-consuming solving it will be.
3. Preview the answer choices.
4. Solve the problem forward and backward (plugging in the multiple-choice answers).

The approach for Problem Solving questions with grid-in answers required:

1. Read the problem through carefully and circle what the question is asking for.
2. Predict how hard the problem is or how time-consuming solving it will be.
3. Solve the problem, double- and triple-checking your equations and calculations.
4. Darken in your answer, being sure to put it in the form requested.

Tips and tricks:

- Easy problems often have easy answers.
- Eliminate illogical (dumb) answer choices.
- Don't choose a "close enough" answer.
- Don't be afraid to skip.
- Give your pencil a workout. Plug in numbers, write down formulas, and draw pictures.

Chapter 16

A Chance to Show Off: Practice Problem Solving Questions

In This Chapter

- Being conned by deceptively easy problems with traps for the unwary
- Suffering through long and tedious (typical!) word problems
- Enjoying simple, straightforward algebra problems
- Enduring geometry headaches demanding application of memorized formulas

Does the mere thought of having a chance to display your proficiency in math give you goose bumps? (Know why we have goose bumps, incidentally? To keep geese from speeding!) Well, here's where you get to show that you understand Chapter 15, know all the important formulas, and can recognize and avoid built-in traps.

Bonus! At the end of every answer explanation, you are told which tip (from Chapter 15) you could and should have used to answer the question correctly. If you missed the question, be sure to look at that specific tip again:

- Tip 1: Remember that easy problems often have easy answers
- Tip 2: Eliminate illogical (dumb) answer choices
- Tip 3: Don't choose a "close enough" answer
- Tip 4: Don't be afraid to skip
- Tip 5: Give your pencil a workout

Okay: Here's your chance to prove your brilliance by acing the following dozen questions.

Please go through the answer explanations for every question, not just for the ones you miss. (How dare I assume you'll miss any!)

1. Bob "B.O." Ostink is trying to get more girls to come to his fraternity party. One of every 3 girls he calls already has plans for that night. Of the girls without plans, 2 of every 5 inform him hastily that they would rather eat lizard sushi than be at his bash. Of the remainder, 1 of every 2 has a headache planned for that evening. If B.O. calls 120 girls, how many are available to come to his party?

   (A) 80

   (B) 48

   (C) 40

   (D) 24

   (E) 12

This problem is not difficult, just tedious and time-consuming. Work backward from 120. First, 1 out of 3 ($\frac{1}{3}$) of the girls is busy that night. That means $\frac{1}{3} \times 120$ or 40 girls are busy, leaving a remainder of 80. Of those 80, 2 of every 5 ($\frac{2}{5}$) would rather ingest raw reptiles than be Bob's date. That means $\frac{2}{5} \times 80 = 32$, leaving 48 girls still in the running. Of those 48 girls, 1 out of 2 intends to have a headache that evening: $\frac{1}{2} \times 48 = 24$. There are 24 girls still in contention for the dubious honor of being present at the B.O. Bash. The correct answer is D. Tip: 5

2. Wolfe drives half of the 600-mile trip to his grandmother's house at 30 mph and the other half at 60 mph. If he returns home along exactly the same route at 50 mph, what is his average speed for the round trip (rounded to the nearest mile)?

(A) 50 mph

(B) 49 mph

(C) 45 mph

(D) 44 mph

(E) 40 mph

You didn't really fall for C, did you? Much too easy. Use the "dirty" formula (discussed in Chapter 12), D-I-R-T: Distance Is Rate times Time. Make a chart as shown.

Distance	=	***Rate***	×	***Time***
300		30		10 hours
300		60		5
600		50		12

Total: 1200 miles in 27 hours. 1200 divided by 27 = 44.4444 m.p.h., which rounds *down* to 44. The correct answer is D. Tip: 5

Time, Rate, and Distance problems often are trickier than they look. Don't just assume an average speed; make the chart and figure it out precisely.

3. If three times a third of a number equals itself, that number could be

I. –1

II. 0

III. 1

(A) I only

(B) II only

(C) I and III only

(D) II and III only

(E) I, II, and III

Three times a third is simply one. One times any number is itself. If you don't see the connection immediately, you can, of course, work the problem out. A third of –1 is $-\frac{1}{3}$; $-\frac{1}{3} \times 3 = -1$. For II, a third of 0 is 0; $3 \times 0 = 0$. For III, a third of 1 is $\frac{1}{3}$; $\frac{1}{3} \times 3 = 1$. The correct answer is E. Tip: 5

4. At a dance, there are 5 nerds for every 4 geeks. If the only people at the dance are geeks and nerds, which of the following could be the total number of people at the dance?

I. 20

II. 45

III. 54

(A) I only

(B) II only

(C) I and III only

(D) II and III only

(E) I, II, and III

When you are given a ratio and asked for a possible total, do the following:

1. **Add the numbers in the ratio.**
2. **Find a number that is evenly divisible by that sum. That is the total.**

Here, the ratio is 5:4; 5 + 4 = 9. Because 9 does not divide evenly into 20, there cannot be a total of 20 people at the party. Nine does divide evenly into 45: there could be 25 nerds and 20 geeks. Nine does divide evenly into 54: there could be 30 nerds and 24 geeks. The correct answer is D. Tip: 5

The question very carefully asks which number *could be* the total. The total *could be* any multiple of 9, such as 9, 18, 27, 36, 45, and so on. If the question were to ask which of the following *is* the total, you would not be able to answer.

5. The sum of the interior angles of a figure is twice the sum of the interior angles of a pentagon. The figure has how many sides?

(A) 10

(B) 9

(C) 8

(D) 7

(E) 6

Did you fall for answer A? Read on to see how you were tricked. (It happens to the best of us.)

The formula for the interior angles of any polygon is $(n - 2)180$ degrees, where n stands for the number of sides. For example, a triangle is $(3 - 2)180 = 1 \times 180 = 180°$. The interior angles of a pentagon (which has 5 sides) = $(5 - 2)180 = 3 \times 180 = 540°$. Twice 540 = 1080.

Now work backward:

$$(n - 2)180 = 1080$$

$$1080 \div 180 = 6$$

$$(n - 2) = 6$$

$$n = 8$$

The correct answer is C.

There are two trap answers here. Choice A is the most obvious trap. Many people assume that the interior angles of a ten-sided figure must be twice as much as the interior angles of a five-sided figure. Not so. A ten-sided figure — a decagon — has an interior angle measure of $(10 - 2)180 = 8 \times 180 = 1440$.

The second trap is choice E. If you got as far as dividing 1080 by 180 and getting 6, you may have forgotten to go on to the next step. When the answers are this close together (10, 9, 8, 7, 6), double-check for traps. Tip: 3

6. Four ounces of Controlled Substance A are added to 16 ounces of Controlled Substance B. What percent of the resulting banned-in-48-states mixture is Controlled Substance A?

(A) 50

(B) 40

(C) $33\frac{1}{3}$

(D) 25

(E) 20

A percent is part/whole. The whole is the entire solution, both Controlled Substance A and Controlled Substance B: 4 + 16 = 20 oz. That's your denominator. The numerator is that part you're looking at, Controlled Substance A. $\frac{4}{20} = \frac{1}{5}$ = 20%. The correct answer is E. Tip: 5

7. 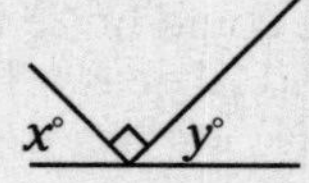

$x + y =$

(A) 180

(B) 90

(C) 80

(D) 45

(E) It cannot be determined from the information given.

This should be a very simple problem. Angles along a straight line sum up to 180 degrees. Because the box in the problem indicates a 90° angle, the remaining angles (x plus y) together sum up to 180 – 90 = 90. The correct answer is B. Tip: 1

If the question asked you for the measure of just angle x or just angle y, you'd have to say you could not determine that. You know that x and y together are 90°; you couldn't solve for either one individually. If you've done the QC (Quantitative Comparisons) material (see Chapter 13), you've seen this same information tested in QC form.

8. $\frac{1}{x}$

$$\frac{\frac{1}{x}}{\frac{1}{x}} + 1 = 11$$

Solve for x.

(A) 13

(B) 10

(C) 9

(D) 1

(E) $\frac{1}{10}$

The question wants to be sure you know that when dividing by a fraction, you invert (turn the number upside down) and multiply.

Begin with the terms on the top. $\frac{1}{x}$ times $\frac{x}{1}$ = 1. Then just plug in and divide 1 by each of the answer choices.

Answer A: $1 / (\frac{1}{13}) = 1 \times \frac{13}{1} = 13$. $1 + 13$ is not equal to 11.

Answer B: $1 / (\frac{1}{10}) = 1 \times \frac{10}{1} = 10$. $1 + 10 = 11$. Ladies and gentlemen, we have a winner. The correct answer is B. Tip: 5

If you chose answer E, you got careless or lazy, or both. When you see variations on a theme such as $\frac{1}{13}$ versus 13, or $\frac{1}{10}$ versus 10, the word *TRAP* should flash like a neon sign in front of your eyes. Slow down and work out the problem.

9. Which of the following represents the expression: three times five less than a fourth of a number is equal to the product of that number and its negative reciprocal?

(A) $3 \times 5 + \frac{1}{4}x = x \times -\frac{1}{x}$

(B) $3 \times 5\ (-\frac{1}{4}x) = x \times -\frac{1}{x}$

(C) $3(\frac{1}{4}x - 5) = x \times -\frac{1}{x}$

(D) $3(\frac{1}{4}x - 5) = x + \frac{1}{x}$

(E) $3(\frac{1}{4}x) + 5 = x + \frac{1}{x}$

This sort of problem tests your ability to convert English into algebra. (Actually, it tests your patience, but that's another story.) Break the problem down. It often pays to work backward, upside down, or inside out. Take "a fourth of a number" — that's easy. Let the number be x. A fourth of that is $\frac{1}{4}x$. "Five less than" means take away 5, or –5. So far you have $(\frac{1}{4}x) - 5$. Take a look at the answer choices. Immediately you can narrow the choices down to C or D. If you're in a rush, go ahead and make a guess; 50-50 odds are worth the risk.

Still sticking it out? Good for you. "Three times" means to multiply by 3. Both C and D do that, so it doesn't help you. "Is equal to" just means an equal sign. "The product of" means to multiply. Whoops! You can cross off D because it adds. I'll finish the problem just for fun. "The negative reciprocal" is negative 1 over x. (A *reciprocal* is simply the number flipped upside down.) The correct answer is C. Tip: 2

10.

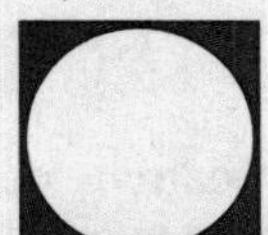

If the diagonal of the square is $4\sqrt{2}$, what is the area of the shaded portion?

(A) $32 - 4\pi$

(B) $16 - 2\pi$

(C) $16 - 4\pi$

(D) $4\sqrt{2} - 4\pi$

(E) $16 - 16\pi$

Think of a shaded area as leftovers. You find an obscurely shaped shaded area (one that isn't a basic triangle, square, and so on) with a three-step approach:

1. ***Total:* Find the area of the large outside figure.**
2. ***Subtotal:* Find the area of the unshaded portion.**
3. **Subtract *Total* minus *Subtotal*. The *leftover* is the shaded area.**

Problem 10 is a little harder than it looks. You need to find the area of the square, which means knowing the length of a side of the square. The diagonal of a square divides that square into two isosceles right triangles. As I review in Chapter 10, the special ratio for the sides of an isosceles right triangle is side:side:side$\sqrt{2}$. If the diagonal, which is actually the hypotenuse of the right triangle, is $4\sqrt{2}$, each side of the triangle, and hence of the square, is 4.

The area of a square is *side* times *side*: $4 \times 4 = 16$. Therefore, your answer is going to be 16 minus something. That narrows the answers down to B, C, and E. (If you think for a minute about E, you'll see that you can eliminate it. Because 16π is greater than 16, the quantity would be negative. You won't find an area less than 0 in an SAT problem.)

Next, find the area of the circle: πr^2. If the side of the square is 4, the diameter of the circle is 4 as well.

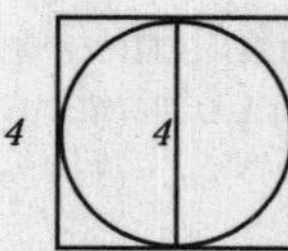

The diameter is twice the length of the radius; that means the radius here is 2. Next, $2 \times 2 = 4$. The area of the circle is 4π.

Finally, subtract: $16 - 4\pi$. The correct answer is C. Tip: 5

The answer is left in this form. Don't head for the calculator and work out 4π. Most answers with π in them just leave in the π; they don't work it out with 3.14. Always check out the answer key before you dive in to do more work, unless you just can't get enough of that SAT math, yum yum.

11. $x^y + y^x =$

(A) 0

(B) 1

(C) x

(D) y

(E) It cannot be determined from the information given.

Everything depends on what the values of x and y are. They could be positive, negative, or 0. They could be odd or even, whole numbers, or fractions. No way is there enough information to solve this problem. The correct answer is E. Tip: 1

The SAT seems to be phasing out the "It cannot be determined" answers. You may not encounter them at all on your test, or you may see only a few. Don't fall into the bad habit of choosing this answer whenever it appears just because it's rare.

12. Given that $a = 2b$ and $a + b = 6\ (c + d)$, the average of a, b, c, and d in terms of a is which of the following?

(A) $\frac{7}{16}a$

(B) $a + 12$

(C) $\frac{1}{2}(a + b)$

(D) a^2

(E) It cannot be determined from the information given.

Just looking at this problem is enough to give you brain cramps. Make things easy: Plug in numbers. I'll start with b and say it's 2. Then $a = 4$. Why did I choose these numbers? Because $2 + 4 = 6$, and $a + b = 6\ (c + d)$. I want a number that's easy to make fit the second part of the equation. I could have plugged in 1 and 2, but then $a + b$ would equal 3 and $(c + d)$ would have to be $\frac{1}{2}$ . . . and fractions are a pain in the hinterlands.

If $a + b = 6$, then $(c + d) = 1$. The average of numbers is found by adding all the numbers and then dividing that sum by the number of items. Here, $a + b + (c + d) = 4 + 2 + 1 = 7$. Divide 7 by 4. Why? Because four terms are being added. Don't fall for the trap of dividing by 3. Even though you have been thinking of $(c + d)$ as one sum, there are two terms there. The average, therefore, is $\frac{7}{4}$.

What is $\frac{7}{4}$ in terms of a? $a = 4$. Plug in the answer choices. For choice A: $\frac{7}{16} \times 4 = \frac{7}{4}$. It fits! The correct answer is A. Tip: 5

But now for the bad news: You have to try the rest of the answers. When you make up your own numbers, you have to do every answer choice just in case more than one is correct. If more than one is correct, you plug in a different set of numbers and try again.

Don't be surprised when hard questions have hard answers. You'd be more likely to get something bizarre like $\frac{7}{4}$ for the last few questions than for the first few, which probably have simple answers of whole numbers. A weird answer like $\sqrt{17} - (\frac{2}{3}x)$ would almost never be the correct answer to question number 1, but it just may be right for number 25.

Part IV

It All Comes Down to This: Full-Length Practice SATs

"If it's okay for them to ask experimental questions, I figure it should be okay for me to give some experimental answers."

In this part . . .

Just when you think your brain can't be stuffed with one more factoid, relief is at hand. You finally get to download some of the information you've been inputting throughout this book. Trust me; you'll feel better when you let it all out.

This unit has two full-length practice exams that are as close to the actual SAT as I can get without having barristers battering down my door. I take these tests seriously, and you should, too — do them under actual test conditions, sitting in a quiet room and timing yourself. But the good news is that the answer explanations don't have to be serious and, in fact, are a lot of fun. Ready? Show me what you can do!

Answer Sheet

Begin with Number 1 for each new section. If any sections have fewer than 35 questions, leave the extra spaces blank.

Section 1

1. Ⓐ Ⓑ Ⓒ Ⓓ Ⓔ	8. Ⓐ Ⓑ Ⓒ Ⓓ Ⓔ	15. Ⓐ Ⓑ Ⓒ Ⓓ Ⓔ	22. Ⓐ Ⓑ Ⓒ Ⓓ Ⓔ	29. Ⓐ Ⓑ Ⓒ Ⓓ Ⓔ
2. Ⓐ Ⓑ Ⓒ Ⓓ Ⓔ	9. Ⓐ Ⓑ Ⓒ Ⓓ Ⓔ	16. Ⓐ Ⓑ Ⓒ Ⓓ Ⓔ	23. Ⓐ Ⓑ Ⓒ Ⓓ Ⓔ	30. Ⓐ Ⓑ Ⓒ Ⓓ Ⓔ
3. Ⓐ Ⓑ Ⓒ Ⓓ Ⓔ	10. Ⓐ Ⓑ Ⓒ Ⓓ Ⓔ	17. Ⓐ Ⓑ Ⓒ Ⓓ Ⓔ	24. Ⓐ Ⓑ Ⓒ Ⓓ Ⓔ	31. Ⓐ Ⓑ Ⓒ Ⓓ Ⓔ
4. Ⓐ Ⓑ Ⓒ Ⓓ Ⓔ	11. Ⓐ Ⓑ Ⓒ Ⓓ Ⓔ	18. Ⓐ Ⓑ Ⓒ Ⓓ Ⓔ	25. Ⓐ Ⓑ Ⓒ Ⓓ Ⓔ	32. Ⓐ Ⓑ Ⓒ Ⓓ Ⓔ
5. Ⓐ Ⓑ Ⓒ Ⓓ Ⓔ	12. Ⓐ Ⓑ Ⓒ Ⓓ Ⓔ	19. Ⓐ Ⓑ Ⓒ Ⓓ Ⓔ	26. Ⓐ Ⓑ Ⓒ Ⓓ Ⓔ	33. Ⓐ Ⓑ Ⓒ Ⓓ Ⓔ
6. Ⓐ Ⓑ Ⓒ Ⓓ Ⓔ	13. Ⓐ Ⓑ Ⓒ Ⓓ Ⓔ	20. Ⓐ Ⓑ Ⓒ Ⓓ Ⓔ	27. Ⓐ Ⓑ Ⓒ Ⓓ Ⓔ	34. Ⓐ Ⓑ Ⓒ Ⓓ Ⓔ
7. Ⓐ Ⓑ Ⓒ Ⓓ Ⓔ	14. Ⓐ Ⓑ Ⓒ Ⓓ Ⓔ	21. Ⓐ Ⓑ Ⓒ Ⓓ Ⓔ	28. Ⓐ Ⓑ Ⓒ Ⓓ Ⓔ	35. Ⓐ Ⓑ Ⓒ Ⓓ Ⓔ

Section 2

1. Ⓐ Ⓑ Ⓒ Ⓓ Ⓔ	8. Ⓐ Ⓑ Ⓒ Ⓓ Ⓔ	15. Ⓐ Ⓑ Ⓒ Ⓓ Ⓔ	22. Ⓐ Ⓑ Ⓒ Ⓓ Ⓔ	29. Ⓐ Ⓑ Ⓒ Ⓓ Ⓔ
2. Ⓐ Ⓑ Ⓒ Ⓓ Ⓔ	9. Ⓐ Ⓑ Ⓒ Ⓓ Ⓔ	16. Ⓐ Ⓑ Ⓒ Ⓓ Ⓔ	23. Ⓐ Ⓑ Ⓒ Ⓓ Ⓔ	30. Ⓐ Ⓑ Ⓒ Ⓓ Ⓔ
3. Ⓐ Ⓑ Ⓒ Ⓓ Ⓔ	10. Ⓐ Ⓑ Ⓒ Ⓓ Ⓔ	17. Ⓐ Ⓑ Ⓒ Ⓓ Ⓔ	24. Ⓐ Ⓑ Ⓒ Ⓓ Ⓔ	31. Ⓐ Ⓑ Ⓒ Ⓓ Ⓔ
4. Ⓐ Ⓑ Ⓒ Ⓓ Ⓔ	11. Ⓐ Ⓑ Ⓒ Ⓓ Ⓔ	18. Ⓐ Ⓑ Ⓒ Ⓓ Ⓔ	25. Ⓐ Ⓑ Ⓒ Ⓓ Ⓔ	32. Ⓐ Ⓑ Ⓒ Ⓓ Ⓔ
5. Ⓐ Ⓑ Ⓒ Ⓓ Ⓔ	12. Ⓐ Ⓑ Ⓒ Ⓓ Ⓔ	19. Ⓐ Ⓑ Ⓒ Ⓓ Ⓔ	26. Ⓐ Ⓑ Ⓒ Ⓓ Ⓔ	33. Ⓐ Ⓑ Ⓒ Ⓓ Ⓔ
6. Ⓐ Ⓑ Ⓒ Ⓓ Ⓔ	13. Ⓐ Ⓑ Ⓒ Ⓓ Ⓔ	20. Ⓐ Ⓑ Ⓒ Ⓓ Ⓔ	27. Ⓐ Ⓑ Ⓒ Ⓓ Ⓔ	34. Ⓐ Ⓑ Ⓒ Ⓓ Ⓔ
7. Ⓐ Ⓑ Ⓒ Ⓓ Ⓔ	14. Ⓐ Ⓑ Ⓒ Ⓓ Ⓔ	21. Ⓐ Ⓑ Ⓒ Ⓓ Ⓔ	28. Ⓐ Ⓑ Ⓒ Ⓓ Ⓔ	35. Ⓐ Ⓑ Ⓒ Ⓓ Ⓔ

Section 3

1. Ⓐ Ⓑ Ⓒ Ⓓ Ⓔ	8. Ⓐ Ⓑ Ⓒ Ⓓ Ⓔ	15. Ⓐ Ⓑ Ⓒ Ⓓ Ⓔ	22. Ⓐ Ⓑ Ⓒ Ⓓ Ⓔ	29. Ⓐ Ⓑ Ⓒ Ⓓ Ⓔ
2. Ⓐ Ⓑ Ⓒ Ⓓ Ⓔ	9. Ⓐ Ⓑ Ⓒ Ⓓ Ⓔ	16. Ⓐ Ⓑ Ⓒ Ⓓ Ⓔ	23. Ⓐ Ⓑ Ⓒ Ⓓ Ⓔ	30. Ⓐ Ⓑ Ⓒ Ⓓ Ⓔ
3. Ⓐ Ⓑ Ⓒ Ⓓ Ⓔ	10. Ⓐ Ⓑ Ⓒ Ⓓ Ⓔ	17. Ⓐ Ⓑ Ⓒ Ⓓ Ⓔ	24. Ⓐ Ⓑ Ⓒ Ⓓ Ⓔ	31. Ⓐ Ⓑ Ⓒ Ⓓ Ⓔ
4. Ⓐ Ⓑ Ⓒ Ⓓ Ⓔ	11. Ⓐ Ⓑ Ⓒ Ⓓ Ⓔ	18. Ⓐ Ⓑ Ⓒ Ⓓ Ⓔ	25. Ⓐ Ⓑ Ⓒ Ⓓ Ⓔ	32. Ⓐ Ⓑ Ⓒ Ⓓ Ⓔ
5. Ⓐ Ⓑ Ⓒ Ⓓ Ⓔ	12. Ⓐ Ⓑ Ⓒ Ⓓ Ⓔ	19. Ⓐ Ⓑ Ⓒ Ⓓ Ⓔ	26. Ⓐ Ⓑ Ⓒ Ⓓ Ⓔ	33. Ⓐ Ⓑ Ⓒ Ⓓ Ⓔ
6. Ⓐ Ⓑ Ⓒ Ⓓ Ⓔ	13. Ⓐ Ⓑ Ⓒ Ⓓ Ⓔ	20. Ⓐ Ⓑ Ⓒ Ⓓ Ⓔ	27. Ⓐ Ⓑ Ⓒ Ⓓ Ⓔ	34. Ⓐ Ⓑ Ⓒ Ⓓ Ⓔ
7. Ⓐ Ⓑ Ⓒ Ⓓ Ⓔ	14. Ⓐ Ⓑ Ⓒ Ⓓ Ⓔ	21. Ⓐ Ⓑ Ⓒ Ⓓ Ⓔ	28. Ⓐ Ⓑ Ⓒ Ⓓ Ⓔ	35. Ⓐ Ⓑ Ⓒ Ⓓ Ⓔ

Section 4

1. Ⓐ Ⓑ Ⓒ Ⓓ Ⓔ	4. Ⓐ Ⓑ Ⓒ Ⓓ Ⓔ	7. Ⓐ Ⓑ Ⓒ Ⓓ Ⓔ	10. Ⓐ Ⓑ Ⓒ Ⓓ Ⓔ	13. Ⓐ Ⓑ Ⓒ Ⓓ Ⓔ
2. Ⓐ Ⓑ Ⓒ Ⓓ Ⓔ	5. Ⓐ Ⓑ Ⓒ Ⓓ Ⓔ	8. Ⓐ Ⓑ Ⓒ Ⓓ Ⓔ	11. Ⓐ Ⓑ Ⓒ Ⓓ Ⓔ	14. Ⓐ Ⓑ Ⓒ Ⓓ Ⓔ
3. Ⓐ Ⓑ Ⓒ Ⓓ Ⓔ	6. Ⓐ Ⓑ Ⓒ Ⓓ Ⓔ	9. Ⓐ Ⓑ Ⓒ Ⓓ Ⓔ	12. Ⓐ Ⓑ Ⓒ Ⓓ Ⓔ	15. Ⓐ Ⓑ Ⓒ Ⓓ Ⓔ

Section 4 (continued)

16.

17.

18.

19.

20.

21.

22.

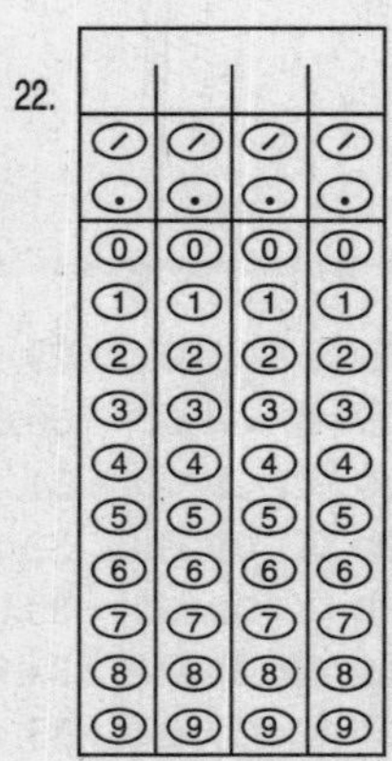

23.

24.

25.

Section 5

1. Ⓐ Ⓑ Ⓒ Ⓓ Ⓔ
2. Ⓐ Ⓑ Ⓒ Ⓓ Ⓔ
3. Ⓐ Ⓑ Ⓒ Ⓓ Ⓔ
4. Ⓐ Ⓑ Ⓒ Ⓓ Ⓔ
5. Ⓐ Ⓑ Ⓒ Ⓓ Ⓔ
6. Ⓐ Ⓑ Ⓒ Ⓓ Ⓔ
7. Ⓐ Ⓑ Ⓒ Ⓓ Ⓔ
8. Ⓐ Ⓑ Ⓒ Ⓓ Ⓔ
9. Ⓐ Ⓑ Ⓒ Ⓓ Ⓔ
10. Ⓐ Ⓑ Ⓒ Ⓓ Ⓔ
11. Ⓐ Ⓑ Ⓒ Ⓓ Ⓔ
12. Ⓐ Ⓑ Ⓒ Ⓓ Ⓔ
13. Ⓐ Ⓑ Ⓒ Ⓓ Ⓔ
14. Ⓐ Ⓑ Ⓒ Ⓓ Ⓔ
15. Ⓐ Ⓑ Ⓒ Ⓓ Ⓔ
16. Ⓐ Ⓑ Ⓒ Ⓓ Ⓔ
17. Ⓐ Ⓑ Ⓒ Ⓓ Ⓔ
18. Ⓐ Ⓑ Ⓒ Ⓓ Ⓔ
19. Ⓐ Ⓑ Ⓒ Ⓓ Ⓔ
20. Ⓐ Ⓑ Ⓒ Ⓓ Ⓔ
21. Ⓐ Ⓑ Ⓒ Ⓓ Ⓔ
22. Ⓐ Ⓑ Ⓒ Ⓓ Ⓔ
23. Ⓐ Ⓑ Ⓒ Ⓓ Ⓔ
24. Ⓐ Ⓑ Ⓒ Ⓓ Ⓔ
25. Ⓐ Ⓑ Ⓒ Ⓓ Ⓔ
26. Ⓐ Ⓑ Ⓒ Ⓓ Ⓔ
27. Ⓐ Ⓑ Ⓒ Ⓓ Ⓔ
28. Ⓐ Ⓑ Ⓒ Ⓓ Ⓔ
29. Ⓐ Ⓑ Ⓒ Ⓓ Ⓔ
30. Ⓐ Ⓑ Ⓒ Ⓓ Ⓔ
31. Ⓐ Ⓑ Ⓒ Ⓓ Ⓔ
32. Ⓐ Ⓑ Ⓒ Ⓓ Ⓔ
33. Ⓐ Ⓑ Ⓒ Ⓓ Ⓔ
34. Ⓐ Ⓑ Ⓒ Ⓓ Ⓔ
35. Ⓐ Ⓑ Ⓒ Ⓓ Ⓔ

Section 6

1. Ⓐ Ⓑ Ⓒ Ⓓ Ⓔ
2. Ⓐ Ⓑ Ⓒ Ⓓ Ⓔ
3. Ⓐ Ⓑ Ⓒ Ⓓ Ⓔ
4. Ⓐ Ⓑ Ⓒ Ⓓ Ⓔ
5. Ⓐ Ⓑ Ⓒ Ⓓ Ⓔ
6. Ⓐ Ⓑ Ⓒ Ⓓ Ⓔ
7. Ⓐ Ⓑ Ⓒ Ⓓ Ⓔ
8. Ⓐ Ⓑ Ⓒ Ⓓ Ⓔ
9. Ⓐ Ⓑ Ⓒ Ⓓ Ⓔ
10. Ⓐ Ⓑ Ⓒ Ⓓ Ⓔ
11. Ⓐ Ⓑ Ⓒ Ⓓ Ⓔ
12. Ⓐ Ⓑ Ⓒ Ⓓ Ⓔ
13. Ⓐ Ⓑ Ⓒ Ⓓ Ⓔ
14. Ⓐ Ⓑ Ⓒ Ⓓ Ⓔ
15. Ⓐ Ⓑ Ⓒ Ⓓ Ⓔ
16. Ⓐ Ⓑ Ⓒ Ⓓ Ⓔ
17. Ⓐ Ⓑ Ⓒ Ⓓ Ⓔ
18. Ⓐ Ⓑ Ⓒ Ⓓ Ⓔ
19. Ⓐ Ⓑ Ⓒ Ⓓ Ⓔ
20. Ⓐ Ⓑ Ⓒ Ⓓ Ⓔ
21. Ⓐ Ⓑ Ⓒ Ⓓ Ⓔ
22. Ⓐ Ⓑ Ⓒ Ⓓ Ⓔ
23. Ⓐ Ⓑ Ⓒ Ⓓ Ⓔ
24. Ⓐ Ⓑ Ⓒ Ⓓ Ⓔ
25. Ⓐ Ⓑ Ⓒ Ⓓ Ⓔ
26. Ⓐ Ⓑ Ⓒ Ⓓ Ⓔ
27. Ⓐ Ⓑ Ⓒ Ⓓ Ⓔ
28. Ⓐ Ⓑ Ⓒ Ⓓ Ⓔ
29. Ⓐ Ⓑ Ⓒ Ⓓ Ⓔ
30. Ⓐ Ⓑ Ⓒ Ⓓ Ⓔ
31. Ⓐ Ⓑ Ⓒ Ⓓ Ⓔ
32. Ⓐ Ⓑ Ⓒ Ⓓ Ⓔ
33. Ⓐ Ⓑ Ⓒ Ⓓ Ⓔ
34. Ⓐ Ⓑ Ⓒ Ⓓ Ⓔ
35. Ⓐ Ⓑ Ⓒ Ⓓ Ⓔ

Chapter 17

How to Ruin a Perfectly Good Day, Part I: Practice Exam 1

You're ready to take a sample SAT test. The following exam consists of four 30-minute sections and two 15-minute sections. Three sections are verbal; three are math.

Please take this test under normal exam conditions. This is serious stuff here!

1. **Sit where you won't be interrupted (even though you'd probably welcome any distractions).**
2. **Use the answer grid provided.**
3. **Set your alarm for 30- or 15-minute intervals.**
4. **Do not go on to the next section until the time allotted for the section you are taking is up.**
5. **If you finish early, check your work for that section only.**
6. **Don't take a break during any one section.**
7. **Give yourself one 10-minute break between sections 2 and 3 and a second 10-minute break between sections 4 and 5.**

When you complete the entire test, check your answers with the answer key at the end of this chapter. Sample scoring charts are provided.

Go through the answer explanations to *all* the questions, not just the ones you missed — see Chapter 18. There's a plethora of worthwhile information — material that provides a good review of everything in the lectures. I've even tossed in a few good jokes to keep you somewhat sane.

Section 1

Time: 30 Minutes

35 Questions

Choose the *best* answer to each question. Blacken the corresponding oval on the answer grid.

Each of the following sentences contains one or two blanks indicating words or phrases that have been omitted. Choose the answer that best completes the sentence.

Example:

Because he ---- the test, John was ----.

(A) flunked .. thrilled

(B) forgot .. brilliant

(C) passed .. happy

(D) ignored .. praised

(E) memorized .. surprised

The correct answer is (C). 

1. Unsurprised by the ---- his documentary received, the filmmaker said he knew from the start that his picture would sweep the Academy Awards.

(A) shock

(B) severity

(C) criticism

(D) praise

(E) complaints

2. Californian Martha King has gathered national ---- for being the first American woman in the history of aviation to be qualified to fly every class of aircraft, including jets, helicopters, and even blimps.

(A) renown

(B) bemusement

(C) despair

(D) glee

(E) vituperation

3. Scientists are developing viral pesticides because just as humans suffer from the common cold, insects are ---- naturally occurring viruses.

(A) immune to

(B) enhanced by

(C) integrated into

(D) susceptible to

(E) unaffected by

4. The most ---- letter in the alphabet is "O" which has remained ---- in shape since being used in the Phoenician alphabet in 1300 B.C.

(A) novel .. similar

(B) ancient .. unchanged

(C) complicated .. round

(D) obsolete .. stable

(E) studied .. fluctuating

5. Well-known for his ---- adherence to the rules, the judge had little patience with those who believed the spirit, not the letter, of the law was the essential point.

(A) dogmatic

(B) benign

(C) impetuous

(D) cryptic

(E) redoubtable

Go on to next page

6. Although originally ---- by the author's scientific colleagues as ---- theory, the idea that an ulcer could be treated with antibiotics soon gained nearly universal acceptance.

(A) denounced .. a rational

(B) derided .. a plausible

(C) dismissed .. an untenable

(D) scoffed at .. a hypothetical

(E) praised .. an unlikely

7. Forced to ---- the parent club because of their own ---- views, the faction immediately began proselytizing, hoping to add new members to their chapter.

(A) leave .. docile

(B) secede from .. unorthodox

(C) integrate into .. rebellious

(D) revile .. heretical

(E) establish .. dogmatic

8. The school adopted a program in which seniors served as ---- to freshmen, giving them advice and helping them adjust to high school.

(A) sentries

(B) mentors

(C) acolytes

(D) pedants

(E) sycophants

9. A(n) ---- animal, the Pallas cat is active primarily at dawn and dusk.

(A) crepuscular

(B) gargantuan

(C) corpulent

(D) querulous

(E) indolent

10. Annoyed at the politician's ---- comments, the reporter pressed harder for a more ---- response.

(A) redundant .. repetitive

(B) tactless .. immediate

(C) phlegmatic .. lackadaisical

(D) disputatious .. heartfelt

(E) circumlocutious .. direct

Each of the following questions features a pair of words or phrases in capital letters, followed by five pairs of words or phrases in lowercase letters. Choose the lowercase pair that most closely expresses the same relationship as that of the uppercase pair.

Example:

HAPPY: SAD::

(A) tall: fat

(B) silly: serious

(C) yellow: red

(D) nervous: anxious

(E) joyful: mysterious

The correct answer is (B).   

11. PUNCH: BRUISE::

(A) toast: bread

(B) cut: scar

(C) laughter: tickle

(D) drought: tempest

(E) name: sobriquet

12. DEHYDRATED: WATER::

(A) regretful: sorrow

(B) impecunious: money

(C) graceful: rhythm

(D) brawny: muscles

(E) effervescent: bubbles

13. CHIMNEY: SMOKE::

(A) straw: liquid

(B) basin: water

(C) binder: papers

(D) bowl: ice cream

(E) label: bottle

14. AMORPHOUS: SHAPELESS::

(A) atypical: common

(B) amoral: loving

(C) abstemious: overindulgent

(D) obstinate: open-minded

(E) deficient: lacking

Go on to next page

15. GYMNAST: AGILE::
(A) specter: substantial
(B) pacifist: irascible
(C) pariah: gregarious
(D) glutton: abstemious
(E) charlatan: duplicitous

16. SPHYGNEMOMETER: BLOOD PRESSURE::
(A) ounce: ton
(B) sundial: sun
(C) microscope: bacteria
(D) copyright: book
(E) scale: weight

17. EXCULPATE: GUILT::
(A) appropriate: credit
(B) rumple: wrinkles
(C) exterminate: pests
(D) synchronize: consistency
(E) exonerate: happiness

18. MISOGYNIST: WOMEN::
(A) prophet: wisdom
(B) hypochondriac: medications
(C) witch: spell
(D) pragmatist: fantasy
(E) reprobate: cruelty

19. ARCHIPELAGO: ISLANDS::
(A) page: book
(B) faucet: water
(C) federation: states
(D) scarf: clothing
(E) pint: liquid

20. CUPIDITY: MONEY::
(A) acclaim: property
(B) zeal: lethargy
(C) taciturnity: discourse
(D) philanthropy: evil
(E) gluttony: food

21. EMBARGO: BLOCK::
(A) incantation: deny
(B) parody: originate
(C) euphemism: denounce
(D) obfuscation: clarify
(E) boycott: shun

22. ASSASSIN: SANGUINARY::
(A) charlatan: deceitful
(B) ruffian: gentle
(C) scapegoat: pragmatic
(D) sage: ignorant
(E) surgeon: inept

23. OBDURATE: STUBBORN::
(A) illegal: inconsiderate
(B) fractious: whole
(C) mild: strident
(D) emaciated: free
(E) wooden: stiff

DIRECTIONS: Each passage is followed by questions that pertain to that passage. Read the passage and answer the questions based on information stated or implied in that passage.

Black Americans have served in the armed forces since the birth of the United States. The following material discusses their service.

Line

The dearth of intelligence made available to the American public concerning blacks in the military has left the impression with many that blacks have really not been involved in combat activities in any significant manner. This belief is erroneous.

Blacks have been in the United States Navy since the early days of the Republic. Unfortunately, circumstances occasioned by the manner of service rendered by black sailors have made it almost impossible to determine how many blacks actually served. One reason for the paucity of information is that service records were not kept by race until a short time before World War I. In addition, many blacks served as substitutes for white men and were not listed by their own names. Blacks were often given their freedom in exchange for such service.

Go on to next page

The impressment of black sailors aboard British ships was one of the primary causes of the problems that occasioned the War of 1812 with Great Britain. The distinguishing action of black soldiers in this war came in the Battle of New Orleans, which ironically took place after the war was officially over. The city had been threatened by the British, and Andrew Jackson insisted that the offer of the Battalion of Free Men of Color to fight against the British be accepted. Around this time in the Navy, some sources estimate that between ten and twenty percent of the sailors were black, although exact numbers are impossible to obtain. When Perry won his great victory on Lake Erie, at least one out of every ten sailors on his ship was black.

In the first and second Seminole wars (1816-1842), blacks fought with the Indians against the whites. Blacks who had settled with the Indians and intermarried with them had established themselves as farmers and elements of a protective militia. They provided much of the resistance to Andrew Jackson's troops. For a considerable period of time, the blacks and Indians fought a very effective war against Jackson's regulars.

Black women also served in the military. The spirit of Harriet Tubman became a moving force for those who valued freedom. This black Union spy, unpaid soldier, volunteer nurse and freedom fighter, friend of the famed white abolitionist John Brown of Harper's Ferry fame, had such a strong love for freedom that she left her husband and brothers who chose not to run the risk of escaping from slavery. Although she could not and did not receive any pay for her services, Tubman was often in the field with the soldiers. She acquired the nickname "General" Tubman.

While the exploits of Harriet Tubman are generally known, less discussed are the services of the former slave Susan King Taylor, who in her time became the most famous black woman who volunteered to help the troops during the Civil War. She escaped from slavery at the age of 12 and became a teacher for freedmen by the age of 16. Her meeting with Clara Barton, founder of the American Red Cross, greatly influenced her activities as a volunteer nurse for black Civil War troops as she traveled with her husband's unit, the 33rd United States Colored Troops. In 1902, Taylor published her wartime memoirs, providing the only written record of the activities of black volunteer nurses during the Civil War.

The Spanish-American War was also one in which black American females played a role. Volunteer nurses were badly needed because the army was not able to make adequate medical personnel available for combat units. Most of the soldiers who became casualties fell from diseases associated with the tropical climate of Cuba, and not from enemy bullets. The Army was so pleased with the black nurses who had served as combat nurses that bills were submitted to Congress (but defeated) to have the Army create a permanent corps of nurses.

World War I was the first major American military conflict in which the black female had a recognized organization to provide leadership and direction. The National Association of Colored Graduate Nurses had been founded in 1909. When America entered World War I in 1917, the co-founder of the organization began to urge black nurses to enroll in the American Red Cross.

24. Which of the following best captures the meaning of the word "intelligence" as it is used in line 1?

(A) wisdom

(B) experience

(C) IQ

(D) information

(E) prejudice

25. The primary purpose of the second paragraph is to

(A) refute a study

(B) correct a misapprehension

(C) develop a philosophy

(D) predict an event

(E) denounce an attitude

26. According to the passage, which of the following is mentioned as a reason for the lack of statistics about the number of blacks who served in the military in our nation's early days?

I. Men's races were not specified in the records.

II. Blacks had no names of their own.

III. Slaves' names were released from the records when the men earned their freedom.

(A) I only

(B) I and II only

(C) II and III only

(D) I and III only

(E) I, II, and III

Go on to next page

27. The practice of having blacks serve as substitutes for whites (lines 15–16) suggests that

(A) many whites were unwilling to serve in the armed forces

(B) blacks were forced to serve in the place of whites

(C) many of the blacks who served in this way were slaves

(D) blacks proved to be better soldiers than the whites they replaced

(E) blacks were mistreated in the armed forces

28. The passage implies that the people of New Orleans

(A) secretly sided with the British in the War of 1812

(B) were the first to establish a regiment of black fighters

(C) were reluctant to have the battalion of black men fight for them in 1812

(D) had a population that was predominantly black

(E) distrusted Andrew Jackson

29. The author mentions the percentage of sailors aboard Perry's ship who were black to make the point that

(A) black men fight better than white men

(B) there were more black sailors than most people realize

(C) Perry was free of the prejudice that afflicted so many of his contemporaries

(D) the Navy was more likely to keep its word about setting free those who fought than was the Army

(E) white men are more likely to get ill at sea than are black men

30. You may infer from the passage that blacks fought alongside the Indians in the Seminole wars because

(A) blacks felt that the Indians' cause was more righteous than was the whites' cause

(B) the Indians offered them land for their services

(C) the whites had been excessively cruel to the blacks

(D) the blacks were protecting their homes and families

(E) the whites didn't want the blacks fighting alongside them and rejected the blacks' offer of service

31. The primary contrast that the author makes between Harriet Tubman and Susan King Taylor is

(A) Tubman nursed the soldiers; Taylor actually fought alongside them

(B) Tubman held a commission; Taylor was a volunteer

(C) Tubman had white friends; Taylor believed in total segregation as the best path for blacks

(D) Tubman took no salary; Taylor was generously paid

(E) Tubman is more famous in our time; Taylor was more well-known in her time

32. You may infer from the passage that the Spanish-American War

(A) was fought in Cuba

(B) led to the creation of a permanent corps of nurses

(C) proved the inadequacy of medical training

(D) was the first war in which black females participated

(E) triggered the establishment of the American Red Cross

Go on to next page

33. The author states that all of the following statements about World War I are true *except*

(A) black women participated as nurses
(B) the American Red Cross was active
(C) American participation began in 1917
(D) black women finally had an organization to provide leadership
(E) black women were actively recruited by white military leaders

34. In lines 84–85, the author uses the phrase "recognized organization" to imply that

(A) everyone had heard of the National Association of Colored Graduate Nurses
(B) military personnel had learned to identify black female nurses in the field
(C) black females had served previously in unofficial capacities
(D) before that time, record-keeping had not distinguished between black and white females
(E) black females were not accepted in the military prior to that time

35. The tone of this passage may best be described as

(A) facetious
(B) lugubrious
(C) inspirational
(D) belligerent
(E) vindictive

STOP

DO NOT TURN THE PAGE UNTIL TOLD TO DO SO.
DO NOT RETURN TO A PREVIOUS TEST.

Section 2

Time: 30 Minutes

25 Questions

Directions: Solve each problem. Blacken the corresponding oval on the answer grid.

Notes:

* You may use a calculator.
* All numbers used in this exam are real numbers.
* All figures lie in a plane.
* All figures may be assumed to be to scale unless the problem specifically indicates otherwise.

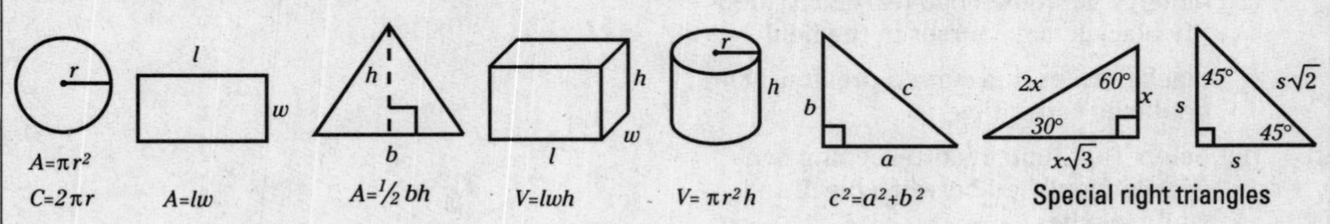

There are 360 degrees of arc in a circle.

There are 180 degrees in a straight angle.

There are 180 degrees in the sum of the interior angles of a triangle.

1. $7x + 18 = 13x$.

   $x =$

   (A) 0

   (B) 1

   (C) 2

   (D) 3

   (E) $\frac{9}{10}$

2. A used car lot has only Cadillacs, Ferraris, and Corvettes. The number of Cadillacs is twice the number of Ferraris and half the number of Corvettes. If there are 20 Cadillacs, how many cars are in the lot?

   (A) 80

   (B) 70

   (C) 60

   (D) 55

   (E) 45

Go on to next page

3. Using Set x = (1, 9, 7, 2, 5), what is the difference between the number obtained by arranging the terms in descending order and the number obtained by arranging the terms in ascending order?

(A) 88,903

(B) 84,942

(C) 82,094

(D) 74,941

(E) 72,090

4. Which of the following is *not* true of a circle whose area is 16π square units?

I. Its radius is 4 units.

II. Its circumference is 32π units.

III. Its longest chord is 8 units.

(A) I only

(B) II only

(C) III only

(D) II and III only

(E) I, II, and III

5. When the angle formed by the hour and minute hands of a clock is 60 degrees, which of the following *could be* the time?

(A) 1:00

(B) 2:00

(C) 3:00

(D) 3:15

(E) 3:30

6. A teacher walks down the aisle, checking homework. He checks the math for the first student, the English for the second, the science for the third, and the history for the fourth and starts over again. If he continues this pattern, what homework will he check for the 38th student?

(A) math

(B) English

(C) science

(D) history

(E) It cannot be determined from the information given.

Go on to next page

7. A bowl contains 42 pieces of fruit. One-third of the pieces of fruit are apples. Half of the pieces of fruit are red. How many pieces of fruit are neither red nor apples?

(A) 40

(B) 35

(C) 22

(D) 6

(E) It cannot be determined from the information given.

8. Let x represent the number of surgeons in a hospital, and y the number of anesthesiologists. The number of surgeons is five times six less than the number of anesthesiologists. Together there are 54 surgeons and anesthesiologists. Which of the following equations expresses the relationship between the number of surgeons and anesthesiologists?

(A) $5x - 6 = y$

(B) $x - 6 = 54$

(C) $5y - 6 = x$

(D) $5y - 30 = x$

(E) $x + 5y = 6$

9. The average of x, y, and z is one third greater than x. Therefore, $y + z$ is what percent greater than x?

(A) 50

(B) 100

(C) 200

(D) 300

(E) 400

10. $\frac{6a^{10}b^5c^7}{3a^5b^9c^7} =$

(A) $2a^2b^4c$

(B) $\frac{2a^2b^4}{c}$

(C) $\frac{2a^5b^4}{c}$

(D) $2a^5b^4$

(E) $\frac{2a^5}{b^4}$

Go on to next page

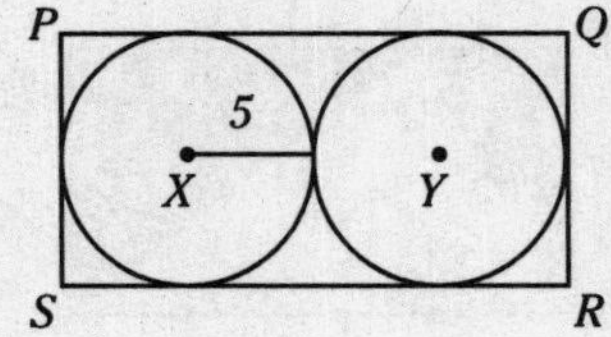

11. The area of circle *X* equals the area of circle *Y*. The circles touch each other and touch the sides of the rectangle as shown. What is the area of rectangle *PQRS*?

(A) 200

(B) 180

(C) 150

(D) 100

(E) 25

12. Marking flags are placed along a building site. If the orange flag is twice as far from the red flag as the red flag is from the green flag, which of the following represents this ratio:

$$\frac{\text{distance from red to orange flag}}{\text{distance from orange to green flag}}$$

(A) 4:1

(B) 3:1

(C) 2:1

(D) 3:2

(E) It cannot be determined from the information given.

13. The length of a rectangle is six times its width. The ratio of perimeter to width equals

(A) 21:1

(B) 21:6

(C) 14:1

(D) 7:1

(E) 6:1

14. A painter is painting poles. One pole is blue; the rest of the poles are black. Starting at the side closer to the painter, the blue pole is the ninth. From the side farther from the painter, the blue pole is the eleventh. How many poles are there altogether?

(A) 18

(B) 19

(C) 20

(D) 21

(E) 22

Go on to next page

15. Cody drops and breaks three dishes for every four that he manages to put away. If there were 63 dishes at the start, how many dishes remain intact at the end of his assistance?

(A) 36

(B) 30

(C) 27

(D) 25

(E) 22

16. Given that $2r = 5s = 3t$, which of the following is a true statement? ($r, s, t > 0$)

I. $3t = 2r + s$

II. $6s = 3t + r$

III. $10s = 3t + 2r$

(A) I only

(B) II only

(C) III only

(D) I and III only

(E) I, II, and III

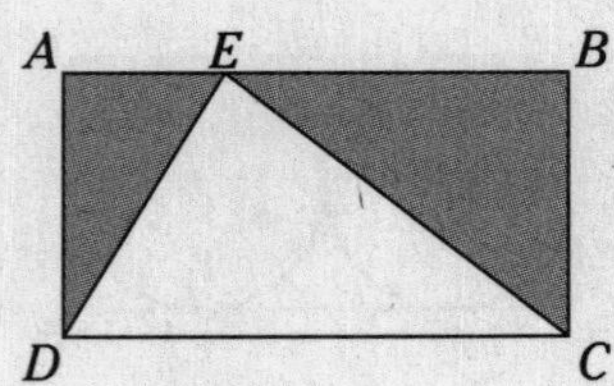

17. Triangle *EDC* touches the sides of the rectangle at points *E, D,* and *C* as shown. Given that the area of triangle *EDC* = 36, what is the area of the shaded portion of the figure?

Note: The figure is not drawn to scale.

(A) 72

(B) 54

(C) 40

(D) 36

(E) 18

18. On a coordinate grid, if point *A* is at (3,5) and point *B* is at (6,4), what is the slope of line *AB?*

(A) –3

(B) –2

(C) –⅓

(D) ⅓

(E) 3

Go on to next page

19. One hundred job applicants show up in response to a classified ad. If 60% of them are female and if ¾ of the female applicants are willing to relocate if the job demands it, how many people are *not* willing to relocate?

(A) 60

(B) 55

(C) 45

(D) 15

(E) It cannot be determined from the information given.

20. A square of diagonal 8 has a perimeter of

(A) 64

(B) 32

(C) 16

(D) $16\sqrt{2}$

(E) $8\sqrt{2}$

21. Yogi weighs seven boxes to ready them for shipping. Their average weight is 80 lbs. If the first five boxes weigh 75, 69, 81, 90, and 73, what is the average weight for the last two boxes?

(A) 65

(B) 74

(C) 82

(D) 86

(E) 92

22. The radius of the smaller circle is ½ the radius of the larger circle. If the area of the shaded region is 12π, which of the following is the area of the small (unshaded) circle?

(A) 2π

(B) 4π

(C) 6π

(D) 8π

(E) 16π

Go on to next page

23. A hubcap with an area of 16π square feet has a radius exactly one-half that of the wheel it is on. If the wheel were to roll down a 400-foot hill, *approximately* how many revolutions would it make?

(A) 16

(B) 10

(C) 8

(D) 6

(E) 4

24. Ⓧ $= x + x^2$ for all prime numbers x

Ⓧ $= x^2 - x$ for all composite numbers x

④ + ⑤ =

(A) 50

(B) 42

(C) 40

(D) 32

(E) 15

25. At a warehouse store, eight cans of frozen concentrated orange juice cost d dollars. If each can makes m milliliters of orange juice when mixed with three cans of water, what will be the total cost, in dollars, to make 400 milliliters of orange juice if one can of water costs c cents?

(A) $3200md + 96c$

(B) $\frac{md + 3c}{400}$

(C) $\frac{d + 3c}{50m}$

(D) $\frac{8d + 96c}{m}$

(E) $\frac{50d + 12c}{m}$

STOP DO NOT TURN THE PAGE UNTIL TOLD TO DO SO. DO NOT RETURN TO A PREVIOUS TEST.

Section 3

Time: 30 Minutes

30 Questions

Directions: Choose the *best* answer to each question. Blacken the corresponding oval on the answer grid.

Each of the following sentences contains one or two blanks indicating words or phrases that have been omitted. Choose the answer that best completes the sentence.

Example:

Because he ---- the test, John was ----.

(A) flunked .. thrilled

(B) forgot .. brilliant

(C) passed .. happy

(D) ignored .. praised

(E) memorized .. surprised

The correct answer is (C). Ⓐ Ⓑ ● Ⓓ Ⓔ

1. The banana tree, which is actually the largest herb in the world, gains its ---- in the mild climates of the subtropics.

(A) toxicity

(B) dominance

(C) pungency

(D) fertility

(E) immensity

2. Though she was unable to change the school's policy on recycling, Dakota did achieve ---- in her crusade to ---- the amount of waste paper generated by the computer labs on campus.

(A) contempt .. destroy

(B) praise .. increase

(C) success .. limit

(D) failure .. curtail

(E) nothing .. expand

3. Rather than being ----, the Constitution is a flexible document that can be amended as necessary.

(A) improper

(B) cohesive

(C) subversive

(D) immutable

(E) insightful

4. The Feileadh Mör, or great kilt, was the ---- of the Feileadh Beag, or modern kilt, which has since become the ---- attire of Scotland.

(A) predecessor .. traditional

(B) precursor .. anonymous

(C) descendent .. habitual

(D) successor .. audacious

(E) conclusion .. attractive

5. The news report was anything but ----, but those of us who have learned to discount such gloomy ---- are optimistic.

(A) moribund .. traps

(B) pessimistic .. confusion

(C) pleasant .. prognostications

(D) malicious .. benefits

(E) trivial .. magnitude

6. Although originally ---- when she erroneously thought her dog Cheerio had been disqualified from the match, Leoni became ---- when she later found out Cheerio had in fact won her division.

(A) lugubrious .. lachrymose

(B) enervated .. exhausted

(C) disgruntled .. annoyed

(D) inconsolable .. ebullient

(E) effervescent .. excited

Go on to next page

7. Previously considered ----, assertions that stomach ulcers were caused by bacteria rather than solely by stress have gained ---- with many physicians.

(A) impossible .. continuity

(B) outlandish .. credibility

(C) plausible .. strength

(D) indisputable .. belief

(E) probable .. acceptance

8. Often people who have been ---- by one group of society will subconsciously try to demonstrate that they are ---- others.

(A) demeaned .. superior to

(B) lauded .. beneath

(C) denigrated .. scuttled by

(D) befriended .. servile to

(E) emasculated .. in conjunction with

9. In an open market, the highly praised new trade agreement is expected to ---- new exports for national firms but not ---- the foreign competition problems the U. S. products already face.

(A) reduce .. lessen

(B) open .. ameliorate

(C) derogate .. solve

(D) spur .. exacerbate

(E) stymie .. decrease

Each of the following questions features a pair of words or phrases in capital letters, followed by five pairs of words or phrases in lowercase letters. Choose the lowercase pair that most closely expresses the same relationship as that of the uppercase pair.

Example:

HAPPY: SAD::

(A) tall: fat

(B) silly: serious

(C) yellow: red

(D) nervous : anxious

(E) joyful: mysterious

The correct answer is (B). 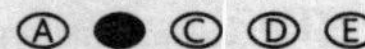

10. OSTRICH: BIRD::

(A) feather: raven

(B) rubber: element

(C) monitor: computer

(D) cuticle: fingernail

(E) denim: fabric

11. ACTOR: THEATER::

(A) judge: court

(B) chef: hospital

(C) tailor: auditorium

(D) physician: pharmacy

(E) goldsmith: market

12. GALLEON: SHIP::

(A) computer: typewriter

(B) book: text

(C) store: mall

(D) anchor: boat

(E) papyrus: paper

13. LEAGUE: DISTANCE::

(A) thermometer: temperature

(B) metronome: time

(C) watt: electricity

(D) knot: ocean

(E) orbit: earth

14. LOQUACIOUS: CHATTER:

(A) inauspicious: favor

(B) seething: fantasy

(C) prevaricating: confusion

(D) skeptical: doubt

(E) obese: confusion

15. VISIONARY: QUIXOTIC::

(A) employer: servile

(B) pugilist: brawny

(C) toady: autonomous

(D) idiot: ingenious

(E) kith: wily

Go on to next page

Directions: Each passage is followed by questions that pertain to that passage. Read the passage and answer the questions based on information stated or implied in that passage.

Questions 16–21 are based on the following passage.

A NASA (National Aeronautics and Space Administration) occupational health program called Enlightened Employee Health featured the following.

Due to the involuntary simultaneous contraction of 15 facial muscles, the upper lip is raised, partially uncovering the teeth and effecting a downward curving of the furrows that extend from the wings of both nostrils to the corners of the mouth. This produces a puffing out of the cheeks on the outer side of the furrows. Creases also occur under the eyes and may become permanent at the side edges of the eye. The eyes undergo reflex lacrimation and vascular engorgement. At the same time, an abrupt strong expiration of air is followed by spasmodic contractions of the chest and diaphragm, resulting in a series of expiration-inspiration microcycles with interval pause. The whole body may be thrown backward, shaken, or confused due to other spasmodic skeletal muscle contractions. We call this condition laughter.

Laughter is considered to be an innate human response that develops during the first few weeks of life. Evidence of the innate quality of laughter is seen in its occurrence in deaf and blind infants and children who are completely without visual or auditory clues from their environment. Darwin propounded in his *Principle of Antithesis* that laughter develops as the infant's powerful reward signal of comfort and well-being to the nurturing adult. This signal is totally antithetical perceptually to the screams or cries of distress associated with discomfort. Laughter seems to play an important role in the promotion of social unity, production of a sense of well-being, communication of well-being, and as a mechanism for coping with stressful situations.

Psychologically, both reflexive (tickle response) and heart-felt (mental response) laughter effect changes to the human system that may be significant in the treatment and prevention of illness. These include laughter's association with an increase in pulse rate, probably due to increased levels of circulatory catecholamines. There is an increase in respiration. There is a possible increase in secretion of brain and pituitary endorphins — the body's natural anesthetics, which relieve pain and reduce suffering. There is a decrease in red blood cell sedimentation rate (*sed rate* is associated with the body's level of infections or inflammation).

The possibility exists that laughter and other salutary emotions have a placebo effect upon the body. This in no way minimizes the therapeutic potential for these emotions. Hippocrates propounded that the mind and body are one. It may be possible that there is a physical chemistry associated with the will to live. Further investigation of the effects of positive emotions upon health and well-being may give us the keys to unlocking the power of the life force.

Immanuel Kant, in his *Critique of Pure Reason*, wrote that laughter is the physician of the body. Echoing Kant's thesis nearly two centuries later, Norman Cousins, author, senior lecturer at the UCLA School of Medicine, and editor of *Saturday Review*, has become the modern-day patron saint of self-potentiation through the healing power of laughter.

16. The purpose of the first paragraph is to

(A) describe the physical features of laughter

(B) list the causes of laughter

(C) urge people to laugh more

(D) propose a plan for developing muscular control

(E) analyze the damaging effects of laughter on the central nervous system

17. In lines 22–25, the author uses the example of blind and deaf infants to make the point that

(A) laughter has salubrious physical effects

(B) all children love to laugh

(C) the ability to laugh is inborn, not acquired

(D) sighted and hearing children laugh at different things and in different ways than do blind and deaf children

(E) laughter is a socializing event, drawing people together

Go on to next page

18. Which of the following is the best rewording of the author's explanation of Darwin's *Principle of Antithesis* in this context?

(A) Children learn more quickly than do adults.

(B) Children communicate contentment to condition adults to distinguish between children's pleasure and displeasure.

(C) Adults are unable to understand or communicate with infants.

(D) Younger parents are better able to communicate with their infants than are older parents.

(E) Children have different concepts of what is funny than do adults.

19. According to the passage, the *sed rate*

(A) increases with laughter

(B) is proportionally related to heartbeat and pulse rate

(C) is associated with the body's level of infection

(D) stimulates the laughter response

(E) increases the level of circulatory catecholamines

20. In line 50, you may infer that "placebo effect" means something that is

(A) stationary

(B) toxic

(C) inflammatory

(D) outdated

(E) beneficial

21. The best title for this passage might be

(A) How to Develop a Sense of Humor

(B) Why We Laugh

(C) Cultural Differences in Humor

(D) The Physical and Emotional Effects of Laughter

(E) Laughter: America's Favorite Medicine

Questions 22–30 are based on the following passage.

There is much concern nationwide about air quality. The following is from a 1985 report by the Tennessee Valley Authority.

Sulfur dioxide, a colorless and odorless gas in typical outdoor concentrations, is formed naturally through biological decay and volcanic eruptions. Natural background levels are intensified by man-made emissions from fossil-fueled power plants, industrial and commercial boilers, ore smelters, cement plants, and petroleum refineries.

When a blanket of pollution enveloped the Meuse Valley, Belgium in 1933, 60 people died and 6,000 people became ill. When similar events occurred in Donora, Pennsylvania in 1948 and London, England in 1952, the scientific community was forced to locate and identify a culprit. During these incidents, the estimated excessive concentrations of sulfur dioxide and particulate matter (many times greater than today's standards) made them obvious choices as the problem pollutants.

Sulfur dioxide becomes most dangerous to people when, clinging to small particulates, it is carried into the lungs. When this happens, as it did in the deadly incidents of the mid-1900s, it may kill or incapacitate sensitive individuals such as the very young or very old or those with serious preexisting heart or lung problems. It can also cause increased illness in normally healthy people.

Particulates are small liquid droplets or solid particles of airborne "dust," which range in size from those visible as soot or smoke to those too small to be seen without a high powered microscope. The health effects of particulates depend on their size and composition. The larger particulates are usually filtered out in the nose and throat and rapidly cleared from the body. Smaller particles may be carried deeper into the lungs. Particles reaching sensitive deep lung areas are considered relatively more important for health purposes. Particle composition is also important because some compounds are relatively harmless whereas others — such as asbestos and beryllium — can result in serious health problems. Welfare effects caused by particulates have to do with soiling clothes and surfaces, and in combination with some gases, such as sulfur dioxide, corroding materials.

Go on to next page

Acid rain, or more accurately, acidic deposition (which refers to both wet and dry deposition of acidifying compounds), is one of the most controversial and important environmental issues of the day. It is the subject of both international concern and worldwide research.

Acidity is measured using a logarithmic scale of 0 to 14 called the pH scale. On this scale, a neutral substance has a pH of 7. An acidic substance, like vinegar, has a pH value less than 7. An alkaline or basic substance, like baking soda, has a pH value higher than 7. Theoretically, pure rainfall has a pH of 5.6 and is acidic because the water has combined with carbon dioxide in the air to form weak carbonic acid. Rain with a lower pH than 5.6 is called acid rain.

There is no reliable way to estimate what the acidity of rainfall may have been at various times and places throughout history. Preserved as ice in glaciers, arctic snows that fell in the 1800s were generally above pH 5, and some in Greenland even range from 6 to 7.6. Because of the remote location, however, these values might not be typical, and because snow and rain form by different processes and at different temperatures, values for rain and snow may not be directly comparable.

Recent evidence suggests that natural rain (in the absence of man-made pollution) is several times more acidic than previously thought. In several remote areas of the globe, rainfall pHs of 4.5 to 5.0 are routinely encountered. Some scientists suggest that these low pH values indicate the global extent of the acid rain problem.

In some areas, there have been fishkills associated with acidic stream runoff following heavy rains. If the water in the streams, rivers, and lakes becomes too acidic, fish cannot survive. Spring snowmelt or heavy rain may abruptly change the water acidity level. Scientists are also studying the effects of acid rain on crops, plants and land animals. For sensitive environments, an increase in the acidity of rainfall could be very serious. However, it would be unwise to investigate every aspect of acid rain before action is taken. Clearly something must be done.

22. According to the passage, the dangers of sulfur dioxide increase when

(A) biological decay occurs

(B) pollution laws are rescinded

(C) particulates carry it into the lungs

(D) acid rain increases

(E) drought conditions exist for extended periods of time

23. With which of the following would the author *disagree*?

I. Sulfur dioxide rarely harms normally healthy people, adversely affecting only the ill.

II. Particulates' effects depend on their sizes.

III. If man-made emissions were to cease worldwide, there would be no danger from harmful particulates.

(A) II only

(B) III only

(C) I and II only

(D) I and III only

(E) I, II, and III

24. Which of the following does the author list as a means of controlling the harmful effects of particulates?

(A) crop rotation

(B) body filters

(C) forest fires

(D) increased vigilance

(E) decreased cattle grazing

25. In line 44, the author uses the word "welfare" to mean

(A) charity

(B) condition

(C) poverty

(D) hopelessness

(E) subsistence payments

26. It can be inferred from the passage that the highest pH for snows that fell in Greenland in the 1800s was

(A) alkaline

(B) neutral

(C) acidic

(D) variable

(E) dangerous

Go on to next page

27. The author gives the same information about which of the following in his discussion of sulfur dioxide, particulates, and acid rain?

(A) the solution to the problem

(B) the leading scientists working on the problem

(C) the economic repercussions of the problem

(D) examples of difficulties caused by each

(E) the number of deaths attributable to the problem

28. By stating in lines 79–81, "Some scientists suggest that these low pH values indicate the global extent of the acid rain problem," the author

(A) indicates that there may be disagreement on the point

(B) denigrates as scaremongers those scientists who are attempting to frighten us

(C) lampoons the scientists who claim that acid rain is a theory, not a fact

(D) predicts that global warming is finally coming under control

(E) proves that global warming is the most serious consequence of acid rain

29. The rest of the last paragraph of this passage most likely would discuss which of the following?

(A) the steps to take to decrease acid rain

(B) the importance of swift action on the problems

(C) the economic difficulties of implementing acid rain controls

(D) the programs that have already been attempted and have failed to decrease acid rain

(E) the folly of being too hasty in enacting stringent antipollution laws

30. Which of the following is the primary focus of the passage?

(A) the number of people killed by sulfur dioxide

(B) the harmful effects of sulfur dioxide and acid rain

(C) how chemistry is destroying the planet

(D) the benefits of clean air

(E) why stronger antipollution laws are needed

STOP

DO NOT TURN THE PAGE UNTIL TOLD TO DO SO.
DO NOT RETURN TO A PREVIOUS TEST.

Section 4

Time: 30 Minutes

25 Questions

Directions: Solve each problem. Blacken the corresponding oval on the answer grid.

Notes:

* You may use a calculator.
* All numbers used in this exam are real numbers.
* All figures lie in a plane.
* All figures may be assumed to be to scale unless the problem specifically indicates otherwise.

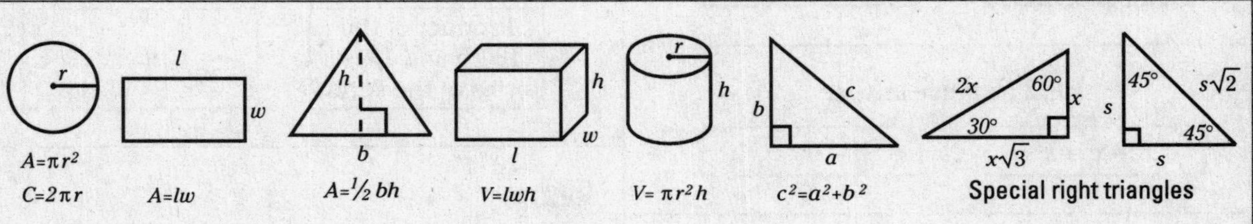

There are 360 degrees of arc in a circle.

There are 180 degrees in a straight angle.

There are 180 degrees in the sum of the interior angles of a triangle.

Directions for Quantitative Comparison questions:

Questions 1–15 feature two columns with a quantity in each. Compare the quantities and choose

A if the quantity in Column A is greater

B if the quantity in Column B is greater

C if the two quantities are equal

D if the relationship cannot be determined from the information given

AN E RESPONSE WILL NOT BE SCORED

General information:

A letter (*a, b, c,* or *x, y, z*) or symbol means the same thing throughout one problem but may not be the same in different problems.

Information that is centered between two columns applies to both columns in that problem.

Examples:

	Column A	Column B	Sample ovals
1.	2^3	4	● Ⓑ Ⓒ Ⓓ Ⓔ

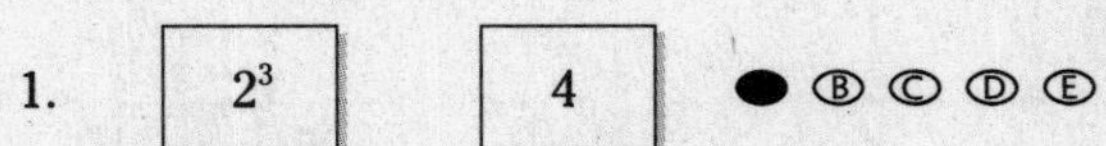

	Column A	Column B	Sample ovals
2.	$x°$	45°	Ⓐ Ⓑ Ⓒ ● Ⓔ

3. $3x + y = 3x$

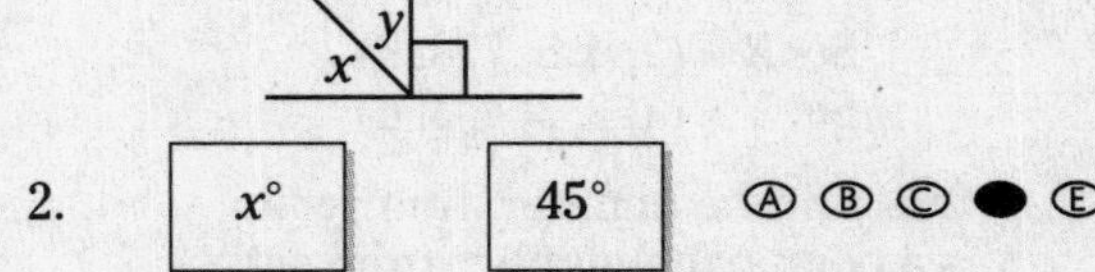

	Column A	Column B	Sample ovals
	0	y	Ⓐ Ⓑ ● Ⓓ Ⓔ

Go on to next page

	Column A	Column B
1.	$10 \geq a \geq 5$ $ab = 55$	
	b	5
2.	When a jar contains 5,000 marbles, it is half full.	
	Capacity of jar	2,500 marbles
3.	$x \neq 0$	
	$1/x$	x
4.	x is a negative integer	
	$x^2 + x^3 + x^4$	0
5.	Perimeter of a square of side R	Area of a square of side R

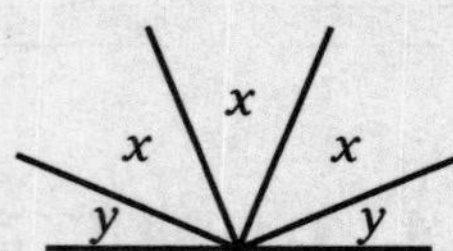

	Column A	Column B
6.	$x = 2y$	
	y	25
7.	Set X = (2, 4, 6, 7, 8, 9) Set Y = (1, 2, 3, 4, 5, 6) x is a prime number from set X y is a composite number from set Y	
	The greatest possible value of $x + y$	13
8.	$11/15 + 17/23 + 28/29$	$5/18 + 9/25 + 21/50$
9.	The test scores of a group of five students are 72, 70, 68, 75, 80	
	The median test score	73
10.	–3, –2, –1, 0, –3, –2, –1, 0 . . . The sequence repeats as shown.	
	Product of the 100th and 101st terms of the series	0
11.	$x > 1$	
	$x^8 \cdot x^{-8}$	$8 \cdot x^8$
12.	The psychiatry lab is 200 yards from the gym, which is 600 yards from the parking lot.	
	Distance from the lab to the parking lot	800 yards
13.	Surface area of a cube of edge 5 units	150 square units
14.	$3m + 2n = 13$; $2n + 6m = 22$	
	m	n
15.	$\boxed{A} = (3A)^3 + A/3$	
	$\boxed{1/3}$	4

Go on to next page

Directions for student-produced responses: Questions 16–25 require you to solve the problem and then blacken the oval corresponding to the answer, as shown in the following example.

Example: Note the fraction line and decimal points.

Answer: 7/2

Answer: 3.25

Answer: 853

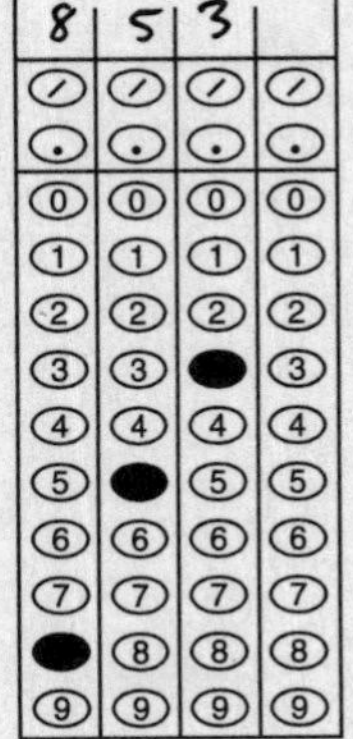

Write your answer in the box. You may start your answer in any column.

- Although you do not *have* to write the solutions in the boxes, you *do* have to blacken the corresponding ovals. It is strongly suggested that you fill in the boxes to prevent confusion. *Only the blackened ovals, however, will be scored.* The numbers in the boxes will not be read.
- There are no negative answers.
- Mixed numbers, such as 3½, may be gridded in as a decimal (3.5) or as a fraction (7/2). Do *not* grid in 3½; it will be read as 31/2.
- Grid in a decimal as far as possible; do not round it. If your answer is $.\overline{33}$, for example, fill in as many 3s as you have spaces for. Do *not* round down to .33 or .3 unless the problem specifically tells you to do so.
- A question may have more than one answer; grid in only one.

16. Roses cost $45 a dozen — three times as much as carnations. If Flora wants to buy two dozen carnations and three dozen roses, how much will she have to spend? (Disregard the dollar sign when gridding in your answer.)

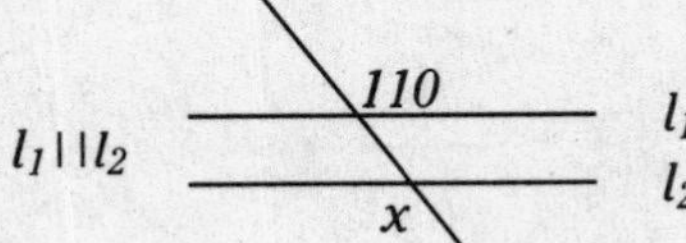

17. What is the number of degrees in angle *x*?

Go on to next page

18. $(a + b)^2 = 36$. If $ab = 4$, how much is $a^2 + b^2$?

19. From the beginning to the end of 1990, the price of a rare book rose 20%. In 1991, it dropped 25%. In 1992, it rose 20%. What percent of 1990's starting price is 1992's price?

20. A pair of fair, six-sided dice is rolled. The probability that the sum of the numbers on the faces up is 12 is what percent less than the probability that the sum of the faces up is 2?

21. The ages of children at a party are 5, 6, 6, 9, 5, 8, 7, 7, 9, 6, 5, 6, 6, 10, and 6. Let A stand for the median of their ages, and a for the mode of their ages. What is $A - a$?

Go on to next page

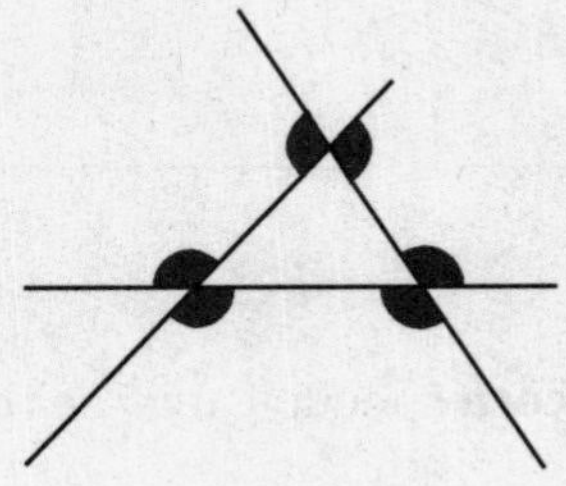

22. What is the sum of the degree measures of the shaded angles? (Ignore the degree sign when gridding in your answer.)

23. n, o, p, q, and r are integers in a sequence. $n = 4$, $o = 11$. The sequence is formed by doubling the last term and then adding that result to one less than the second-to-last term. For example, p would be 25 because $11 \times 2 = 22$; $22 + 3 = 25$. What is the value of r?

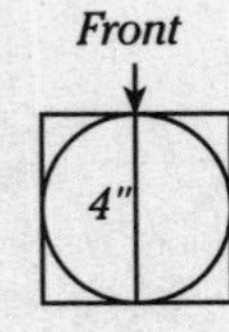

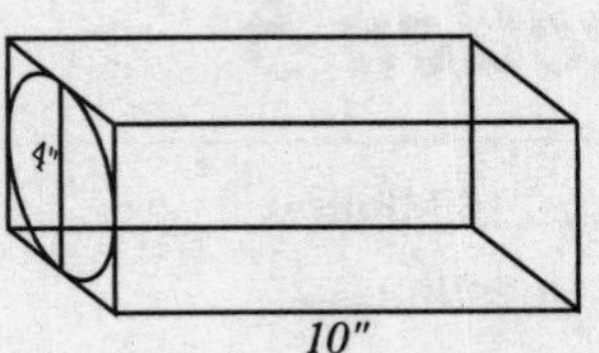

24. Abe is going to whittle a rectangular piece of wood down to make a dowel (a cylindrical rod). The diameter of the dowel will not change. What amount of wood, in cubic inches, will be removed from the piece of lumber to make the dowel? (Use 3.14 for π.)

25. What is the smallest positive integer that results in an integer when its square is divided by ½ of the original integer?

DO NOT TURN THE PAGE UNTIL TOLD TO DO SO.
DO NOT RETURN TO A PREVIOUS TEST.

Section 5

Time: 15 Minutes

13 Questions

Directions: Choose the *best* answer to each question. Blacken the corresponding oval on the answer grid.

Answer the questions following the pair of passages below based on information stated or implied in the passages and in the introductory material. Questions are based on the content of the passage and on the relationship between the pair of passages.

Questions 1–13 are based on the following passages.

Passage 1 is adapted from a guide used by teachers to develop a program to teach children about the environment. Passage 2 is from a 1985 Bureau of Land Management article on the Cleveland-Lloyd Dinosaur quarry.

Passage 1

Plants and animals are found in a wide variety of environments. Certain factors limit where each of these organisms can live. Possible limiting factors are temperature, light conditions, water conditions, content of atmospheric gases, availability of nutrients and minerals, soil conditions, fire conditions, and currents and pressures. The degree of influence each factor has may well depend on whether a terrestrial, marine, or freshwater environment is involved.

Each species has its own minimum requirements. Some plants and animals have a wider range of tolerance; they may be found over a broader geographical area and may also be more resistant to environmental changes. If you are trying to identify the factors that limit a particular species, this may be easiest at the margin, or edge, of its geographical range. Thus, if environmental conditions change — for example, an extremely cold winter, a very dry season, an increase in water salinity — you can study directly the effects of these factors upon the organism and can determine whether the factors are limiting.

Some organisms require different environmental conditions during different phases of their life cycle. For example, the eggs or larvae of animal species may be far more sensitive to changes than the adult organisms are.

Scientists believe that, in the long run, only one species can occupy a specific niche or play a specific role in the ecological community. If two species compete for one role, one will eventually be driven out. This does not mean that very similar species — among birds, for example — cannot occupy very similar niches. Interestingly enough, scientists have found that different species occupy nearly identical niches in ecological communities in different parts of the world. These species, which have developed to perform certain functions in the ecological community they belong to, are called "ecological equivalents."

General ecologic concepts help you to understand why organisms live where they do and how they interact with other organisms around them. If we recognize the environmental conditions that promote stability and productivity for different species, we can then protect or use natural resources in a way that will minimize man's adverse effects on ecological relationships.

Passage 2

When the bones of many large animals are found concentrated in great graveyards, the question of how they died and were gathered together comes naturally to mind. Did the animals congregate of their own free will and die peacefully of old age, as the elephants of Africa were once thought to do? Did they die one at a time over many years or decades, or did they perish all at once, huddled together in the face of a sudden deadly natural catastrophe? Were they drawn to their doom because something attracted them in an irresistible way, cowing them into submission? Were they trapped as groups or as individuals by something they unsuspectingly blundered into like rabbits into snares? Finally, did they actually die on the spot, or were they scattered here and there to have their remains picked up and carried to a central locality by some natural agent, such as a flood of water?

Go on to next page

Each of the possibilities appears to be represented somewhere in the fossil record. Only occasionally does enough evidence exist to give definite answers to the problem of natural concentrations such as that of the Cleveland-Lloyd Quarry. Because we have no eyewitnesses and only indirect evidence about what went on in the distant past, all we can do is speculate within the framework of what can be observed. What follows is merely one man's opinion.

The simple facts are these. Dinosaurs of all but the very smallest size (youngest) are represented. Many more carnivorous types and individuals are represented than are herbivores. The bones are separated and mingled together, but individual bones are not broken, gnawed, or visibly weathered. The bones are buried in the clayey, water-deposited sediments associated with fresh-water organisms.

Putting these facts together, a first conclusion must be that this graveyard has something to do with water. Either the dinosaurs died on the surface and were covered immediately by water-deposited mud or they sank into the mud after it was deposited but while it was still very soft and at the surface. Because the bones are not distributed in distinct layers, are not spread very widely, and show little evidence of having been exposed on the surface, I conclude that the dinosaurs sank into the sediment so that it enclosed them instead of being deposited on top of them.

Objections to this theory come to mind. If the dinosaurs sank one by one into the mud, why didn't they remain intact or at least show less scattering of the bones? My answer is that, as the bodies inevitably decayed, the bones were released and dispersed by the internal movement of the bog. Bogs slowly bubble and boil due to the circulation of water rising into them. It is worth pointing out that this is not strictly a quicksand situation. The matrix is clay and limestone with no sand whatsoever. But the action of quicksand does tell us one thing that helps our memory: Animals may easily be trapped and sink out of sight in sediment that has already been deposited.

1. From passage 1, you may infer that a marine environment

(A) leads to quick plant deterioration

(B) can be found in the Northern hemisphere only

(C) severely limits the availability of nutrients and minerals for animals

(D) is neither terrestrial nor freshwater

(E) encourages natural gas formation

2. The author would most likely agree that which of the following is true of a species whose members are widely scattered?

I. It has a high tolerance for limiting factors.

II. It has few natural enemies.

III. It is resistant to environmental change.

IV. It is capable of surviving in both marine and freshwater environments.

(A) I only

(B) III only

(C) I and III only

(D) I, II and III only

(E) I, II, III and IV

3. The author cites which of the following as a factor that contributes to the difficulty of identifying the cause of a decrease in the number of members of a species?

(A) Predators may prey upon the very young.

(B) Species may cover a broad geographical area.

(C) Species may adapt from a terrestrial to a marine environment.

(D) The salinity and turbidity of water may suddenly change.

(E) It may be necessary to examine all the stages of the life cycle of the organism.

Go on to next page

4. Using the author's reasoning as demonstrated in passage 1, which of the following would most likely be ecological equivalents?

(A) bottomfeeders and scavengers

(B) vultures and robins

(C) cockroaches and butterflies

(D) goats and tigers

(E) humans and elephants

5. The author presents the information that appears in lines 45–49 of passage 1

(A) to criticize man for his waste of resources

(B) to encourage man to learn how to reduce his negative impact on the environment

(C) to explain why certain species become extinct

(D) to predict animal migration patterns

(E) to compare ecological equivalents

6. The author of passage 2 would most probably consider the theory that the dinosaurs became extinct as a result of a large meteor hitting Earth as

(A) improbable given that water was involved

(B) a far-fetched hypothesis

(C) a proven theory

(D) something on which scientists cannot speculate

(E) a possible explanation

7. In line 61, the word "cowing" most nearly means

(A) grazing

(B) galloping

(C) cannibalizing

(D) intimidating

(E) confusing

8. The author of passage 2 would accept as proven which of the following?

(A) All dinosaurs perished at approximately the same time.

(B) Dinosaurs were more frequently carnivorous than herbivorous.

(C) Natural sites attracted dinosaurs who knew they were going to die.

(D) A great flood caused the extinction of dinosaurs.

(E) None of the above

9. The author concludes in lines 86–92 that the graveyards were around water

(A) because of the sediment in which the bones were buried

(B) because the earliest dinosaurs were amphibious

(C) because the bones were not weathered

(D) because the bones were found in several strata or layers

(E) because the youngest dinosaurs' bones are absent

10. The best title for passage 2 may be

(A) What Dinosaurs Tell Us

(B) A Theory of the Causes of the Extinction of Dinosaurs

(C) One Man's Search for Dinosaurs

(D) Bogs and Other Burial Sites

(E) Dinosaurs' Effects on Their Environment

11. Which of the following best describes the attitude of the author of passage 2?

(A) sanctimonious

(B) improbable

(C) expository

(D) enigmatic

(E) huffy

Go on to next page

12. One primary difference between passage 1 and passage 2 is

(A) passage 1 discusses marine mammals; passage 2 discusses land mammals

(B) passage 1 encourages a course of action; passage 2 supports a hypothesis

(C) passage 1 is based on opinion that is refuted by facts in passage 2

(D) the theory in passage 2 is based upon the facts discussed in passage 1

(E) passage 1 is correct; passage 2 is full of errors

13. The authors of both passages would most likely agree with which of the following?

(A) Environment contributes to the life and death of animal species.

(B) Large animals are less prone to extinction than are small animals.

(C) A species' life span is directly influenced by its geographical range.

(D) Fresh water availability is the primary influence on animals' migratory patterns.

(E) Species may be distinguished by their contact with man.

STOP DO NOT TURN THE PAGE UNTIL TOLD TO DO SO. DO NOT RETURN TO A PREVIOUS TEST.

Section 6

Time: 15 Minutes

10 Questions

Directions: Solve each problem. Blacken the corresponding oval on the answer grid.

Notes:

* You may use a calculator.
* All numbers used in this exam are real numbers.
* All figures lie in a plane.
* All figures may be assumed to be to scale unless the problem specifically indicates otherwise.

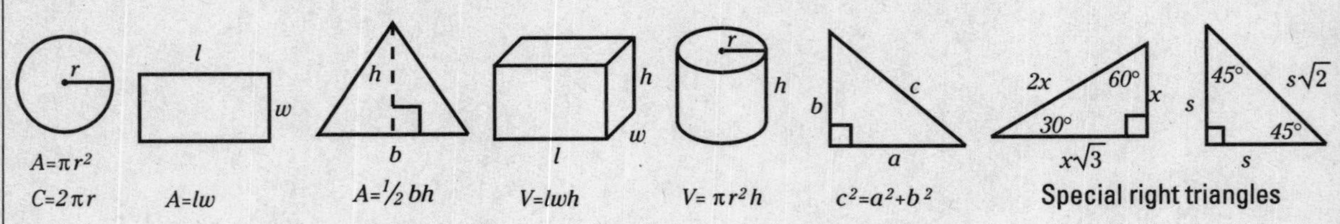

There are 360 degrees of arc in a circle.

There are 180 degrees in a straight angle.

There are 180 degrees in the sum of the interior angles of a triangle.

1. The square root of which of the following is equal to 50% of the original number?

(A) 64

(B) 49

(C) 25

(D) 16

(E) 4

$$x^2 + x^2 + x^2 > x^6$$

2. x could be which of the following?

I. ½

II. 0

III. 1

(A) I only

(B) II only

(C) III only

(D) I and III only

(E) I, II, and III only

Go on to next page

3. The sum of four consecutive odd integers is 32. What is the difference between the greatest and the least of these integers?

(A) 10

(B) 9

(C) 7

(D) 6

(E) 5

Questions 4 and 5 are based on the following chart, which represents the number of points cafeteria workers get in their quest to be the worker of the month.

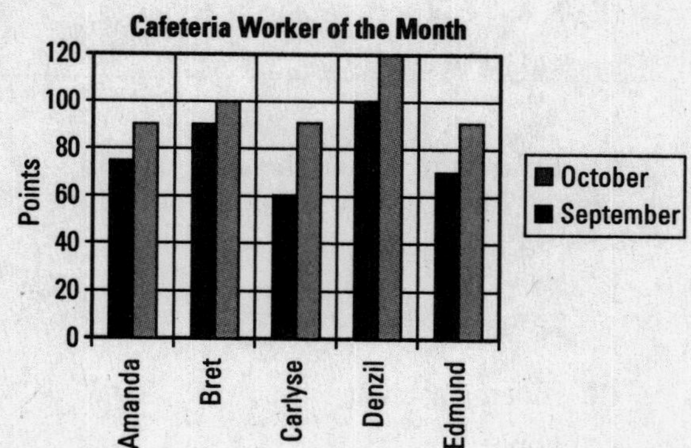

4. Which of the five workers has had the greatest percentage increase in points from September to October?

(A) Amanda

(B) Bret

(C) Carlyse

(D) Denzil

(E) Edmund

5. In November, the number of points Denzil earned drops 25% from his October point total. The November point total is what percent of his original (September) point total?

(A) 95

(B) 90

(C) 80

(D) 75

(E) 70

6. A circle is divided into 8 equal sectors. If the area of one sector is 8π, what is the circumference of the circle?

(A) 4π

(B) 8π

(C) 16π

(D) 64π

(E) 88π

Go on to next page

7. Rachel and Shayna are looking at a shelf of 84 books at the library. The difference between the number of books that they look at and put back and the number of books that they look at and check out is 20. How many books did they put back? (They put back more books than they took out.)

(A) 24

(B) 32

(C) 35

(D) 52

(E) 64

A B

10

D C

8. Which of the following represents the area of the shaded region around the circle with diameter *BC*?

(A) $100\pi - 100$

(B) $100\pi - 50$

(C) $50 - 50\pi$

(D) $50 - 25\pi$

(E) $50 - 12.5\pi$

Questions 9 and 10 refer to the following diagram.

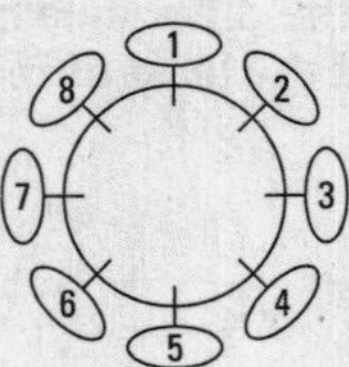

The diagram above represents a circular table with 8 equally spaced chairs labeled 1 through 8. Five diners — A, B, C, D, and E — will each sit in one of the chairs, with the following restrictions:

* B will sit next to A.
* C will sit directly opposite B.
* There will be exactly one chair between C and D.
* A will sit in seat 5.
* Three chairs will remain empty.

9. If the diners sit at the table so that there is no empty chair between any two of them, the empty chairs could be which of the following?

(A) 1, 2, 7

(B) 1, 3, 6

(C) 1, 7, 8

(D) 2, 3, 7

(E) 3, 6, 7

10. If E sits next to and to the right of A, E may sit directly across from which of the following?

I. C

II. D

III. An empty chair

(A) I only

(B) II only

(C) III only

(D) II and III

(E) I, II, and III

STOP

DO NOT TURN THE PAGE UNTIL TOLD TO DO SO.
DO NOT RETURN TO A PREVIOUS TEST.

Answer Key for Practice Exam 1

Section 1	Section 2	Section 3	Section 4	Section 5	Section 6
1. D	1. D	1. E	1. A	1. D	1. E
2. A	2. B	2. C	2. A	2. C	2. D
3. D	3. B	3. D	3. D	3. E	3. D
4. B	4. B	4. A	4. A	4. A	4. C
5. A	5. B	5. C	5. D	5. B	5. B
6. C	6. D	6. D	6. B	6. E	6. C
7. B	7. E	7. B	7. C	7. D	7. D
8. B	8. D	8. A	8. A	8. E	8. E
9. A	9. C	9. D	9. B	9. A	9. C
10. E	10. E	10. E	10. C	10. B	10. C
11. B	11. A	11. A	11. B	11. C	
12. B	12. E	12. E	12. D	12. B	
13. A	13. C	13. C	13. C	13. A	
14. E	14. B	14. D	14. A		
15. E	15. A	15. B	15. B		
16. E	16. C	16. A	16. 165		
17. C	17. D	17. C	17. 110		
18. D	18. C	18. B	18. 28		
19. C	19. E	19. C	19. 108		
20. E	20. D	20. E	20. 0		
21. E	21. D	21. D	21. 0		
22. A	22. B	22. C	22. 720		
23. E	23. C	23. D	23. 144		
24. D	24. B	24. B	24. 34.40		
25. B	25. E	25. B	25. 1		
26. A		26. A			
27. C		27. D			
28. C		28. A			
29. B		29. B			
30. D		30. B			
31. E					
32. A					
33. E					
34. C					
35. C					

Scoring Your Exam

For both verbal and math, you have two scores. The Raw Score is in double digits (53 or 21, for example); the Converted Score is in triple digits (690 or 350, for example). You have to do the math to get the Raw Score, find your Raw Score on the chart, and then locate the Converted Score. Before you begin calculating your scores, compare the answers you recorded on your answer sheet with the answer key. You may want to use these codes:

- Mark each answer you get right with a check mark (✔).
- Mark each answer you skip with a zero (0).
- Mark each answer you get wrong with an X.

Scoring verbal sections

All the verbal questions are multiple choice, with five answer choices. To score verbal sections 1, 3, and 5, follow these steps:

1. **In the worksheet below, write the total number of correct answers in Line 1.**
2. **Multiply the total number of incorrect answers in sections 1, 3, and 5 by ¼ and write that total (even if it's a fraction) in Line 2.**
3. **Subtract the number in Line 2 from the number in Line 1 and write that number on Line 3.**

   That's your total raw score for the verbal section of the test.

Verbal Raw Score Worksheet
Sections 1, 3, and 5

1. Total number of correct answers in Sections 1, 3, and 5 ______ 1

2. Total number of incorrect answers in Sections 1, 3, and 5______x ¼ – ______ 2

3. Total Verbal Raw Score ______ 3

Finding your converted ("final") verbal score

Your Raw Score is the ugly duckling that turns into a swan when you look at the Conversion Table. Find your Raw Score on the left and then find your corresponding Converted Score on the right. That Converted Score is what people mean when they talk about their SAT scores.

SAT Verbal Conversion Table

Raw	*SAT*	*Raw*	*SAT*	*Raw*	*SAT*
78	800	50	580	22	430
77	800	49	580	21	420
76	800	48	570	20	410
75	800	47	570	19	410
74	790	46	560	18	400
73	780	45	560	17	390
72	760	44	550	16	390
71	750	43	540	15	380
70	740	42	540	14	370
69	730	41	540	13	360
68	720	40	530	12	360
67	710	39	520	11	350
66	700	38	520	10	340
65	690	37	510	9	330
64	680	36	510	8	320
63	670	35	500	7	310
62	660	34	500	6	300
61	650	33	490	5	290
60	650	32	490	4	280
59	640	31	480	3	270
58	630	30	470	2	260
57	620	29	470	1	240
56	620	28	460	0	230
55	610	27	460	–1	220
54	610	26	450	–2	200
53	600	25	440	and below	200
52	600	24	440		
51	590	23	430		

Scoring math sections 2, 4, and 6

The math is a little more complicated to score than the verbal because you have three different types of questions. The questions in Sections 2 and 6 are multiple choice and are scored the same way as the multiple choice verbal questions: You get one point for every correct answer, you lose ¼ for every wrong answer, and omitted answers don't count for or against you.

However, scoring the questions in Section 4 is different. Fifteen of the questions are Quantitative Comparisons — with only four possible answers. For these, you still get one point for every right answer and no points for an omitted answer, but you lose ⅓ of a point (rather than ¼ of a point) for a wrong answer.

Finally, ten of the questions are grid-ins — with no answer choices. You have good news on these. You get one point for every right answer, no points for every omitted answer, but you do not lose any points for a wrong answer. (This is the only style question on the whole SAT that is penalty-free.)

Confused? It's easier than it sounds. Just follow these steps:

1. **In the worksheet below, write the total number of correct answers for sections 2 and 6 in Line 1.**
2. **Multiply the total number of incorrect answers in section 2 and 6 by ¼ and write that total (even if it's a fraction) in Line 2.**
3. **Subtract the number in Line 2 from the number in Line 1 and write that number in Line 3.**
4. **Write the total number of correct answers for questions 1–15 from section 4 in Line 4.**
5. **Multiply the total number of incorrect answers for questions 1–15 from section 4 by ⅓ and write that total (even if it's a fraction) in Line 5.**
6. **Subtract the number in Line 5 from the number in Line 4 and write that number in Line 6.**
7. **Write the total number of correct answers for questions 16–25 from section 4 in Line 7.**
8. **Add the numbers in Lines 3, 6, and 7 and write that number in Line 8.**

   That's your total raw score for the math section of the test.

Math Raw Score Worksheet
Sections 2, 4, and 6

1. Total number of correct answers in Sections 2 and 6		_____ 1
2. Total number of incorrect answers in Sections 2 and 6_____x ¼	–	_____ 2
3. Subtotal in Sections 2 and 6 (Step 1 minus Step 2)		_____ 3
4. Total number of correct answers in questions 1–15 in Section 4		_____ 4
5. Total number of incorrect answers in Sections 2 and 6_____x ⅓	–	_____ 5
6. Subtotal from questions 1–15 (Step 1 minus Step 2)		_____ 6
7. Total number of correct answers in questions 16-25 in Section 4		_____ 7
8. Total Math Raw Score (Add lines 3, 6, and 7)		_____ 8

Finding your converted ("final") math score

You're finally ready to look up your 200–800 math score in the conversion table. Find your Raw Score on the left, and then find your corresponding Converted Score on the right. That Converted Score is what people mean when they talk about their SAT scores.

SAT Math Conversion Table

Raw	SAT	Raw	SAT	Raw	SAT
60	800	38	570	16	410
59	790	37	560	15	410
58	770	36	550	14	400
57	750	35	540	13	390
56	730	34	530	12	380
55	720	33	530	11	370
54	700	32	520	10	370
53	690	31	520	9	360
52	680	30	510	8	350
51	670	29	500	7	340
50	660	28	500	6	320
49	650	27	490	5	310
48	650	26	480	4	300
47	640	25	480	3	280
46	630	24	470	2	270
45	620	23	460	1	250
44	610	22	460	0	230
43	600	21	450	–1	210
42	600	20	440	–2	200
41	590	19	440	and below	200
40	580	18	430		
39	570	17	420		

Chapter 18

Practice Exam 1: Answers and Explanations

The following are the answers to the questions found in Chapter 17. Don't forget — any words marked ***like this*** are vocabulary words to add to your vocabulary list.

Section 1

1. **D.** If the picture swept the Academy Awards, it was very highly thought of. Therefore, the filmmaker would not be surprised by the praise or ***accolades*** he received.

   If you don't know the meaning of a word, the answer is probably too hard for question number one. (Questions go from easier to harder in a section.)

2. **A.** Predict that you're looking for a positive word, something good (eliminating *despair*). ***Renown*** means fame. The first woman to achieve such an impressive accomplishment is famous. Bemusement means confusion. While ***glee,*** meaning joy or happiness, is positive, it doesn't fit the sentence logically (Ms. King herself might be gleeful, or happy, but doesn't "gather national happiness.") ***Vituperation*** means criticism or hasty speech and is just the opposite of what the sentence calls for.

3. **D.** You can predict that insects are capable of suffering from viruses. Eliminate choices A and E, which state just the opposite. Choice C makes no sense: You don't integrate an insect into a virus! A virus can go into an insect, not vice versa. Choice B is also illogical. To ***enhance*** is to improve, to make better. If a scientist is developing a pesticide, it is to kill insects, not to improve or enhance them.

4. **B.** If the letter has been around since 1300 B.C., predict that you're looking for an answer like old or aged or ancient.

   Often you can predict what type of word fits the blank. After you've found it, however, be sure to reread the entire sentence with both words inserted, so you don't fall for a cheesy trick of one word that fits but a second that doesn't. (***Bonus trivia:*** The longest alphabet is Cambodian, which has 74 letters compared to 26 in the English alphabet.)

5. **A.** The sentence itself is simple enough. Predict that the judge was really hard-nosed, very strict. The problem now is the difficult vocabulary. Use roots to narrow down the choices. Eliminate benign, based on the root "ben" which means good. (A ***benign*** tumor is a "good" tumor, at least better than a "malignant" tumor.) If you know that *crypt* means secret or mysterious, you can eliminate ***cryptic.*** The judge was well-known, not at all mysterious. That narrows the choices down to three.

   Impetuous means hasty, rash. You're impetuous if you meet someone at a rock concert this Friday and marry him on Saturday. (This honestly happened to my best friend in high school. The marriage lasted about three months.) ***Redoubtable*** means awesome, fearsome, formidable. (Do you speak French? A redoubt is a fortress, a stronghold.) The right answer, dogmatic, is based on the word dogma. Dogma are rules. A ***dogmatic*** judge or lawyer follows the rules.

Bonus: Speaking of lawyers, here's my favorite lawyer joke: Know why they bury lawyers 12 feet under, instead of 6?

Because deep down, they're all nice guys!

6. **C.** Predict positive or negative. Both words must be negative because the sentence begins with "although" and ends with a positive thought. Eliminate choices A (rational), B (plausible) and E (praised) as having positive words. While the first word in choice D works, the second is not logical: All theories are, by nature, hypothetical.

7. **B.** A ***faction*** is a splinter group, a small group that has split off from the larger group (*fac* means break or part). To ***secede from*** is to leave or break off from (*se-* means apart or away from). ***Unorthodox*** means unconventional, not conforming to normal doctrine. ***Docile*** means tame, submissive. ***Heretical*** means unorthodox. ***Dogmatic*** means opinionated, narrow-minded. (When I used to argue with my dad, I'd tell him he was close-minded. He'd always respond, "Better than being so open-minded your brains fall out!")

Always be sure to check *both* blanks; often more than one answer choice can work in one of the two blanks. Here, answers A and B work for the first blank, and B, C, and D work for the second blank, but only B works for both blanks.

8. **B.** A ***mentor*** is a teacher or an advisor, one who takes you under his wing to help. (The original Mentor, with a capital M, was a character in Greek mythology. He was the teacher of the hero Odysseus.) A ***sentry*** is a guard. An ***acolyte*** is a follower, a disciple. A ***pedant*** is a teacher (you may know this word in its more common form, pedantic, meaning overly teacherly or fussy.) A ***sycophant*** is a servile flatterer, a kiss-up, a yes man.

Although the question itself was very easy, the vocabulary was extremely difficult. This would be an excellent question to skip.

9. **A.** This question is a classic example of an easy question with hard vocabulary. Remember that if everything depends on the vocab and you just plain don't know the words, skip the question. ***Crepuscular*** means active at dawn and dusk. ***Gargantuan*** means huge. ***Corpulent*** means overweight (from the same root meaning body, as corp or corpse). ***Querulous*** means complaining (don't confuse querulous with ***quarrelsome,*** which does mean to fight or quarrel). ***Indolent*** means lazy.

10. **E.** Predict that the first word is negative, because the reporter is annoyed. Unless you know ***phlegmatic*** (and most people don't — it means calm, even sluggish), you can't eliminate any answers so far. Predict that the second blank is positive, something the reporter is pressing to get. That eliminates answer A. (Who wants a repetitive answer? Reporters are looking for fresh news.) It also eliminates answer C (***lackadaisical*** means lacking spirit or interest).

If you, like most students, don't know the words in this question, skip it quickly and go on. It's the last Sentence Completion question, meaning it's supposed to be hard. No shame in skipping it.

Circumlocutious means talking in circles, beating around the bush (*circum-*= around; *loc* = speech or talk; *-ous* = full of, very). A circumlocutious answer is the opposite of a direct one. ***Redundant*** means repetitive (or did I already say that?). ***Tactless*** means without any manners or diplomacy.

My friend is very tactful. When my mom asked him to guess her age, he hesitated and then said, "I don't know whether to guess ten years younger because of your ***pulchritude*** (beauty), or ten years older because of your ***sagacity*** (wisdom)." ***Disputatious*** is full of debate, argumentative. ***Heartfelt*** is with deep feeling, sincere.

11. **B.** A punch causes, or leaves behind, a bruise. A cut causes, or leaves behind, a scar.

Choice C is backward. Laughter doesn't cause people to tickle; tickling usually causes laughter. In choice D, a ***tempest*** is a storm, just the opposite of a drought. A ***sobriquet*** is a nickname, like Sweet Cheeks or Hungry Hips. Wasn't it W.C. Fields who said that "People with cutesy nicknames should be used for food!"?

12. **B.** Use your roots on this question. ***Dehydrated*** means lacking water, desiccated (*de-* = away from). ***Impecunious*** means without money, broke (*im-* = not; *-ous* = full of).

    Brawny means having muscles, strong (think of the lumberjack on the wrapper of Brawny paper towels). ***Effervescent*** means bubbly, like soda or champagne or a hyper cheerleader. ***Graceful*** is having rhythmic beauty — unlike me. (I once had a dance partner ask me whether I'd had a rhythmectomy!)

13. **A.** A chimney funnels smoke up and out; a straw funnels liquid up and out. A basin contains water, but doesn't move it. A binder contains papers. A bowl contains ice cream. A label is on a bottle. ***Bonus trivia:*** Take a guess when ice cream was available to the general public? It was saved for royalty for a hundred years, but finally allowed in a public café in Paris in 1670.

14. **E.** Your roots will help you make the sentence here. The prefix a- means without or not; morph means shape; -ous means full of. Something ***amorphous*** is not full of shape, or shapeless. The words are synonyms. Something ***deficient*** is lacking, as in, "Your vocabulary, rather than being sufficient, is deficient, which is why you need to learn your roots." In choice A, ***atypical*** means not typical, not common. Choice B, ***amoral*** is not moral. Choice C, ab- means away from. Abstemious is a form of the more common word, abstain. To be ***abstemious*** is to do without, just the opposite of being overindulgent. ***Obstinate*** means stubborn (ob- is a root meaning block or against), the opposite of open-minded.

15. **E.** If you don't know the words, assume they are synonyms. A gymnast is ***agile*** (flexible, limber). Now the problem lies in the answer choices. A ***pacifist*** (a person in favor of peace) is not ***irascible*** (easily angered).

    A ***specter*** (ghost, spirit) is not substantial. A ***pariah*** (an outcast) is not ***gregarious*** (*greg* = group or herd; *-ous* = full of, very). If you are "full of the group," you are sociable, friendly. A ***glutton*** (a pig, an overindulger) is not ***abstemious*** (doing without). The prefix *ab* = away from; an ***abstemious*** person abstains or stays away from something. A ***charlatan*** (a fake, a fraud) is ***duplicitous*** (deceptive, tricky).

A word of encouragement: Don't despair if you don't know a lot of these words. I've planned the book this way. Sure, I can give you all words you know and stroke your ego, but that won't help you much when you get to the real exam. Or I can destroy you now and force you to learn what you don't know, thus helping you ace the exam. Any word I use in this book could show up on the SAT. However, I use all the hardest words in greater concentrations than the real SAT would. For example, I may put eight super-hard words into a question that would have only four super-hard words on the real exam. This is for your own good. Think of yourself as a batter who swings a practice bat with three or four doughnuts (weights) on it to make it heavier and more difficult to swing. By the time you pick up the real bat (or get to the real test, in your situation), things seem much easier.

16. **E.** A ***sphygmomanometer*** measures blood pressure; it's that little machine with the cuff that goes around your arm. You could figure that out from the ***-meter*** ending, which means to measure (think speedometer, odometer, pedometer, and so on). A scale measures weight.

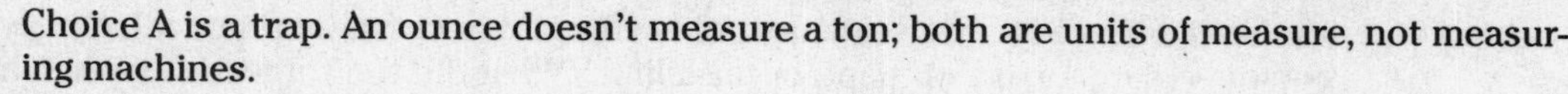

Choice A is a trap. An ounce doesn't measure a ton; both are units of measure, not measuring machines.

17. **C.** To ***exculpate*** is to "make guilt go away" (*ex-* = out of or away from; *culp* = guilt; *-ate* = to make), to remove guilt, to vindicate. To ***exterminate*** is to remove pests. To ***rumple*** is to make wrinkled, just the opposite of what you want.

Often, one of the answer choices is an exact opposite of the correct relationship. If you're totally bewildered by the vocabulary and don't have a clue, look among the answer choices for two that have opposite relationships. One of them is probably correct, and you can make a 50-50 guess.

To ***exonerate*** is to free from blame. If your incensed (burning mad) mother asks who borrowed her new car and dented the fender, you'd better have a good alibi to *exonerate* you. To ***synchronize*** is to do at the same time.

18. **D.** A ***misogynist*** is a person who hates women (*miso-*= hate; *gyn* = woman; *-ist* = a person). A ***pragmatist*** (a realist, a practical person) may not actually *hate* fantasy, but he's opposed to it. (Hey, not all the questions are totally clear-cut. Because no choice says "None of the above," you have to choose the "best" — not perfect, just the best — answer.)

    Use your common sense to eliminate A (even if you don't know what a prophet is, nobody really "hates" wisdom). In C, a witch likes and uses spells. (*Question*: Do witches run "spell" checkers?) A ***hypochondriac*** always thinks he's sick and loves medications. A ***reprobate*** is someone who has no morals. (An easy way to remember this word is to think of "re-probation." A *reprobate* is so awful that she goes to court, gets put on probation, does something awful again, and gets put on re-probation, over and over.)

19. **C.** An ***archipelago*** is a group of islands. A ***federation*** is a group of states.

    If you didn't know the word *archipelago,* you could use the tip: Assume unknown words are synonyms. Just say: "Archipelago is islands." The other answers don't quite fit: A page is a part of a book; a tap spouts water. (Know how to get rid of water on the brain? A tap on the head!) A scarf is a type of clothing; a pint is a unit of liquid measure.

    Don't automatically skip an Analogy question just because you don't know the meaning of the word. Assume unknown words are synonyms.

20. **E.** *Cupidity* is a very hard word, but think about it: Cupid is the god of what? The god of love. Now look at the question. ***Cupidity*** is excessive love, usually of money. ***Gluttony*** is the love of food (a glutton is a pig, one who overindulges).

    Acclaim is praise (you always hear the expression "the critically *acclaimed* movie"). ***Zeal*** is enthusiasm; ***lethargy*** is laziness, languor. ***Taciturnity*** is being silent or not talkative; *-ity* just makes a word into a noun. ***Discourse*** is conversation. ***Philanthropy*** is generosity. (*phil-* = love; *anthro* = human; *-ity* makes a word a noun. One who loves fellow human beings is often generous or philanthropic.)

21. **E.** The purpose of an ***embargo*** (which comes from the same root as bar or barricade) is to block. You may have heard of an arms embargo, during which one country blocks firearms from reaching another nation. The purpose of a ***boycott*** is to shun. (***Bonus trivia:*** Boycott comes from the name of a man. Charles C. Boycott was an English land agent in Ireland in the late 1800s. The locals shunned or ostracized him when he refused to reduce rents.) An incantation has nothing to do with "can't." An ***incantation*** is a spell, like a witch's incantation. A ***parody*** makes fun of something that already exists, but doesn't originate something new. A ***euphemism*** is a good or polite way of saying something ("study-challenged" instead of "lazy as a dog"). To ***denounce*** is to criticize (de- means to put down). To ***obfuscate*** is to muddle, confuse, make unclear or obscure (ob- means to block or oppose).

22. **A.** Assume that unknown words are synonyms: An assassin is *sanguinary.* ***Sanguinary*** means bloodthirsty. A ***charlatan*** is a fraud, a quack, a fake. A ***ruffian*** is someone who is not at all gentle, a rough person. A ***scapegoat*** is the fall guy, the person who takes the blame. ***Pragmatic*** means practical. Although you may think it is practical to have a scapegoat ("I didn't spill soda all over your computer, Dad. It must have been Skip. Yeah, that's right; it was Skip; Skip did it."), a scapegoat himself is not necessarily practical. A ***sage*** is a wise person. A surgeon is not inept, or unskillful. (What did the surgeon say when he took out the class clown's appendix? "That'll be enough out of you!")

23. **E.** You may not know *obdurate.* Assume that unknown words are synonyms. Make this sentence: "***Obdurate*** is stubborn" (which in fact is exactly what it means). ***Wooden*** means stiff, inflexible. Think of Pinocchio, who moved in a very, uh, wooden manner, not smoothly or fluidly.

    D is the trap answer. The word is ***emaciated,*** meaning excessively skinny, not ***emancipated,*** meaning free (gotcha!).

    In A, although something illegal may be *inconsiderate* ("You say you stole my car? How *inconsiderate* of you!"), the words aren't really synonyms. ***Fractious*** means hard to manage, unruly, like a three-year-old or a class when a substitute teacher is in charge. ***Strident*** means harsh or grating, like a strident voice that makes the hairs on the back of your neck stand up. (Think of a Stridex acne pad, which is "strong" or harsh medicine.)

24. **D.** International students, don't worry if you don't know American history. You don't have to know any history to answer the questions on the SAT. All the questions can be answered based on what is stated or implied in the passage. Besides, the American kids don't know this stuff, either!

The ***dearth*** (lack) is of information — something the author mentions in the passage, saying that we have only estimates and can't be sure of the numbers.

If you chose A or C, you didn't go back to the passage to see how the word is used in context. When you are asked for the definition of a word, the right answer rarely is the commonsense, everyday definition, but something that's less frequently used.

25. **B.** The primary purpose of a passage is usually given in the first paragraph. Here, however, the author uses the second paragraph to correct the misapprehension that blacks have not been involved in combat activities in any significant manner.

Negative answers — like A and E here — are rarely correct. To ***refute*** is to disprove. To ***denounce*** is to criticize or put down. The purpose of a passage rarely is to put someone or something down.

26. **A.** When a question begins "According to the passage," you can usually go back and skim for the precise answer. You know from line 13 that statement I is correct. Eliminate choice C.

Statement II holds a trap for the careless reader. Lines 14–17 tell you that black men were listed by the names of the white men for whom they substituted, *not* that blacks had no names of their own. In fact, the line specifically says that they were not listed by their own names, which means such names existed. Cross off any answers that include statement II, choices B, C (already eliminated), and E.

Although the second paragraph tells you that slaves often were given their freedom in exchange for service, the passage does not say that the names of such slaves were erased. Don't read more into the passage than it contains.

Because Roman numeral questions can be confusing, tricky, and just plain time-consuming, they are often good ones to skip. Save them for last; go back and answer them if and only if you have enough time left. If you don't get to them, no sweat; many people miss this sort of question, anyway.

27. **C.** When given a line reference, be sure to read the surrounding material, especially on an inference question. Here, the key is to read the next sentence, which says that blacks were often given their freedom in exchange for serving in place of whites. To be given freedom, the blacks had to have been something other than free before serving. Choice C, which mentions that blacks were slaves, fits in very well with this reasoning and is the answer.

Choice A infers too much, primarily because of the word *many*. You have no way of knowing exactly how frequently the exchange of a black for a white took place (what do you consider "many" when you don't know the number who were serving in the first place)? The word *unwilling* is also inappropriate. The whites who let blacks take their place may have been willing to serve; it's just that a better prospect, namely having blacks take their place, may have been available. Don't eliminate choices just because they are ambiguous. A wishy-washy choice is often easier for the test maker to defend (and thus more likely to be correct) than is a choice that makes an extreme statement.

The word *forced* makes choice B a bad one. The fact that the blacks were offered freedom in exchange for service implies that they had a choice in the matter. The blacks were certainly forced to serve as slaves, but they were not forced to serve in the military, at least according to the information in the passage.

Choice D comes from out of nowhere. The passage does say that blacks often performed admirably in the armed forces, but it does not compare their ability with that of whites and says nothing about how well they did in the service referred to in lines 14–18.

Choice E has no connection either to lines 14–18. The spirit of the passage is that many blacks served in the military and that they did well while doing so. While another SAT I passage might focus on the mistreatment of blacks in the military, this particular passage does not. Don't use your outside knowledge to come up with a correct answer. You must make sure that your answer is based on what is stated or implied in the passage.

28. **C.** Lines 26–28 tell you that Andrew Jackson *insisted* that the battalion's offer be accepted. From that word, you can infer that the populace didn't want to accept the offer and had to be persuaded to do so.

    Choice A is not implied anywhere in the passage; don't read too much into the city's reluctance to accept the black fighters. Choice B may or may not be true. Lines 25–28 tell you that Louisiana accepted black fighters in 1812, but not that the people of New Orleans were the first to have a black battalion. Choice D has absolutely no information to support it. Choice E is the opposite of the correct answer. If the people did as Jackson insisted, they probably trusted, not distrusted, him.

29. **B.** An example is usually given to support the main idea or primary purpose of the passage. The primary purpose of this passage is to correct a wrong idea that people have (that blacks weren't actively engaged in fighting for America).

    Choices A and E are value judgments. Who is to say whether black men or white men fight better or are more subject to seasickness? Don't try to foist your own ideas off onto the author. You can answer a question based only on what is stated or implied in the passage.

    International students, you have an advantage on a question like this. American kids who grew up learning American history and values have all sorts of preconceived notions that make them fall for trap answers. You come to the passage without those prejudices and can do a great job of answering the questions based only on what is stated or implied in the passage.

    Choice C is a trap. Maybe Perry had more black sailors because he was free of prejudice; maybe there was another reason why he had more blacks. You can't stretch your reasoning that far.

30. **D.** Lines 36–39 tell you that the blacks intermarried with the Indians and established lives in Indian territory. They were part of a protective militia, meaning that they fought to protect their land, their property, and their families. Although the other answers may be true, you have no way of knowing that from the information in the passage.

31. **E.** Lines 56–60 tell you that Taylor was better known in her time, whereas Tubman is better known in ours.

    Choice A is backward. Tubman both nursed and fought alongside the soldiers; remember that she had the nickname "General" Tubman. According to the passage, Taylor didn't fight; she only nursed. Choice B is true, but it is not the main distinguishing characteristic between the two women. Choice D is wrong; both women were unpaid. The passage provides no information on the women's beliefs about segregation, so choice C may or may not be true.

32. **A.** Lines 75–78 tell you that most of the soldiers died from diseases associated with Cuba, not from bullets. If soldiers were dying in Cuba, Cuba must have been where the war was.

    Did you choose B? Lines 78-82 tell you that the Army was so pleased with the nurses that it *tried* to establish a permanent corps of nurses, but the bill was defeated in Congress.

    Choice C is also tricky. The war didn't necessarily prove the inadequacy of medical training. Lines 73–75 merely say that the Army was unable to make adequate medical personnel available. Maybe there weren't enough people, but maybe there was some other cause.

33. **E.** This question is a time-waster. The last paragraph mentions all the answers except E. The passage contains no information, one way or the other, about white recruitment of black women.

34. **C.** The SAT has a habit of using common words in uncommon ways. You may think of "recognize" as meaning "know or identify," as in, "I recognized the girl as an old friend from the neighborhood." Often, the "normal" meaning is the first meaning given and is also the trap answer (here, choices A and B). In this case, the sentence implies that the recognized organization is an official organization, such that the previous ones were not official. Choice E is tempting, but too strong. It's not that black females weren't in the military (you heard about black females' service in various other wars) but that they weren't in an acknowledged group.

35. **C.** This question goes back to the primary purpose of the passage, which is to correct the mistaken idea that blacks didn't participate actively in the American military. The author appears to want to inspire people with the stories of the bravery of the blacks — the courage they showed in fighting, not just the enemy, but the prejudices and constraints of their time.

    Facetious means joking, humorous, amusing. Nothing is humorous about the SAT. (***Trivia:*** What's so special about the word *facetiously?* It contains all the vowels in alphabetical order, even the "sometimes y.")

    Lugubrious (choice B) means sad or gloomy. Choice D has a trap. ***Belligerent*** means warlike (*belli* = war). Although the subject matter is war, the tone of the passage itself is not warlike. In choice E, ***vindictive*** means seeking revenge. The author was seeking ***redress*** (trying to right a wrong), not revenge. You seek *redress* when you ask the friend who got a hole in your sweater to buy you a new one. You seek revenge when you rip a hole in his sweater to get even.

Words like *lugubrious, belligerent,* and *vindictive* are negative. The test makers would not use a passage — especially a humanities passage — that has a mean-spirited or negative tone.

Section 2

1. **D.** Move the $7x$ to the right of the equal sign, remembering to change it to $-7x$. That gives you $18 = 13x - 7x$. $18 = 6x$. Divide both sides through by 6, the number next to the variable. $3 = x$. If you chose E, you forgot to convert $7x$ to $-7x$ when you moved it from one side to the other. The test makers know that this mistake is common, and they usually put in a trap answer to catch careless students.

2. **B.** If Cadillacs = 20, Ferraris = 10 (because there are twice as many Cadillacs as Ferraris), and Corvettes = 40 (because there are half as many Cadillacs as Corvettes). $20 + 10 + 40 = 70$.

3. **B.** Descending order: 97521. Ascending order: 12579.

   You did *not* have to use your calculator to subtract or work this problem out at all. Look at the units digits (the ones column). Because it has to be $1 - 9$ or $11 - 9 = 2$, only choice B works. Save yourself a few seconds.

4. **B.** The area of a circle is π radius^2. If the area is 16π, the radius is 4 (because $4^2 = 16$). Statement I is true.

   The question asks which is *not* true. Eliminate any answers with I in them, choices A and E.

   The circumference of a circle is 2πradius. Here, that's 8π, not 32π. Statement II is false, which is what the problem does want. Cross off any answer without II in it, choice C.

   The longest chord of any circle is its diameter, which is 2 radii. Here, that's 8. Statement III is true, meaning you cross off any answer including it. Only B is left.

   For any Roman numeral question, circle each true statement and X out any false statement. Then a quick glance at the statements lets you answer quickly which is true and which is not true. Doing this prevents your getting confused in the middle of what should be an easy problem.

5. **B.**

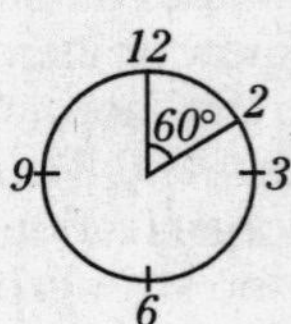

A clock has 12 divisions (from 12 to 1, from 1 to 2, from 2 to 3, and so on). Like any circle, a clock has 360 degrees; $^{360}/_{12} = 30$. That means that each interval is 30 degrees. Two intervals constitute 60 degrees. When the clock shows 2:00, the hands show two intervals.

You can look at this problem in another way. A clock is a circle, meaning that it has 360 degrees; 60 is $\frac{1}{6}$ of 360. A clock has 12 numbers; $\frac{1}{6}$ of 12 = 2.

6. **B.** The pattern is a set of 4. Divide 4 into 38, and you get 9 with a remainder of 2. That means that the 36th student ($4 \times 9 = 36$) finishes a set of 4. The 37th student starts a new set with math. The 38th student has his English homework checked.

This question is a classic example of a situation in which the calculator cannot help you. For remainder problems, you don't want something like .5 or $\frac{1}{2}$.

Fewer and fewer SAT math questions have "It cannot be determined" answer choices. Your exam may not have any or may have just a few. Don't automatically assume, however, that just because it shows up, it must be correct. This answer has the same one in five chance as any other answer.

7. **E.** If you fell for choice B, your quest for the right answer was fruitless (ah, you saw that one coming, didn't you?). One-third of the pieces of fruit are apples, meaning that there are $42 \div 3 = 14$ apples. One-half of the pieces of fruit are red, meaning that the bowl contains 21 red pieces of fruit. However, you don't know whether all of the apples are red (and count as part of the 21), some of the apples are red, or none of the apples are red. You don't have enough information to answer this question.

8. **D.** If the number of anesthesiologists is y, then surgeons is 6 less than that: $y - 6$. The number of surgeons is five times that: $5(y - 6)$.

If you chose C, you fell for the trap answer. You forgot to distribute, to multiply the 5 by both the y and the 6. Tsk, tsk. I'm sure the surgeons would have a cutting remark to make right about now.

If you got this question correct, you get to enjoy the following joke: What do you get when you cross an anesthesiologist with a rabbit? The ether bunny!

9. **C.** Good problem. Set it up as follows:

$$\frac{x+y+z}{3} = \frac{4}{3}x$$

An average is the sum of all the terms divided by the number of terms. You know that one-third more than something is the same as $1\frac{1}{3}$ of that something.

To get rid of the fraction, multiply both sides through by 3. You now have $x + y + z = 4x$. Subtract an x from both sides. $y + z = 3x$.

If you chose D, you got suckered. If a number is *three times* as much as another number, it is *two times greater,* or 200% greater. If this is confusing, talk it through in simple terms, such as dollars and cents. If you have three dollars, you have three times as much as one dollar but only two dollars, or 200 cents, more than one dollar. You have to "subtract" the original 100 cents — or, in this case, 100%.

10. **E.** If you chose A, you fell for one of the ***myriad*** (many), even ***superfluity*** (overabundance) of traps here. Dividing like bases means subtracting the exponents. For a^{10} divided by a^5, subtract: $10 - 5 = 5$. Divide 6 by 3 to get 2. You know that the first term is $2(a^5)$, so you can narrow the choices down to C, D, and E.

b^5 divided by b^9 is b^{-4}, or $\frac{1}{b^4}$. That result eliminates choices C and D; you can stop now.

Just for fun, though, I'll finish this calculation. c^7 divided by c^7 is 1. Any number divided by itself is 1. (Or you could think of it as being 7 – 7 = 0; any number to the zero power is 1.) The answer 1 doesn't change anything in the multiplication; ignore it.

Choices A and B were traps for people who tried $\frac{10}{5}$ = 2 instead of subtracting exponents.

Choices C and D were traps for people who forgot that a negative exponent is in the denominator, not the numerator. Remember: 2 to the negative third really is $\frac{1}{2^3}$. If you forgot this, return to Chapter 11.

International students: Some of the word problems are very difficult for people whose English is a little weak (actually, some of the word problems are *impossible* even for those of us who grew up speaking English!). Because you may need to skip some of the more confusing and wordy problems, you *must* be absolutely certain you can do all the algebra problems that are just numbers and no words. Spend a little extra time making sure you can do anything algebraically.

11. **A.** This problem is a real brain picnic, much easier than it looks. If two circles have the same area, they have the same radius because the area of a circle = πradius^2. The radius of circle *Y* is 5 as well. The diameters of the two circles are 10 each because the diameter of a circle is twice its radius. The length of the rectangle is 20, therefore, and the width is 10.

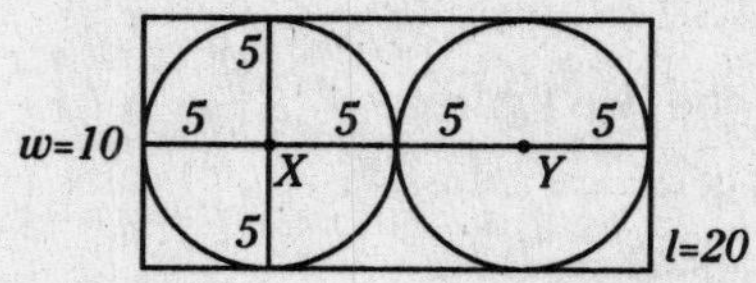

The area of a rectangle is *length* times *width:* 20 × 10 = 200.

12. **E.** Did I get you, or did you remember this type of problem from the Part III of this book? When a question asks you to put items in a line, the answer often depends on the order in which the items are arranged — that is, the figure could be like this:

or like this:

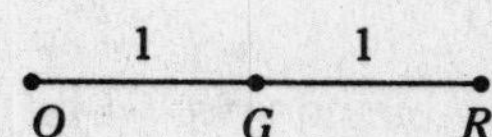

or even like this:

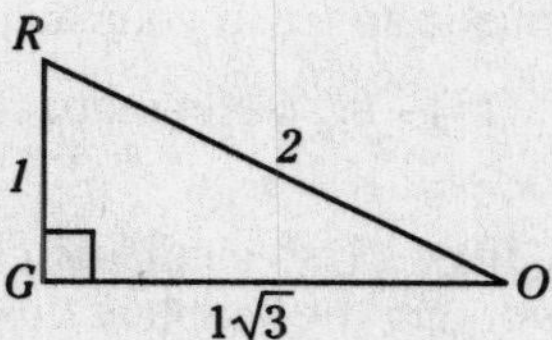

Because you don't know the layout of the flags, you can't answer the question.

Fewer and fewer SAT math questions have "It cannot be determined" answer choices. Your test may not have any or may have just a few. Don't automatically assume, however, that just because it shows up, it must be correct. This answer has the same one in five chance as any other answer.

13. **C.** Draw the figure and plug in easy numbers: 1 for the width and 6 for the length. (Of course, the sides could be in any multiple of this ratio, like 2:12 or 3:36, but why make life hard?) The length is six times the width. The perimeter of a figure is the sum of all the sides; 6 + 1 + 6 + 1 = 14. Because the width is 1, the ratio is 14:1.

If you chose D, you outsmarted yourself and did too much work. The sum of the widths is 1 + 1 = 2. The ratio 14:2 can be reduced to 7:1. The question, however, doesn't ask you for the ratio of the perimeter to both widths, only for the ratio of the perimeter to "the" width, which is 1.

14. **B.** This problem is much easier than it looks. Forget about straining the brain with formulas and algebraic equations. Instead, draw yourself a simple picture. Make eight dashes and put BLUE in the ninth space, as follows:

   - - - - - - - - BLUE

   Now, count the blue pole as the 11th and count backward, making more dashes, like this:

   BLUE - - - - - - - - - -

   11 10 9 8 7 6 5 4 3 2 1

   Finally, combine the two figures:

   - - - - - - - - BLUE - - - - - - - -

   and count the spaces: 19.

15. **A.** Think of this problem as a ratio: three dishes broken for every four intact. Now use the ratio formulas in the order that follows. (See Chapter 11.)

1. Add the numbers in the ratio: 3 + 4 = 7.
2. Divide that sum into the total: $^{63}/_{7}$ = 9.
3. Multiply that number by each term in the ratio. 9 × 3 = 27. 9 × 4 = 36.
4. Add to make sure that those numbers sum back up to the total. 27 + 36 = 63. Yup, no careless errors here.

Did you choose C? Tsk, tsk. And I had such high hopes for you. The trap answer, 27, represents the number of *broken* dishes; the question asks for the number of *intact* dishes. Circling what the question is asking for is a good idea. You just *know* that the test makers are going to have a trap answer in the choices; why give them the satisfaction of making a fool of you?

16. **C.** You can solve this problem in two ways. One easy way is to find a common multiple and then *plug in numbers*. Because 2, 5, and 3 all divide evenly into 30, use that multiple. Calculate $2r = 30$; $r = 15$. Next, calculate $5s = 30$; $s = 6$. Then calculate $3t = 30$; $t = 10$. Now you can work through each answer choice.

Be sure to write down what each variable equals; don't try to remember those values even if you have a lot of unused space in your head.

I. 3(10) is not equal to 2(15) + 6, so eliminate choices A, D, and E. (Eliminating as you go is always a good idea.)

II. 6(6) is not equal to 3(10) + 15, so eliminate choice B. Choice C must be right; you don't have to spend time working the problem through. If you want proof, however, here it is:

III. 10(6) = 3(10) + 2(15).

These answers will work out, regardless of what numbers you plug in, as long as you plug in something that is true in the equation $2r = 5s = 3t$. For example, you could have plugged in $r = 30$, $s = 12$, $t = 20$ (although why you'd want to make your life that hard, I have no idea).

If you don't want to plug in numbers, you can talk the problem through.

I. 3*t*, you know, is equal to 2*r* on its own; adding *s* would make the sides unequal. Eliminate choices A, D, and E.

II. Let's skip to III. If it works, the answer is C. If III doesn't work, the answer is B.

III. Because 10*s* is twice 5*s*, it *would* equal 3*t* (5*s*) + 2*r* (another 5*s*). Either method — plugging in numbers or talking the problem through — will work.

17. **D.** A triangle perfectly inscribed in a rectangle has an area exactly half the area of the rectangle. This blessed event happens because the base of the triangle is the same as the length of the rectangle. The height of the triangle is the same as the width of the rectangle.

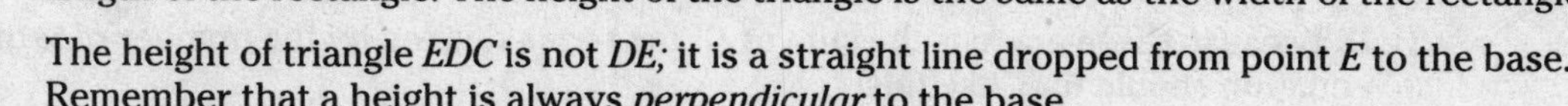

The height of triangle *EDC* is not *DE;* it is a straight line dropped from point *E* to the base. Remember that a height is always *perpendicular* to the base.

Because the area of a triangle = ½ *base* × *height,* the area of the triangle here is ½ *length* × *width,* or ½ the area of the rectangle.

If the area of the triangle is half the area of the rectangle, the shaded or leftover area must be the other half. The halves are equal.

18. **C.** Don't worry; you don't have to be a Mathlete to do this problem. You need only one fact: The slope of a line may be found using Rise/Run. Simply put, make a fraction. The numerator (top number) is the difference between the *y* variables (how much the number goes up or down). The denominator (bottom number) is the difference between the *x* variables (how much the number goes right or left). Here, the *y* value goes from 5 to 4, for a difference of –1. The *x* value goes from 3 to 6, for a difference of 3. Make the fraction: –⅓.

Students tend to make two careless mistakes on slope problems. Did you put the *x* difference on top and the *y* difference on bottom? That gets you choice A. Did you forget the negative sign? That's choice D. You know, you just *know*, the test makers are going to put every possible trap choice among the answer choices; double-check for these two common mistakes.

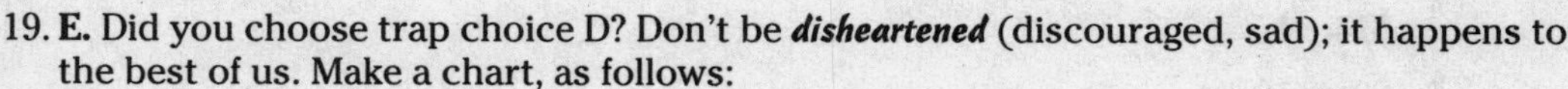

19. **E.** Did you choose trap choice D? Don't be ***disheartened*** (discouraged, sad); it happens to the best of us. Make a chart, as follows:

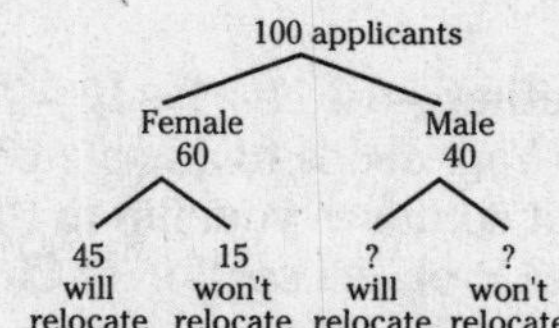

As you can see, 15 of the female applicants are not willing to relocate. However, you have no clue how many of the *male* applicants are not willing to relocate. Maybe all of the men will relocate, so the total number of applicants who are unwilling to relocate is 15 — choice D. Maybe none of the men will relocate, so the total number of applicants who are unwilling to relocate is 55 — choice B. You don't have enough information to answer the question.

Fewer and fewer SAT math questions have "It cannot be determined" answer choices. Your exam may not have any or may have just a few. Don't automatically assume, however, that just because it shows up, it must be correct. This answer has the same one in five chance as any other answer.

20. **D.** A diagonal of a square is the same thing as a hypotenuse of an isosceles right triangle (see Chapter 14 for more information). One of the Pythagorean theorem shortcuts that you learned (or were supposed to learn) is that the sides of an isosceles right triangle are in a ratio of $s:s:s\sqrt{2}$. That ratio also can be written as $\frac{s}{\sqrt{2}}:\frac{s}{\sqrt{2}}:s$ (*s* stands for side). Because the diagonal here is 8, each side must be $\frac{8}{\sqrt{2}}$.

The perimeter of a figure is the sum of all sides: $\frac{8}{\sqrt{2}}+\frac{8}{\sqrt{2}}+\frac{8}{\sqrt{2}}+\frac{8}{\sqrt{2}}=\frac{32}{\sqrt{2}}$.

To get rid of a square root in the denominator (the fancy term is "rationalizing the denominator," if those words strike a familiar chord), multiply both the top and bottom through by the square root.

$$\frac{32}{\sqrt{2}} \times \frac{\sqrt{2}}{\sqrt{2}} =$$

$$\frac{32\sqrt{2}}{\sqrt{4}}$$

$$\frac{32\sqrt{2}}{\sqrt{2}} = 16\sqrt{2}$$

21. **D.** Because the average is the sum of all the terms divided by the number of terms, your equation should look like this:

$$80 = \frac{75 + 69 + 81 + 90 + 73 + x}{7}$$

Cross-multiply: $80 \times 7 = 560$.

$560 = 388 + x$. Therefore, $x = 172$.

You're probably lucky that there was no trap answer of 172; you may have chosen it and gone on your merry way. The question, however, asks for the average weight of the last *two* boxes. $^{172}\!/_{2} = 86$.

If you just divided 388 (the sum of the six numbers) by 6, you got 64.66 and may have been tempted to choose E, rounding up to 65. But that answer is just the average of those six numbers — not at all what the question is asking for.

Because of all these traps, I prefer just to talk this problem through. Calculate how far each weight is from the average.

75 = –5

69 = –11

81 = +1

90 = +10

73 = –7

Add the numbers together: –5 – 11 + 1 + 10 – 7 = –12. If the two boxes sum up to –12, each box is –6. That means Yogi needs to add six pounds more per box, or 86. This way seems much easier to me; if it confuses you, flip to the much more detailed explanation in the Missing Term Averages Problem section of Chapter 12.

And speaking of Yogi, do you know why there's only one Yogi Bear? When they tried to make another, they made a Boo Boo.

22. **B.** Think of the shaded region as a leftover. It's what's "left over" after you have subtracted the unshaded portion from the area of the larger figure. Because the numbers are relatively small, this problem is probably best answered by plugging in numbers. Say the radius of the small circle is 1, making the radius of the large circle 2. Then the area of the large circle is 4π, which isn't big enough. Try making the radius of the small circle 2, which means that the radius of the large circle is 4. The area of the large circle is 16π; the area of the small circle is 4π. 16π – 4π = 12π.

If you chose E, you completely forgot what the question was asking. It wanted the area of the small circle, not the area of the large circle.

23. **C.** If the area of the hubcap is 16π, its radius is 4 (because the area of a circle is πr^2). That means that the radius of the wheel is twice that figure, or 8. The circumference of the wheel would be 16π (because circumference = $2\pi r$, or πd). A wheel rolls the length of its circumference in one revolution. Multiply 16 by 3.14 (an approximation for π); you get 50.24. Divide that figure into 400 to get 7.96, or approximately 8 revolutions.

The important point to remember here is that a wheel travels the length of its circumference in one revolution. Finding the circumference isn't the hard part; the hard part is knowing that finding the circumference is what you're supposed to do.

24. **B.** Understand what the explanation means. (The explanation is made up for this particular problem. There is no such thing as a "circle" operation in the real world — only in the ***microcosm*** [little universe] of the SAT. Lucky you.) The explanation says that you have a number in the circle. If that number in the circle is a prime number (meaning that it can be divided only by itself and 1), you add the number in the circle to the square of the number in the circle.

If the number in the circle is a composite number (one that *can* be divided by something other than just 1 and itself), you square that number and subtract the number in the circle from the square.

Ugh. You may have to repeat those instructions to yourself a few times. You're really just substituting the number in the circle for the x in the appropriate equation.

Because 4 is composite, you use the second line of the explanation. Square 4: $4^2 = 16$. Subtract from that the number in the circle: $16 - 4 = 12$.

Because 5 is prime, you add it to its square: $5 + 25 = 30$.

Add the two results: $12 + 30 = 42$.

This problem has all sorts of trap answers. If you used the first line $(x + x^2)$ for both terms, you got 50. If you used the second line $(x^2 - x)$ for both terms, you got 32. If you confused prime and composite numbers, using the composite rule for 5 and the prime rule for 4, you got 40.

25. **E.** Did you get brain cramp just reading the problem? If you're totally confused, you may want to skip this advertisement for Tylenol and come back to it later . . . or just forget you ever saw it. Remember: A good test-taker knows which problems are worth investing time in, and which ones are not.

When dealing with variables, I suggest you plug in numbers. In this case, try the following:

d = 16 I chose that number so that 8 cans of juice cost $16, meaning each can costs $2.00.

m = 800 so that each can makes 800 milliliters.

c = 2 so that each can of water cost 2 cents.

Take this one step at a time. One can of juice costs $2. One can of water costs 2 cents. You need to add three cans of water, or 6 cents' worth of water. Your grand total is now $2.06.

This $2.06 is the cost for 800 milliliters. The problem asks for the cost of 400 milliliters; divide by 2 to get $1.03, the cost for 400 milliliters. (Why didn't I let m = 400? Sometimes when dealing with 1, several of the answer choices come out correct, and you have to substitute new numbers anyway. I like using a 2 in these longer, harder problems.)

Next, plug d = 16, m = 800, and c = 2 into each choice and eliminate those choices that don't yield 1.03 dollars:

(A) 3200(800)(16) + 96(2). You can tell without doing all the work that this answer will be much too large.

(B) $\frac{800(16)+3(2)}{400} = \frac{12,806}{400}$, which is certainly more than 1.03.

(C) $\frac{16+3(2)}{50(800)} = \frac{22}{40,000}$. This number is going to be a fraction.

(D) $\frac{8(16)+96(2)}{800} = \frac{320}{800}$, which is a fraction less than 1. The answer had better be choice E, or we're in trouble.

When you get to this point, and you've decided the answer has to be E, still go ahead and solve choice E. Why? What if you've made a careless mistake in one of the earlier answers (something easy to do with all these numbers)? When choice E doesn't come out right, you'll realize you bungled somewhere, go back, and check your work.

(E) $\frac{50(16)+12(2)}{800} = \frac{824}{800} = 1.03$. At last!

If you're an algebra whiz, you may find it easier to do the straightforward algebra. Write down the units to make sure that you're left with dollars. For the cans of orange juice:

$$\frac{\text{d dollars}}{\text{8 cans}} \times \frac{\text{1 can}}{\text{m milliliters}} = \frac{\text{d dollars}}{\text{8m milliliters}} \text{ (the cans cancel)}$$

Because you want 400 milliliters, multiply as follows:

$$\frac{\text{d dollars}}{\text{8 m milliliters}} \times 400 \text{ milliliters} = \frac{\text{50d dollars}}{\text{m}} \text{ (the milliliters cancel)}$$

Now for the water, remembering that you must convert the cents to dollars:

$$\frac{\text{3c cents}}{\text{can}} \times \frac{\text{1 dollar}}{\text{100 cents}} = \frac{\frac{3c}{100}\text{ dollars}}{\text{can}} \text{ (the cents cancel)}$$

Work in the milliliters:

$$\frac{\frac{3c}{100}\text{ dollars}}{\text{can}} \times \frac{\text{1 can}}{\text{m milliliters}} = \frac{\frac{3c}{100m}\text{ dollars}}{\text{milliliter}} \text{ (cans cancel)}$$

As with the juice, multiply by 400:

$$\frac{\frac{3c}{100m}\text{ dollars}}{\text{milliliter}} \times 400 \text{ milliliters} = \frac{12c}{m} \text{ dollars (milliliters cancel)}$$

You now have 50d/m for the cost of the juice and 12c/m for the cost of the water, so add to get $\frac{50d+12c}{m}$ dollars (choice E).

Section 3

1. **E.** Because the sentence specifies that the tree is a large herb, predict that you are looking for a word meaning large. ***Immensity*** (which is just the noun form of immense) means largeness, bigness. Choice A, ***toxicity,*** means poisonousness. Choice C, ***pungency,*** means having a sharp taste or smell (think of a very stinky cheese as being pungent).

2. **C.** *Though* tells you that even though Dakota failed at one thing, she must have succeeded at something else. Therefore, you need a positive word for the first blank, so you can eliminate choices A, D, and E. As for the second blank, Dakota would not want to increase the amount of waste paper, but rather limit the amount. To ***curtail*** is to shorten or lessen. (Associate this term with its sister word, curt, which means short and to the point. "Would you like me to *curtail* my explanation?" asked the teacher. "Yes!" was the student's *curt* response.)

3. **D.** To ***amend*** is to change, to alter. The phrase "rather than" means that you are looking for something that is the opposite of changeable. ***Immutable*** means not able to change. (You can deduce the meaning from the roots: *im-* means not; *mut* means change.)

4. **A.** The word "modern" later in the sentence implies that the Feileadh Mör came before the Feileadh Beag. The first blank must be filled with a word that means before, narrowing your choices down to A or B (***successor,*** in D, means something that comes after). The ***anonymous,*** meaning having no name, attire makes no sense; you've just been told the name.

5. **C.** Predict that the news report is negative because those who ***discount*** it (attach no importance to it, ignore it) are optimistic or positive. The *anything but* means not, such that the first blank must be positive. If the first word has to be positive, you can eliminate A (if you know what it means; if not, leave it as a "maybe"), B, D, and maybe E (***trivial*** means minor,

unimportant). Choice A makes no sense; how can a trap be gloomy? If you fall for traps, you may be gloomy, but the trap itself isn't gloomy. ***Moribund*** means stagnant, nearing death or extinction (your few remaining brains cells may be *moribund* after suffering through questions like this one). A ***prognostication*** is a prediction, something foretold (*pro-* = before; *gnos* = knowledge).

If English is not your first language, this would be a good question to skip. The construction "anything but" can be very confusing. I suggest that, when you encounter such weird expressions throughout this book (and I've tried to put in a few that I know often bewilder international students), you make a list of them and their meanings and just memorize them.

6. **D.** Predict that the first blank will be negative, as Leoni would probably be unhappy to have her dog disqualified. That eliminates choice E because ***effervescent*** means bubbly, excited, and has a connotation of happy. Predict that the second blank will be positive; Leoni would be happy when her dog was a winner. That eliminates choices B and C — and A, if you know what lachrymose means. Hint: Where are your lachrymal glands? They are your tear ducts. ***Lachrymose*** means tearful, unhappy. By the process of elimination, choice D is the answer. ***Inconsolable*** means not able to be consoled or comforted. If you are totally distraught and unhappy, you are inconsolable. ***Ebullient*** is the same as effervescent, bubbling and overflowing with enthusiasm. (***Bonus trivia:*** Speaking of Cheerios, the next time you have some for breakfast, you can show off your ***erudition*** [wisdom, learning] by explaining to your munching companions that the original name of the cereal was Cheerioats.)

7. **B.** The key word *previously* tells you that the words in the two blanks must be opposites. Something has changed. Eliminate choices C (***plausible*** means believable), D (***indisputable*** means there is no dispute; the concept is believable), and E (something probable is acceptable). As quickly as that, you have narrowed the choices down to two.

   The first word in choice A is logical, but the second makes no sense. How can an assertion "gain continuity" with physicians? ***Continuity*** means continuing or constancy. For example, you want to have continuity in your SAT prep program, to put in study time every day. By the process of elimination, choice B is correct. ***Outlandish*** means outrageous, bizarre, or as one of my students put it so well when talking about a friend's outlandish neon pink hair, "socially defective." ***Credibility*** means believability (the root *cred* means belief or trust).

8. **A.** ***Lauded*** means praised (think of app*laud*). ***Denigrated*** (demeaned, put down) would fit the first blank, but ***scuttled by,*** which means sunk by, makes no sense in the second blank. To ***befriend*** is to make friends with. To ***emasculate*** is to deprive of strength, weaken. Again, that works for the first blank, but *in conjunction with* doesn't fit in the second blank.

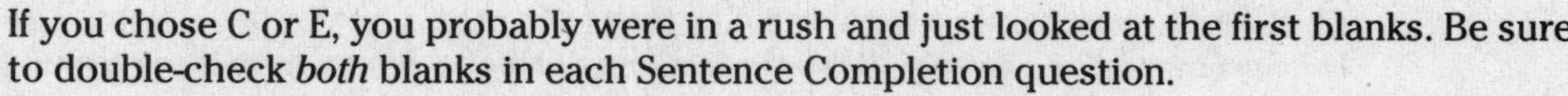

If you chose C or E, you probably were in a rush and just looked at the first blanks. Be sure to double-check *both* blanks in each Sentence Completion question.

9. **D.** You know that the word choice for the first blank should be something positive because the agreement is praised. You can probably predict that the agreement will encourage or bring about new exports. To ***derogate*** is to speak badly of to put down (*de-* = down from, away from). ***Spur*** means to impel or stimulate. Think of what spurs do when you tap a horse with them: They stimulate him to move faster. To ***stymie*** is to block or hamper.

   For the second blank, you need a word like "while not increasing" the current problems. ***Ameliorate*** is to improve, to make more tolerable. (Sitting next to the most gorgeous person in the school will *ameliorate* your feelings about having to take Latin.) ***Exacerbate*** is to make worse. (Sitting next to the biggest nerd in school will *exacerbate* your feelings about having to take Latin.)

As is usual with questions near the end of the section, the vocab here is very hard. If you weren't sure of the words and couldn't narrow the answers down to two, skip the question. Your ***incipient*** (just beginning) ulcers will thank you.

10. **E.** Make the sentence: An ostrich is a type of bird; denim is a type of fabric. (***Bonus trivia:*** You probably wear denim frequently: Do you know the origin of the word? It's a corruption of the French, *de Nimes,* meaning from the city of Nimes, where the fabric was popularized.)

Note trap answer A. Yes, a raven is a bird, but a feather is not a type of raven. Remember that a trap answer often has the same general meaning as the question (ostriches and ravens may be birds of a feather, but that's not the point!).

11. **A.** An actor performs his or her job in a theater; a judge performs his or her job in a court. In E, a goldsmith is someone who works with gold. (Stay away from goldsmiths: Gold merchants have association by gilt.)

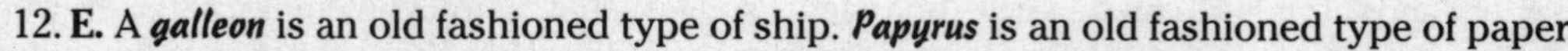

12. **E.** A ***galleon*** is an old fashioned type of ship. ***Papyrus*** is an old fashioned type of paper.

Don't choose D just because anchor and boat have to do with ship. The answer with "sorta the same" meaning as the question is often the trap answer. Look at the *relationships* between the words, not at the meanings of the words.

Trivia: Did you know that Columbus was the first ecologically minded explorer? Yeah, he got thousands of miles to the galleon.

13. **C.** A ***league*** is a unit of measure of distance, approximately three miles. A ***watt*** is a unit of measure of electrical power. Choice A is a trap: A ***thermometer*** measures temperature, but it is a tool, a device, not a unit of measure. The same is true for B. A ***metronome*** beats time, and helps a person to establish a tempo (for example, when playing the piano). It is an instrument, not a unit of measure. A ***knot*** in choice D is a unit of measure, but of speed, not of the ocean. (***Bonus trivia:*** Know why we measure nautical speed in knots? The expression came from the sailors' habit of tying knots in a rope at regular intervals, tossing it over, and seeing how many knots the ship could pass in a set time.)

14. **D.** Someone ***loquacious*** is full of chatter or talk (*loq* = speech, talk; *-ous* = full of, very). Someone skeptical is full of doubt.

Inauspicious means not favorable. ***Seething*** means simmering with anger. (The evening your parents are *seething* about their high taxes is an *inauspicious* moment to ask for a raise in your allowance.) ***Prevaricating*** is lying, telling falsehoods. ***Obese*** means fat, overweight, like Miss Piggy. (Miss Piggy gave my all-time favorite dieting tip, one I strive hard to follow: Never eat more than you can lift!) *Obese* has no connection to *confusion*.

15. **B.** You probably didn't know the word *quixotic;* that's normal.

Assume that unknown words are synonyms. A visionary (a dreamer, one who looks into the future and is not necessarily practical) is quixotic (idealistic). A ***quixotic*** person has his head in the clouds, is impractical.

Servile means humble and submissive (like a servant) and is more likely the characteristic of an employee than an employer. A ***pugilist*** (a fighter, a boxer; *pug* = fight; *-ist* = a person) is ***brawny*** (muscular, strong). ***Autonomous*** means self-governing, or self-controlling, and is probably not a characteristic of a ***toady*** (a yes man, an over-flatterer).

Did the word *ingenious* trick you into thinking it meant "not a genius," or stupid? True, the prefix *in-* usually means not, but it can also mean inside. An ***ingenious*** person is very smart, with "a genius inside" of him or her.

It's a good idea to memorize a few words that begin with *in-* but don't mean not- something. For example, ***invaluable*** means very valuable (not "not valuable"). ***Inflammable*** means highly flammable (not "not flammable"). Can you think of any others? And finally in choice E, ***kith*** are your friends and neighbors. (You may have heard the expression "kith and kin," meaning "friends and family.") ***Wily*** means sneaky, devious, deceptive. Your friends — I hope — are not noted for being sneaky.

16. **A.** The first paragraph describes the physical changes that occur when we laugh. (I have a physician friend who describes laughter as an internal massage.)

Three words are often correct answers to primary purpose questions: *describe, discuss,* and *explain.* Many times, the main idea or primary purpose of a passage is to describe, discuss, or explain something.

17. **C.** The purpose of any example is to support the main idea, either of the passage as a whole or of one individual paragraph. The main idea of this paragraph is given in the topic sentence: "Laughter is considered to be an innate human response that develops during

the first few weeks of life." In other words, the ability to laugh is pretty much there when a baby is born; it is not acquired later.

The word *innate* is tricky if you use roots. The root *nat* means birth (a mother-to-be goes to the hospital for pre*nat*al care). The prefix *in-*, usually means not, but it can also mean inside or beginning. Here, use *in-* to mean inside, such that something *innate* is "inside at birth," or *inborn.*

Beware of answers that give true statements, but don't answer this specific question. For example, choice A may be true, but it is not the reason the author uses the example of blind and deaf infants.

18. **B.** Lines 28–30 explain that laughter is ***antithetical,*** or opposite, to the cries of distress. Laughter is called the infant's "powerful reward signal of comfort." The child rewards the parents with laughter when he's feeling good and lets the parents know, in no uncertain terms, when it's time for a new diaper!

19. **C.** At last, a straightforward "According to the passage" question that can be answered quickly and precisely. Identify the key words (*sed rate*) in the question and skim the passage for them. Line 47 says that the sed rate is associated with the body's level of infection. The only way to miss this question is to be too lazy ("motivationally challenged") to go back to find the answer.

When a question begins "According to the passage," it should be almost a freebie for you. If you're running short of time and you know you won't do every single question, head for this one. You can nearly always get this type of question correct with a minimum of time and effort.

20. **E.** The right answer rarely appears in the line to which you are directed. You need to read a little bit above (not logical here, because line 49 is the first of the paragraph) or a little bit below. The next line tells you that "this in no way minimizes the therapeutic potential."

    The rest of the passage leads you to believe that a placebo effect is more in the mind than in the body. In fact, a ***placebo*** is a harmless substance given as a "medicine" to humor a patient. When a notorious hypochondriac makes her weekly visit to the doctor, she may receive sugar pills as a *placebo,* a substance that she thinks is working to cure her and that will be *beneficial.*

21. **D.** The best title has to incorporate the main idea of the passage, which is laughter. Eliminate choices A and C, which don't feature that word. B is beyond the scope of this passage, which describes only how we laugh and what laughter does for us, not why we laugh. Choice E is the trap. The passage says that laughter may have a curative effect, but that is not the main point of the passage.

A main point is usually quite broad and general. The main idea, or best title, often appears in the first sentence or the first paragraph. In question 16, you decided that the purpose of the first paragraph is to describe the physical features of laughter; develop that answer a little further to come up with the best title.

22. **C.** An "according to the passage" question is often answered ***verbatim*** (word for word) in the passage. Identify the key words in the question (here, dangers of sulfur dioxide) and skim the passage for those exact words. Lines 20–22 tell you that sulfur dioxide is most dangerous when it clings to small particles and is carried into the lungs.

23. **D.** Lines 26–28 tell you that sulfur dioxide also can cause increased illness in normally healthy people. Because statement I is false, the author would disagree with it. Circle I and eliminate any answers without it (choices A and B).

    If you used only your common sense, you probably thought this was a true statement. Be sure to invest a few seconds to go back and find the answer based on what the *author* thinks, not on what *you* think.

Lines 33–34 state that the effects of the particulates depend on their size and composition. Therefore, II is a true statement, and the author would not disagree with it. Eliminate answers with II (choices C and E).

By eliminating as you go, you find that only choice D is left. You don't even have to bother looking at statement III. The process of elimination is especially useful in Roman numeral questions.

Okay, here's the rest of the question, if you need closure: The author lists several natural sources of dangerous particulates in lines 1–4. Therefore, statement III is wrong, and the author would disagree with it.

24. **B.** Lines 34–36 state that some of the harmful particulates are filtered out by the body. If you think about this, the other answers may help to decrease the particulates themselves, but only B decreases the *effects* of the particulates.

25. **B.** The author talks about how particulates affect one's ***welfare,*** or condition (*welfare* = faring well). If you fell for any of the trap answer choices — A, C, and E — you didn't go back to the passage to see how the word was used in context.

When you are asked to define a word on the SAT, remember that the sick and twisted ghouls who write this jazz (not me, I only teach it) rarely use the commonsense, everyday definition, but one that you can identify only by going back and reading the word in context. Don't try to save time here; go back to the passage and find the exact way the word is used.

26. **A.** This question requires you to put together a couple of facts presented in the passage. Lines 66–69 reveal that some snows in Greenland ranged from 6 to 7.6. The highest pH value, therefore, is 7.6, which, according to the information in the previous paragraph, is alkaline or basic. Choice A follows as the answer.

    For a substance to be neutral, the pH must be 7, while acidic substances have pH values below 7. A pH of 7.6 doesn't fit either of these, eliminating choices B and C.

    Don't fall for choice D just because you see a range. Yes, the pH value of snows in Greenland in the 1800s varied, but "the highest value" is a single number. Values vary, but the highest value is fixed at the top.

    Acid rain can be dangerous, but the passage provides no information on whether the snows at the highest pH range were dangerous. Eliminate choice E.

27. **D.** This would have been an excellent question to skip if the answer wasn't obvious to you immediately. If you didn't remember that the author talked about the examples of difficulty, you'd have to reread the entire passage. You can't afford the time to do so.

If you didn't understand the passage, but just skimmed it trying to find specific answers, you absolutely need to skip this sort of question. This is a comprehensive question, demanding that you truly understand the passage as a whole. Given the short amount of time you have for reading in this section, you probably didn't get more than the basics of the passage. Any answer you take here would most likely be a guess, and random guessing can hurt you on the SAT. Remember that you lose a quarter point on your raw score for every wrong answer, and when the raw score changes to the converted score, those quarter points can really add up and take their toll.

28. **A.** Use your common sense. When *some* people suggest a point, it is fair to assume that *not all* people agree on the point.

Eliminate negative answers, which are rarely correct. To ***denigrate*** is to criticize or insult. (Many *de-* words mean to put down, insult.) To ***lampoon*** is to ridicule (think of the funny and sarcastic National Lampoon movies).

Eliminate dramatic answers, like choice E. *Proves* is too strong a word; things are rarely proven in an SAT passage. A wishy-washy answer, one that hedges madly, is a good choice.

29. **B.** If it would be unwise to investigate *every* aspect of acid rain before action is taken, action is important and should be taken sooner rather than later.

    You need to go back to the last sentence of the passage to answer this sort of question. The next paragraph continues the theme of its topic (or main idea) sentence.

30. **B.** A primary focus is main and general in its scope. Choice A is tempting, but B is better because it incorporates both sulfur dioxide and acid rain.

If you chose A, you probably read only the first sentence of the passage. With a passage this long . . . and boring (don't forget booooooring), quite a bit of material is covered. Check all the answer choices to see which one encompasses the most ideas.

Because negative answers are rarely correct, choice C is a weak choice. Almost any SAT reading passage will discuss even bad things in a good way (not "How I Lost My Admission Ticket the Night before the SAT" but rather "How I Aced the SAT Even Though I Lost My Ticket the Night before the Test").

Section 4

1. **A.** Try both extremes for *a*. First, make $a = 10$ because *a* could be less than *or equal to* 10. If $a = 10$, $b = 55/10 = 5.5$. Column A is greater. Now go to the other extreme. Make $a = 5$ because *a* could be greater than *or equal to* 5. If $a = 5$, $b = 55/5 = 11$. Column A is greater again. Because all the other possible values of *a* must fall between these two extremes, the answer will not change: Column A is greater.

Notice how tricky this problem can be. Although variable *b* may be greater than variable *a*, Column A is greater than Column B.

2. **A.** This problem is not a Power Math problem; it's a talk-it-through problem. If the jar is half full at 5,000, it would be all the way full at 10,000. If you chose C, you fell for the trap. (If the columns look equal, it's probably a trap. You should have double-checked your result.) Half of 5,000 is 2,500, but that's not what the problem is asking.

3. **D.** The answer depends on the value of *x*. Plug in numbers and play the *what if* game. *What if* $x = 1$? Then Column A = $1/1$ or 1, and Column B = 1; the columns are equal. *What if* $x = 2$? Then Column A = ½, and Column B = 2; now Column B is greater. If the answer *could be* B or C, it *depends* on what you plug in; the answer is D.

   The problem tells you that *x* is not equal to 0 because division by 0 is undefined.

4. **A.** Plug in numbers. *What if* $x = -1$? Then Column A = $1 + (-1) + 1 = 1$. *What if* $x = -2$? Then Column A = $4 + (-8) + 16 = 12$. You can keep going if you want to, but the answer always will be A.

You may be able to see, without actually plugging in numbers, that Column A is greater. Because the final term is to the fourth power, and because some integer (other than 1) to the fourth power is going to be greater than the sum of that same integer to the second and third powers, Column A is going to be greater than 0. And you get that result without even considering the fact that the middle term (x^3) is going to be negative. If you can just see this, great. If you can't, plug in numbers.

What if Column A were $x^3 + x^4 + x^5$? Then Column A would be negative and B would be the answer.

5. **D.** The answer depends on how long each side of the square is. Suppose that each side of the square is 1. Then the perimeter (the sum of all the lengths of the sides of the figure) equals $1 + 1 + 1 + 1 = 4$. The area (the area of a square is *side*²) equals $1^2 = 1$. So far, Column A is greater.

   Now make the side of the square equal 2. The perimeter is $2 + 2 + 2 + 2 = 8$. The area is $2^2 = 4$. The answer still is Column A. If you are tempted just to choose Column A and go on your merry way, fight that urge! Try plugging in a bigger number and see what happens.

   Suppose that the side of the square is 10. Then the perimeter is $10 + 10 + 10 + 10 = 40$. The area of the square is $10^2 = 100$. Aha! Now Column B is greater. If the answer could be A or B, it depends, and you should choose D.

How did I know to plug in a big number such as 10? Why didn't I use 1, 2, 0, –1, –2, or ½ — the sacred six? First, you don't plug in negatives for distance or the sides of a figure. Second, remember the major tip given in the Quantitative Comparisons lecture: The answer to a geometry problem with no picture usually is D. Assume guilty (choice D) until proven innocent. As soon as you see a geometry problem that's words, words, and more words without any pictures, decide that the answer probably is going to be D and try several times to make it so.

6. **B.** Angles along a straight line sum up to 180 degrees. Substitute $2y$ for each x in the figure, which gives you $2y + 2y + 2y + y + y = 180$. $8y = 180$. $y = 22.5$. Column B is greater than Column A. Hey, there's no need to let a geometry problem psych you out. Just do it by degrees.

7. **C.** You need to know math vocabulary (given in Chapters 10, 11, and 12). A *prime number* has no positive integral factors other than one and itself. The greatest prime number in Set X is 7 (8 and 9 are not prime, because they have factors other than one and themselves). A *composite number* does have positive integral factors other than one and itself (in other words, it's composed of more factors). The largest composite number in Set Y is 6. To find the greatest possible value for x + y, add 7 + 6 = 13.

8. **A.** STOP! Do not reach for your calculator! Sure, you could work this problem out to the bitter end, but no one really cares what the actual answer is. All you're obligated to do is find out which column is larger. Use one of the tricks from Chapter 15: Compare each element of Column A to its counterpart in Column B. Which is larger, $^{11}/_{15}$ or $^{5}/_{18}$? Because $^{11}/_{15}$ is more than half while $^{5}/_{18}$ is less than half, Column A is larger. Continue. Because $^{17}/_{23}$ is more than half while $^{9}/_{25}$ is less than half, the second element of Column A is larger as well. And finally, because $^{28}/_{29}$ is more than half while $^{21}/_{50}$ is less than half, the last element of Column A is larger than its counterpart in Column B. A is larger.

No, the test makers will not — repeat, will *not* — give you a problem in which part of Column A is bigger and part of Column B is bigger. Doing so would defeat the little trick they want you to use here. Keep in mind that the test makers are not checking that you know how to use your calculator, but that you know how to use your brain to *prevent* having to do a lot of calculating.

9. **B.** If you chose C, you fell for the trap. The mean (average) of the scores is 73, but the median is 72. A median is the middle term when all terms are arranged in order: 68, 70, 72, 75, 80 (Hint: To remember a median, think of the median strip when you're driving down the road: It's in the middle.)

   If you're rusty on the three Ms — mean (average), median (middle term) and mode (most occurring term) — flip to Chapter 12.

10. **C.** The series contains four terms: –3, –2, –1, 0. Divide 100 by 4 to get 25. In 100 numbers, the series repeats exactly 25 times, ending in the last term of the series, 0. Stop! As soon as you know that one of the terms in a multiplication problem is 0, you know that the product of the problem is 0 (because 0 times anything is 0). The columns are equal. (I guess you could say you did all that work for naught. . . .)

Suppose you decide that dividing by 10 is an easy way to go. Count out 10 terms in the series: –3, –2, –1, 0, –3, –2, –1, 0, –3, –2. Now figure that if the 10th term is –2, the 100th term must be –2 as well. Wrong. As you've already seen, the 100th term is 0. The point is that you can't change the series. Find out how many terms are in the series and divide by that number. Because this series has four terms, you must divide by 4.

11. **B.** When you have a number with a negative exponent, that number is the same as the reciprocal of itself. Here, $x^{-8} = 1/x^8$. Multiply $x^8 \times 1/x^8 = x^8/x^8 = 1$. This will be true regardless of the value of x because any number over itself equals 1.

    Column B must be greater than 1 because 8 times a number is greater than that number (when the number is greater than 1).

Did you find the great, built-in shortcut that allows you to do this problem in just a few seconds? As you can read up on in Chapter 11, when multiplying like bases, add the exponents. This problem has like (identical) bases, the x's; just add the exponents: $8 + (-8) = 0$. You find out in Chapter 11 (good stuff there; it's never too late to read it, hint, hint) that any number to the zero power equals 1. Regardless of the value of x, x^0 equals 1. Knowing these two rules for working with bases and exponents saves you a lot of time.

12. **D.** You've seen this type of problem before and should remember that the answer *depends on* how you line up the different buildings. You could line up the buildings different ways, as shown in the following figure.

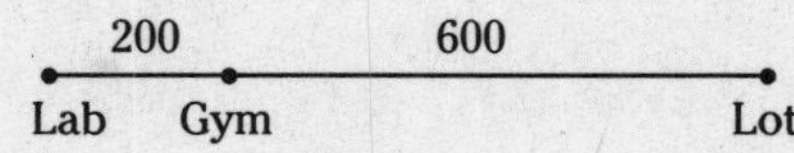

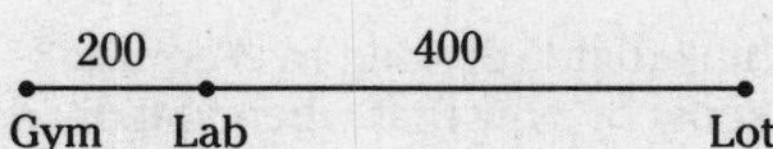

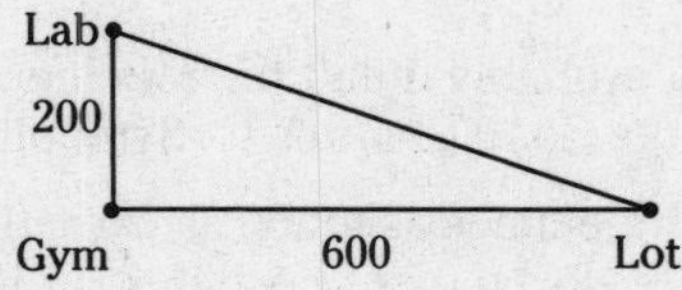

When you have a problem that makes you draw a picture, the answer usually is D because it will depend on how you *draw* that picture. Speaking of buildings, when I was in college, we put a sign on the Psych Lab door: "Telepath Wanted. You know where to apply."

13. **C.** The surface area is the sum of the areas of all surfaces. A surface of a cube is a square. The area of a square is *side* × *side;* here, that is 5 × 5 = 25. A cube has six surfaces, or faces (think of the six sides on a die, which is one of a pair of dice). 25 × 6 = 150.

If you chose B, you probably tried to find the volume of the cube instead of its surface area. The volume of a cube is *edge* × *edge* × *edge.* Here, that would be 5 × 5 × 5 = 125. Be sure to note what the question is asking for; don't rewrite the question to fit what you know, tempting though that may be.

Did you fall for the trap and choose D for this problem? True, when a figure is not given in a geometry problem, the answer is *usually* D because *usually* you don't have enough information to compare the two columns. This question is an exception just to keep you on your toes. As I'm always reminding you, don't count on the tips to the point of shutting off your own brain. Your *first* thought should be that this type of problem is *usually* choice D . . . but your *second* thought should be to double-check.

14. **A.** When you have two equations with the same variables, line them up vertically and either add or subtract to make one of the variables drop out. Here, that would be

$6m + 2n = 22$ (you switch m and n to make subtraction easier)

$3m + 2n = 13$

Subtract to get $3m = 9$. (Notice that the n's drop out: $2n - 2n = 0$.) $m = 3$.

Now substitute 3 for m in the equation. (You can use either equation. I like to use the one with smaller, "easier" numbers.)

$3(3) + 2n = 13$

$9 + 2n = 13$ (When you can cancel, as with the 3s here, you know that you're on the right track.)

$2n = 4$

$n = 2$

15. **B.** If you chose C, you fell for the trap. If you chose D, you didn't work this problem out at all.

This is a symbolism problem. The box is made up just for this problem; there is no such operation as "box" in the real world. Say it to yourself in English. "I have a number in a box. I'm supposed to multiply that number by three and then cube the product. Next, I take a third of that original number. Finally, I add the two numbers." Now substitute ⅓ for the *A* in the equation.

$$(3 \times \tfrac{1}{3})^3 + \frac{(\tfrac{1}{3})}{3}$$

$1^3 + \tfrac{1}{3} \times \tfrac{1}{3} = 1 + \tfrac{1}{9} = 1\tfrac{1}{9}$

It's tempting to think that ⅓ divided by 3 equals 3. Then you'd add 1 + 3 and get 4: the trap answer. But you know by now that when you divide by a fraction, you invert (turn upside down) and multiply. ⅓ divided by 3 is the same as ⅓ divided by $\tfrac{3}{1}$. Invert $\tfrac{3}{1}$ to get $\tfrac{1}{3} \times \tfrac{1}{3} = \tfrac{1}{9}$. Don't let yourself be carried along by what you expect to see; work the problem through entirely.

If you chose D, you probably didn't have a clue what the stupid box means or what you were supposed to do. Go to Chapter 11. Symbolism is actually a lot easier than it looks.

16. **165.** If roses cost three times as much as carnations, carnations are $\tfrac{45}{3} = 15$ a dozen. Two dozen cost 30. Three dozen roses cost $45 \times 3 = 135$. Add: $135 + 30 = 165$.

17. **110.** Number the angles as shown in the figure.

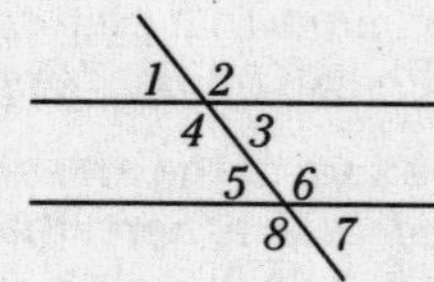

All odd-numbered angles are equal; all even-numbered angles are equal. Because *x* is an odd-numbered angle, it is equal to 110, also an odd-numbered angle.

This problem is very simple if you know how to number angles of parallel lines around a transversal. (See Chapter 10.) This concept works regardless of where you start numbering the angles, as long as you number them clockwise and start in the same position for both sets of angles.

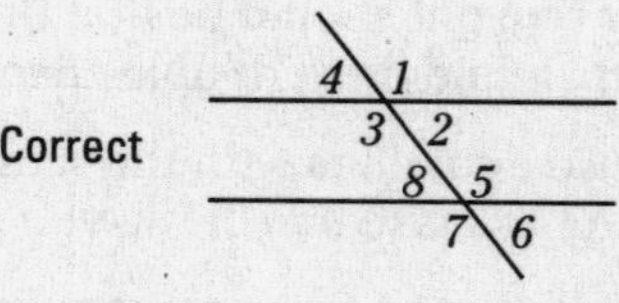

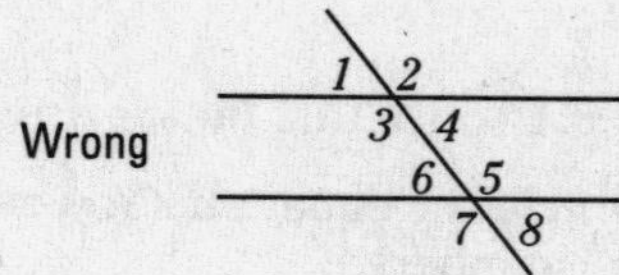

18. **28.** You should memorize from Chapter 11 that $(a + b)^2 = a^2 + 2ab + b^2$. If $ab = 4$, then $2ab = 8$. Plug this into the equation: $a^2 + 8 + b^2 = 36$; $a^2 + b^2 = 28$.

If you didn't have $(a + b)^2$ memorized, you could FOIL (First, Outer, Inner, Last) it out as follows:

$(a + b)\ (a + b) =$

Multiply the First terms: $a \times a = a^2$.

Multiply the Outer terms: $a \times b = ab$.

Multiply the Inner terms: $b \times a = ba$ (which is the same as ab).

Multiply the Last terms: $b \times b = b^2$.

Combine like terms: $a^2 + ab + ab + b^2 = a^2 + 2ab + b^2$.

You can save yourself a lot of time by memorizing three basic algebra problems:

$(a + b)^2 = a^2 + 2ab + b^2$.

$(a - b)^2 = a^2 - 2ab + b^2$.

$(a + b)(a - b) = a^2 - b^2$.

These are discussed in excruciating detail in Chapter 11.

19. **108.** Plug in 100 for percentages, remember? Make the starting price for 1990 be 100. By the end of 1990, the price had risen 20% to 120.

In 1991, the price dropped 25%, *but* it dropped from 120, not from the original 100. In other words, the price went from 120 to 90 (25% of 120 = 30; 120 – 30 = 90).

In 1992, it went up 20%, *but* it went up from 90, not from 100 or from 120. That means that the price went from 90 to 108 (20% of 90 = 18; 18 + 90 = 108).

If 1992 is 108, and if 1990's beginning price is 100, 108 is 108% of 100.

The question does not ask how much the price went up (or down), which would lead you to choose 8% as the answer; it asks you what percent of 1990's price is 1992's price. A percentage = $\frac{is}{of}$. So, 108 is/100 of.

You may have been tempted not to work the problem out but to say that the obvious answer is 95 because the price went up 20, down 25, and up 20 again for a net loss of 5%. AAAARGH! Anytime you think that something is obvious, think again.

20. **0.** In this problem, the math is easy, but the wording is hard. (International students, if the English is confusing you, you could waste a lot of time trying to figure out this problem. Forget it. Because the grid-in questions have no penalties for wrong answers, fill in something, anything, and hope you make a lucky guess, but don't waste more than a few seconds on this problem.) The face of a die has six numbers. The only way to get a total of 12 is to roll two sixes. There is only one chance of doing that: $\frac{1}{36}$ (as a ratio 1:36). The only way to get a sum of 2 is to roll two ones. There is only one chance of doing that: $\frac{1}{36}$. Therefore, the difference between the two chances is 0. You don't even have to deal with fractions. (If you don't know where in the world I got the $\frac{1}{36}$, head to the probabilities portion of Chapter 11. All is explained in detail there.)

21. **0.** This is a pure math vocabulary problem. The *median* is the middle term when all the numbers are arranged in order. (You know what a median is. Think of the median strip in the middle of the road.) If you found the middle number without first arranging the numbers in order, you thought the median was 7. When you arrange the numbers in order, you have 5, 5, 5, 6, 6, 6, 6, 6, 6, 7, 7, 8, 9, 9, 10. There are 15 terms; the middle, or median, is 6.

The *mode* is the most frequently occurring number. There are more 6s than anything else, so 6 is the mode. 6 - 6 = 0. (Medians and modes are discussed in Chapter 12.)

22. **720.** The exterior angles of any polygon add up to 360 degrees. (See Chapter 10.) If you said that 360 was the answer, you fell for the trap. (Shame on you. This question is almost the last one in the section. Did you really think it would be that easy? Have I taught you nothing?)

The trick here is that the figure represents *two sets* of exterior angles. Think of them this way:

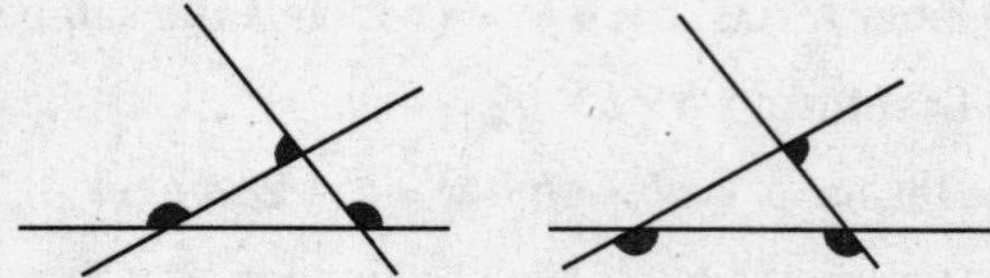

Because each set sums to 360, $360 \times 2 = 720$.

23. **144.** Talk the problem through. You get a number by doubling the last term. Then you take one less than the second-to-last term. Finally, you add those two numbers.

To get *q*, you first double the last term, *p*. $25 \times 2 = 50$. Then take one less than the second-to-last term (second to last goes by the name ***penultimate,*** if you remember your vocabulary lessons). $11 - 1 = 10$. Add: $50 + 10 = 60$. $q = 60$.

To get *r*, you first double the last term, *q*. $60 \times 2 = 120$. Then you take one less than the second-to-last term. $25 - 1 = 24$. Add: $120 + 24 = 144$.

24. **34.40.** First, find the volume of the piece of wood. The volume of a rectangular solid is *length* × *width* × *height.* The length here is given as 10. The width must be 4 because the circle has a diameter of 4. The height also is 4 for the same reason. The volume of the piece of wood is $10 \times 4 \times 4 = 160$.

Second, find the volume of the dowel or rod, which is a cylinder. The volume of a cylinder is πr^2 height. Because the diameter of the circle is 4, the radius is 2. $2^2 = 4$. The height of the cylinder is how long it is: the length of the rod, or 10. The volume of the cylinder or rod, therefore, is $4\pi \times 10$ or 40π or (using 3.14 for π, as the problem instructed) 125.6.

Finally, subtract. Think of the wood to be removed as being the leftover after the dowel has been whittled out. $160 - 125.60 = 34.40$.

Confused? This question is like a shaded-area problem, with the amount of wood to be removed substituting for the shaded area. See Chapter 10.

25. **1.** It's the wording, not the math, that is deadly here. (This would be a great question for international students to skip.) You know that an integer is a whole number, as opposed to a fraction. Integers are . . . –3, –2, –1, 0, 1, 2, 3 . . . . Because the question asks for a positive integer, start with 1.

Did you want to start with 2? Don't confuse *even and odd* with *positive and negative*. That happens a lot, and the test makers know it.

Talk your way through the problem slowly. The square of 1 is 1. One-half of the original integer is one-half of 1, or ½. Divide the square, 1, by one-half of the original integer, ½. 1 divided by ½. When you divide by a fraction, you invert (turn upside down) and multiply (you've seen this a gazillion times by now). $1 \times 2/1 = 2$. Because 2 is an integer, you know that all this rigamarole did in fact result in an integer. Because 1 is the smallest positive integer (again, not the smallest *even* integer, just the smallest *positive* integer), you're done.

Section 5

This reading section may be very difficult for you to finish on time. You have to read two complete passages and answer as many as 13 questions, all in just 15 minutes. If you know you won't finish everything on time, my advice is to concentrate on just one passage. Determine which passage has more questions about it and read it carefully. Skip the other passage entirely. Keep in mind that you can skip a lot of questions on the SAT and still get a very good score.

1. **D.** The last sentence of the first paragraph talks about a "terrestrial, marine, or freshwater environment," allowing you to conclude that they must be three separate types. ***Terrestrial*** means dwelling on land, as opposed to ***aquatic,*** dwelling in the water. You can associate these words with aquarium, where fish live, and terrarium, where lizards and turtles live.

   Question: Why did the turtle cross the road? ***Answer:*** To get to the Shell station!

2. **C.** Like most Roman numeral questions, this one is time-consuming. If you are running short on time, I suggest you leave this passage for last and go back to it if you have the time. Otherwise, you may not make it to the last three or four questions. Obviously, it's better to skip just one question than to leave three or four blank.

   The second line of the first paragraph introduces the concept that certain factors limit where species live. You may therefore deduce that those species that have high tolerance for limiting factors can live in a greater range of places. Because statement I is true, eliminate choice B.

   Statement II is tricky. Although common sense tells you that a species with few natural enemies would wander far and wide, nothing on that topic is addressed in the passage. You must answer questions based only on what the passage states or implies. Because statement II is wrong, eliminate choices D and E. You can now narrow the choices to I only or I and III only. Don't even bother looking at IV because it can't be the right answer. Why waste time?

   The last line of paragraph 2 tells you that animals with a wide range of tolerances are found over a wider range (more confirmation that statement I is true) and are more resistant to environmental changes. Statement III is true.

   Statement IV is a trap (those of you who didn't even bother looking at it were smart). Although it's logical to think that a species that can live in both freshwater and marine environments would have a wider range (assuming that such species do, in fact, exist), answer the question based on what the author says or would believe, not what you believe.

3. **E.** Lines 25–29 state that it's difficult to identify factors that cause a change in the number of a population unless all stages of the animal's life cycle are considered. That's choice E.

4. **A.** Lines 36–42 tell you that ecological equivalents have developed to perform certain functions in their communities. In other words, different species perform the same tasks. You can choose A by process of elimination, even if you're not sure what a bottom feeder is.

   There's a big difference between a question like this that actually expects you to think and reason and a straightforward detail or "according to the passage" question. If you're rushed for time, this is a good question to postpone. Come back to the question later if you have the time, but don't worry if you don't get to it. Your time is better spent on questions with very direct answers.

5. **B.** Because this is the last question about passage 1, go to the end of passage 1 to find the answer. The last three lines say, ". . . we can then protect or use natural resources in a way that will minimize man's adverse effects . . . ." The author apparently hopes this information can be used to reduce the harm man does to the environment.

   Did you eliminate choice A right away? Negative answers are rarely correct (but, of course, you should always at least look at them, just in case).

   The passage mentions choices C and E, but neither choice is the main purpose of the passage. Just because a statement is true or is mentioned in the passage does not mean that the statement is the main idea or primary purpose of the passage.

6. **E.** The author asks a series of rhetorical questions in the first paragraph to present a number of reasonable explanations for the presence of great graveyards. While the passage provides no evidence that the extinction of dinosaurs resulted in a great graveyard, lines 65–69 present a catastrophic event as a real possibility for widespread death. Choice E is correct, and the author discusses a catastrophe as an idea that deserves some merit and study. The first sentence of the second paragraph reinforces the notion along with the other possibilities mentioned in the first paragraph.

If you picked choices A or D, you are concentrating too much on what the author says when discussing the Cleveland-Lloyd quarry. In fact, the author says that we can speculate (line 78), suggesting that he would be open to any reasonable speculation. Eliminate choice D. Water is discussed in the fourth paragraph, but this speculation does not preclude the possibility that the dinosaurs worldwide were wiped out by a meteor. Eliminate choice A. The water has to do with what happened to the dinosaur remains once the animals died. It does not deal with the manner of death. Furthermore, the passage is concerned with a particular group of dinosaurs. For all you know, most of the dinosaurs in the world lived for millions of years after the Cleveland-Lloyd dinosaurs perished. In short, the passage does not deal with dinosaur extinction, so the author would have no trouble with the meteor idea as a viable explanation.

Choices B and C are much too extreme for this passage, in which the author makes it clear that everything proposed is just one man's opinion. In general, extreme answers are unlikely to be correct on the SAT I because they are so easy to dispute. Most SAT I passages avoid dramatic or strong statements, meaning you should be very wary of extreme answer choices.

7. **D.** To ***cow*** is to intimidate or frighten. (If you are *cowed,* you *cower* in a corner, and I mock you for being a *coward.*) Don't worry, you don't have to know that word (most people don't) in order to answer the question correctly. Go back to the context. If the animals become ***submissive*** (humble, docile, subservient), they have been intimidated or frightened into becoming so.

   If you chose any of the other answers, you were thinking about four-footed bovines, not about how the word is used in context. For any vocabulary question in Critical Reading passages, force yourself to go back to the passage to see how the word is actually used. You'll probably be surprised.

8. **E.** This question gets my vote for Lead Loser; it's both tricky and time-consuming. (This is the type of question that makes one of my favorite students exclaim, "Dial 1-800-SAT SUCKS!") Throughout the passage, the author mentions that each answer may possibly be true, but doesn't actually consider any one of them proven. Choice B is especially tricky. Lines 83–84 say that many more carnivorous types were at this particular site than herbivorous ones. However, the author didn't use just one site to generalize that there were more carnivores than herbivores among dinosaurs in general.

9. **A.** Lines 87–89 tell you that the bones are buried in the types of sediments associated with freshwater organisms; the next paragraph begins with the theory that the graveyard has something to do with water.

   Yes, all the answers are mentioned in the passage, but not as answers to this particular question. Just because something is mentioned or is true does not mean it answers the question.

10. **B.** Usually, the first sentence of the passage gives the best title. However, because this question is near the end, it is unlikely that the answer would be found near the beginning of the passage or be so obvious. This is a read-between-the-lines question. Ask yourself what the passage is about: a writer discussing his theory of the causes of the dinosaurs' extinction.

    Choice C is very tempting because of the idea of *one man's search.* However, this passage is not about a search for dinosaurs; the dinosaurs have already been found. The search is for the cause of their extinction.

    Choice D is also tempting because the passage mentions bogs. Unfortunately, there are no "other burial sites." Besides, because the whole passage is about dinosaurs, don't you think the word *dinosaur* should be in the title somewhere?

11. **C.** Skip a question that depends *entirely* on unknown vocabulary. You may be able to predict what the attitude was; but if you can't define any of the words, your knowledge does you no good. (If I'm underestimating your brilliant vocabulary, I abjectly apologize.)

    Sanctimonious means pretending to be very holy or righteous (*sanc* = holy; *-ous* = full of, very). Improbable means unlikely to take place and is a fun word to use on your parents. "You want me to get a 1600 on the SAT? How *improbable!*") ***Expository*** means explanatory. (Keep your eyes open for this word. It is often the correct answer to an "attitude or tone" question, because so many passages simply explain the facts or an opinion.)

    Enigmatic means puzzling, confusing. ***Huffy*** means quick to take offense, likely to storm off in a huff. (There's a great Groucho Marx line I often quote when someone is walking away from me, disgusted by my jokes: "Hey, don't leave in a huff! Wait a minute and a huff!")

12. **B.** Did you notice that you have actually already answered this question? Here, the question is in effect asking you the purpose of each passage: why the author put you through all this. The purpose of passage 1 (as you deduced in question 5) is to motivate man to stop wasting resources. The purpose of passage 2 (as you realized from question 10) is to present one man's hypothesis or theory behind the extinction of the dinosaurs.

    Do you know the word ***refute?*** It means disprove. The facts of passage 1 are not disproved by passage 2's theories.

    As for choice E, do you really think the SAT would give you a passage full of errors (full of grief, yes; full of errors, no)? Besides, unless you are a professional paleontologist in your spare time, how would you know whether passage 2 has errors or not?

13. **A.** The last two questions in a double-passage section usually require you to compare or contrast the two passages. Skip these questions if you are not entirely committed to your answers.

    The correct answer here is nice and vague — always a good selling point for an SAT question. The first passage speaks about how the environment affects animals; passage 2 discusses how the dinosaurs were affected by their environment (leading to their demise in bogs). No, it's not a great answer, but it's the best of the sorry lot presented for your viewing pleasure.

Never hesitate to skip the last two, or even three, questions in any section. You may feel I'm asking you to skip a lot — and you're right. Go back to the scoring table and see how many questions you can skip and still get the goal score you want. For example, say you want a 550 verbal. You can get as few as 44 out of 78 questions correct. That means that (assuming you get right the questions you actually *do* answer) you can skip 34 questions! That's a heckuva lotta questions. Even if you want a 600, you can skip 26 questions. Want a 700? You can skip 12 questions.

Section 6

1. **E.** This is another Nike problem. (Just Do It!) Try each of the answer choices. In A, $\sqrt{64} = 8$; 8 is not half of 64. In B, $\sqrt{49} = 7$; 7 is not half of 49. In C, $\sqrt{25} = 5$; 5 is not half of 25. In D, $\sqrt{16} = 4$; 4 is not half of 16. Choice E had better work, or you're in trouble. In E, $\sqrt{4} = 2$; 2 *is* half of 4.

2. **D.** $\frac{1}{2}^2 = \frac{1}{2} \times \frac{1}{2} = \frac{1}{4}$. Three of those are $\frac{3}{4}$. That result is greater than $\frac{1}{2} \times \frac{1}{2} \times \frac{1}{2} \times \frac{1}{2} \times \frac{1}{2} \times \frac{1}{2} = \frac{1}{64}$. Because I must be true, eliminate choices B and C.

    II does not work. 0 to any power is 0. $0 + 0 + 0 = 0$. And 0 is not greater than 0. Eliminate choice E.

    III works. $1^2 + 1^2 + 1^2 = 3$, which is greater than 1^6, or 1.

3. **D.** Did you actually *solve* this problem? No way. Don't spend a minute actually solving for the values of the terms; use your common sense. If there are four consecutive odd integers, they are each two units apart. For example, four consecutive odd integers could be 1, 3, 5, 7 or 11, 13, 15, 17. In any case, each integer is two away from the others. The last integer in the series will be six more than the first integer. You don't actually have to solve the problem to find out which four values add up to 32.

Did you fall for the trap answer, 8? If so, you probably figured that four numbers, two apart, must equal 8. However, there are two units between the first and second terms, two units between the second and third terms, and two units between the third and fourth terms, for a total of 6.

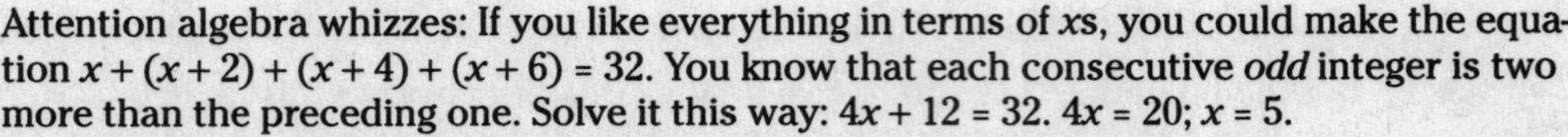

Attention algebra whizzes: If you like everything in terms of *x*s, you could make the equation $x + (x + 2) + (x + 4) + (x + 6) = 32$. You know that each consecutive *odd* integer is two more than the preceding one. Solve it this way: $4x + 12 = 32$. $4x = 20$; $x = 5$.

That's one of the answer choices; careless readers could fall for that one big-time. If $x = 5$, the series is 5, 7, 9, 11, and the difference between the first and last terms is $11 - 5 = 6$.

Once more, with feeling. There is yet another way to solve this problem. Find the average: $^{32}/_{4} = 8$. Because the average is the middle term, you have a series like this: _ _ 8 _ _. The odd integers on either side of 8 must be 7 and 9, again giving you the series 5, 7, 9, 11.

4. **C.** A percent increase (or decrease) is the number increase (or decrease) over the original whole. You don't have to find the actual percentages in this case; a look at the basic fractions is enough.

   Amanda: $^{15}/_{75}$

   Bret: $^{10}/_{90}$

   Carlyse: $^{30}/_{60}$

   Denzil: $^{20}/_{100}$

   Edmund: $^{20}/_{90}$

   Because Carlyse's is 1/2 (just reduce $^{30}/_{60}$), significantly more than the fractions for the others, she had the greatest increase.

5. **B.** If you chose A, you fell for the trap. The key here is recognizing that the drop was not 25 points, but 25 percent of 120, which is 30 points. $120 - 30 = 90$. Choice E is also a trap answer, which you get if you subtract $100 - 30$.

6. **C.** A sector is a segment of a circle, part of the circle's area. If there are 8 equal sectors, and one sector is 8π, multiply $8\pi \times 8$ to find that the area of the entire circle is 64π.

Note that choice D is the trap answer 64π. Just because the "answer" you got is staring you in the face doesn't mean that you have answered what the question is asking. The answer choices on the SAT often feature "intermediate" answers, those numbers you get in the course of eventually getting around to the right answer.

The formula for the area of a circle is πr^2. If the area of the circle is 64π, then $\pi r^2 = 64\pi$. Solve that $64 = r^2$ and $r = 8$. (Notice that the trap answer, choice B, has an 8 in it.) You're almost done; hang in there. The circumference of a circle is $2\pi r$. This gives you 16π, the right answer at last.

7. **D.** Make x stand for the number of books that they check out and make $x + 20$ represent the number of books that they put back. The equation now is $x + (x + 20) = 84$. $2x + 20 = 84$. $2x = 64$. $x = 32$.

If you chose B, you forgot to answer the question, which wants to know how many books were put back, not how many were checked out. $84 - 32 = 52$.

You can use a great shortcut to narrow down the answers. You know that more books were put back than were checked out. That means that more than half of the books were put back and fewer than half the books were checked out. Half of 84 is 42; more than that must have been put back. Only answers D and E could fit. Instead of working through all the garbage algebra, use those two answers. If 52 books were put back, 20 fewer than 52, or 32, were checked out. Do 52 + 32 = 84? Yup, they do, and you've finished the problem. If you want to check, try choice E. If 64 books were put back, 20 fewer than 64, or 44 books, were checked out. Do 64 + 44 = 84? Nope. Choice D was right all along.

8. **E.** Think of a shaded area as a "leftover." Find the area of the whole figure. Find the unshaded area. What's "leftover" when you subtract is the shaded area.

   The area of a rectangle is *length* times *width.* The *length* is 10. The *width* is the same as the radius of the circle. Because the diameter of the circle is line *BC,* which is 10 (just like line *AD*), the radius is 5. (A radius is half a diameter.) The area of the rectangle is $10 \times 5 = 50$. Immediately eliminate choices A and B.

   The area of a circle is πr^2, which here is 25π. Choice D is the trap answer. You are not subtracting the entire circle from the rectangle, but only half the circle. Half of 25 is 12.5.

   Even if you don't have a clue how to do this problem, you can eliminate choice C. Because 50π is greater than 50, the answer would be negative. You can't have a negative area.

9. **C.** Set up a few diagrams, indicating the possible arrangements of the diners. The easiest restriction to start with is that A will sit in seat 5, so put A in seat 5 in the diagram. Next, use the restriction that B will sit next to A. The problem is that you don't know which side of A, so put B in seat 4 and then draw another circle, with numbered seats as in the diagram, and put A in seat 5 and B in seat 6.

   Put C across from B in each of the two diagrams that you now have: C will be in seat 8 (across from seat 4) in the first diagram that you draw and will be in seat 2 (across from seat 6) in the second diagram.

   Now you have to place D. Once again, you don't know in which direction. To start, copy the two diagrams that you have. (You now have a total of four diagrams.) Two of these diagrams have C in seat 8, so put D in seat 6 in one of them, and put D in seat 2 in the other. The two remaining diagrams have C in seat 2, so put D in seat 8 in one of them, and put D in seat 4 in the other.

   To summarize (and now you know why these are the last, hardest questions in the section), you now have the following possibilities:

   - You have four diagrams with seats 1-8.
   - Each diagram has diner A in 5.
   - Diagram one has B in 4, D in 6, and C in 8.
   - Diagram two has B in 6, D in 4, and C in 2.
   - Diagram three has B in 4, D in 2, and C in 8.
   - Diagram four has B in 6, D in 8, and C in 2.

   Now you're finally ready to answer the question (which isn't actually hard so much as just annoyingly time-consuming). The diagrams show you that the only way to place the five diners so that there are no empty seats in between any two of them is to use the diagrams in which D is in seat 4 (circle two) or seat 6 (circle one). If D is in seat 6, you may put E in seat 5, leaving seats 1, 2, and 3 empty. Unfortunately, this choice isn't offered. If D is in seat 4, you may put E in seat 3, leaving seats 1, 7, and 8 empty — and this is the arrangement given in answer choice C.

Choices A and D could work with the diagram in which B is in 4, D is in 6, and C is in 8 if you didn't have that requirement of having no empty seats between the five diners. Similarly, choice B and E would work with D in 2, B in 4, and C in 8, but once again, you'll have an empty seat between two diners. Be sure you follow all of the constraints given in the facts of the question.

10. **C.** If you're next to clueless (no, no, don't worry; Clueless is not another diner, added to this table!), eliminate choices A and E. Why? C must sit directly opposite B, so it's impossible to have E sit opposite C. Option I is impossible, meaning you can toss the choices that include this option, choices A and E.

The only diagram that can accommodate E next to and to the right of A is the one that has C in 2, B in 6, and D in 8. E will go in chair 4, directly across from D in seat 8.

Answer Sheet

Begin with Number 1 for each new section. If any sections have fewer than 35 questions, leave the extra spaces blank.

Section 1

1. Ⓐ Ⓑ Ⓒ Ⓓ Ⓔ	8. Ⓐ Ⓑ Ⓒ Ⓓ Ⓔ	15. Ⓐ Ⓑ Ⓒ Ⓓ Ⓔ	22. Ⓐ Ⓑ Ⓒ Ⓓ Ⓔ	29. Ⓐ Ⓑ Ⓒ Ⓓ Ⓔ
2. Ⓐ Ⓑ Ⓒ Ⓓ Ⓔ	9. Ⓐ Ⓑ Ⓒ Ⓓ Ⓔ	16. Ⓐ Ⓑ Ⓒ Ⓓ Ⓔ	23. Ⓐ Ⓑ Ⓒ Ⓓ Ⓔ	30. Ⓐ Ⓑ Ⓒ Ⓓ Ⓔ
3. Ⓐ Ⓑ Ⓒ Ⓓ Ⓔ	10. Ⓐ Ⓑ Ⓒ Ⓓ Ⓔ	17. Ⓐ Ⓑ Ⓒ Ⓓ Ⓔ	24. Ⓐ Ⓑ Ⓒ Ⓓ Ⓔ	31. Ⓐ Ⓑ Ⓒ Ⓓ Ⓔ
4. Ⓐ Ⓑ Ⓒ Ⓓ Ⓔ	11. Ⓐ Ⓑ Ⓒ Ⓓ Ⓔ	18. Ⓐ Ⓑ Ⓒ Ⓓ Ⓔ	25. Ⓐ Ⓑ Ⓒ Ⓓ Ⓔ	32. Ⓐ Ⓑ Ⓒ Ⓓ Ⓔ
5. Ⓐ Ⓑ Ⓒ Ⓓ Ⓔ	12. Ⓐ Ⓑ Ⓒ Ⓓ Ⓔ	19. Ⓐ Ⓑ Ⓒ Ⓓ Ⓔ	26. Ⓐ Ⓑ Ⓒ Ⓓ Ⓔ	33. Ⓐ Ⓑ Ⓒ Ⓓ Ⓔ
6. Ⓐ Ⓑ Ⓒ Ⓓ Ⓔ	13. Ⓐ Ⓑ Ⓒ Ⓓ Ⓔ	20. Ⓐ Ⓑ Ⓒ Ⓓ Ⓔ	27. Ⓐ Ⓑ Ⓒ Ⓓ Ⓔ	34. Ⓐ Ⓑ Ⓒ Ⓓ Ⓔ
7. Ⓐ Ⓑ Ⓒ Ⓓ Ⓔ	14. Ⓐ Ⓑ Ⓒ Ⓓ Ⓔ	21. Ⓐ Ⓑ Ⓒ Ⓓ Ⓔ	28. Ⓐ Ⓑ Ⓒ Ⓓ Ⓔ	35. Ⓐ Ⓑ Ⓒ Ⓓ Ⓔ

Section 2

1. Ⓐ Ⓑ Ⓒ Ⓓ Ⓔ	8. Ⓐ Ⓑ Ⓒ Ⓓ Ⓔ	15. Ⓐ Ⓑ Ⓒ Ⓓ Ⓔ	22. Ⓐ Ⓑ Ⓒ Ⓓ Ⓔ	29. Ⓐ Ⓑ Ⓒ Ⓓ Ⓔ
2. Ⓐ Ⓑ Ⓒ Ⓓ Ⓔ	9. Ⓐ Ⓑ Ⓒ Ⓓ Ⓔ	16. Ⓐ Ⓑ Ⓒ Ⓓ Ⓔ	23. Ⓐ Ⓑ Ⓒ Ⓓ Ⓔ	30. Ⓐ Ⓑ Ⓒ Ⓓ Ⓔ
3. Ⓐ Ⓑ Ⓒ Ⓓ Ⓔ	10. Ⓐ Ⓑ Ⓒ Ⓓ Ⓔ	17. Ⓐ Ⓑ Ⓒ Ⓓ Ⓔ	24. Ⓐ Ⓑ Ⓒ Ⓓ Ⓔ	31. Ⓐ Ⓑ Ⓒ Ⓓ Ⓔ
4. Ⓐ Ⓑ Ⓒ Ⓓ Ⓔ	11. Ⓐ Ⓑ Ⓒ Ⓓ Ⓔ	18. Ⓐ Ⓑ Ⓒ Ⓓ Ⓔ	25. Ⓐ Ⓑ Ⓒ Ⓓ Ⓔ	32. Ⓐ Ⓑ Ⓒ Ⓓ Ⓔ
5. Ⓐ Ⓑ Ⓒ Ⓓ Ⓔ	12. Ⓐ Ⓑ Ⓒ Ⓓ Ⓔ	19. Ⓐ Ⓑ Ⓒ Ⓓ Ⓔ	26. Ⓐ Ⓑ Ⓒ Ⓓ Ⓔ	33. Ⓐ Ⓑ Ⓒ Ⓓ Ⓔ
6. Ⓐ Ⓑ Ⓒ Ⓓ Ⓔ	13. Ⓐ Ⓑ Ⓒ Ⓓ Ⓔ	20. Ⓐ Ⓑ Ⓒ Ⓓ Ⓔ	27. Ⓐ Ⓑ Ⓒ Ⓓ Ⓔ	34. Ⓐ Ⓑ Ⓒ Ⓓ Ⓔ
7. Ⓐ Ⓑ Ⓒ Ⓓ Ⓔ	14. Ⓐ Ⓑ Ⓒ Ⓓ Ⓔ	21. Ⓐ Ⓑ Ⓒ Ⓓ Ⓔ	28. Ⓐ Ⓑ Ⓒ Ⓓ Ⓔ	35. Ⓐ Ⓑ Ⓒ Ⓓ Ⓔ

Section 3

1. Ⓐ Ⓑ Ⓒ Ⓓ Ⓔ	8. Ⓐ Ⓑ Ⓒ Ⓓ Ⓔ	15. Ⓐ Ⓑ Ⓒ Ⓓ Ⓔ	22. Ⓐ Ⓑ Ⓒ Ⓓ Ⓔ	29. Ⓐ Ⓑ Ⓒ Ⓓ Ⓔ
2. Ⓐ Ⓑ Ⓒ Ⓓ Ⓔ	9. Ⓐ Ⓑ Ⓒ Ⓓ Ⓔ	16. Ⓐ Ⓑ Ⓒ Ⓓ Ⓔ	23. Ⓐ Ⓑ Ⓒ Ⓓ Ⓔ	30. Ⓐ Ⓑ Ⓒ Ⓓ Ⓔ
3. Ⓐ Ⓑ Ⓒ Ⓓ Ⓔ	10. Ⓐ Ⓑ Ⓒ Ⓓ Ⓔ	17. Ⓐ Ⓑ Ⓒ Ⓓ Ⓔ	24. Ⓐ Ⓑ Ⓒ Ⓓ Ⓔ	31. Ⓐ Ⓑ Ⓒ Ⓓ Ⓔ
4. Ⓐ Ⓑ Ⓒ Ⓓ Ⓔ	11. Ⓐ Ⓑ Ⓒ Ⓓ Ⓔ	18. Ⓐ Ⓑ Ⓒ Ⓓ Ⓔ	25. Ⓐ Ⓑ Ⓒ Ⓓ Ⓔ	32. Ⓐ Ⓑ Ⓒ Ⓓ Ⓔ
5. Ⓐ Ⓑ Ⓒ Ⓓ Ⓔ	12. Ⓐ Ⓑ Ⓒ Ⓓ Ⓔ	19. Ⓐ Ⓑ Ⓒ Ⓓ Ⓔ	26. Ⓐ Ⓑ Ⓒ Ⓓ Ⓔ	33. Ⓐ Ⓑ Ⓒ Ⓓ Ⓔ
6. Ⓐ Ⓑ Ⓒ Ⓓ Ⓔ	13. Ⓐ Ⓑ Ⓒ Ⓓ Ⓔ	20. Ⓐ Ⓑ Ⓒ Ⓓ Ⓔ	27. Ⓐ Ⓑ Ⓒ Ⓓ Ⓔ	34. Ⓐ Ⓑ Ⓒ Ⓓ Ⓔ
7. Ⓐ Ⓑ Ⓒ Ⓓ Ⓔ	14. Ⓐ Ⓑ Ⓒ Ⓓ Ⓔ	21. Ⓐ Ⓑ Ⓒ Ⓓ Ⓔ	28. Ⓐ Ⓑ Ⓒ Ⓓ Ⓔ	35. Ⓐ Ⓑ Ⓒ Ⓓ Ⓔ

Section 4

1. Ⓐ Ⓑ Ⓒ Ⓓ Ⓔ	4. Ⓐ Ⓑ Ⓒ Ⓓ Ⓔ	7. Ⓐ Ⓑ Ⓒ Ⓓ Ⓔ	10. Ⓐ Ⓑ Ⓒ Ⓓ Ⓔ	13. Ⓐ Ⓑ Ⓒ Ⓓ Ⓔ
2. Ⓐ Ⓑ Ⓒ Ⓓ Ⓔ	5. Ⓐ Ⓑ Ⓒ Ⓓ Ⓔ	8. Ⓐ Ⓑ Ⓒ Ⓓ Ⓔ	11. Ⓐ Ⓑ Ⓒ Ⓓ Ⓔ	14. Ⓐ Ⓑ Ⓒ Ⓓ Ⓔ
3. Ⓐ Ⓑ Ⓒ Ⓓ Ⓔ	6. Ⓐ Ⓑ Ⓒ Ⓓ Ⓔ	9. Ⓐ Ⓑ Ⓒ Ⓓ Ⓔ	12. Ⓐ Ⓑ Ⓒ Ⓓ Ⓔ	15. Ⓐ Ⓑ Ⓒ Ⓓ Ⓔ

Section 4 (continued)

16. 17. 18. 19. 20.

21. 22. 23. 24. 25.

Section 5

1. Ⓐ Ⓑ Ⓒ Ⓓ Ⓔ	8. Ⓐ Ⓑ Ⓒ Ⓓ Ⓔ	15. Ⓐ Ⓑ Ⓒ Ⓓ Ⓔ	22. Ⓐ Ⓑ Ⓒ Ⓓ Ⓔ	29. Ⓐ Ⓑ Ⓒ Ⓓ Ⓔ
2. Ⓐ Ⓑ Ⓒ Ⓓ Ⓔ	9. Ⓐ Ⓑ Ⓒ Ⓓ Ⓔ	16. Ⓐ Ⓑ Ⓒ Ⓓ Ⓔ	23. Ⓐ Ⓑ Ⓒ Ⓓ Ⓔ	30. Ⓐ Ⓑ Ⓒ Ⓓ Ⓔ
3. Ⓐ Ⓑ Ⓒ Ⓓ Ⓔ	10. Ⓐ Ⓑ Ⓒ Ⓓ Ⓔ	17. Ⓐ Ⓑ Ⓒ Ⓓ Ⓔ	24. Ⓐ Ⓑ Ⓒ Ⓓ Ⓔ	31. Ⓐ Ⓑ Ⓒ Ⓓ Ⓔ
4. Ⓐ Ⓑ Ⓒ Ⓓ Ⓔ	11. Ⓐ Ⓑ Ⓒ Ⓓ Ⓔ	18. Ⓐ Ⓑ Ⓒ Ⓓ Ⓔ	25. Ⓐ Ⓑ Ⓒ Ⓓ Ⓔ	32. Ⓐ Ⓑ Ⓒ Ⓓ Ⓔ
5. Ⓐ Ⓑ Ⓒ Ⓓ Ⓔ	12. Ⓐ Ⓑ Ⓒ Ⓓ Ⓔ	19. Ⓐ Ⓑ Ⓒ Ⓓ Ⓔ	26. Ⓐ Ⓑ Ⓒ Ⓓ Ⓔ	33. Ⓐ Ⓑ Ⓒ Ⓓ Ⓔ
6. Ⓐ Ⓑ Ⓒ Ⓓ Ⓔ	13. Ⓐ Ⓑ Ⓒ Ⓓ Ⓔ	20. Ⓐ Ⓑ Ⓒ Ⓓ Ⓔ	27. Ⓐ Ⓑ Ⓒ Ⓓ Ⓔ	34. Ⓐ Ⓑ Ⓒ Ⓓ Ⓔ
7. Ⓐ Ⓑ Ⓒ Ⓓ Ⓔ	14. Ⓐ Ⓑ Ⓒ Ⓓ Ⓔ	21. Ⓐ Ⓑ Ⓒ Ⓓ Ⓔ	28. Ⓐ Ⓑ Ⓒ Ⓓ Ⓔ	35. Ⓐ Ⓑ Ⓒ Ⓓ Ⓔ

Section 6

1. Ⓐ Ⓑ Ⓒ Ⓓ Ⓔ	8. Ⓐ Ⓑ Ⓒ Ⓓ Ⓔ	15. Ⓐ Ⓑ Ⓒ Ⓓ Ⓔ	22. Ⓐ Ⓑ Ⓒ Ⓓ Ⓔ	29. Ⓐ Ⓑ Ⓒ Ⓓ Ⓔ
2. Ⓐ Ⓑ Ⓒ Ⓓ Ⓔ	9. Ⓐ Ⓑ Ⓒ Ⓓ Ⓔ	16. Ⓐ Ⓑ Ⓒ Ⓓ Ⓔ	23. Ⓐ Ⓑ Ⓒ Ⓓ Ⓔ	30. Ⓐ Ⓑ Ⓒ Ⓓ Ⓔ
3. Ⓐ Ⓑ Ⓒ Ⓓ Ⓔ	10. Ⓐ Ⓑ Ⓒ Ⓓ Ⓔ	17. Ⓐ Ⓑ Ⓒ Ⓓ Ⓔ	24. Ⓐ Ⓑ Ⓒ Ⓓ Ⓔ	31. Ⓐ Ⓑ Ⓒ Ⓓ Ⓔ
4. Ⓐ Ⓑ Ⓒ Ⓓ Ⓔ	11. Ⓐ Ⓑ Ⓒ Ⓓ Ⓔ	18. Ⓐ Ⓑ Ⓒ Ⓓ Ⓔ	25. Ⓐ Ⓑ Ⓒ Ⓓ Ⓔ	32. Ⓐ Ⓑ Ⓒ Ⓓ Ⓔ
5. Ⓐ Ⓑ Ⓒ Ⓓ Ⓔ	12. Ⓐ Ⓑ Ⓒ Ⓓ Ⓔ	19. Ⓐ Ⓑ Ⓒ Ⓓ Ⓔ	26. Ⓐ Ⓑ Ⓒ Ⓓ Ⓔ	33. Ⓐ Ⓑ Ⓒ Ⓓ Ⓔ
6. Ⓐ Ⓑ Ⓒ Ⓓ Ⓔ	13. Ⓐ Ⓑ Ⓒ Ⓓ Ⓔ	20. Ⓐ Ⓑ Ⓒ Ⓓ Ⓔ	27. Ⓐ Ⓑ Ⓒ Ⓓ Ⓔ	34. Ⓐ Ⓑ Ⓒ Ⓓ Ⓔ
7. Ⓐ Ⓑ Ⓒ Ⓓ Ⓔ	14. Ⓐ Ⓑ Ⓒ Ⓓ Ⓔ	21. Ⓐ Ⓑ Ⓒ Ⓓ Ⓔ	28. Ⓐ Ⓑ Ⓒ Ⓓ Ⓔ	35. Ⓐ Ⓑ Ⓒ Ⓓ Ⓔ

Chapter 19

How to Ruin a Perfectly Good Day, Part II: Practice Exam 2

Are you ready to have another go at it? The following exam consists of four 30-minute sections and two 15-minute sections. Three sections are verbal; three are math. You should be familiar with the question formats by now.

Please take this test under normal exam conditions. This is serious stuff here!

1. **Sit where you won't be interrupted (even though you'd probably welcome any distractions).**
2. **Use the answer grid provided.**
3. **Set your alarm for 30- or 15-minute intervals.**
4. **Do not go on to the next section until the time allotted for the section you are taking is up.**
5. **If you finish early, check your work for that section only.**
6. **Do not take a break during any one section.**
7. **Give yourself one 10-minute break between sections 2 and 3, and a second 10-minute break between sections 4 and 5.**

When you complete the entire test, check your answers with the answer key at the end of this chapter. Sample scoring charts are provided.

Go through the answer explanations to *all* the questions, not just the ones you missed (see Chapter 20). There is a plethora of worthwhile information, material that provides a good review of everything in the lectures. I've even tossed in a few good jokes to keep you somewhat sane.

Section 1

Time: 30 Minutes

35 Questions

Choose the *best* answer to each question. Blacken the corresponding oval on the answer grid.

Each of the following sentences has one or two blanks indicating words or phrases that are omitted. Choose the answer that best completes the sentence.

Example:

Because he ---- the test, John was ----.

(A) flunked .. thrilled

(B) forgot .. brilliant

(C) passed .. happy

(D) ignored .. praised

(E) memorized .. surprised

The correct answer is (C). 

1. Our culture finds it paradoxical that in Bulgaria a nod means no, while a shaking of the head side to side signifies ----.

(A) nothing

(B) contempt

(C) agreement

(D) friendship

(E) dissent

2. Although very few people will ever achieve ---- of more than six and a half feet (78 inches), every one of us has about sixty thousand miles of vessels that carry blood to the parts of our bodies.

(A) an involvement

(B) a girth

(C) a weight

(D) a height

(E) a direction

3. ---- by the enormity of the task in front of her, Counselor Knostman ---- and finally managed to find the perfect college for the candidate who had very unusual requirements for a school.

(A) Undeterred .. persevered

(B) Undaunted .. resigned

(C) Bored .. continued

(D) Intimidated .. quit

(E) Frightened .. relaxed

4. While obviously intending to ---- the reader's appetite to learn more about its fascinating and intriguing subject, the biography was written so ---- that it had the reverse effect.

(A) dull .. quickly

(B) whet .. poorly

(C) sharpen .. well

(D) suppress .. brilliantly

(E) stymie .. badly

5. The effects of overfishing on whole ecosystems are ---- to monitor and assess accurately, but they must be ---- if ocean ecosystems are to be managed successfully.

(A) useless .. evaluated

(B) important .. ignored

(C) difficult .. understood

(D) challenging .. overlooked

(E) easy .. criticized

Go on to next page

6. Although he lacked the ---- that he would like to have in the field, Dr. Wissen felt confident enough of his premise to continue arguing ---- against the physician, whom he considered to be a dangerous quack and a charlatan.

(A) fidelity .. exhaustively

(B) grace .. indifferently

(C) skill .. vaguely

(D) expertise .. vehemently

(E) ability .. tentatively

7. The terms "poison oak" and "poison ivy" are ---- because the plants are neither oak nor ivy, but members of the cashew family (Anacardiaceae).

(A) apropos

(B) misnomers

(C) euphonious

(D) indefinite

(E) florid

8. Jarchow, in his seminal work on India, neglected to note the public's ---- to complete a thousand page ---- and lost sales to Wender's more concise travelogue.

(A) disinclination .. tome

(B) eagerness .. book

(C) refusal .. pamphlet

(D) willingness .. paragraph

(E) consternation .. brochure

9. Impressed by the ---- of the job applicant, Mr. Ramon hired her, saying that her attitude was a refreshing change from the ---- and duplicity that the other applicants had demonstrated.

(A) candor .. hypocrisy

(B) vacillation .. integrity

(C) perfection .. opulence

(D) mendacity .. presumptuousness

(E) didacticism .. idiocy

10. Unlike most of his more garrulous friends, Lou was ----, especially in the presence of ---- women, when he became even more tongue-tied than usual.

(A) contentious .. beautiful

(B) gregarious .. attractive

(C) loquacious .. aggressive

(D) laconic .. pulchritudinous

(E) affable .. haughty

Each of the following questions features a pair of words or phrases in capital letters, followed by five pairs of words or phrases in lowercase letters. Choose the lowercase pair that most closely expresses the same relationship as that of the uppercase pair.

Example:

HAPPY: SAD::

(A) tall: fat

(B) silly: serious

(C) yellow: red

(D) nervous: anxious

(E) joyful: mysterious

The correct answer is (B). 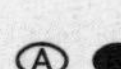 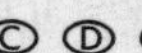

11. BEAKER: FLASK::

(A) feather: weapon

(B) valise: luggage

(C) computer: monitor

(D) silverware: drawer

(E) pencil: pen

12. STAMP: LETTER::

(A) clasp: purse

(B) label: package

(C) crumbs: cake

(D) bark: tree

(E) ribbon: gift

Go on to next page

13. HUSK: RICE::
(A) shellac: varnish
(B) kernel: corn
(C) shell: walnut
(D) leotard: dancer
(E) necklace: neck

14. PINCERS: CRAB::
(A) ears: elephant
(B) hands: human
(C) hide: crocodile
(D) warts: frog
(E) eyes: monkey

15. FISSURE: EARTH::
(A) strata: atmosphere
(B) soil: dirt
(C) electron: molecule
(D) rift: stone
(E) monitor: computer

16. INSURGENT: GOVERNMENT::
(A) iconoclast: religion
(B) cadet: military
(C) lawyer: judiciary
(D) minister: church
(E) worker: corporation

17. ADEQUATE: SUPERFLUOUS::
(A) annoying: infuriating
(B) humorous: amusing
(C) insincere: honest
(D) partial: incomplete
(E) innovative: conservative

18. BAGPIPES: CACOPHONY::
(A) buzzers: knell
(B) bells: peal
(C) chimes: hiss
(D) watches: clatter
(E) lights: flicker

19. CURSORY: METICULOUS::
(A) clandestine: swift
(B) languorous: listless
(C) novel: new
(D) placid: agitated
(E) parched: wrinkled

20. HAZARDOUS: INNOCUOUS::
(A) serene: placid
(B) jealous: envious
(C) lucid: ambiguous
(D) immature: immaterial
(E) expensive: costly

21. PREMONITION: AFTERTHOUGHT::
(A) demand: suggestion
(B) conclusion: interference
(C) prologue: peroration
(D) product: prototype
(E) consensus: agreement

22. DUPLICITOUS: DECEIVE::
(A) carping: praise
(B) analytical: dismiss
(C) innovative: profane
(D) stultifying: bore
(E) pious: scorn

23. WARREN: RABBIT::
(A) neigh: horse
(B) leaves: giraffe
(C) burrow: mole
(D) wing: vulture
(E) blubber: whale

Go on to next page

Each passage is followed by questions that pertain to that passage. Read the passage and answer the questions based on information stated or implied in that passage.

Questions 24–35 are based on the following passage.

The following passage is from a memoir by a young woman who is reminiscing about how her childhood shaped her future.

Growing up in the Midwest, I always felt I was missing out on the excitement offered "out there," on the coasts. The teenagers in New York City sported the latest fashions and listened to the edgiest music. Teens in Los Angeles, according to the television shows we avidly watched, were all tanned surfers who created the modern slang that their parents couldn't comprehend, and attended non-stop outrageous beach parties. Those of us in the center of the country, in my opinion, were years behind the times, wearing antediluvian clothes, listening to obsolete music, using expressions that would make us look provincial in the eyes of the more modish Coasters. My friends and I were certain that our parents had ruined our lives by making us live in the rural areas of the Midwest, and constantly complained that our lives weren't as exciting or interesting as those of the teenagers elsewhere. No matter how much our parents told us that life wasn't like we read about it in the fashion magazines or saw it unfold on the sitcoms on tv, we were positive that those teenagers living on the coasts were the luckiest people on earth.

Because of these beliefs, I was ambivalent about attending college on the East Coast. Although I was excited about getting into the college of my choice, proud that I had met the exacting standards, I knew I would be meeting new people who had grown up in the East. I was sure that they would consider me hopelessly antiquated. I agonized for three months over what clothes to take, what to wear on the first day of classes, what image to project. Should I be cool and haughty? Should I be warm and approachable? What would make me look friendly without seeming desperate? I'm sure my insecurities concerned my parents too. My mother would often leave brochures of local colleges sitting on the kitchen table, or casually mention a friend's daughter who was very happy at the community college.

I did decide to accept the East Coast college's offer of admission, and was lucky enough to get a scholarship that took some of the pressure off my parents . . . and put more on me. I had to keep up my grades academically or risk losing the scholarship. However, all I could really think about was the social aspect of my future. That nervousness carried over when I began college. Although I'm usually a very gregarious person, I wasn't comfortable around groups of people my first few weeks at school. I was wary of anyone who wanted to be my friend, wondering what they could possibly see in me, what I could offer to anyone. It wasn't until I heard some girls talking about what a snob I was that I realized they thought I was keeping my distance because I felt they had nothing to offer me! I had to laugh at the irony, and made an effort to become friends with everyone after that. I learned the truth of my father's favorite adage, "Just be the best You that you can be."

Years later, my education behind me, I moved from school back to the Midwest. Again, my insecurities surfaced. I was cowed by the cliques of women who had grown up together, been each other's bridesmaids, served as godmothers to each other's children. I decided this time not to start out a recluse as I had done when I was at school, but to reach out and try to make friends. I joined several volunteer organizations and attended local political functions. I even surprised myself by agreeing to run for the school board!

After serving two terms on the school board, I worked my way through most local political offices, everything from dogcatcher to Mayoral assistant. These days I'm often asked to give speeches to groups, and love addressing high school students. When I was in my old hometown last month, I spoke to a young girl who told me she was afraid that growing up in her small town meant she wouldn't be able to fit in in the larger cities. I told her my story, gave her my business card, and offered to mentor her when she came to my town. I like to think that by helping her, I'll complete a circle that started a long time ago.

Go on to next page

24. The primary purpose of this passage is to

(A) refute the idea that people on the coasts are more stylish than people in the Midwest

(B) encourage students to broaden their horizons by attending out-of-state colleges

(C) describe how the author's feelings affected her actions

(D) ridicule the author's original insecurities

(E) analyze the differences between people in different parts of the country.

25. Which of the following could best be substituted for the word "ambivalent" in line 25?

(A) conflicted

(B) afraid

(C) eager

(D) unhappy

(E) ignorant

26. The tone of the description in lines 33–36 is one of

(A) admiration

(B) excitement

(C) entreaty

(D) indecisiveness

(E) hopelessness

27. The author mentions her mother's leaving brochures from local colleges on the table (lines 39–40) for which of the following reasons?

(A) to reassure her daughter that she could change her mind and attend a college closer to home

(B) to help her daughter to decide on a major at college

(C) to encourage her daughter to attend the same school as her parents did

(D) to prove that community colleges are just as good as four year colleges

(E) to request that her daughter save the family money by attending a less expensive college

28. How does the second paragraph function in relation to the first paragraph?

(A) It refutes a theory that was presented in the first paragraph.

(B) It introduces a new theory and changes the primary focus of the passage.

(C) It dismisses one set of concerns and introduces a second.

(D) It answers a question and resolves a problem discussed in the first paragraph.

(E) It continues and expands upon the topic of the first paragraph.

29. The passage answers all of the following questions *except*

(A) Why was the author concerned about going away to college?

(B) How did the author come to hold her opinion about West coast teenagers?

(C) Why did the author move back to the Midwest?

(D) What political offices did the author hold?

(E) Why was the author nervous about moving back to the Midwest?

30. Which of the following best describes what the author means by "I had to laugh at the irony," lines 59–60?

(A) She enjoyed the sense of humor her college friends displayed.

(B) She was deeply hurt on the inside but masked it with humor on the outside.

(C) She found it amusing that her actions were perceived exactly the opposite of how she had intended them.

(D) She was excited by the possibility of making friends at last.

(E) She felt that she would be more likeable if she showed a strong sense of humor.

31. The author uses the expression "cowed by" in line 66 to mean

(A) disdainful of

(B) intimidated by

(C) angered by

(D) repulsed by

(E) deceived by

Go on to next page

32. Which of the following may best be substituted for "not to start out as a recluse" (lines 69–70) without changing the meaning of the original?

(A) not to keep to myself

(B) not to worry about how I appeared to others

(C) not to try so desperately to make friends

(D) not to plan ahead, but to let things happen naturally

(E) not to reject others

33. Which of the following may you most reasonably infer from the author's statement in lines 73–75 that, "I even surprised myself by running for the school board!"?

(A) She filed just in time to make the deadline to become a candidate.

(B) She believed she would not be eligible to run as she had attended an out-of-state college.

(C) She had not previously been involved in politics.

(D) Politics were considered an ignoble profession in the Midwest.

(E) Someone else registered her as a candidate without her knowledge.

34. The author uses the expression, "from dog-catcher to Mayoral assistant" (line 78–79) for which of the following reasons?

(A) She wants to impress the reader with the variety of abilities she has.

(B) She wants to inject a tone of humor over how many offices a previously inexperienced person could hold.

(C) She wants to encourage career fields outside of traditional ones.

(D) She wants to prove that even a small-town person from the Midwest could become a success.

(E) She wants to predict what kind of career the students she mentors will have.

35. The author's style in writing the passage is best described as

(A) introducing a theory and then providing supporting examples

(B) providing pros and cons of a pair of possible actions

(C) explaining actions and then justifying them

(D) describing how a history of events led to the current situation

(E) discussing a plan of action and then ridiculing the results

STOP

You may check your work on this section only.
Do not go back to any previous section.

Section 2

Time: 30 Minutes

25 Questions

Directions: Solve each problem. Blacken the corresponding oval on the answer grid.

Notes:

* You may use a calculator.
* All numbers used in this exam are real numbers.
* All figures lie in a plane.
* All figures may be assumed to be to scale unless the problem specifically indicates otherwise.

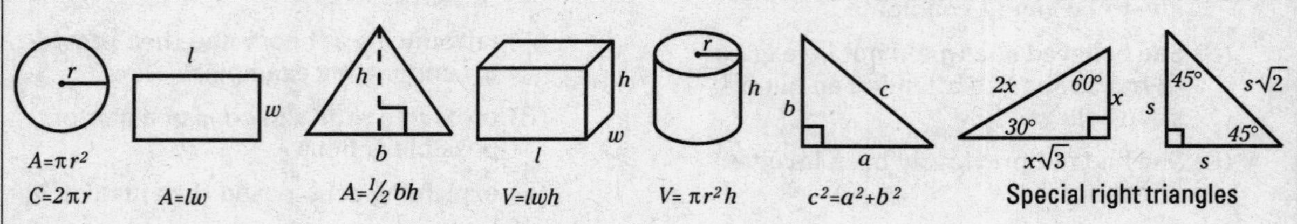

There are 360 degrees of arc in a circle.

There are 180 degrees in a straight angle.

There are 180 degrees in the sum of the interior angles of a triangle.

1. What is the perimeter of an equilateral triangle of side ⅔?

(A) 6

(B) 3

(C) 2

(D) ⅔

(E) It cannot be determined from the information given.

2. $x > 2$. Solve for $\frac{(x^3)^{10}}{x^4}$

(A) x^{36}

(B) x^{24}

(C) x^7

(D) x^5

(E) x^0

Go on to next page

3. Which one of the following terms is *not* equal to the others?

(A) $\frac{1}{3}$

(B) $\frac{3}{9}$

(C) $\frac{12}{36}$

(D) $\frac{13}{39}$

(E) $\frac{24}{62}$

4. A blimp travels at 10 miles per hour for 3 hours from point A to point B and then increases its speed by 50% when it returns home along the same route. What is the blimp's average speed for the round trip?

(A) 15 mph

(B) 13.5 mph

(C) 12.5 mph

(D) 12 mph

(E) 11 mph

Questions 5 and 6 are based on the following chart.

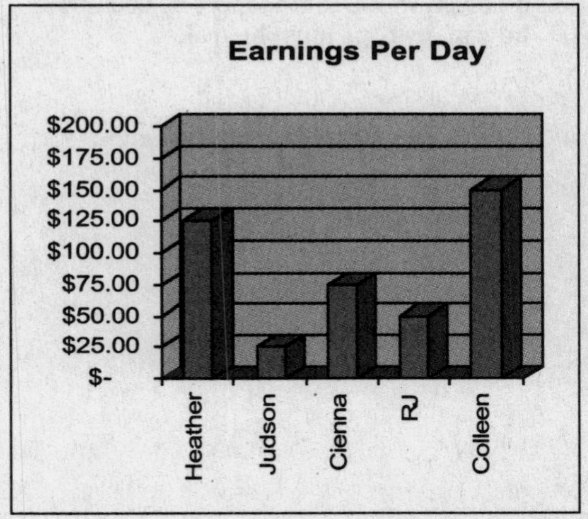

5. This chart represents the amount of money each person earns per day. How many days must Judson work to earn as much as Heather would earn in four days?

(A) 500

(B) 125

(C) 100

(D) 20

(E) 12.5

6. The amount of money that Heather and Judson earn in four days is what percent of the amount of money that Colleen working alone could earn in two days?

(A) 400

(B) 200

(C) 100

(D) 2

(E) 1

Go on to next page

7. A carton contains three dozen CDs. Steven's small plane can carry 432 cartons at a time. If Steven wants to transport 60,000 CDs, how many trips must he make?

(A) 6

(B) 5

(C) 4

(D) $3\frac{4}{5}$

(E) 3

8. Given a triangle with sides of 3 and 7, which of the following could be the length of the third side?

(A) 1

(B) 2

(C) 3

(D) 4

(E) 5

$$x * y * z = \frac{\frac{1}{2}x + y^3}{y - z}$$

9. Solve for 6 * 2 * 9.

(A) 108

(B) 21

(C) 17

(D) $-\frac{11}{7}$

(E) $-\frac{1}{6}$

10. Dan is twice as old as Jason, who is six years younger than Courtney. If Courtney's age is *x*, which of the following in terms of *x* is Dan's age?

(A) $x - 6$

(B) $x + 6$

(C) $2x - 6$

(D) $2x + 6$

(E) $2x - 12$

Go on to next page

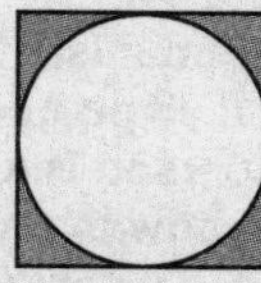

11. The area of the shaded portion of the figure is

(A) $100 - 25\pi$

(B) $100 - 10\pi$

(C) $40 - 25\pi$

(D) $40 - 10\pi$

(E) It cannot be determined from the information given.

12. The perimeter of 30:60:90 triangle ABC is $30 + 10\sqrt{3}$. What is its area in square units?

(A) $100\sqrt{3}$

(B) 100

(C) $50\sqrt{3}$

(D) 50

(E) $25\sqrt{23}$

13. Solve for $(a + b)^2 - (a - b)^2$ when $ab = 15$.

(A) 150

(B) 75

(C) 60

(D) 15

(E) 0

14. The first two terms in a sequence are 3 and 5. Each consecutive term is found by taking the square of the first number and adding it to the sum of the last two numbers. For example, the third term in the series is 17. What is the fifth term of this sequence?

(A) 16

(B) 26

(C) 29

(D) 57

(E) 353

Go on to next page

15. Bob traveled 40 percent of the distance of his trip from Carmel, Indiana, to Bean Blossom Junction, went another 20 miles with Anthony, and then finished the last half of the trip alone. How many miles long was the trip?

(A) 240

(B) 200

(C) 160

(D) 100

(E) 50

16. $\frac{8a^8b^3c^0}{4a^4b^2c^3}$

(A) $2a^2bc^3$

(B) $\frac{2a^2b}{c^3}$

(C) $\frac{2a^4b}{c^3}$

(D) $\frac{2a^4}{bc}$

(E) $2a^4b$

17. The ratio of communists to capitalists at a seminar is 7:2. If 63 people are in the seminar (and each person is either a communist or a capitalist), how many more communists than capitalists are in the seminar?

(A) 52

(B) 45

(C) 35

(D) 9

(E) 5

18. A recipe calls for a mixture of ⅔ cup sesame seeds and ⅓ cup nuts. If Yuri adds one cup of nuts to the mixture for a total of 2 cups, what percent of the total mixture is now nuts?

(A) 66⅔

(B) 33⅓

(C) 17

(D) 1⅓

(E) ⅔

Go on to next page

19. If $x \neq -1$ or 0 and $y = \frac{1}{x}$, then $\frac{1}{x+1} + \frac{1}{y+1} =$

(A) 1

(B) 3

(C) x

(D) $x + 1$

(E) $x + \frac{1}{x} + 2$

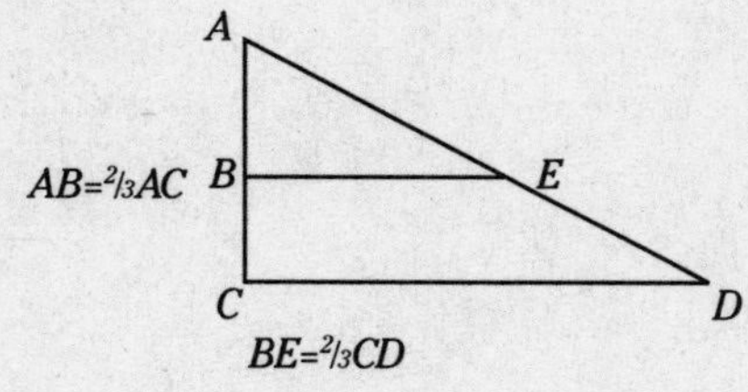

20. The ratio of the area of isosceles right triangle *ABE* to triangle *ACD* is how much? Express your answer as a fraction.

(A) $\frac{4}{18}$

(B) $\frac{4}{9}$

(C) $4\frac{1}{3}$

(D) $4\frac{1}{18}$

(E) $\frac{3}{2}$

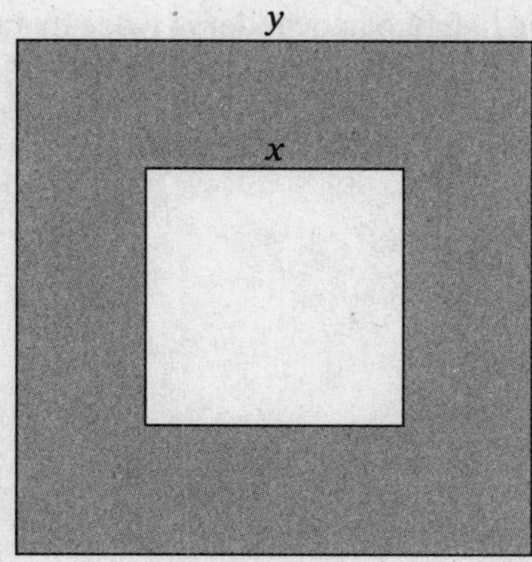

21. Given two squares of sides x and y as shown, which of the following represents the shaded area?

(A) $x^2 - y^2$

(B) $y^2 - x^2$

(C) $2xy - 2yx$

(D) $2yx - 2xy$

(E) $4xy$

22. If the average (arithmetic mean) of nine consecutive integers is 0, what is the average of the last four of these integers?

(A) –2.5

(B) –1

(C) 0

(D) 1

(E) 2.5

Go on to next page

23. The height of a cylinder is twice its radius. The circumference of the base of the cylinder is 8π. What is the number of cubic units in the volume of the cylinder?

(A) 8π

(B) 16π

(C) 48π

(D) 108π

(E) 128π

A university has put a magnetic strip on all its student identification cards since 1985. Since 1988, some of these cards have included a photograph. All of the photographs have been taken in color since 1993.

24. If Megan has a 1991 identification card from this university, which of the following must be true?

I. The card has a magnetic strip.

II. The card has a photograph.

III. The card does not have a color photograph.

(A) I only

(B) III only

(C) I and II

(D) I and III

(E) I, II, and III

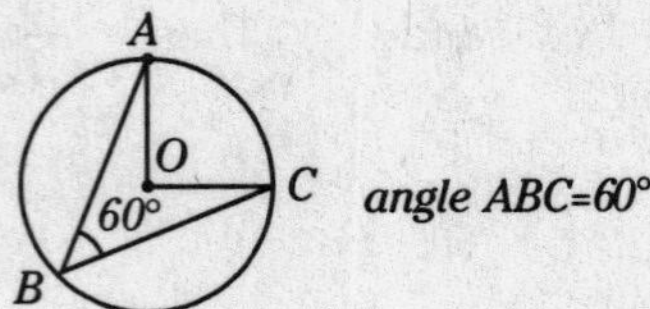

25. If O is the center of the circle, angle AOC =

(A) 360 degrees

(B) 180 degrees

(C) 120 degrees

(D) 60 degrees

(E) 30 degrees

You may check your work on this section only. Do not go back to any previous section.

Section 3

Time: 30 Minutes

30 Questions

Choose the *best* answer to each question. Blacken the corresponding oval on the answer grid.

Each of the following sentences contains one or two blanks indicating words or phrases that are omitted. Choose the answer that best completes the sentence.

Example:

Because he ---- the test, John was ----.

(A) flunked .. thrilled

(B) forgot .. brilliant

(C) passed .. happy

(D) ignored .. praised

(E) memorized .. surprised

The correct answer is (C). Ⓐ Ⓑ ● Ⓓ Ⓔ

1. Thor Heyerdahl's ---- voyage in a reed raft proved his hypothesis that early sailors were in fact able to traverse the distance between islands.

(A) successful

(B) unambitious

(C) failed

(D) inappropriate

(E) dismaying

2. Fire protection, in modern buildings, not only establishes a ---- environment but allows for ---- insurance costs.

(A) clean .. an increase in

(B) tainted .. a revision of

(C) controlled .. a raise in

(D) safe .. a reduction of

(E) polluted .. a lowering of

3. The billboard promotes milk as ---- beverage, claiming that those who consume dairy products feel better and live longer.

(A) a noxious

(B) a salubrious

(C) a superfluous

(D) a legitimate

(E) an inexpensive

4. Ginger and Cody said that although the income selling used books from their small store would never make them ----, they enjoyed the ---- of being able to read everything that customers brought in.

(A) affluent .. perquisite

(B) wealthy .. duty

(C) opulent .. obligation

(D) impoverished .. privilege

(E) poor .. facility

5. Renowned aviators and flight instructors John and Martha King are ---- and ---- people, despite being revered by their students nationwide.

(A) objective .. bombastic

(B) modest .. unpretentious

(C) obscure .. reserved

(D) prolix .. arrogant

(E) dominant .. servile

Go on to next page

6. Although my friends disagree, I argue that being ---- in some matters is preferable to being ----, especially, for example, in medical matters.

(A) persuasive .. convincing

(B) controversial .. belligerent

(C) immoral .. staunch

(D) wayward .. capricious

(E) dogmatic .. ambivalent

7. Our course, by ---- all costs up front, contributes to your peace of mind, as you can be ---- that there are no hidden expenses.

(A) exaggerating .. comfortable

(B) disclosing .. confident

(C) eliminating ..suspicious

(D) increasing .. uncertain

(E) decreasing .. doubtful

8. The ---- nature and ---- numbers make the clouded leopard difficult to study in the wild.

(A) gregarious .. increasing

(B) sociable .. diminishing

(C) reclusive .. decreasing

(D) obstreperous .. growing

(E) amiable .. plummeting

9. Blessed with ---- land and abundant rainfall, the valley produced most of the crops grown in the otherwise ---- region.

(A) sere .. torrid

(B) fecund .. verdant

(C) arable .. sufficient

(D) parched .. sporadic

(E) fertile .. arid

Each of the following questions features a pair of words or phrases in capital letters, followed by five pairs of words or phrases in lowercase letters. Choose the lowercase pair that most closely expresses the same relationship as that of the uppercase pair.

Example:

HAPPY: SAD::

(A) tall: fat

(B) silly: serious

(C) yellow: red

(D) nervous : anxious

(E) joyful: mysterious

The correct answer is (B).  

10. SUPERMARKET: BANANAS::

(A) sawmill: sawdust

(B) television: program

(C) haberdashery: hash

(D) health spa: health

(E) nursery: plants

11. SHEAF: PAPERS::

(A) document: arguments

(B) collection: items

(C) parchment: skins

(D) quiver: arrows

(E) quarter: dimes

12. ARMOR: BODY::

(A) thimble: finger

(B) hat: neck

(C) sock: foot

(D) corset: girth

(E) braces: teeth

13. IRON: BLACKSMITH::

(A) fabric: mason

(B) wood: carpenter

(C) cleavers: butcher

(D) brides: matchmaker

(E) rumors: jester

Go on to next page

14. PARADIGM: MODEL::

(A) example: statistic

(B) apogee: apology

(C) intrusion: lie

(D) diatribe: group

(E) convention: norm

15. EUPHONIOUS: SOUND::

(A) pusillanimous: pus

(B) savory: taste

(C) dissonant: shade

(D) wizened: moisture

(E) hapless: luck

Each passage is followed by questions that pertain to that passage. Read the passage and answer the questions based on information stated or implied in that passage.

Questions 16–21 are based on the following passage.

This material discusses the ways in which Cherokee people differed from Whites in the West of the mid- to late 1800s.

Line In many ways, a Cherokee woman in the time of the "Wild West" had more power within her social group than did a European woman. It was through the mother of the family that membership in clans and general kinship were determined. A Cherokee (the name comes from a Creek Indian word "Chelokee" meaning "people of a different speech"; however, today many Cherokee prefer to be called Tsalagi from their own name for the Cherokee Nation, Tsalagihi Ayili) woman was not forced to marry someone whom her family had chosen in advance for her, as was the practice in European families. Instead, the Cherokee woman had the right to choose her own mate. That mate then had the job to build a house for the woman, which was considered the woman's property. If the woman already had a house of her own, the man would go live there. Should the man be unable or unwilling to build a house, the couple would live with the woman's parents.

A Cherokee house was wattle and daub. Often described as looking like an upside-down basket, it was a simple circular frame with interwoven branches. The house was plastered with mud, and sunken into the ground. Although many people do not associate log cabins with Native Americans, these became common among the Cherokee later in their history. They also built large council houses to keep the sacred fire, which was never allowed to go out.

Divorce was very simple. The woman would place her husband's possessions outside of the house, which was considered sufficient notice to free the woman and the man each to remarry. The woman kept the house her husband built for her. It was very common for a woman to have one husband after another. Adultery in the marriage, therefore, was relatively uncommon.

Any children born to the couple were considered the woman's, as well. The father had very few child-rearing responsibilities; instead, the wife and her brothers took charge of the children, showing them the tribal ways. The woman also controlled how many children would survive. She had the legal right to destroy any children who were not born healthy, or any children she felt were beyond the number she was capable of feeding and caring for. The father had no such right.

Rights for women were just one aspect of the "civilization" of the Cherokees. During the early 1800s, the Cherokee developed a formal written constitution. Cherokees had their own courts and schools, considered by some to be of a higher standard than those of their white counterparts. Even today, the Cherokee level of education and living standard ranks among the highest of all Native American tribes.

16. The passage serves primarily to

(A) ridicule the idea that Cherokee women were less advanced than White women

(B) compare and contrast the educational systems of Cherokees and Whites

(C) praise the advances that Cherokees made in the face of White resistance

(D) inform the reader of the rights of Cherokee women

(E) refute the theory that Cherokee women were less capable of fighting than were Cherokee men

Go on to next page

17. Which of the following questions is *not* answered in the passage?
   (A) When did the Cherokee nation begin following a written constitution?
   (B) What do the Cherokee people call themselves?
   (C) How is a Cherokee house constructed?
   (D) Who educated Cherokee children?
   (E) How did a Cherokee woman choose a mate?

18. Which of the following could best be substituted for the word "practice" (line 13)
   (A) effort
   (B) attempt
   (C) repetition
   (D) sport
   (E) custom

19. The tone of the description in lines 52–53 of the civilization of Cherokees is one of
   (A) strong impatience
   (B) mild sarcasm
   (C) bitter ridicule
   (D) pitying condescension
   (E) heartfelt sympathy

20. Which of the following would be the most appropriate example to add to the two points of courts and schools mentioned in lines 55–56?
   (A) medical care
   (B) sports arenas
   (C) amphitheaters
   (D) kindergartens
   (E) tribal councils

21. The author's strategy in this passage is best described as
   (A) presenting a chronological history of events
   (B) presenting and then refuting a theory
   (C) proposing a theory and then anticipating a countertheory
   (D) stating an idea and then giving supporting examples
   (E) proving an hypothesis

Questions 22–30 are based on the following passage.

The following is an excerpt from a speech delivered to a convention of educators in the 1980s.

Americans must decide as a nation whether arts education should be part of a basic education in this country. First, as we approach this decision, we must recognize that in England, Germany, and Japan, arts education is considered essential.

These nations see a formal grounding in the arts as a fundamental part of the education of all their citizens, and an important contributor to cultural and economic vitality. Furthermore, their experience shows that arts education can be made integral to the core of a strong educational system. It is equally important to recognize that there are many ways to make it work. The variety of national practices is as noteworthy as the many similarities.

Countless specific examples from other countries are worthy of consideration as the United States works toward voluntary national standards and assessments in arts education. Of the many that could be cited, here are just three.

Japan demonstrates a philosophy that takes for granted every student's ability to learn and focuses teaching and evaluation on student effort. It does not "track" students according to ability, even in the field of art, a discipline in which some students clearly show more aptitude than others. As the Council for Basic Education study notes, "The widely reported international comparisons of student achievement confirm the success the Japanese have had with this system. Not only are their students overall world leaders in mathematics, sciences, and geography, but they show much greater uniformity at a high level of attainment." This observation resonates with those made about exemplary schools in this country: Strong programs that include all students are like rising tides that lift all boats.

In Germany, educators use the arts in teaching other subjects. Bavaria's visual arts curriculum for college preparatory students in grades five through thirteen has ambitious goals for the skills and knowledge it hopes to impart. It also encourages integrated learning across the curriculum by linking art subject themes to other disciplines. The written curriculum includes specific interdisciplinary approaches for teams of teachers. For example, "imagination" exercises are used in biology, ethics, and geography

Go on to next page

classes; and teaching about medieval culture is linked to history, religion, German language, and literature.

In England's national curriculum, design gets a high priority among the foundation subjects. Within the technology curriculum in England and Wales, four of the five attainment targets (or learning objectives) address the capabilities all students are to acquire in design and technology. These are identifying needs and opportunities for design activities in such contexts as home, school, the community, business, and industry; being able to conceive a design proposal and then develop it into an achievable design; making objects, systems, and environments with an emphasis on procedures and techniques that result in high quality products; and being able to evaluate design products and processes, including ones from other times and cultures.

These objectives are supported in the curriculum by a program of study that places an emphasis on students' designing and making objects, systems, and environments. The national curriculum also indicates that students should "draw on their knowledge and skill in other subjects, particularly the foundation subjects of science, mathematics, and art, to support their designing and making activities."

Japan, Germany, and England clearly see that the arts can be an integral part of today's problem-solving strategies, but there is an even more compelling reason to have a foundation in the arts. While the pursuit of natural and social sciences allows humans to etch out an existence on Earth, it is only through the arts that human life springs forward.

22. It can be inferred from the first three paragraphs that

(A) arts education is underfunded in the United States

(B) young artists receive more training in England, Germany, and Japan than they do in the United States

(C) there are currently no generally accepted standards for arts education in the United States

(D) many students in the United States currently receive no schooling in the arts

(E) science is an integral part of education in the United States

23. The author mentions the great variety of approaches to arts education in order to

(A) argue that some approaches are superior to others

(B) challenge the United States to find the most appropriate course of action

(C) support the author's contention that the United States ought to treat arts education as basic

(D) introduce the notion that Japan, Germany, and England employ particularly diverse methods in arts education

(E) contend that the issue of arts education is too complex to consider at this time

24. The discussion of Japanese education (lines 22–38) suggests that

(A) tracking students on the basis of ability impedes the progress of the most gifted students

(B) some educational systems treat students on the basis of what they are believed to be able to achieve

(C) exceptional schools in the United States are modeled after the Japanese system

(D) other countries will rival the Japanese in educational achievement if they cease grouping students according to ability

(E) Japanese children comprise a more heterogeneous group than do their counterparts around the world

25. In line 35, "resonates" is used to mean

(A) vibrates

(B) reverberates

(C) clashes

(D) corroborates

(E) equates

Go on to next page

26. A curriculum developer in Bavaria (Germany) would be most likely to agree with which of the following statements?

(A) Arts education need not begin until fifth grade.

(B) Students not bound for college will receive little benefit from arts education.

(C) The arts should always be taught in relation to other disciplines.

(D) Teachers are more effective when they are part of a team.

(E) The arts are useful in helping students learn a variety of material.

27. As it is used in line 50, "medieval culture" refers to

(A) medieval German language and literature

(B) social customs during the medieval period

(C) various groups of people during the Middle Ages

(D) artistic expression during the Middle Ages

(E) the dominant role religion played during the Middle Ages

28. The English approach to arts education differs most significantly from the German approach in that the English

(A) stress the relationship between design and technology

(B) give arts education a very high priority

(C) integrate the foundation subjects of science, mathematics, and art

(D) include instruction from other times and cultures

(E) emphasize that other disciplines improve art as an end product

29. Which of the following best summarizes the author's argument in the last paragraph?

(A) The United States should borrow from the approaches of Japan, Germany, and England in implementing arts education.

(B) Arts education should remain an option in the United States, but it should be encouraged because it is vital to one's education.

(C) Arts education is important for all and should be made part of basic education in the United States.

(D) More time should be devoted to arts education in the United States than to natural and social science education.

(E) Existence on Earth would be very difficult if humans were ignorant in the natural and social sciences.

30. The passage is best described as

(A) a survey of successful implementations

(B) a recommendation based on a parallel situation

(C) a critique of the status quo

(D) an endorsement of a particular approach

(E) a discussion of the pros and cons of a proposal

STOP

You may check your work on this section only.
Do not go back to any previous section.

Section 4

Time: 30 Minutes

25 Questions

Directions: Solve each problem. Blacken the corresponding oval on the answer grid.

Notes:

* You may use a calculator.
* All numbers used in this exam are real numbers.
* All figures lie in a plane.
* All figures may be assumed to be to scale unless the problem specifically indicates otherwise.

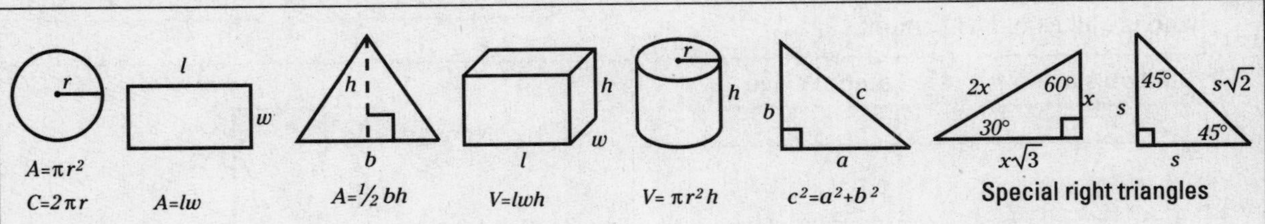

There are 360 degrees of arc in a circle.

There are 180 degrees in a straight angle.

There are 180 degrees in the sum of the interior angles of a triangle.

Directions for Quantitative Comparison questions:

Questions 1–15 feature two columns with a quantity in each. Compare the quantities and choose

A if the quantity in Column A is greater

B if the quantity in Column B is greater

C if the two quantities are equal

D if the relationship cannot be determined from the information given

AN E RESPONSE WILL NOT BE SCORED

General information:

A letter (*a, b, c,* or *x, y, z*) or symbol means the same thing throughout one problem but may not be the same in different problems. Information that is centered between two columns applies to both columns in that problem.

Examples:

	Column A	***Column B***	***Sample ovals***
1.	2^3	4	● Ⓑ Ⓒ Ⓓ Ⓔ
2.	$x°$	45°	Ⓐ Ⓑ Ⓒ ● Ⓔ
3.	$3x + y = 3x$		
	0	y	Ⓐ Ⓑ ● Ⓓ Ⓔ

Go on to next page

Column A	Column B

1.

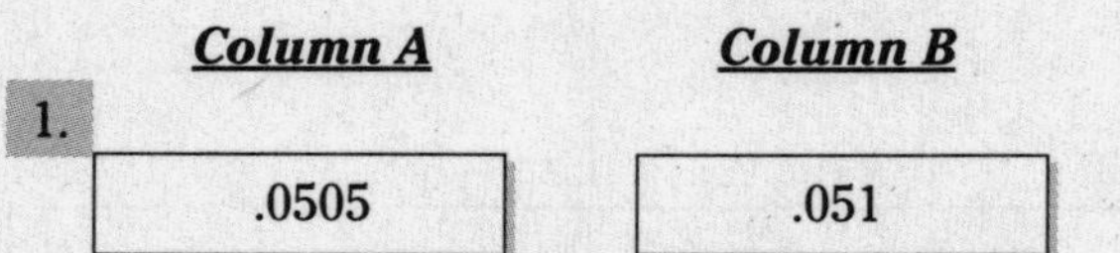

.0505	.051

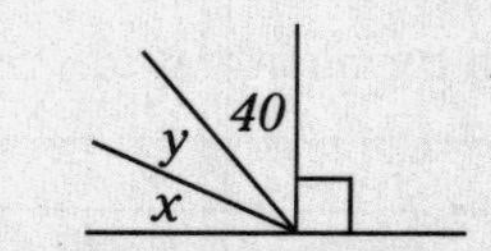

Note: Figure not drawn to scale

2.

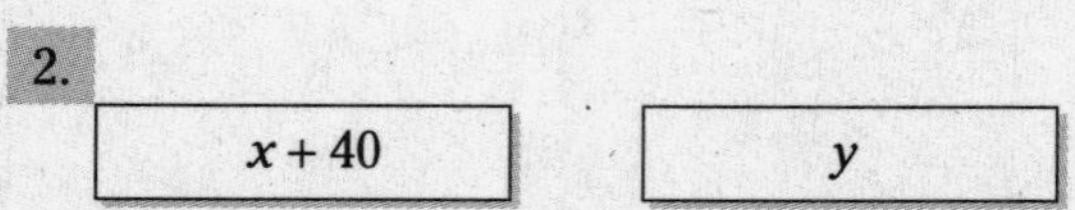

$x + 40$	y

3. Jacob is twice as old as Leroy, who is half as old as Lamont.

Jacob's age	Lamont's age

4.

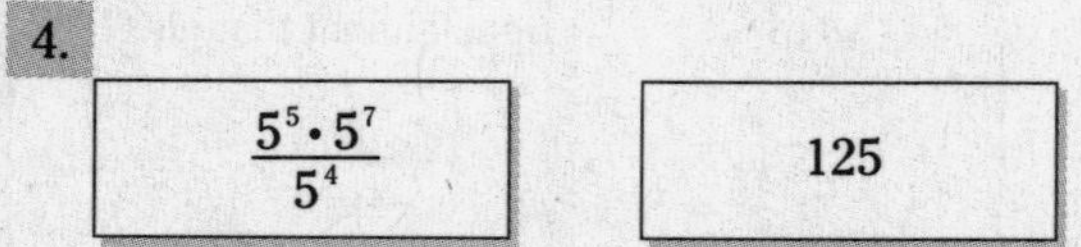

$\frac{5^5 \cdot 5^7}{5^4}$	125

5. A number of red, yellow, and black marbles are in a jar. One marble is chosen at random.

Probability of choosing a red, yellow, or black marble	300%

6.

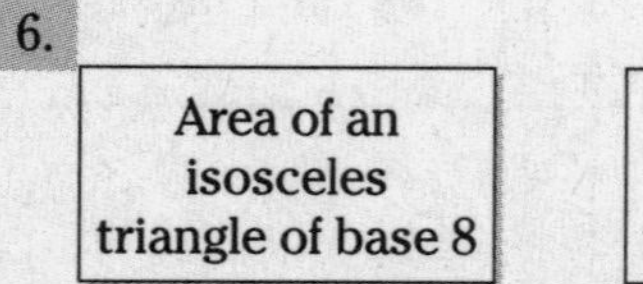

Area of an isosceles triangle of base 8	Area of an equilateral triangle of base 8

7. $x < 1 < y$
$x^2 > y^2$

$(x + y)^2$	$x^2 + y^2$

Column A	Column B

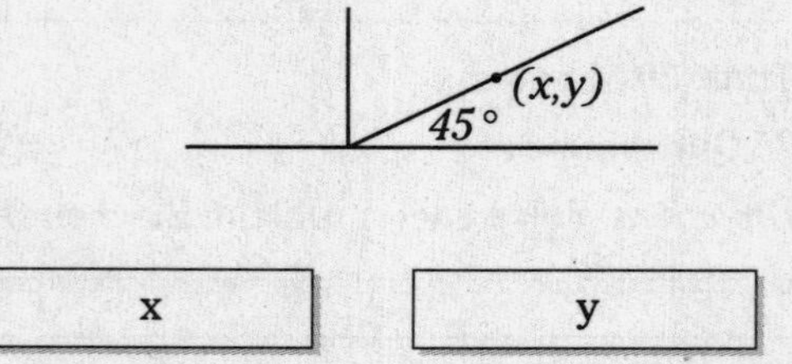

8.

x	y

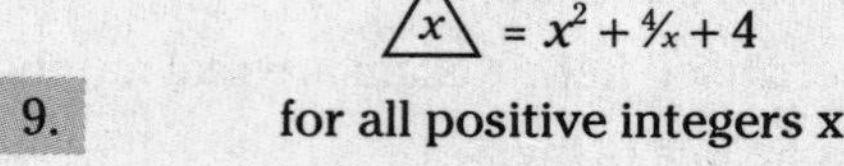

$\triangle x = x^2 + 4/x + 4$

9. for all positive integers x

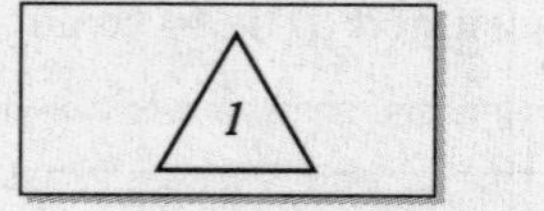

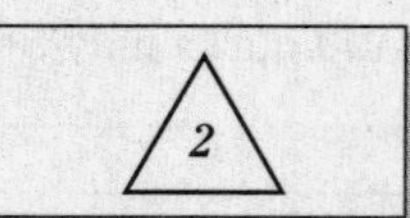

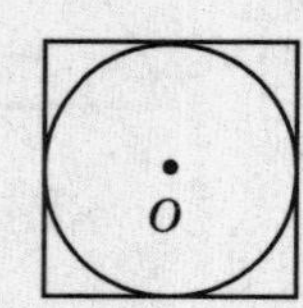

10. Area of square = 144
O is the center of the circle

Circumference of Circle *O*	36

11. $a + b + c = 47$
$a + b - 2c = 14$

$a + b$	33

12. Marcy and Jessica assemble the same products on the assembly line. Marcy can assemble 15 products in 45 minutes. Jessica can assemble 45 products in 15 minutes.

Number of products that Marcy and Jessica, working together, can assemble in 45 minutes	150

Go on to next page

	Column A	Column B
13. $m < 0$, $n > 0$	m^2	n^2

14. x is an even integer greater than 2.

Column A	Column B
The remainder when x is divided by ½x	The remainder when x^2 is divided by x

15. The hypotenuse of an isosceles right triangle is 10.

Column A	Column B
Perimeter of the triangle	20

Directions for student-produced responses: Questions 16–25 require you to solve the problem and then blacken the oval corresponding to the answer, as shown in the following example.

Example: Note the fraction line and decimal points.

Answer: 7/2

Answer: 3.25

Answer: 853

853

Write your answer in the box. You may start your answer in any column.

- Although you do not *have* to write the solutions in the boxes, you *do* have to blacken the corresponding ovals. It is strongly suggested that you fill in the boxes to prevent confusion. *Only the blackened ovals, however, will be scored.* The numbers in the boxes will not be read.
- There are no negative answers.
- Mixed numbers, such as 3½, may be gridded in as a decimal (3.5) or as a fraction (7/2). Do *not* grid in 3½; it will be read as 31/2.
- Grid in a decimal as far as possible; do not round it. If your answer is $.\overline{33}$, for example, fill in as many 3s as you have spaces for. Do *not* round down to .33 or .3 unless the problem specifically tells you to do so.
- A question may have more than one answer; grid in only one.

Go on to next page

16. If $9x + 7 = 41 + \frac{1}{2}x$, solve for x.

17. A circle with a diameter of 5 intersects a circle with a diameter of 8 at two points. The distance between the centers of the circles is x units. What is one possible value for x?

Set A: (1, 21, 30, 32, 33)

18. A number "sparkles" if the sum of its distinct prime factors is 10. Set A has how many terms that "sparkle"?

19. Three friends bring old clothes to the school rummage sale. The ratio of their contributions is 2:3:5. If they bring in a total of 50 items, how many more items did the most generous student bring than the least generous student?

Go on to next page

Question 20 refers to the following chart.

Candidate	*Number of Votes Received*
Amanda	21
Boden	14
Cassidy	x
Dennis	y
Lynda	z

20. There were exactly 350 votes cast for the five candidates shown above. Each voter voted exactly once. If Cassidy got more votes than Dennis, and Dennis got more votes than Lynda, and no candidate received zero votes, what is the most votes Dennis could have received?

Question 21 is based on the following graph.

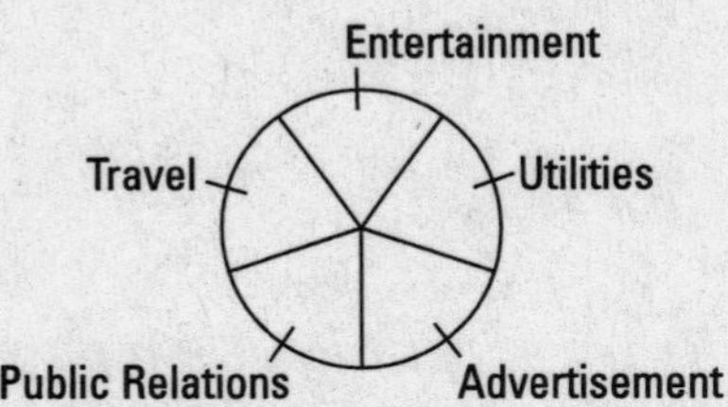

21. A company's monthly budget is evenly divided into five segments as shown above. If half of the company's entertainment budget is $300, what is the total monthly budget?

22. Lael took seven exams. Her average score was 82. Her first six scores were 75, 91, 85, 89, 74, and 79. What was her seventh score?

23. Circle A is perfectly inscribed in the semi-circle B. If the area of circle A is 16π, what is the circumference of circle A?

Go on to next page

24. A witch's cauldron contains 10 eyes of newt, 8 toes of toads, and 15 bat's wings. (Nothing else is in the cauldron.) What is the maximum number of times the witch must yank out exactly one goodie from the cauldron to *ensure* removing one of each goodie (one eye of newt, one toe of toad, one bat's wing)?

25. Barb, Jim, Angie, Mike, Laura, Carissa, and Sara enter a tournament. Each contestant must compete once against every other contestant, one match at a time, in each of the following five activities: hot-air balloon race, golf, mile run, one-on-one basketball, and a talent competition. How many matches will be played in the tournament?

STOP DO NOT TURN THE PAGE UNTIL TOLD TO DO SO. DO NOT RETURN TO A PREVIOUS TEST.

Section 5

Time: 15 Minutes

13 Questions

Directions: Choose the *best* answer to each question. Blacken the corresponding oval on the answer grid.

Answer the questions following the pair of passages below based on information *stated* or *implied* in the passages and in the introductory material provided. Questions are based on the content of the passage and on the relationship between the pair of passages.

Questions 1–13 are based on the following passages.

The following passages, written during the 1980s, present navigational information.

Passage 1

The UTM grid location, or reference, of a point may easily be found if the point can be located on a map with UTM grid marks along its edges or with a UTM grid superimposed. USGS (United States Geographical Survey) quadrangles published since 1959, and many published before then, have these ticks, which are printed in blue. If no USGS map with UTM ticks exists for a location, latitude and longitude coordinates, or certain local grid coordinates, may be converted to UTM references by a mathematical formula. However, computer programs are necessary to perform such a task. It is always preferable to record locations initially in UTM terms rather than to use translated values.

The simplicity of the UTM grid method follows from certain assumptions, which do not seriously compromise the accuracy or precision of measurements made on the common types of USGS topographical maps. The primary assumption is that narrow sections of the earth's nearly spherical surface may be drawn on flat maps with little distortion. Larger sections, however, such as the contiguous United States, cannot be drawn on a single flat map without noticeable distortion.

In the UTM system, the earth is divided into 60 zones, running north and south, each six degrees wide. Mapping on flat sheets within one of these narrow zones is satisfactory for all but the most critical needs. Each zone is numbered, beginning with zone 1 at the 180th meridian near the International Date Line, with zone numbers increasing to the east. Most of the United States is included in Zones 10 through 19. On a map, each zone is flattened, and a square grid is superimposed upon it. Any point in the zone may be referred to by citing its zone number, its distance in meters from the equator ("northing") and its distance in meters from a north-south reference ("easting"). These three figures — the zone number, easting, and northing — make up the complete UTM Grid Reference for any point and distinguish it from any point on earth.

Northings for points north of the equator are measured directly in meters, beginning with a value of zero at the equator and increasing to the north. To avoid negative northing values for points south of the equator, the equator is arbitrarily assigned a value of 10 million meters, and points are measured with decreasing, but positive, northing values heading southward. For clarity, a minus sign usually precedes northing figures for points south of the equator. The explanation may seem complicated, but experience has shown that dealing with negative values for measurements and having to specify the direction of measurements from a reference line are more complex and less reliable. When actually working with maps, especially at the scales commonly used for locating historic sites, the UTM grid system becomes extremely clear and straightforward to use.

Passage 2

A topographic map tells you where things are and how to get to them. These maps describe the shape of the land. They define and locate natural and man-made features. They show the distance between any two places, and they also show the direction from one point to another.

Distances and directions take a bit of figuring, but the topography and features of the land are easy to determine. The topography is shown by contours. These are imaginary lines that follow the ground surface at a constant elevation. They are usually printed in brown, in two thicknesses.

Go on to next page

The heavier lines are called index contours and are usually marked with numbers, which give the height in feet or meters. The contour interval, a set difference in elevation between the brown lines, varies from map to map. Its value is given in the margin of each map.

Maps are made to scale; that is, there is a direct relationship, a ratio, between a unit of measurement on the map and the actual distance in the same unit of measurement on the ground. A convenient way of representing map distance is by a graphic scale. Most Survey topographic maps have a scale, or scales, in the margin, such as 1:24,000 or 1:62,500.

To determine the direction, or bearing, from one point to another, you need a compass as well as a map. Most compasses are marked with the four cardinal points — north, east, south, and west — but some are marked additionally with the number of degrees in a circle. Both kinds are easy to use with a little practice.

One thing to remember is that a compass does not really point north — not true north, except by coincidence in some areas. The compass needle is attracted by magnetic force, which varies in different parts of the world and is constantly changing.

1. The author in passage 1 uses the word "ticks" (line 7) to mean

(A) beats

(B) sounds

(C) insects

(D) marks

(E) watches

2. The author of the first passage prefers not to use translated values because they

(A) are inaccurate

(B) are difficult or inconvenient to obtain

(C) are appropriate only for large-scale maps

(D) measure longitude but not latitude

(E) quickly become obsolete

3. In line 18, the word "compromise" means

(A) lessen

(B) come to an agreement

(C) promise

(D) match

(E) predict

4. Which of the following can you infer from passage 1?

I. The zone number of Florida is higher than the zone number of California.

II. The zone numbers of the United States and Mexico are identical.

III. Zone 15 is farther north of the equator than is Zone 10.

(A) I only

(B) II only

(C) III only

(D) I and II only

(E) I, II, and III

5. The purpose of the last sentence of the first passage is to

(A) list possible uses for UTM grids

(B) criticize the use of negative numbers in the UTM grid system

(C) justify the choice of arbitrary values for points

(D) distinguish northing from easting

(E) reassure readers as to the feasibility of using the grid system

6. The primary purpose of passage 2 is to

(A) compare and contrast topographical and other types of maps

(B) lament the fact that few people know how to interpret topographical maps

(C) discuss topographical maps and how to use them

(D) deride topographical maps and those who use them

(E) urge that classes in topographical map reading be made mandatory in schools

7. Which of the following terms is *not* defined in passage 2?

(A) index contours

(B) contour interval

(C) bearing

(D) cardinal points

(E) elevation

Go on to next page

8. The author of passage 2 would *disagree* with which of the following?

I. A topographical map shows the direction from one point to another.

II. A topographical map alone is sufficient to find the bearing of a point.

III. A topographical map does not show the distance between curved points.

(A) I only

(B) II only

(C) III only

(D) I and II only

(E) I and III only

9. The tone of passage 2 is

(A) passionate

(B) expository

(C) sardonic

(D) fawning

(E) dogmatic

10. The author of the second passage probably expects her audience to be which of the following?

(A) professional cartographers

(B) students

(C) researchers

(D) civil engineers

(E) outdoor guides

11. According to the second passage, a compass needle may not point to true north when

(A) magnetic north does not point to true north

(B) high tide affects the compass reading

(C) there are mountains between the compass and the North Pole

(D) sunspots are active

(E) it is the October through December season

12. Which of the following is most likely to be true?

(A) A person who is interested in passage 1 would probably be interested in the information in passage 2 as well.

(B) The author of passage 1 taught the author of passage 2.

(C) The authors of passages 1 and 2 disagree on earth science.

(D) A reader must understand passage 1 to proceed to passage 2.

(E) The author of passage 1 based his analyses and conclusions on information in passage 2.

13. The primary difference between passage 1 and passage 2 may be described as

(A) passage 2 expands on the information in passage 1

(B) passage 2 disagrees with the information in passage 1

(C) passage 2 discusses measurements on a smaller scale than does passage 1

(D) passage 1 is more technical than passage 2

(E) passage 1 uses American map-reading techniques; passage 2 uses international techniques

STOP

DO NOT TURN THE PAGE UNTIL TOLD TO DO SO.
DO NOT RETURN TO A PREVIOUS TEST.

Section 6

Time: 15 Minutes

10 Questions

Directions: Solve each problem. Blacken the corresponding oval on the answer grid.

Notes:

* You may use a calculator.
* All numbers used in this exam are real numbers.
* All figures lie in a plane.
* All figures may be assumed to be to scale unless the problem specifically indicates otherwise.

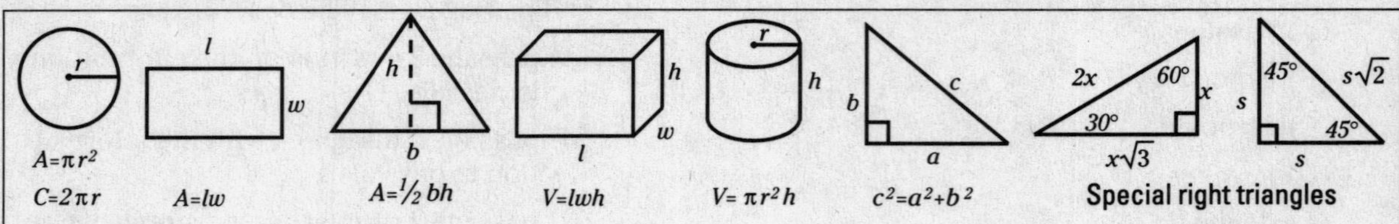

There are 360 degrees of arc in a circle.

There are 180 degrees in a straight angle.

There are 180 degrees in the sum of the interior angles of a triangle.

1. Given that $x > 1$, what is the number of square units in the total surface area of a cube of edge x?
   (A) $6x$
   (B) $6x^2$
   (C) $6x^3$
   (D) $12x$
   (E) $12x^2$

2. The average of nine numbers is 0. The sum of four of the numbers is –8. What is the sum of the remaining five numbers?
   (A) –16
   (B) –8
   (C) 0
   (D) 8
   (E) 16

Go on to next page

Questions 3 and 4 refer to the following graph.

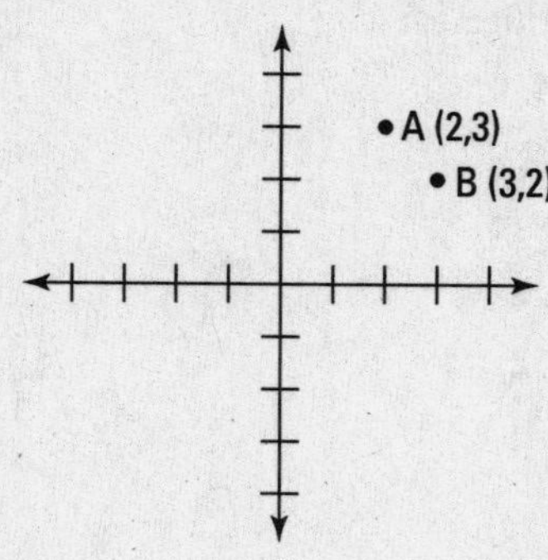

3. What is the slope of line AB?

(A) –2

(B) –1

(C) –⅔

(D) 1

(E) 2

4. Assume that point A rises four units and moves four units to the right. Assume that point B drops four units and moves four units to the left. What is the slope of line AB?

(A) –9/7

(B) –1

(C) –7/9

(D) 0

(E) 9/7

5. A number of friends are at a party. At 11:00 p.m., one-quarter of the friends leave. At midnight, one-third of the remaining friends leave. At 1:00 a.m., as many people leave as left at 11:00. Exactly 30 people remain. How many people were at the party to begin with?

6. A box of candy contains three types of candy: 20 creams, 15 chews, and 12 nuts. Each time LaVonne reaches into the box, she pulls out a piece of candy, takes a bite out of it, and throws it away. She pulls out a cream, a nut, a chew, a nut, a cream, a chew. What is the probability that on the next reach she will pull out a nut?

(A) 15/47

(B) 13/41

(C) 10/41

(D) 13/15

(E) 11/15

Go on to next page

7. Gigi and Neville, working together at the same rate, can mow the estate's lawn in 12 hours. Working alone, what fraction of the lawn can Gigi mow in 3 hours?

(A) $\frac{1}{24}$

(B) $\frac{1}{12}$

(C) $\frac{1}{8}$

(D) $\frac{1}{4}$

(E) $\frac{1}{3}$

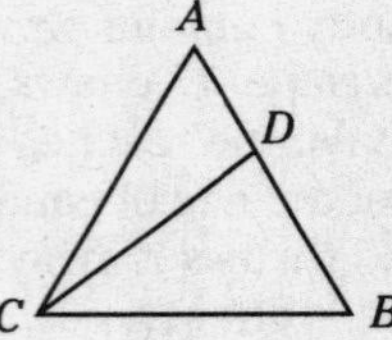

8. In this figure, the number of interior degrees in triangle *ABC* is what percent of the number of interior degrees in triangle *ADC*?

(A) 45

(B) 50

(C) 100

(D) 200

(E) It cannot be determined from the information given.

9. $x^2 - 16x + 48 = 0$. Which of these are possible values for x?

(A) 24, 0

(B) 24, 2

(C) 12, 4

(D) 6, 8

(E) −12, −4

10. The volume of a cube with a surface area of 60 cm^2 is how many times the volume of a cube with a surface area of 6 cm^2?

(A) $\sqrt{10}$

(B) 10

(C) $10\sqrt{10}$

(D) 100

(E) 1000

STOP DO NOT TURN THE PAGE UNTIL TOLD TO DO SO. DO NOT RETURN TO A PREVIOUS TEST.

Answer Key for Practice Exam 2

Section 1	Section 2	Section 3	Section 4	Section 5	Section 6
1. C	1. C	1. A	1. B	1. D	1. B
2. D	2. B	2. D	2. D	2. B	2. D
3. A	3. E	3. B	3. C	3. A	3. B
4. B	4. D	4. A	4. A	4. A	4. E
5. C	5. D	5. B	5. B	5. E	5. 120
6. D	6. B	6. E	6. D	6. C	6. C
7. B	7. C	7. B	7. B	7. E	7. C
8. A	8. E	8. C	8. C	8. B	8. C
9. A	9. D	9. E	9. B	9. B	9. C
10. D	10. E	10. E	10. A	10. B	10. C
11. B	11. A	11. B	11. B	11. A	
12. B	12. C	12. A	12. C	12. A	
13. C	13. C	13. B	13. D	13. C	
14. B	14. D	14. E	14. C		
15. D	15. B	15. B	15. A		
16. A	16. C	16. D	16. 4		
17. A	17. C	17. E	17. $1.5 < x < 6.5$ or $3/2 < x < 13/2$		
18. B	18. A	18. E	18. 2		
19. D	19. A	19. B	19. 15		
20. C	20. B	20. A	20. 156		
21. C	21. B	21. D	21. $3,000		
22. D	22. E	22. C	22. 81		
23. C	23. E	23. C	23. 4π		
24. C	24. A	24. B	24. 26		
25. A	25. C	25. D	25. 105		
26. D		26. E			
27. A		27. D			
28. E		28. E			
29. C		29. C			
30. C		30. A			
31. B					
32. A					
33. C					
34. C					
35. D					

Scoring Your Exam

For both verbal and math, you have two scores. The Raw Score is in double digits (53 or 21, for example); the Converted Score is in triple digits (690 or 350, for example). You have to do the math to get the Raw Score, find your Raw Score on the chart, and then locate the Converted Score. Before you begin calculating your scores, compare the answers you recorded on your answer sheet with the answer key. You may want to use these codes:

- Mark each answer you get right with a check mark (✓).
- Mark each answer you skip with a zero (0).
- Mark each answer you get wrong with an X.

Scoring verbal sections

All the verbal questions are multiple choice, with five answer choices. To score verbal sections 1, 3, and 5, follow these steps:

1. **In the worksheet below, write the total number of correct answers in Line 1.**
2. **Multiply the total number of incorrect answers in sections 1, 3, and 5 by ¼ and write that total (even if it's a fraction) in Line 2.**
3. **Subtract the number in Line 2 from the number in Line 1 and write that number on Line 3.**

   That's your total raw score for the verbal section of the test.

Verbal Raw Score Worksheet
Sections 1, 3, and 5

1. Total number of correct answers in Sections 1, 3, and 5 ______ 1
2. Total number of incorrect answers in Sections 1, 3, and 5______x ¼ – ______ 2
3. Total Verbal Raw Score ______ 3

Finding your converted ("final") verbal score

Your Raw Score is the ugly duckling that turns into a swan when you look at the Conversion Table. Find your Raw Score on the left and then find your corresponding Converted Score on the right. That Converted Score is what people mean when they talk about their SAT scores.

SAT Verbal Conversion Table

Raw	SAT	Raw	SAT	Raw	SAT
78	800	50	580	22	430
77	800	49	580	21	420
76	800	48	570	20	410
75	800	47	570	19	410
74	790	46	560	18	400
73	780	45	560	17	390
72	760	44	550	16	390
71	750	43	540	15	380
70	740	42	540	14	370
69	730	41	540	13	360
68	720	40	530	12	360
67	710	39	520	11	350
66	700	38	520	10	340
65	690	37	510	9	330
64	680	36	510	8	320
63	670	35	500	7	310
62	660	34	500	6	300
61	650	33	490	5	290
60	650	32	490	4	280
59	640	31	480	3	270
58	630	30	470	2	260
57	620	29	470	1	240
56	620	28	460	0	230
55	610	27	460	–1	220
54	610	26	450	–2	200
53	600	25	440	and below	200
52	600	24	440		
51	590	23	430		

Scoring math sections 2, 4, and 6

The math is a little more complicated to score than the verbal because you have three different types of questions. The questions in Sections 2 and 6 are multiple choice and are scored the same way as the multiple choice verbal questions: You get one point for every correct answer, you lose ¼ for every wrong answer, and omitted answers don't count for or against you.

However, scoring the questions in Section 4 is different. Fifteen of the questions are Quantitative Comparisons — with only four possible answers. For these, you still get one point for every right answer and no points for an omitted answer, but you lose ⅓ of a point (rather than ¼ of a point) for a wrong answer.

Finally, ten of the questions are grid-ins — with no answer choices. You have good news on these. You get one point for every right answer, no points for every omitted answer, but you do not lose any points for a wrong answer. (This is the only style question on the whole SAT that is penalty-free.)

Confused? It's easier than it sounds. Just follow these steps:

1. **In the worksheet below, write the total number of correct answers for sections 2 and 6 in Line 1.**
2. **Multiply the total number of incorrect answers in section 2 and 6 by ¼ and write that total (even if it's a fraction) in Line 2.**
3. **Subtract the number in Line 2 from the number in Line 1 and write that number in Line 3.**
4. **Write the total number of correct answers for questions 1–15 from section 4 in Line 4.**
5. **Multiply the total number of incorrect answers for questions 1–15 from section 4 by ⅓ and write that total (even if it's a fraction) in Line 5.**
6. **Subtract the number in Line 5 from the number in Line 4 and write that number in Line 6.**
7. **Write the total number of correct answers for questions 16–25 from section 4 in Line 7.**
8. **Add the numbers in Lines 3, 6, and 7 and write that number in Line 8.**

   That's your total raw score for the math section of the test.

Math Raw Score Worksheet
Sections 2, 4, and 6

1. Total number of correct answers in Sections 2 and 6		______ 1
2. Total number of incorrect answers in Sections 2 and 6______x ¼	–	______ 2
3. Subtotal in Sections 2 and 6 (Step 1 minus Step 2)		______ 3
4. Total number of correct answers in questions 1-15 in Section 4		______ 4
5. Total number of incorrect answers in Sections 2 and 6______x ⅓	–	______ 5
6. Subtotal from questions 1-15 (Step 1 minus Step 2)		______ 6
7. Total number of correct answers in questions 16-25 in Section 4		______ 7
8. Total Math Raw Score (Add lines 3, 6, and 7)		______ 8

Finding your converted ("final") math score

You're finally ready to look up your 200–800 math score in the Conversion Table. Find your Raw Score on the left, and then find your corresponding Converted Score on the right. That Converted Score is what people mean when they talk about their SAT scores.

SAT Math Conversion Table

Raw	SAT	Raw	SAT	Raw	SAT
60	800	38	570	16	410
59	790	37	560	15	410
58	770	36	550	14	400
57	750	35	540	13	390
56	730	34	530	12	380
55	720	33	530	11	370
54	700	32	520	10	370
53	690	31	520	9	360
52	680	30	510	8	350
51	670	29	500	7	340
50	660	28	500	6	320
49	650	27	490	5	310
48	650	26	480	4	300
47	640	25	480	3	280
46	630	24	470	2	270
45	620	23	460	1	250
44	610	22	460	0	230
43	600	21	450	–1	210
42	600	20	440	–2	200
41	590	19	440	and below	200
40	580	18	430		
39	570	17	420		

Chapter 20

Practice Exam 2: Answers and Explanations

Look for words in ***this special type*** throughout this chapter for more additions to your vocabulary list.

Section 1

1. **C.** The word "while" indicates that the two actions are different. (You could, therefore, get this question correct even if you didn't know that a ***paradox*** refers to contrary ideas or concepts.) The opposite of no is yes, or signaling agreement.

If you chose ***dissent*** (meaning disagreement), you're so far from the right answer that you should pack a lunch! You missed the point of the question. Don't be surprised if one of the answer choices is the exact opposite of the correct answer.

2. **D.** This should have been an easy question, just warming up your brain. Six and a half feet would be the maximum height of a person, not weight or direction or involvement. A ***girth*** is a circumference — I doubt your waistline would go up to six and a half feet!

Questions go from easy to hard. When the question is only number 2, the big hard word you don't know (girth) is rarely the answer. Easy questions have easy answers; hard questions have hard answers.

3. **A.** In Sentence Completion sentences, the second blank is often the key. The question tells you that Counselor Knostman "finally managed to find the perfect college." That expression implies that she worked hard at the task, or ***persevered.*** She did not succeed by ***resigning*** (giving up), quitting, or relaxing. Choice C, continued, is a possibility, but the first word doesn't make sense in the sentence. If the task is ***enormous,*** or big and hard, the counselor wouldn't be bored by it.

4. **B.** Narrow the answer choices down by predicting whether you need a positive or a negative word for each blank. The first word should be positive: Because the subject of the biography was fascinating, the book was written to make the readers want to learn about that person. Eliminate choices A, D, and E (to ***stymie*** is to obstruct, frustrate, thwart). Now you have narrowed the choices down to two. Even if you're totally confused or in a hurry, a 50-50 guess is worthwhile. (What if you don't know what the word *whet* means? You can't eliminate it yet. Leave it as a "maybe.")

The second word should be negative, as the biography had the reverse effect, making the readers *not* want to learn more. Eliminate choice C. By the process of elimination, only choice B is left. Note that you can get the right answer without having a clue what the word *whet* means, just by using good test-taking skills. ***Whet,*** incidentally, means to sharpen. Ever see a cartoon in which a Viking or some other warrior is using something that looks like a spinning wheel to sharpen the edge of his ax or knife? That wheel is a whetting stone. To use a cliché, to "whet your appetite" is to sharpen or stimulate your appetite.

5. **C.** This is the type of question that you really need to get correct, even if doing so means that you take a lot of time to read and reread and reread the question. When the answer choices have easy vocabulary (you probably knew every word in the answer choices), you have no excuse for missing the question except laziness. (My students always tell me they aren't lazy; they are "motivationally impaired!")

Often, tackling the second blank first can help. Predict that the word must be positive. Eliminate choices B, D, and E. Ignoring, overlooking, and criticizing ecosystems don't help to manage them successfully. Did you confuse *overlooked* in choice D with *looked over*? To ***overlook*** is to ignore something. For example, you may have overlooked the importance of brushing your teeth after every meal and ended up with cavities. To look over is to examine. The dentist looks over your mouth to find and fill those cavities.

You've narrowed the answers down to A and C. Predict that the first word must be positive, as the systems are to be assessed accurately. That leaves only choice C. Even though you have narrowed your choices down to one, be sure to plug that choice back into the sentence and read the entire sentence again. If you've made a careless mistake, you'll catch it here.

6. **D.** Focus on the second blank. If Dr. Wissen felt that the man against whom he was arguing was dangerous, he would argue pretty strongly, or ***vehemently,*** against him.

Choice A may fit the second blank; ***exhaustively*** means thoroughly. (It does not mean the same thing as exhausted, however; for example, an exhaustive search for something would leave you exhausted.) Fidelity, however, doesn't work for the first blank. ***Fidelity*** is faithfulness (*fid* = faith; *-ity* makes a word a noun). Dogs are named Fido because they are faithful.

Indifferently means not caring one way or the other (it "makes no difference"). ***Vaguely*** means in an unclear way. ***Tentatively*** means hesitantly and uncertainly. Did you know the words in the question? A ***charlatan,*** or a ***quack,*** is a fraud or a nonexpert. An SAT tutor who tells you that you'll get a 1600 if you stand naked in the light of the full moon and bury a toad in your backyard is a charlatan. (It's your *front* yard, actually.)

7. **B.** If the plants are neither oak nor ivy but something else, they are misnamed. The root ***nom*** means name (think *nombre* in Spanish or *nom* in French); a ***misnomer*** is a wrong name. Choice A is just the opposite. Something ***apropos*** is something appropriate. In choice C, eu- means good, phon means sound, and -ous means full of. Something ***euphonious*** is good-sounding. Choice D, indefinite, isn't logical. The terms are definite, although definitely wrong. And choice E, ***florid,*** means flowery (like *flores,* meaning flowers, in Spanish). Florid language is very showy, very la-ti-da (like calling something "gustatorially appealing" instead of saying it tastes good).

8. **A.** Predict that the second blank must refer to some BIG project. Eliminate choices C, D, and E. Because the public probably wouldn't be eager to read a thousand-page project, but rather ***disinclined*** (unwilling, not eager), choose A. A ***tome*** is a long literary project, like *War and Peace* or some SAT prep books that give a list of 10,000 words and a math review that starts with 1 + 1. ***Consternation*** is concern or upset. You would view such SAT prep tomes with great consternation.

9. **A.** Eliminate answers by predicting "positive" or "negative" words. Predict that the second word will be negative because the other applicants did something that Mr. Ramon didn't like.

Eliminate B, because ***integrity*** means honesty and sincerity. Predict that the first word will be positive, because Mr. Ramon was impressed by this quality. Eliminate E. Now it all comes down to vocabulary. ***Candor*** is openness, honesty, and forthrightness. (You may know this word in another form: candid. A candid photograph is not posed, but is honestly catching you just as you are at the moment it is taken.) ***Duplicity*** (used in the question) is deception, the quality of being two-faced or insincere (*dup* = double). Therefore, ***hypocrisy,*** which means saying one thing and doing another, works well in the second blank.

Vacillation means hesitation and wavering — a quality that wouldn't impress an interviewer. ***Opulence*** means affluence, wealth. ***Mendacity*** means dishonesty. (You may also see this word in another form, mendacious.) ***Didacticism*** means preacherliness.

10. **D.** This is a very hard question. You can predict that Lou would be tongue-tied in the presence of a beautiful woman (choices A, B, and D) or a strong woman (choices C and E). Because all the answers fit the second blank, the first blank here is the key. If Lou was tongue-tied, he didn't speak well. ***Laconic*** means brief or ***terse,*** short and to the point. Lou sputtered out just what needed to be said and didn't go into flowery, romantic talk.

    Contentious means argumentative. ***Gregarious*** means sociable, friendly, outgoing (*greg* = group; *-ous* = full of, very). ***Loquacious*** means talkative (*loq* = speech or talk; *-ous* = full of, very). ***Affable*** means friendly. And ***pulchritudinous*** (did you remember this word from the Analogies lecture?) means beautiful. (***True story:*** I met my boyfriend at a party. He pulled out the back of the collar of my tee-shirt and said, "You're so pulchritudinous, I was just checking to see whether you were made in heaven!" The smarmy line left me cold, but he won me with his vocabulary!)

11. **B.** A ***beaker*** is a type of flask; a ***valise*** is a type of luggage. No one really expects you to know the word "valise." You can get this question right by the process of elimination. A feather is not a type of weapon, unless you're using it to tease and torment your baby sister. A computer has a monitor, but is not a type of monitor. Silverware goes in a drawer, but is not a type of drawer. And a pencil is not a type of pen.

12. **B.** You put a stamp on a letter to send it; you put a label on a package to send it. (Bonus trivia: Licking a postage stamp gives you approximately 1⁄10 of a calorie. At last, an excuse for putting on weight over the holidays: "But I had to send all those Christmas cards with all those fattening stamps!")

13. **C.** A ***husk*** is the outer protection of rice. A ***shell*** is the outer protection of a walnut. If you chose B, you were thinking about the meanings of the words (rice, corn) rather than the relationships between the terms. A leotard may be a dancer's outer "husk," but its purpose isn't protection.

    Trivia: By the way, do you know where the word *leotard* came from? It was named after Jules Leotard, a French trapeze artist, who popularized the garment. (You never know what you're going to learn in this book, do you?)

14. **B.** Pincers are the claws of the crab, what it uses to grab and hold things. Hands are the claws of a human.

    Trivia: Speaking of monkeys as we were in answer E, here's a piece of trivia you can use to wow your friends and impress them with your erudition. Can you name the three monkeys that "see no evil, hear no evil, and speak no evil"? They are Mizaru, Mikazaru, and Mazaru. (How could you have lived without knowing that?)

15. **D.** Here's a reward for learning your roots. A ***fissure*** is a break or split in the earth (*fiss* means break or part; think of nuclear *fission* in which molecules are split apart). A rift is a break in the stone. You may have heard this word used metaphorically, dealing with relationships: Diana and Martin have a *rift* in their relationship and aren't going to be seeing each other anymore.

    Bonus! You'll never forget *fissure* or the root *fiss* if you learn this little limerick:

    A valiant young sportsman named Fisher
    Once fished from the edge of a fissure
    A fish with a grin
    Pulled the fisherman in
    Now they're fishing the fissure for Fisher!

    What if you don't know the word *rift*? (In other words, what if you're normal?) Work with what you've got. You know that a *fissure* is a break in the earth because of the root *fiss*. Soil is not a break in the dirt. (If you chose this answer, you probably fell for the trap of thinking earth and dirt had to go together. Remember that you're looking for the relationship between the words, not the meanings of the words.) An ***electron*** is not a break in the molecule, but a part of the molecule. (Two atoms are talking. One turns to the other and says, "Uh-oh, I've lost an electron." The other says, "Are you sure?" The first replies, "Yeah, I'm POSITIVE!") A monitor is not a break in the computer, but a part of the computer. That leaves you with only choices A and D. When you can narrow the answers down to two, even a wild guess is worthwhile. ***Strata*** are the layers of the atmosphere (think of the more common word *stratosphere*), and thus a part of it, not a break in it.

16. **A.** An ***insurgent*** is a rebel, a revolutionary, one against authority or the government. (The prefix *in-* means not or against; from this, you can deduce that the word is negative). An ***iconoclast*** is also a rebel; the word is often used to describe someone who rebels against religion. Even if you don't know these two relatively difficult words, you can get the right answer by the process of elimination. A ***cadet*** is a young member of the military, one just starting out, not one seeking to overturn or fight against the military. A ***lawyer*** is not against the judiciary (the judges or the system of law courts) but works within it. A ***minister*** is part of the church. A ***worker*** is part of the corporation.

17. **A.** The relationship is lesser to greater: Something adequate is less than something superfluous. You can define superfluous by the roots: *super-* means extra or above; *-ous* means full of. Something ***superfluous*** is excessive, or full of extra. Ever see a bottle of Nair, the hair remover for legs? The label says, ". . . for superfluous body hair." Something annoying is less than something infuriating. In choice E, innovative may have tricked you. Nov is a root meaning new, as in novel. The prefix *in-* has three meanings: not, inside, and beginning. In this case, something innovative has "newness inside of it," or is simply new. An ***innovative*** idea is original.

18. **B.** Ever hear the squalling of the bagpipes? That rather discordant whine and shriek is ***cacophony,*** a harsh, unpleasant sound. The sound that bells make is called a ***peal*** (the phrase "the pealing of bells" is a phrase often found in poetry).

    A ***knell*** is also a sound made by a bell (not a buzzer). The distinction between a peal and a knell is rather interesting. Bells knell when they are rung slowly and solemnly, as on some sad occasion ("the death knell"). Bells peal when they are rung quickly and joyously, on some happy occasion (bells peal at the end of a wedding).

    The sound of chimes is not a hiss. The sound of a watch is not a clatter . . . unless you drop it. (Know what watch repairmen do on weekends? Unwind!) Choice E may trap some students who don't make a specific enough sentence. While you want to zoom through analogies, if more than one answer seems to fit, go back and fine-tune your sentence.

19. **D.** In any set of analogies, there is usually one built-in mistake, a question that cannot be answered by using the "assume unknown words are synonyms" tip. In this case, ***cursory*** (brief, superficial, not careful with detail) is the opposite of ***meticulous*** (painstaking, careful with detail). Although you can get a great score by using just tricks, the test makers don't want you to get a perfect score unless you actually know what all the words mean, so they put in a few questions on which the cheap tricks just don't work. ***Placid*** means calm (*plac* = calm, peace). ***Agitated*** means upset, active.

    Clandestine means secretive. (I'm clandestine myself. Whenever some guy I don't like approaches with that weak line, "Where have you been all my life?" I respond, "I'd tell you, but then I'd have to find a new place to hide!") ***Languorous*** means listless, sluggish, not energetic. ***Novel*** means new (*nov* = new). ***Parched*** means dry.

20. **C.** ***Hazardous*** means dangerous, full of hazards or dangers. Use your roots to define innocuous. *In* means not, *noc* means poison, and *-ous* means full of: not full of poison, harmless. ***Lucid,*** meaning clear (luc means light or clear) or understandable (like a lucid explanation) is the opposite of ambiguous. *Ambi* means both; *-ous* means full of. Something ***ambiguous*** is "full of both," in the sense of having both meanings, being unclear. If I shave my head and ask you what you think, you may say, "Ahhh, Suzee. It's so YOU!" I don't know from that ambiguous statement whether you love or hate my new look; I could interpret your comments both ways.

If you don't know the meaning of the question words (and you forgot your roots), you can narrow down your choices by the process of elimination. Choices A, B, and E are synonyms (and because you can't have three correct answers, all three must be wrong). ***Serene*** means placid, or peaceful (*plac* means calm, peace). ***Jealous*** is envious. ***Expensive*** means costly. (I heard a good line from a comedian who said that Beverly Hills was such an expensive place to live that now the parking meters accept only Krugerrands!)

21. **C.** A ***premonition*** comes before (*pre-* means before); an afterthought, logically enough, comes after. A ***prologue*** comes before (*pro-* means before; log means speech or talk), as in the prologue of a play or a book. A ***peroration*** is the conclusion or summary. Yes, peroration is a hard word, but you can get the answer right by the process of elimination. Choice A is backward: Usually a demand comes after — not before — a suggestion. Choice B is tricky: Did you misread the second word as "inference," not *interference?* Interference may or may not come before a conclusion, but a conclusion certainly does not come before interference. Choice D is also backward. A prototype, meaning a first model, comes before the product (you may have heard the phrase "a working prototype," to describe a rough draft or first version). In choice E, consensus is a general agreement, an opinion held by all. It doesn't come before an agreement; it *is* an agreement.

22. **D.** Try assuming that unknown words are synonyms and make the sentence: "Duplicitous means deceptive." Something ***duplicitous*** will deceive; something ***stultifying*** (boring, dull) will bore, like a stultifying lecture from Mom and Dad. To ***carp*** is to complain or criticize. (***Hint:*** You probably know that a carp is a type of fish, right? Think of a fish-faced grump, always complaining and nit-picking.)

    Innovative means new, creative. *Nov* means new. Usually, *in-* means not, but it actually has three meanings: not, inside, and beginning. Here, *innovative* does not mean "not new" but "new beginning." When you have a root with more than one meaning, be sure to memorize — and use — *all* the meanings, not just the first one.

    The SAT often gives common words in uncommon forms. To ***profane*** is to make unholy or obscene. You probably know this word in another form, profanity. If a word looks familiar, but you can't quite get it, see whether you can use it in another form (*candor* and *candid* are another example, as are *ruthless* and *ruth*). ***Pious*** means religious, worshipping.

23. **C.** A ***warren*** is where a rabbit lives; a ***burrow*** is where a mole lives.

    This is one of the rare — very, very rare — times I would suggest skipping an analogy. If you didn't know the words, any answer could fit. If a warren is the sound a rabbit makes, A is correct. If a warren is something a rabbit eats, B is right. If a warren is a part of a rabbit, D is right. A wing is a part of a vulture, not where a vulture lives. (Know what kind of luggage a vulture takes on a trip? Carrion only!) And if a warren is the meat of a rabbit, E is right. Because there are no roots, prefixes, or suffixes to help you to analyze the word, and because assuming the words are synonyms doesn't help, you're better off just skipping this question.

24. **C.** The first question after the passage is usually the main idea. A main idea is broad and general. It is usually positive or neutral, as the passages are almost never negative. Words like "ridicule" rarely describe the main idea or primary purpose of a passage. In the Critical Reading chapter, you learned that "vague" words like discuss, explain and describe are often correct answers to a primary purpose question.

    In choice A, discussing style was not the primary purpose of the passage ("refute" is often a wrong word choice). Choice B is too strong. The passage simply tells a story; it doesn't encourage an action (strong words like "encourage," "urge," and "propose" are often wrong). Choice D uses the word "ridicule." Passages rarely ridicule anyone, especially the hero of the passage. And choice E is too general: The passage talks about one person, not about differences between all persons.

25. **A.** The author feels two ways. On the one hand, she's excited about meeting new people. On the other hand, she's very worried about how those people will perceive her. She has conflicting feelings.

    If you know your roots, you can figure this word out. *Ambi-* means both (if you are ***ambidextrous,*** you can use both hands) and *val* means values. An ***ambivalent*** person has "both values," sees both sides.

26. **D.** The author is undecided about what type of persona to project. She hasn't yet determined whether to play it cool or be friendly and risk coming across as too desperate.

Did you choose C, entreaty? Do you know what it means? Too often, insecurities can trap you: "Oh, big hard word, it must be right." Usually, the hardest word is in fact the trap wrong answer. ***Entreaty*** means begging or pleading.

27. **A.** Many critical reading questions can be answered using common sense. The answers are not given directly in the passage, but are implied. The author mentions that she was worried about going away to college, and that her parents picked up on her insecurities. It's logical, therefore, to assume that the mother wanted to reassure her daughter, and left the brochures to show the daughter her options. Choice B is illogical; majors were not mentioned or implied in the passage. Choice C is also outside the scope of the passage. You know nothing about which college the student's parents attended. Choices D and E go too far. No one said that community colleges were less challenging or academically rewarding than four year colleges; no one suggested that the family's decision on the college revolved around finances. Be careful not to read more into the passage than is given.

28. **E.** The first paragraph discusses the author's worries about not being as sophisticated as the teenagers on the coasts. The second paragraph continues and even expands upon that theme, as the author worries about whether she'll fit in with people on the coast, what they'll think of her, how she should act.

29. **C.** This negatively phrased or *except* question can be answered by the process of elimination. Answering it takes quite a bit of time, as you are actually answering four questions, finding first what was mentioned. If you know you run short of time on reading passages, a question like this one is good to skip and come back to at the end only if you have time left.

    Choice A was discussed in the first paragraph, which tells how the author thought she would not fit in, that she wasn't sophisticated enough to leave the Midwest. Choice B was answered in the first paragraph which mentions the television shows that she watched to learn about the west coast teenagers. Choice D was answered in paragraph five, in which you read that the author had been on the school board and "everything from dogcatcher to Mayoral assistant." Choice E was answered in paragraph four which tells how the author was intimidated by the fact that everyone in the Midwest had grown up together and been involved in each other's lives over many years. Only Choice C was not discussed. You know that the author did move back to the Midwest, but not why she did so.

30. **C.** Irony is the humorous or somewhat sarcastic expression in which the intended meaning is just the opposite of the usual sense (calling someone a brain surgeon to mean he's not very smart, for example).

31. **B.** The author mentions that her "insecurities surfaced," that she was around women who had been each other's bridesmaids and had grown up together. She was intimidated by, or frightened by, these women and their close bonds.

32. **A.** A recluse is a hermit, a loner, a solitary person. Even if you didn't know that, you could understand the meaning from the rest of the sentence, which goes on to state that the author decided to reach out and make friends. That means she was not going to keep to herself. Choice E is the only other tempting choice. However, there is nothing in the passage to indicate that the author actually rejected people when she was at college; she merely didn't reach out to them at that time.

33. **C.** To surprise herself means she did something she had not anticipated doing, something that was out of character for herself. If she had not been involved in politics previously, running for an elected office was quite out of character and surprising. Note that choice D would be a bad answer based on common sense. The SAT would never say that politics is an ***ignoble*** (meaning not noble, bad) profession!

34. **C.** The word "dogcatcher" should have made you smile as you read it. That word is used to inject some humor, to make a point that she also held both the most minor and most important of offices. Choice D may have trapped you. While it is true that this small-town girl did become a success, mentioning that she had been a dogcatcher (and it would be reasonable to infer that she wasn't really a dogcatcher, that she simply used that as a figure of speech) wasn't a way to prove it!

35. **D.** The author takes you through her life chronologically, from high school until the current time. Choice E would be a totally illogical choice, given that the SAT rarely ridicules anything or anyone. Negative answers are almost never correct on the SAT. Choice A is wrong; even if you thought the original theory was that the students at college would dislike the provincial Midwesterner, there were no supporting examples of that theory. Instead, the theory was disproved. Choice B is tempting because of the second paragraph in which the author worries about going away to college. However, there are not really pros and cons discussed. Choice C is wrong because there was no justification given in the passage.

Section 2

1. **C.** An equilateral triangle has three equal sides. The perimeter of a figure is the sum of all sides. $\frac{2}{3} + \frac{2}{3} + \frac{2}{3} = \frac{6}{3} = 2$.

If you added both the numerators and the denominators, you got $\frac{2}{3} + \frac{2}{3} + \frac{2}{3} = \frac{6}{9} = \frac{2}{3}$, which is choice D. Simple logic should tell you this answer is wrong. How can the *sum* of all sides be equal to one side?

2. **B.** International students: This is the type of problem you should skim for and do first, because you can usually get this correct (as opposed to one of those *awful* word problems). When taking a base and an exponent to a power outside of a parenthesis, multiply the exponents: $3 \times 10 = 30$; x^{30}. When dividing like bases, subtract the exponents: $30 - 6 = 24$; x^{24}.

Choice D is a trap you'd fall into if you divided, rather than subtracted, the exponents ($\frac{30}{6} = 5$). Choice C is a trap for those of you who added the exponents first: $x^3 + x^{10} = x^{13}$ and then subtracted $x^{13} - x^6 = x^7$.

3. **E.** Each of the other fractions reduces to $\frac{1}{3}$.

It's easy to think that 24 is one third of 62 because 2 is a third of 6 and 4 is a third of 12 (looking at the 2 in the units column). Here's one of the times when your calculator was truly useful. If your first thought was that all the numbers were the same, you should have punched some buttons and double-checked. Whereas A, B, C, and D divide out to approximately .33, choice E comes out to .387.

4. **D.** If you chose C, you fell for the trap. You can't just add 10 + 15 and divide that by 2. Use the formula Rate × Time = Distance to make the following chart:

$R \times T = D$

$10 \times 3 = 30$

$15 \times 2 = 30$

If the 10 mph speed increased by 50%, it accelerated to $10 + \frac{1}{2}(10) = 15$ mph. Note that the route going and coming for the blimp was the same. If it took 3 hours at 10 miles per hour, the route must have been $10 \times 3 = 30$ miles. Therefore, the return route was 30 miles as well. Zooming along at 15 miles per hour for 30 miles takes 2 hours.

Finally, to find the rate, divide the distance (which totals 60) by the time (which totals 5). $60 \div 5 = 12$.

And speaking of time, know how long it takes to construct a blimp? Oh, a Good Year . . . .

5. **D.** At $125 a day, Heather would earn $500 in four days (125 × 4). At $25 a day, Judson has to work ($\frac{500}{25}$) 20 days. Here's a time when a calculator is handy. You may as well take advantage of this sort of problem because there is a ***surfeit*** (overabundance, excess) of problems in which the calculator doesn't do you much good — problems that test logic and reasoning, not arithmetic.

6. **B.** Heather and Judson, working together, earn $150 a day. In four days, they earn $600. Colleen earns $150 a day working alone, or $300 in two days. Six hundred is twice as much, or 200 percent, of three hundred. If you chose D, you said that Heather and Judson earned only 2 percent of what Colleen earned; "two percent of" is not the same as "twice."

7. **C.** Multiply 432×36 (three dozen is 36) = 15,552 to find the number of CDs the plane can carry at one time. Divide that into 60,000 to get *more than* 3 but *less than* 4. The trap answer is E, 3. However, even though the plane is partially empty on the fourth trip, it does have to make four complete trips or some of the cartons will be left behind. Answer D is illogical: How can the plane make $\frac{4}{5}$ of a trip? Don't be tricked into choosing this just because your answer is approximately 3.8 or $3\frac{4}{5}$. If the plane makes that $\frac{4}{5}$ trip, it crashes short of its destination.

8. **E.** The sum of any two sides of a triangle must be greater than the third side. For example, you could not have a triangle of sides 3, 3, and 7, because $3 + 3$ is not greater than 7. The same is true for 1, 2, and 4. Only 5 works here — $3 + 5 > 7$. (Because the sum of *any* two sides must be greater than the third, you also check: $5 + 7 > 3$ and $3 + 7 > 5$.)

   You *cannot* assume that this is a right triangle and begin using the Pythagorean theorem ($a^2 + b^2 = c^2$). You are not told there is a 90° angle in the triangle. Don't get so carried away by Pythagoras that you look for him and his darn theorem every time you see a triangle.

9. **D.** Substitute numbers for letters in the original formula: Put a 6 where the *x* is, a 2 for the *y*, and a 9 for the *z*. This gives you $\frac{1}{2}(6) + 2^3$ all divided by $2 - 9$. This equals $\frac{(3+8)}{-7}$ or $-\frac{11}{7}$. This problem tests the concept of symbolism, which often requires substitution. Notice that there's no such thing as a * operation; the * means something different in every problem and applies only to that particular problem.

10. **E.** If Courtney is x, Jason is $x - 6$ because he is six years younger (or six years "less") than Courtney. Dan is twice Jason, which is $2(x - 6) = 2x - 12$.

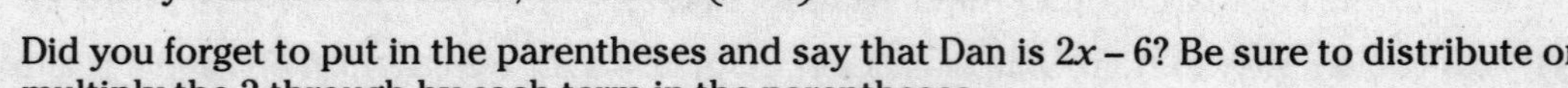

Did you forget to put in the parentheses and say that Dan is $2x - 6$? Be sure to distribute or multiply the 2 through by each term in the parentheses.

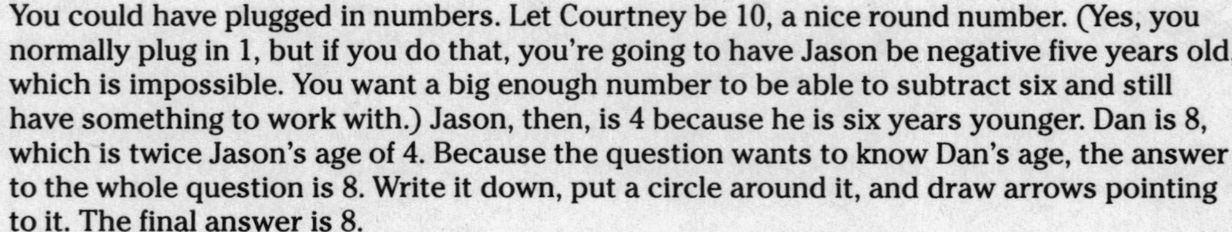

You could have plugged in numbers. Let Courtney be 10, a nice round number. (Yes, you normally plug in 1, but if you do that, you're going to have Jason be negative five years old, which is impossible. You want a big enough number to be able to subtract six and still have something to work with.) Jason, then, is 4 because he is six years younger. Dan is 8, which is twice Jason's age of 4. Because the question wants to know Dan's age, the answer to the whole question is 8. Write it down, put a circle around it, and draw arrows pointing to it. The final answer is 8.

Now, work backward through the answer choices to see which one comes out to be 8. Remember that x represents Courtney's age, 10. Choice A: $10 - 6 = 4$. Choice B: $10 + 6 = 16$. Choice C: $2(10) - 6 = 20 - 6 = 14$. Choice D: $2(10) + 6 = 20 + 6 = 26$. (Choice E had better work or we're in trouble now.) Choice E: $2(10) - 12 = 20 - 12 = 8$. Whew!

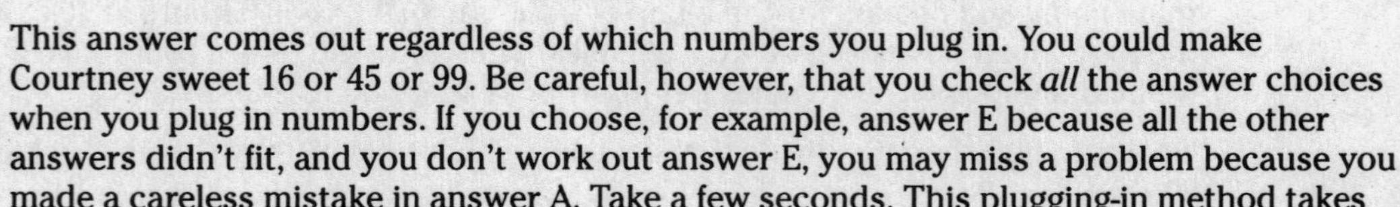

This answer comes out regardless of which numbers you plug in. You could make Courtney sweet 16 or 45 or 99. Be careful, however, that you check *all* the answer choices when you plug in numbers. If you choose, for example, answer E because all the other answers didn't fit, and you don't work out answer E, you may miss a problem because you made a careless mistake in answer A. Take a few seconds. This plugging-in method takes time, but you're *sure* you're correct.

11. **A.** To find a shaded area, subtract the area of the unshaded portion from the area of the total figure. If the diameter of the circle is 10, the side of the square is 10.

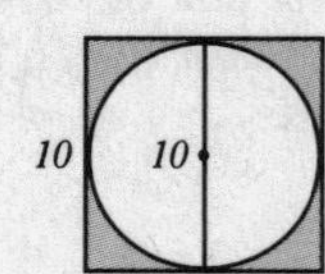

Because the area of a square is side^2, the area of this square is $10 \times 10 = 100$. If the diameter of a circle is 10, the radius is 5. The area of a circle is πradius^2, or $5 \times 5 \times \pi = 25\pi$. Subtract: $100 - 25\pi$. ***Note:*** Don't actually multiply π out. In most problems, π is left in that form. Look at the answer choices before you do too much work.

The easy way to do a shaded area problem is to think of it as a "leftover," what remains when the area of the unshaded part has been subtracted from the area of the entire figure. Shaded areas are covered in Chapter 10.

If you got choice B, you found the circumference ($2\pi r = 10\pi$) of the circle, instead of the area. If you chose C, you used the perimeter of the square ($10 + 10 + 10 + 10 = 40$) rather than the area. If you chose D, you messed up absolutely everything (!); you found the perimeter of the square instead of its area and found the circumference of the circle instead of its area. Isn't it vicious how the test makers anticipate just about every mistake you can make? They must be psychic . . . or is that psycho?

12. **C.** The sides of a 30:60:90 triangle are in the ratio $s : s\sqrt{3} : 2s$. If you forgot this, go back and look at the directions, which are kind enough to provide the information (and you thought the SAT had no heart!). The sides, therefore, must be $10 : 10\sqrt{3} : 20$. The area of a triangle is ½ *base* times *height,* which here is $\frac{1}{2}(10\sqrt{3})(10) = 50\sqrt{3}$.

13. **C.** Write out both full expressions (which I suggest you memorize so that you don't have to FOIL them each time):

$(a + b)^2 = a^2 + 2ab + b^2$

$(a - b)^2 = a^2 - 2ab + b^2$

Subtract the second term from the first (change the signs on the second term):

$$\begin{array}{r} a^2 + 2ab + b^2 \\ \underline{-a^2 + 2ab - b^2} \\ +4ab \end{array}$$

Because $ab = 15$, $4ab = 60$.

If you chose E, you forgot to change the sign of $-2ab$ to $+2ab$.

14. **D.** Just talk it through. Take the square of the first number: $3^2 = 9$. Add it to the sum of the last two numbers: $9 + (3 + 5) = 17$. Now do the same thing, changing the last two numbers. $9 + (5 + 17) = 31$ (trap answer C). So far, your series is 3, 5, 17, 31. Do the same thing one final time: $9 + (17 + 31) = 57$.

15. **B.** If the last half of the trip to the Bean Blossom Junction was alone, the 40% and the 20 miles are the first half, or 50%. Because 50% - 40% = 10%, 20 miles = 10%. It may be easier to think in terms of fractions: 10% = $\frac{1}{10}$. One tenth of something is 20; that something is 200. (Arithmetically: $\frac{1}{10}x = 20$. Divide both sides through by $\frac{1}{10}$, which means inverting and multiplying by $\frac{10}{1}$. $20 \times 10 = 200$.) This was a good problem to talk through; you needed reasoning, not arithmetic.

16. **C.** To divide like bases, subtract the exponents. (Here, the $\frac{8}{4} = 2$, which is irrelevant because every answer choice has a 2.) $a^8 \div a^4 = a^4$. Eliminate answers A and B. Next, $b^3 \div b^2 = b^1$, which is just plain b. Eliminate choice D. (If you had b^{-1}, the b would be in the denominator, but because it's b^1, it's in the numerator.) Finally, c^0 divided by c^3 is c^{-3}, meaning a c^3 in the denominator.

Bases and exponents should be one of the easiest types of problems for you. If you're confused, check out the bases section of Chapter 11.

17. **C.** The total is a multiple of the sum of the numbers in the ratio. The numbers in the ratio, 7:2, sum up to 9. There are seven groups of 9 in 63 ($\frac{63}{9} = 7$). That means there are seven groups of 7, for a total of 49, and seven groups of 2, for a total of 14. Now subtract: $49 - 14 = 35$. If you're confused, go and look at how to do ratios the easy way in Chapter 11.

18. **A.** Make a chart.

Seeds	***Nuts***	***Mixture***
⅔	⅓	3⁄3 (= 1 cup)
	+3⁄3	+3⁄3
⅔	4⁄3	6⁄3 (= 2 cups)

The nuts are 4⁄3 out of 6⁄3 cups, or 4⁄6 = 66⅔% of the mixture.

Choice E is out to getcha. If you chose that, you said the nuts were ⅔% or $.00\overline{666}$, not the $.\overline{66}$ that you want. Choice D is also slick. The nuts are 4⁄3 or 1⅓ cup, but that's not what the question is asking. It's a good idea to circle what the question is looking for, which in this case is not a number of cups, but a *percentage* of the total.

Trivia: In your childhood, you probably saw cartoons in which Ali Baba yells, "Open Sesame!" to gain entrance to a locked cave. Did you ever wonder where the expression came from? When a sesame seed is ripe, it pops, scattering seeds all around. The expression was derived from the fact that the hulls seem to open quickly, like a door hatch.

19. **A.** There's an easy way, and there's a hard way to approach this problem. Let's start with the easy way: Plug in numbers. Substitute numbers for the variables. Let x = 3. (It doesn't make much difference what number you substitute; I just choose 3 because it's small and easy to deal with. You don't want to use 1 because of the fractions: 1⁄1 doesn't help much.) If x = 3, then y = ⅓.

Now plug these numbers into the entire equation:

$$\frac{1}{x+1}+\frac{1}{y+1}=\frac{1}{3+1}+\frac{1}{\frac{1}{3}+1}=\frac{1}{4}+\frac{1}{\frac{4}{3}}=\frac{1}{4}+\frac{3}{4}=1$$

Although in this case, choice A is correct, you must go through the final step of checking every answer choice. Here, choice B is obviously wrong. Choice C: x = 3 is wrong (remember that you're looking for a final answer of 1). Choice D: 3 + 1 = 4. Choice E: $\frac{3+1}{3+2}=\frac{4}{5}$. Why bother with this last step of checking every answer? Depending on what number you plug in, more than one answer could work. In that case, you'd have to change your numbers and try again.

If you're a more abstract thinker and prefer to use basic algebra, think of this as a substitution problem. Substitute y = 1⁄x for y in the expression $\frac{1}{y+1}$:

$$\frac{1}{x+1}+\frac{1}{\frac{1}{x}+1}$$

To get rid of that ugly second part of the expression, multiply $\frac{1}{\frac{1}{x}+1}$ by $\frac{x}{x}$:

$$\frac{1}{x+1}+\frac{1}{\frac{1}{x}+1}\times\frac{x}{x}=\frac{1}{x+1}+\frac{x}{1+x}.$$

Don't forget to distribute! Now you have a common denominator (remember that x + 1 is the same as 1 + x), so add the fractions:

$\frac{1+x}{x+1}=1$ (choice A)

20. **B.** The triangles are similar figures with sides in proportion. A very easy way to solve this problem is to plug in numbers. If *AB* = ⅔ of *AC,* let *AB* = 2 and *AC* = 3. (Hey, I'm all for an easy life — go with what the test gives you.) Because the triangle is isosceles (the question tells you that), *BE* = 2 and *CD* = 3. The area of a triangle is ½ *base* × *height.* Here, the area of triangle *ABE* = ½ (2)(2) = 2. The area of triangle *ACD* = ½ (3)(3) = 4½. Get rid of the fraction by doubling both sides: 4:9.

You can use basic algebra, but there's all sorts of potential for careless mistakes here. Although ratios may be written either horizontally (2:3) or vertically (⅔), I use fractions here to make the multiplication simple. The ratio of the areas is ½(*b*)(*h*): ½ (⅔) (⅔). Multiply it out: ½*bh* = 4⁄18 or ½*bh* = 2⁄9. To get rid of the fraction (½), multiply both sides through by 2: *bh*= 4⁄9.

Most people erroneously multiply both the top and the bottom of $\frac{2}{9}$ by 2 and get $\frac{4}{18}$, which leads you right back to $\frac{2}{9}$. It's an easy mistake to make. Even if you're great at algebra, plugging in numbers takes only a few seconds and can reveal careless mistakes.

There is one very easy, very quick way to solve this problem, *if* you know the formula. *The ratio of the areas of similar figures is the square of the ratio of their sides.* Here, the sides are in the ratio 2:3 (which you can also write as $\frac{2}{3}$). Square that to find the ratio of their areas: $\frac{2}{3} \times \frac{2}{3} = \frac{4}{9}$.

21. **B.** To find a shaded area, find the area of the larger figure and the area of the unshaded figure, and subtract. The larger square has a side of y. The area of the larger square therefore is y^2. The side of the smaller square is x. The area of the smaller square is x^2. Simply subtract: $y^2 - x^2$.

    Although this is a relatively simple problem, the answers can be tricky. Choice A is backward. You don't subtract the larger area from the smaller area, or you would have a negative answer. You can't have a negative area. Give yourself a pat on the back if you noticed that choices D and C are exactly the same. Because $xy = yx$ (you can multiply forward or backward), $2xy - 2yx = 0$. The same is true of choice D. You can tell by looking at the figure that the area is not 0.

22. **E.** *Consecutive* means *in a row,* one after another. The average of consecutive integers is the middle term. Draw the lines and fill in 0 for the middle term, and then fill in the rest of the blanks.

    ___ ___ ___ ___ 0 ___ ___ ___ ___

    –4 –3 –2 –1 0 1 2 3 4

    $1 + 2 + 3 + 4 = 10$

    $\frac{10}{4} = 2.5$

Because all the numbers are consecutive, they increase. That means that the last four numbers are greater than 0, and their average must be greater than 0 as well. Eliminate answer choices A, B, and C automatically.

23. **E.** The volume of any solid is (area of the *base*) × *height*. The base of a cylinder is a circle, so the volume of a cylinder is $\pi r^2 \times$ height. If the circumference of the base is 8π, the radius is 4π (because circumference is $2\pi r$). The area of the base, a circle, is πr^2 or16π. The height is 8 (twice the radius). Multiply $16\pi \times 8 = 128\pi$.

24. **A.** Option I is true because all cards have had magnetic strips since 1985, and Megan's card was issued after that date. Eliminate choice B.

    Option II is not necessarily true (and the question asks which *must* be true) because even though photos started appearing in 1988, three years before the date of Megan's card, the question states merely that some, which means at least one but not necessarily all, of the cards from then on have photos. Given that II is wrong, you know that the answer has to be choice A or D.

If you're running short on time at this stage, it might be worth your making a quick guess (a 50/50 guess is usually worthwhile). Option III is probably the toughest for most people because many will assume that there can't be a color photo prior to 1993. Not so! Just because all photos have been taken in color since 1993 does not mean that a color photo couldn't have appeared earlier. Megan could have had a photo ID because her ID is from later than 1988, and this ID could have been taken in color. Eliminate III, leaving you with choice A.

25. **C.** An inscribed angle is ½ the measure of the central angle with the same endpoints. Because A and C are the endpoints of both angle ABC and angle AOC, angle ABC = ½ of angle AOC, which, therefore, equals 120. (This concept is covered in Chapter 10.)

    Choice E is backward because it is half of angle ABC instead of twice angle ABC. You could just look at the angles and know that angle AOC is more than angle ABC, eliminating answers D and E. ***Remember:*** Unless a problem *specifically* says that a figure is not drawn to scale, it *is* drawn to scale, and you may use it to help you find an answer.

Section 3

1. **A.** If the voyage *proved* Thor Heyerdahl's premise, the voyage must have been a success. Predict that the word is positive. Quickly eliminate choices B, C, D, and E. And yes, some of the SAT questions really are this easy. Remember that the questions go from easier to harder. The first few questions serve just to warm up your brain.

2. **D.** Often, the second blank is easier to figure out than the first. Fire protection should lessen insurance costs, because the building is less likely to burn down when protection has been installed. Eliminate choices A and C. For the first blank, predict that you need a positive word, because fire protection helps a building. Eliminate choices B and E. By the process of elimination, choice D is correct. (***Bonus trivia:*** You've heard the saying, "no smoke without fire." Who said that first? Answer: John Heywood, circa 1497–1580, who actually said, "There is no fire without some smoke." Did you think the line was that old?)

3. **B.** All those hours spent studying your roots and prefixes paid off here. The root *sal* means health (if you speak Spanish, you know that *salud* means health). The suffix *-ous* means full of or very. Therefore, the word ***salubrious*** means healthful, or good for you.

   Choice A uses roots as well. *Nox* means poison; *-ous* means full of or very. ***Noxious*** means full of poison, poisonous — not at all what the billboard is saying. (Know how billboards communicate? With sign language.) In choice C, *super* means above or extra (Superman is "extra man"), and once again, *-ous* means full of or very. ***Superfluous*** means excessive, "full of extra," too much. You may think that some of my jokes in this book are superfluous (extra and unnecessary)!

4. **A.** Predict that the first word would mean getting rich, because the "small income" would not bring in a lot of money. You can eliminate E and D.

   Even though the prefix *im-* often means not, as in impossible or improbable, in this case, it means inside. Someone impoverished is "in poverty," or poor. Be sure when you learn a prefix that you find out all its meanings, not just one. For the second blank, you need a positive word, something that is enjoyed. The words duty and obligation imply something that is done because it has to be, not because doing it is a joy. By the process of elimination, A is correct. ***Affluent*** means wealthy. A ***perquisite*** is something extra or additional to regular pay. You may have heard the expression, "the perks," as in, "Meeting cute girls at the beach is one of the perks of being a lifeguard." Perks is actually short for perquisites. In choice C, ***opulent*** means wealthy or rich.

5. **B.** Because of the "and," the words that will complete the two blanks are going to be somewhat similar, if not precisely synonyms. ***Unpretentious*** means modest, without any pretense or arrogance. The "despite being revered" means that even though the Kings are honored, they are not pompous or haughty, but modest.

   Objective means neutral, unbiased. ***Bombastic*** means big-talking, pretentious. ***Obscure*** means not readily understood. ***Arrogant*** means stuck-up, conceited. ***Servile*** means subservient, like a servant (the opposite of dominant). ***Prolix*** isn't an expensive brand of watch; it means excessively talkative.

6. **E.** Predict that the blanks must be opposites, because being one thing is *better than* being something else. If you've gone through this book in order, this is about the gazillionth time you've seen ***dogmatic,*** which means narrow-minded, opinionated, stubborn. ***Ambivalent*** means unclear, imprecise, wishy-washy (*ambi-* = both; *val* = values).

Belligerent means argumentative and is too close to "controversial" to be correct in the sentence. ***Staunch*** means constant, strong. ***Wayward*** means headstrong, willful. ***Capricious*** means unpredictable, whimsical.

7. **B.** Predict that the second blank must be something like "sure" or "guaranteed." Eliminate answers C, D, and E. In A, it's unlikely that exaggerating all costs contributes to peace of mind. Therefore, B is the answer.

8. **C.** Predict that if the animal is difficult to study, it must be hard to find. Start with the second blanks first. Eliminate choices A and D; if the numbers are increasing or growing, the animal would be easy to find. In choice B, an animal with a sociable nature would be easy to find and study, as he would be more approachable. Eliminate choice A by using your roots: *greg-* means group or herd (think congregate, segregate) and *-ous* means full of or very. A ***gregarious*** animal is "very groupy" or part of a group, just the opposite of what you want here. You've narrowed the choices down to C or E. The second words work in both, as ***plummeting*** means decreasing rapidly, going down. ***Reclusive*** means solitary, away from the world (a recluse is a hermit). In choice E, ***amiable*** means friendly, sociable, just the opposite of what you want (think *ami* as in the French *mon ami,* or the Spanish, *amigo*).

9. **E.** Predict that the first blank needs a positive word because the land is "blessed." That eliminates D, because ***parched*** means dried out. You may not know the rest of the words, so leave them as "maybes." Predict that the second blank needs a negative word, because the rest of the region is not blessed. Eliminate choice C. That narrows the answers down to A, B and E.

You need to make a personal choice whether you want to guess when you can eliminate one or two answers. I, myself, won't guess unless I can get the choices down to two, because I think a 50/50 fight is a fair fight. However, if you're a good guesser, you may want to try when you get the choices down to three. Here, ***sere*** means dry; ***torrid*** means hot. ***Fecund*** means fertile; ***verdant*** means green and blooming (think of *verde,* which means green in Spanish). ***Fertile*** means able to grow crops; ***arid*** means dry. ***Sporadic*** means off and on, not constant.

10. **E.** A supermarket sells bananas. A nursery sells plants. You didn't fall for the trap in D, did you? A health spa promotes health, but it doesn't stick health in a bag and sell it for you to take home. A ***haberdashery*** is a men's clothing store.

My greengrocer has a sign on her counter: "Time flies like an arrow; fruit flies like a banana." It took me a minute to get it.

Don't choose a word you can't define for one of the so-called "easy" questions at the beginning (unless, of course, you're absolutely positive that all the words you can define are wrong). An easy question usually has an easy answer.

11. **B.** A ***sheaf*** is a collection or bundle of papers. (You may have heard the lyric, "Bringing in the sheaves," referring to harvesting sheaves, or bundles, of wheat.) A ***collection*** is a bundle of items. A document is not necessarily a bundle of arguments (think love letters). A parchment may be made of skins, but is not a collection of them. A ***quiver*** contains arrows. A quarter is not a collection of dimes. (***Bonus trivia:*** A quarter has exactly 119 grooves on its circumference. A dime has 118.)

12. **A.** Armor protects a body. A thimble protects a finger.

You probably made as your original sentence, "Armor goes on a body." But then choices A, C, and E (and maybe D) all work. That's a clue to go back and fine-tune your sentence, trying to make it more specific. Find the salient, or distinguishing, feature of armor. Armor is not just apparel, but apparel with a purpose: protection.

A sock covers, but doesn't really protect, a foot. A corset controls, but doesn't protect, your girth. ***Girth*** means circumference; your waistline is your girth. Braces straighten, but don't protect, teeth. And television features, not protects, programs. (Did ya ever hear the Fred Allen quote: "Television is my favorite medium because it's so rarely well-done!")

13. **B.** Iron is the raw material with which a blacksmith works; wood is the raw material with which a carpenter works. Choice D is a pathetic and feeble attempt at humor. Brides are not "raw material" of a matchmaker. Answers that are funny — or that are supposed to be funny — are almost never right. The SAT is about as funny as a zit on the end of your nose.

14. **E.** Try assuming that unknown words are synonyms and make the sentence: "A paradigm is a model." (For all you smart alecks out there, no, a paradigm is not twenty cents! I've heard that one before, you know.) A ***convention*** (the standard) is a norm (something normal). You probably know convention in another form, ***conventional.*** A conventional person is normal, not bizarre.

An ***apogee*** is the top point. The apogee of your life may be when you see your great SAT score. A ***diatribe*** is a tirade, a bitter and abusive speech. If you see someone trying to cheat off you during the SAT, you launch into a diatribe, telling her she has to study, just the way you did.

15. **B.** ***Euphonious*** means full of good sound (*eu* = good; *son* = sound; *-ous* = full of, very), pleasant-sounding. ***Savory*** means full of good taste, tasty. Pusillanimous does not mean full of pus. (Did you really think that the SAT would feature a word that means "full of pus"? No way.) ***Pusillanimous*** means fearful or timid. ***Dissonant*** means not harmonious; dissonant sounds are clashing sounds. ***Wizened*** means withered, shriveled, dried up. ***Hapless*** means luckless (*hap* = luck).

16. **D.** Because the "primary purpose" or "main idea" question is so common in Critical Reading passages, you should read the passage with an eye toward identifying those points. Although the passage gets more general at the end, it is primarily about the rights of the Cherokee women.

17. **E.** A negatively-phrased question, such as "Which is *not* true" or "All of the following are true *except*" is often very difficult or tricky or just plain time-consuming. Good test-takers often skip this question, going back to it at the end. Here, although the passage said the Cherokee woman has the right to choose her own mate, nowhere were you told the procedure for her doing so.

18. **E.** A vocabulary question like this is usually one of the easier types of questions. If you're running short on time and know you won't get to all the questions, try this one. The exact line number is given to you; all you have to do is "plug 'n' chug," plug the answer choices into the sentence and see which one makes sense. In this case, it was the custom in European families to choose the mate for the women.

If you chose A or B or even C, you probably didn't take the time to go back to the passage and see how the word was used. A word is often used differently in the context of the passage than you would expect (if you're confused on this concept, flip to Chapter 8).

19. **B.** You could almost get this question right without going back to the passage. Answer choices to reading questions are rarely strong or mean or negative (eliminating answers A, C, and D). By putting the word "civilization" in quotes, the author is being slightly sarcastic, implying that Whites may have thought they were the only civilized group.

20. **A.** This is a rather subjective question (meaning it's your personal opinion, rather than an objective fact). If you missed it, don't feel too bad. A "standard of living" more likely includes medical care than sports arenas or amphitheaters. A kindergarten is part of the education system already mentioned; tribal councils might be considered part of the courts already mentioned.

21. **D.** The best way to answer this question is through the process of elimination. There is no chronology (time line) of events (choice A). There is no refutation (disproving) of a theory (choice B) or counterexample to a theory (choice C). There is no hypothesis (choice E). All the author does is state his idea and then give examples to support what he's said.

Did you think this question was very easy for the last one? Remember that Critical Reading is the only part of the SAT in which questions do not necessarily go from easy to hard. Questions in Critical Reading simply follow the order of the passage. Question one might be the most difficult question, but the answer is at the beginning of the passage. Question 10 might be the easiest question, but the answer is at the end of the passage.

22. **C.** Choice C follows very nicely from lines 17–20. Because the U.S. is moving toward national standards and assessments, it stands to reason that those national standards and assessments are not yet there.

    Choice A is very plausible, but it cannot be directly inferred from the passage, which does not mention funding. Perhaps sufficient money is spent on arts education, but the money is simply distributed only to a few.

    Choice B is out primarily because there is no mention of artists, or of people who specialize in art. The emphasis is on the arts and basic education. Furthermore, choice B could very well be false. The children who show a lot of promise in the arts might get plenty of training in the U.S.

    Choice D is yet another example of a choice that is too extreme. The passage certainly implies that arts education in the U.S. is not considered basic, but you cannot interpret that to mean that many students receive absolutely no education in the arts.

    Does the passage say anything about science education in the U.S.? Choice E is the time-wasting answer. If you don't recall reading anything about science education, you can probably trust your memory and not go back and reread the entire passage (especially when another answer is so tempting).

23. **C.** The author has a very upbeat attitude when discussing the different approaches to arts education. The author is of the opinion that because so many methods can work, it's time just to get on with making arts education basic in the United States. Choice C echoes this thought.

    If you picked choice D, you need to practice selecting the *why* of a detail rather than the *what* of a detail when the question uses the phrasing "in order to." The author is not interested in Japan, Germany, and England per se.

    You may eliminate choice A because the author never endorses one approach over another. Get rid of choice B for a similar reason. The author is not concerned with how the job gets done but simply wants to get the job done.

    Choice E would be great if the author were pessimistic. If this were his attitude, you would certainly be justified in saying that he presents the variety of approaches to urge further study. However, it is readily apparent that the author supports making arts education basic in the U.S.

24. **B.** Choice B is not directly stated in the fourth paragraph, but that's the point of an inference question like this one. By saying that the Japanese focus on student effort and don't track, the author implies that some systems focus on something else and do track. Furthermore, the author follows the mention of the approach by discussing how exceptional the Japanese are. Putting these ideas together leads to choice B as the answer.

    The fourth paragraph emphasizes how students do better without tracking. It does not discuss the most gifted students. The author seems to feel that tracking on the basis of ability impedes the progress of the majority of students, but you don't know what he thinks about the most gifted students. Eliminate choice A.

    At the end of the fourth paragraph, the author points out that the best U.S. schools employ an approach similar to that used by the Japanese ("raising all the boats"), but nowhere does he hint that the exceptional U.S. schools were modeled after the Japanese schools. For all you know, the Japanese schools studied the most successful U.S. schools. Cross off choice C.

    The author clearly believes that much of the Japanese success is attributable to the non-tracking method, but he doesn't claim that this is the only factor that separates the Japanese from the rest of the world. Choice D goes too far and can be eliminated.

    The author implies that Japanese children differ in terms of ability, but he provides no information about the diversity found in Japan compared to that found in the rest of the world. Because you have no way of knowing exactly how mixed, or ***heterogeneous,*** students are in any country, choice E is wrong.

25. **D.** Choices A and B fit very well with a common definition of ***resonates*** (sounding over and over), but such choices are usually incorrect on vocabulary-in-context questions. The author supports the Japanese and their nontracking approach by pointing out that successful U.S. schools also attempt to consider everybody at the same time. You need to find a word similar to "support," and "corroborate" (choice D) does the trick. Choice E is tempting but *equates* goes too far and doesn't "sound right" when plugged back into the sentence. Remember, one way to check whether your answer to a vocabulary-in-context question is correct is to reread the entire sentence with your new choice inserted. The sentence must read easily and clearly, not be awkward or confused. Choice C is the opposite of what you are looking for.

26. **E.** The entire paragraph on education in Germany, specifically Bavaria, addresses the relationship between arts education and the teaching of other subjects. Choice E is very consistent with the thrust of the paragraph and is the answer.

    Choices A and B infer too much from the paragraph about Germany. Just because arts education is given a lot of emphasis for college preparatory students from grades five through thirteen does not mean that arts education is only for those students.

    Choice C is wrong because of the word "always." Perhaps the educator would feel that the arts should often be taught in relation to other disciplines, but that's about it. For all you know, the educator also endorses some instruction in the arts for the arts' sake.

    Choice D does too much with the next-to-last sentence in the paragraph. The written curriculum may include approaches for teams of teachers, but you can't tell from this whether the educator would say that teams are always the way to go.

27. **D.** ***Medieval*** refers to the Middle Ages, but this definition is not any help here because all the choices include medieval or Middle Ages. Culture can refer to people and their customs or art, music, theater, and other related sources of expression. Given that the entire paragraph on German education relates arts education to education in other disciplines, the latter reference makes the most sense, making choice D the correct answer. Choices B and C are tempting, but they do not match the point made by the paragraph.

    Choice A is designed to catch those who read the last sentence in the German paragraph too quickly. Medieval culture is linked to German language and literature, so medieval culture has to be something different from German language and literature.

    Religion certainly is related to culture, but the paragraph in question does not discuss religion. Don't use your outside knowledge about the dominance of religion during the Middle Ages to make you pick choice E. It's okay to use outside knowledge to get a handle on the reading passage and eliminate wrong answer choices, but you must make sure that a correct answer is stated or clearly implied by the passage.

28. **E.** Choices A and B include key words from the first paragraph about English arts education, but they are not correct. The Germans certainly stress the relationship between the arts and other disciplines, so choice A does not differ significantly from the German approach. Choice B is even worse because Germans clearly consider arts education to be very important.

    The exact subjects mentioned in choice C may not be directly stated in the German paragraph, but that paragraph continually discusses integration in education. It is safe to infer that choice C is something that is done in Germany as well as in England.

    The last sentence of the German paragraph indicates that choice D is a point of similarity between the Germans and English. Eliminate choice D.

    All this elimination leaves choice E. The English paragraphs keep discussing how the English want their students to be good at design. The last English paragraph mentions that other fields should be used to support design. The German approach uses the arts to support other disciplines. The German paragraph makes no mention of art as an end product, so choice E is the answer.

29. **C.** By saying that there is a compelling reason for people to have a foundation in the arts, the author sums up what the entire passage has hinted: that arts education should be part of basic education in the United States.

    Choice A can be eliminated for a basic SAT reason: The author of a passage rarely endorses a particular approach. The author's attitude is that the method doesn't matter, it's just important to do something. You will often find on the SAT I the same wrong idea appearing in question after question. You will save yourself time and be more accurate if you learn to identify this wrong idea quickly and dispense with the choice.

    The second part of choice B is fine, but the first part is not.

    The author states that the arts are what ultimately makes life worth living, but this notion should not be construed to mean that the number of hours devoted to arts education exceeds the number of hours dedicated to other disciplines. Perhaps science, by its very nature, requires more instructional hours than do the arts, even if the arts are ultimately more important. Therefore, eliminate choice D.

    Choice E is a tough answer choice to eliminate because it is something with which the author agrees. The problem with choice E is that it does not answer the question. You need to summarize the author's argument, not simply pick up on a true, but minor, point.

30. **A.** The author devotes most of his time to discussing some ways that arts education can be accomplished. By showing that arts education can be approached in a variety of ways, the author is implying that the United States should make arts education part of the basic educational core in this country and not delay due to simple inability to figure out how to do the job. Choice A fits well because the author is presenting an overview, or survey, of ways to implement a worthy idea.

    In choice B, "recommendation" is not the best word because the author is not recommending or advocating one specific, particular approach. Although you may feel that the author is recommending that arts education become basic in this country, he does not focus on one particular situation.

    The author does think that the status quo of not having arts education as part of the core curriculum is not a good idea, but his emphasis is on presenting what other countries do. He is not spending his time criticizing the United States. On the SAT, it is unlikely that a passage will have a negative focus, denouncing or criticizing someone or something. Therefore, many negative answer choices, like this one, can be quickly eliminated.

    Choice D is similar to choice B. You may get rid of it primarily because the author does not favor a particular approach.

    Although the author discusses the pros of arts education, he doesn't address any cons. That's one good reason to knock out choice E. You may also eliminate it for the same reason used to eliminate choices B and D: The author discusses more than one approach.

Section 4

1. **B.** Compare each numeral in the decimal. The 0s are equal. The 5s are equal. But then column A has a 0 and column B has a 1, making column B larger.

2. **D.** As soon as a problem says "Note: Figure not drawn to scale," think D, but double-check. $x + y + 40 = 90$. $x + y = 50$. You don't know how much of that 50 is x and how much of that 50 is y. There isn't enough information to answer the question.

   If you chose C, you assumed that the angles were equal just because they look equal. This trap is easy to fall for. (And that's the voice of experience speaking — I've fallen for it several times myself.) If the figure is *not* drawn to scale (and the problem always makes it clear if that's the case), you can't make comparisons based on appearances.

3. **C.** Assign values hypothetically. (This is just a fancier way of restating my favorite tip: Plug in numbers.) If Leroy is 1 and is half as old as Lamont, you know that Lamont is 2. Because Jacob is twice as old as Leroy, he also is 2. The relationship between their ages is the same, regardless of which number you put in. The problem requires thinking and logic, not Power Math.

4. **A.** Multiplying like bases means adding the exponents, making the numerator 5^{12}. Dividing like bases means subtracting the exponents, making the answer 5^8, which is greater than 125.

If you chose C, you divided the exponents ($5^{12} \div 5^4$) and fell into the trap. Because choice C is so often a trap, you should immediately be suspicious of any C answer you get; scrutinize it as closely as you would the blind date your mother tries to set you up with.

Make sure that you understand how to work with exponents; once you know the rules, this type of problem is among the easiest on the test. Exponents are covered in Chapter 11.

5. **B.** This is a good trick question. A probability is always between 0 (there's no possibility of something's happening) and 100 (there's a 100 percent possibility of its happening). In other words, probability is always between 0 percent and 100 percent; it can never be negative and it can never be more than 100 percent. Therefore, Column B is greater.

Choice C is the trap answer. If you assume that each marble has a 100 percent chance of being pulled out, you add: 100 + 100 + 100 = 300. Always double-check and triple-check your C answers. It's amazing how often they're just waiting to get you.

Answer D may look good at first glance, but careful thinking shows you the error. (They expect you to have time to *think* on this test? Who do they think you are, Einstein?) Although it's true that you can't find the probability of drawing out a red, drawing out a black, or drawing out a yellow (because you don't know how many of each type of marble the jar contains), the probability of drawing out every single marble in the jar is 100 percent. Again, probabilities cannot be above 100 percent.

6. **D.** Although you can find the area of the equilateral triangle (don't bother doing so), you can't determine the area of the isosceles triangle because you don't know whether the 8 is one of the two equal sides or the third unequal side.

If a geometry question has no picture, the correct answer is often choice D because the answer *dee*-pends on how you *dee*-raw the figure.

7. **B.** Did you fall for trap answer A? That's wrong because $(x + y)^2 = (x + y)(x + y) = x^2 + 2xy + y^2$. Column A has $2xy$, which Column B doesn't have. Don't jump to choice A because you see that Column A has something extra. You know that y is positive because $y > 1$, but for x^2 to be greater than y^2 while $x < y$, x must be negative. With a negative x and a positive y, $2xy$ will be negative, making Column A, with the extra $2xy$, less than Column B.

HEADS UP

Don't like algebra? Try a simple way to do this problem: Plug in numbers. You need to be absolutely sure that the numbers you plug in fit the constraints given by the centered information. For example, you could not say $x = 1$, because you are told $x < 1$. Suppose you choose $x = 0$ and $y = 2$. Wait, wait: Those numbers don't work with the second equation. 0 squared is *not* larger than 2 squared. Try some different numbers. How about $x = -1$, $y = 2$? No, –1 squared is not larger than 2 squared. Try -3 for x and 2 for y. Ah, that works: –3 squared, which is 9, is larger than 2 squared, which is 4. (Note that this plug 'n' chug technique, while easy, can be tricky and time-consuming.) Now plug these values into the question: $(-3 + 2)^2 = -1^2 = 1$.

Column B: $-3^2 + 2^2 = 9 + 4 = 13$. Column B is correct. But you need to plug in again, just to be sure. Try -4 and 3. $(-4 + 3)^2 = 1^2 = 1$. $-4^2 + 3^2 = 16 + 9 = 25$. Column B is still greater.

8. **C.** A 45-degree angle is formed by points having the same (x,y) coordinates, such as (1,1), (2,2), and (3,3). You just have to memorize this hard-and-fast rule. (Most students think geometry formulas are about as useless as a helmet on a kamikaze pilot, but they're necessary for this type of situation.)

9. **B.** Substitute the number for the *x* in the equation.

$\triangle_{1} = 1^2 + 1/1 + 4 = 9$

$\triangle_{2} = 2^2 + 2/2 + 4 = 10$

Symbolism questions often look imposble. Your first reaction may be one of complete bewilderment or indignation, such as "Hey, that's not fair, my teacher never taught us this stuff!" Keep in mind that these crazy symbols mean nothing in real life; they're made up for this specific problem. Just talk your way through the problem, plugging the numbers into the "explanation" you get.

10. **A.** The circumference of a circle is $2\pi radius$. If the area of the square is 144, the side of the square is 12 (because the area of a square is *side* × *side*). The side of the square is the same as the diameter of the circle.

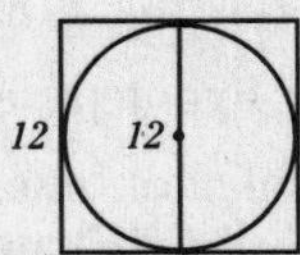

The radius is ½ the diameter, or 6. Circumference = $2\pi 6 = 12\pi$.

Trap! Because π is slightly greater than 3, 12π is slightly greater than 36.

Son-of-Trap! Did you luck out and get A without doing the problem the correct way? If you figured that the area was $\pi r^2 = \pi 6^2 = 36\pi$ and then reasoned that 36π is greater than 36, you got lucky . . . this time. Because you can't count on being that lucky on the SAT, be sure to note carefully what the question is asking for: circumference? area? arc? sector? It's a good idea to circle the word that tells you what to find.

11. **B.**

$$a + b + c = 47$$
$$-(a + b - 2c = 14)$$
$$a - a = 0$$
$$b - b = 0$$
$$c - (-2c) = 3c$$

Don't forget that you're subtracting a negative: a negative negative is a positive. In other words, "minus minus 2c" is +2c: 47 – 14 = 33. 3c = 33. c = 11.

If you chose C, you probably got confused on the negative signs and said –(–2c) = c, then c = 33.

12. **C.** Marcy assembles 15 products in those 45 minutes. Jessica assembles 45 in 15 minutes, another 45 in the next 15 minutes, and yet another 45 in the next 15 minutes, for a total of 135 products in 45 minutes. Add 15 + 135 = 150. Don't even bother creating a formula or equation here; talk through the problem logically. By the time the kid in the seat next to you comes up with an equation (which more than likely will be wrong anyway), you'll have talked the problem out, gotten the right answer, and be sweating through the next question.

13. **D.** If (for example) $m = -1$ and $n = 1$, then the two columns are equal. If $m = -2$ and $n = 1$, then the columns are not equal. You don't have enough information to determine the relationship between the columns.

Whenever you see a variable, your first reaction should be to plug in numbers. By the time you finish this book, plugging in numbers should be as instinctive as bending down to tie your shoelace in order to be inconspicuous when the teacher scans the room looking for volunteers.

14. **C.** The key to this problem is noting that the question asks not for the quotient, but for the *remainder.* Plug in numbers. For Column A, let $x = 4$. Then $4 \div 2 = 2$ with a remainder of 0. Let $x = 6$. Then $6 \div 3 = 2$ with a remainder of 0. When you divide an even number by an even number, you have a remainder of 0.

    For Column B, if $x = 4$, then $16 \div 4 = 4$ with a remainder of 0. If $x = 6$, then $36 \div 6 = 6$ with a remainder of 0. The remainder is always going to be 0. The two columns are equal.

15. **A.** An isosceles right triangle has two equal sides. The ratio of the sides of an isosceles right triangle is side: side: side$\sqrt{2}$.

Did you forget this ratio? Not only is it in Chapter 11 (which you may have memorized as closely as your best friend's phone number by now), but it is given to you in the directions. Ah, people tend to forget how much good info is in those directions. Take a moment to go back and look now. You shouldn't need that information, but it's there as a security blanket for you, just in case.

Back to the problem. Here's where things get a little nasty. If the sides are in the ratio side: side: side$\sqrt{2}$, you can also write that ratio as $\frac{\text{side}}{\sqrt{2}}$: $\frac{\text{side}}{\sqrt{2}}$: side. That is, you divide the whole ratio by $\sqrt{2}$. Therefore, if the hypotenuse (the longest side) is 10, the other sides are $\frac{10}{\sqrt{2}}$. You can't have a $\sqrt{\ }$ in the denominator. You must "rationalize the denominator" (remember that term from algebra class?) by multiplying both the top and bottom by $\sqrt{2}$, as follows:

$$\frac{10}{\sqrt{2}} \times \frac{\sqrt{2}}{\sqrt{2}} =$$

$$\frac{10\sqrt{2}}{\sqrt{4}}$$

Simplify to $\frac{10\sqrt{2}}{2}$, or $5\sqrt{2}$.

If each side of the right triangle is $5\sqrt{2}$, the final perimeter is $5\sqrt{2} + 5\sqrt{2} + 10$. Here's where your calculator is worth its weight in gold. Because $\sqrt{2}$ is a just a little greater than 1.4, $5\sqrt{2}$ is just over 7. Add $7 + 7 + 10 = 24$, greater than column B.

16. **4.** Multiply through by 2 to get rid of the fraction: $18x + 14 = 82 + x$. (Be very careful not to make the x into $2x$. This is an easy mistake to make.) Move the x from the right to the left, making it $-x$. Move the +14 to the right, making it –14. Combine like terms: $17x = 68$. Divide both sides through by 17: $x = 4$.

If you put 5.647, you forgot to change +14 to –14. If you put 3.578, you forgot to change $+x$ to $-x$. Forgetting to change the sign when you move a term from one side of the equal sign to the other is one of the most common careless mistakes. Always double-check your figures.

17. **$1.5 < x < 6.5$ or $\frac{3}{2} < x < \frac{13}{2}$.** The answer must be greater than 1.5 and less than 6.5.

If you filled in exactly 1.5 or 6.5, don't give yourself credit. If you expressed your answer as a fraction, x must be greater than $\frac{3}{2}$ and less than $\frac{13}{2}$. Remember not to grid in mixed numbers (for example, $2\frac{1}{2}$) as they will be read by the scoring computer as improper fractions ($\frac{21}{2}$).

Start off by thinking of one extreme situation: One circle is almost completely outside the other so that the centers are as far apart as possible. If the circles touch at only one point, the distance between the centers would be the sum of the two radii, 2.5 and 4, or 6.5. For the circles to touch at two points, the centers must be pushed a little closer together. In this case, the distance between the centers must be less than 6.5. An easy way to answer the question at this point is to grid in 6.49 (the closest number to 6.5 that the grid can accommodate).

While you don't need to figure the other extreme, for instructional purposes, here it is:

In this situation, the distance between the centers is $4 - 2.5 = 1.5$. For the circles to touch at two points, push the smaller circle a bit outside the larger circle. The centers are now farther apart, so the distance between them is more than 1.5.

You don't need to waste time trying to figure the number that is exactly half way between the two extremes. Any number more than 1.5 and less than 6.5 will do.

18. **2.** Prime numbers are numbers that can be divided evenly only by 1 and themselves. For example, 2, 3, 5, and 7 are prime numbers.

Note that 0 and 1 are neither prime nor composite. Note also that 2 is the only even prime. (Chapter 12 covers prime and composite numbers in more detail.)

In this case, the prime factors of 21 are 3 and 7. Because $3 + 7 = 10$, 21 sparkles. The prime factors of 30 are 2, 3, 5. Because $2 + 3 + 5 = 10$, 30 sparkles. The only prime factor of 32 is 2, because $2 \times 2 \times 2 \times 2 \times 2 = 32$. Therefore, 32 does not sparkle.

If you thought 32 sparkled because $2 + 2 + 2 + 2 + 2= 10$, you didn't read the question carefully enough. The question says a number sparkles if the sum of its *distinct* — meaning different — prime factors is 10. (Gotcha!) Finally, the prime factors of 33 are 3 and 11. Because $3 + 11$ does not equal 10, 32 does not sparkle.

19. **15.** Use the values $2x$, $3x$, and $5x$ for the friends so that $10x = 50$ and $x = 5$. The ***parsimonious*** (cheap, stingy) friend brought in $2x$, or 10 items. The ***munificent*** (generous) friend brought in $5x$, or 25 items. The difference is $25 - 10 = 15$.

This question tests the concept of ratios and totals. If you are confused about this concept (the total is a multiple of the sum of the numbers in the ratio), go to Chapter 11.

20. **156.** The math in this question isn't hard; it's the wording that will give you brain cramp. First, subtract the votes you know, 21 + 14, from 350. That gives you 315. If no candidate got 0 votes, that means that Lynda got at least one vote, dropping the remaining votes left to 314. If Cassidy and Dennis each got exactly the same number of votes, each would get 157. But Cassidy got more votes than Dennis. Let him get 158 and Dennis get 156, his maximum number possible.

21. **$3,000.** The problem tells you the five segments are equal; therefore, each is ⅕ of the total. That means ½ of the entertainment budget is ½ of ⅕, or 1/10 ("of" means you multiply). If ⅒ of the total is $300, you have the equation: ⅒T = 300. Divide both sides by ⅒, which means multiplying by 10 (to divide by a fraction, invert and multiply). $10 \times 300 = 3{,}000$.

22. **81.** There are two ways to do this problem. Here's the "official" way. Find the total number of points by multiplying the average times the number of items: $82 \times 7 = 574$. Find the subtotal by adding all given numbers: $75 + 91 + 85 + 89 + 74 + 79 = 493$. Subtract the subtotal from the total: $574 - 493 = 81$.

Another way of saying this is by using an equation:

$$\text{Average} = \frac{\text{Sum of all terms}}{\text{Number of terms}}$$

$$\text{Here: } 82 = \frac{(75 + 91 + 85 + 89 + 84 + 79 + x)}{7}$$

Cross-multiply: $82 \times 7 = 75 + 91 + 85 + 89 + 84 + 79 + x$.

$574 = 493 + x$. $x = 81$.

Now, here's my favorite shortcut way to do this problem. Figure out how many points away from the average (82) each score is. Your calculations should look like this:

75	–7
91	+9
85	+3
89	+7
74	–8
79	–3

The +3 and –3 cancel each other out. The +7 and the –7 cancel each other out. You're left with +9 and –8, which come out to +1. That tells you that Lael had one *extra* point going into the final test. In order to make things come out even, she is going to *lose* that extra point on the final test, or be one point *below* the average: 82 – 1 = 81. This is my favorite "talk it through" way of doing this problem; no Power Math required.

23. **4π.** Draw yourself a diagram, as shown.

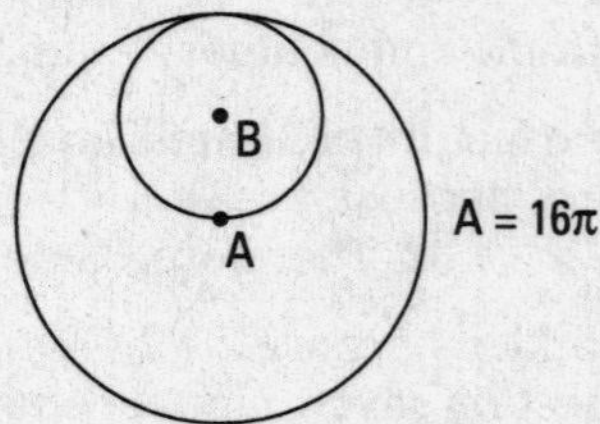

The area of a circle is πr^2. This means that $16\pi = \pi r^2$; $r^2 = 16$; $r = 4$. If the radius of circle A is 4, the diameter of circle B is 4. The circumference of a circle is $2\pi r$ or πd. The circumference of circle B is 4π.

24. **26.** Think of this as a "worst-case scenario." To pick out the maximum, the witch would have to make the worst choice each time. She could pull out all 15 bat wings first and then all 10 newt eyes. At this point, her very next pick would have to be a toad toe because nothing else is left. That means that 15 + 10 + 1 = 26 is the maximum number she would pull out to *ensure* getting one of each type of goodie.

25. **105.** If your first reaction was to bail out, you were thinking the right way. This is a pretty complicated question, well worth skipping. But let's suppose that you like a good challenge. The best way to tackle this problem is to break it down and make some simpler computations before building up to the final answer.

    Let's say you are Barb. How many people will you need to take on in a hot-air balloon race? Six. Now, each of the seven contestants has to race six other people, so it's tempting to say that there will be forty-two hot-air balloon races (7 × 6). The problem with this thinking is that it counts each match twice. Barb racing Jim is the same as Jim racing Barb. So, while each contestant has six races, the total number of hot-air balloon races is 7 × 6 ÷ 2, or 21. Uh, uh — don't fall for that. You need to remember one last step (as is typical on tough SAT problems such as this one): You have to multiply 21 by 5 to account for all the different activities. There are 21 matches in each activity and 5 activities. This means the correct answer is 21 × 5 = 105.

Section 5

1. **D.** The marks along the edge of the maps are the ticks. You can deduce this from the second sentence, which says that ticks are printed in blue. Of the answer choices, only marks can be printed. (You can't print a beat or print an insect, for example.)

    If you chose A, B, or C, you probably didn't go back to the passage to see how the word was used, but merely went on instinct. Always go back, back, back to check how the *author* uses the word; often, he uses it differently than you'd expect.

2. **B.** In line 12, you learned that computers are necessary for this translation. Use this statement to infer (the passage doesn't come right out and say this) that such translation is not always convenient (where's a computer when you need one?).

    Choice A is the trap, but it is illogical. A computer most likely would give better or more precise readings than a human would.

3. **A.** The assumptions do not compromise, or lessen, the accuracy of the measurements.

If you chose B, you probably didn't go back to see how the word was used in the passage. A vocabulary-in-context question like this should be an absolute freebie for you, but *only* if you take the time to go back to see how the word was used by the author (and don't just think of how you yourself would have used it).

4. **A.** Lines 32–33 tell you that zone numbers increase as they go east. Because Florida is east of California, it's a safe bet that its zone number is higher than that of California. Because statement I is correct, eliminate choices B and C. Because the U.S. goes farther east than Mexico, the two countries probably don't have the same zone numbers. Because statement II is wrong, eliminate choices D and E. Only A is left.

   For those of you who like to finish what you start: Statement III is wrong because the zones measure only from west to east, not north to south. This is a little tricky because you read about northing (measuring the distance in meters from the equator) near the spot where you read about zone numbers. You can avoid this trap by eliminating answers as you go, as I did above.

5. **E.** The last sentence reassures readers that the grid system becomes "extremely clear and straightforward to use" with a map. Even if you don't know the meaning of ***feasibility*** (probability or possibility), you could get the correct answer from the word "reassure."

   If you chose B, you forgot a very important SAT concept: The test rarely says anything mean and nasty about anyone. Your answers should be sweet and kind, no matter how grumpy *you* are over having to read all this dull material.

6. **C.** The passage introduces topographical maps, explaining what they are and how to use them.

   Discuss is a nice vague word that often is the correct answer to a "what is the purpose" question.

   Son-of-tip! Eliminate choices B and D quickly, as negative answers are rarely correct. To ***lament*** is to grieve. To ***deride*** is to ridicule.

   Stepson-of-tip! The word *urge*, in choice E, is too strong or dramatic a word to be the right answer. Few passages — except the rare editorial — urge the readers to do anything. An editorial may urge a course of action, but a passage on how to read a map doesn't stimulate any urges that I know of.

7. **E.** Lines 75–77 defines index contours; lines 78–80 define contour interval. Line 89 defines bearing; lines 92–93 define the cardinal points. Elevation is the answer by process of elimination.

   This turkey is a real (time) gobbler. This is a classic time-wasting question, not particularly difficult, but time-consuming. You have to go back and reread quite a bit of material. Even then, you may miss this question. Because elevation is mentioned in the same sentence as the contour interval (lines 78–80), you may be misled into thinking that you read a definition of the word. When a question is phrased negatively, like, "which of the following is not . . .," it is often a good one to skip.

8. **B.** This question contains a double whammy. Roman numeral questions are time-consuming and usually good to skip. Negative questions, questions which contain words like *disagree* or *not*, are good to skip. This question contains both Roman numerals and the word *disagree*, so if you skipped it, ***kudos*** (praises) to you.

   The author would agree with statement I, meaning you can eliminate any answer with statement I (because the question is looking for something with which the author *disagrees*). He states in line 69 that topographical maps "also show the direction from one point to another." Immediately narrow the answers down to B and C. If you're in a hurry, this is a good time to guess, because a 50/50 shot is pretty good odds.

   The author would disagree with statement II. Lines 89–91 say, "To determine the direction, or bearing, from one point to another, you need a compass as well as a map." Notice how far down in the passage this information is from the point at which you found the information in statement I? You practically had to reread the entire passage. You don't have the time — or the burning desire — to do so.

Just to finish this question, the author would agree with statement III. He tells you in paragraph 4 how to use a map to find the distance between curved points.

You may be arguing right now that "you have to use a piece of paper as well as the map to find the distance between curved points." Yeah. So what? The answer doesn't say that the map alone is sufficient to find the distance between curved points, does it? That's why II is a false statement and III is a true statement. And that's why you probably should have skipped this question from the start. How awful to do all that work and miss it anyway.

9. **B.** Were you looking for my favorite word, "objective"? ***Plaudits*** (praises) to you. Alas, it wasn't here this time. Instead, most of the words are incredibly difficult. Sure, you can eliminate A, but what do the rest of those words mean? You know that you want to choose a word that means objective, but which word means that?

Skip a question that depends entirely on unknown vocabulary. The odds are too great for a wild guess. Okay, here are the definitions: ***Expository*** means discussing the facts, explanatory. (Whenever my students blush when saying this word, I know they're confusing it with "suppository." It's highly unlikely you'll see a word like "suppository" on the SAT!) ***Sardonic*** means sarcastic. ***Fawning*** means flattering excessively. ***Dogmatic*** means opinionated and narrow-minded.

10. **B.** The passage explains how to use a map, something students would learn. Professional cartographers — map makers — certainly would know how to read a map. Researchers wouldn't be spoken to in this rather elementary tone. Civil engineers had better already know how to read a map. It's tempting to choose outdoor guides, but there is no clue to indicate that the author is addressing them. Besides, they'd have to be megawandering outdoor guides to need to read maps on this large scale.

11. **A.** My favorite type of question! When a question begins "According to the passage," take the time to go back and find the specific answer, which usually appears word for word in the passage. Here, lines 98–101 state that the compass needle is attracted by magnetic force, which varies in different parts of the world.

12. **A.** This is a commonsense question. Because both passages are about using maps, it's logical to think that someone who's interested in one passage would be interested in the other. The other answers ask you to make wild assumptions that don't seem justified.

If all the answers to a commonsense question look good to you, skip the question. You can't go back to the passage to find a specific fact or word; there's no way to "prove" your answer.

13. **C.** This question is very subjective. You can't go back to the passage to find the specific answer; you have to wing it.

Passage 1 discusses dividing up the earth, finding points north and south of the equator, and talks about the International Date Line. Passage 2 seems more homey, as though it were talking about maps that you'd use in your own neighborhood or in your own country. Hey, if you're arguing with me right now, don't get all hyper. I absolutely agree that this is a matter of interpretation; that's why I recommend that you skip this type of question.

The last two questions in this section, which compare or contrast the two passages, really demand *comprehension* from you. (How dare they!) You can't just use tricks or go back to find a fact; you have to understand what the passages were talking about and where the author was coming from. These are good questions to skip. And given the time constraints in this section (you have to read two entire passages and answer up to 13 questions in just 15 minutes!), you may not get to these questions anyway. No big loss.

Section 6

1. **B.** The total surface area is the sum of the areas of all surfaces. There are six surfaces on a cube. (Think of the six faces of a die, one of a pair of dice.) Each surface is a square. The area of a square is side^2, or x^2. Therefore, there are six x^2, or $6x^2$.

2. **D.** The average of numbers is their sum divided by the number of terms. Let x = the sum of the *five* unknown numbers. The equation can be written as:

   $\text{Average} = \frac{\text{Sum}}{\text{Number of terms}}$

   $0 = \frac{-8 + x}{9}$

   Cross-multiply (remembering that 0 is the same as $\frac{0}{1}$): $0 \times 9 = 0$

   $(-8 + x) \times 1 = -8 + x$

   $0 = -8 + x$

   $x = 8$

   You've done averages in all ways, shapes, and forms by now — forward, backward, upside down, and inside out. You should be able to do any average problem you encounter on the SAT. I've made you suffer through several incarnations of this problem because it's a "go for it!" type, a question that you know you can always, always get right. There may be — who am I kidding here? There *will* be — some impossible questions that make you sorry you were ever born. Knowing this and accepting it as a fact of life means that you're not going to worry about those types. Instead, you're going to focus on making absolutely, positively, categorically sure that you get the "do-able" problems — such as average problems — correct.

   Averages are covered in Chapter 12.

3. **B.** The formula for slope is $\frac{\text{rise}}{\text{run}}$, or $\frac{y^2 - y^1}{x^2 - x^1}$. The numerator, y, is 2 – 3 or –1. The denominator is 3 – 2 or 1. So, –1 ÷ 1 = –1.

4. **E.** The new coordinates of point A are (6,7) and the new coordinates of point B are –1,–2).

   Note that point B moves down and left, not right. The new numerator is (–2 – 7) = –9. The new denominator is (–1 – 6) = –7. The new slope is $-\frac{9}{-7}$ or $\frac{9}{7}$.

5. **120.** Figure out the fraction of people who left. First, $\frac{1}{4}$ of the people left. That means $\frac{3}{4}$ remain. Then $\frac{1}{3}$ of the remaining people leave: $\frac{1}{3}$ of $\frac{3}{4} = \frac{1}{3} \times \frac{3}{4} = \frac{3}{12} = \frac{1}{4}$. At 1:00 another $\frac{1}{4}$ of the people leave.

   Be sure not to say $\frac{1}{4}$ of the *remaining* people leave. If as many people leave at 1:00 as left at 11:00 p.m., then $\frac{1}{4}$ of the original number left. Add all the fractions: $\frac{1}{4} + \frac{1}{4} + \frac{1}{4} = \frac{3}{4}$. If $\frac{3}{4}$ of the people have left, then only $\frac{1}{4}$ remain. The new equation is: 30 = $\frac{1}{4}$ T (T standing for Total). Divide both sides through by $\frac{1}{4}$, which is the same as multiplying by $\frac{4}{1}$ (invert the fraction). 30 × 4 = 120.

6. **C.** You can find the probability by using this formula:

   $\frac{\text{\# of possible desired outcomes}}{\text{\# of total possible outcomes}}$

   The first thing to do is to find the denominator: the number of candies that will be left after LaVonne has chomped into the others. She starts with 47 candies (20 + 15 + 12). You know that she throws some of them away. You can eliminate choice A immediately because the denominator must be less than 47.

   She throws away a cream (down to 46), a nut (down to 45), a chew (down to 44), a nut (down to 43), a cream (down to 42), and a chew (down to 41). The denominator for the probability of the next candy that she pulls out is 41 because she'll have some chance in 41 of pulling out a nut. That narrows the answers down to B and C.

   As a shortcut, subtract 6 (the number of candies that she already pulled out) from 47 (the number of candies that originally were in the box). I solved the problem the long way to show you where the 41 really comes from.

   Now find the numerator. LaVonne starts with 12 nuts, pulls out one (down to 11), and then pulls out another (down to 10). The probability that the next candy will be a nut is $\frac{10}{41}$. (Still confused? This type of problem is discussed in Chapter 11.)

7. **C.** The key to this problem is knowing that Gigi and Neville work *at the same rate.* If they finish the lawn in 12 hours, each did half the job in 12 hours, meaning that it would have taken Gigi working alone 24 hours to finish the lawn. Because 3 hours is $\frac{1}{8}$ of 24 hours, she could have done $\frac{1}{8}$ of the job in that time.

   Here's another case of brain over brawn . . . or brain over buttons. You don't need your calculator for this type of problem. Don't let the grass grow under your feet (!); talk this problem through quickly.

8. **C.** This problem is much easier than it looks. The number of degrees in the interior angles of *any* triangle is 180, regardless of that triangle's size or shape (so much for answer choice E!). Therefore, $\frac{180}{180} = 1$, which is 100 percent.

   If you chose D, you thought that because the big triangle looks to be twice the size, or area, of the little one, the big triangle's angles must be twice as large as the little triangle's. When it comes to what's inside, all triangles are created equal. Regardless of the size or shape of the triangle, its interior angles sum up to 180 degrees.

9. **C.** Factor down the $x^2 - 16x + 48 = 0$ into $(x - 12)(x - 4) = 0$. (If you are unclear on how to factor, flip to Chapter 11, where the process is explained in exceedingly tedious detail.) Recognize that either $(x - 12) = 0$ or $(x - 4) = 0$ because any number times 0 is 0. That means x could be 12 or 4.

   If you chose E, you didn't actually work out the whole problem. You thought you could break 48 down into 12, 4. You thought you needed negatives because of the -16 in the middle. You would then have $(-12 - 12)(-4 - 4)$ which does *not* equal 0. When you have "variations on a theme," like this (two answers that are the positive/negative versions of each other), be especially alert.

10. **C.** Don't simply think that $\frac{60}{6} = 10$, making the answer choice B. (Would I give you anything that easy?) The volume ratio, which depends on three dimensions, differs from the surface area ratio, which depends on two dimensions.

    A cube has six square faces, so each face of the small cube has an area of 1 cm^2, making each side 1cm. The volume of this cube is 1 cm × 1 cm × 1cm = 1 cm^3. (Don't forget that the actual SAT gives this volume formula in the directions of each math section. The surface area formula, alas, is not given.) Each face of the large cube has an area of 10 cm^2, so each side of this cube is the square root of 10 cm. The volume is $\sqrt{10}$ cm times $\sqrt{10}$ cm times $\sqrt{10}$ cm = 10 times $\sqrt{10}$ cm^3. Divide the volume of the large cube by the volume of the small cube to find the ratio asked for in the problem:

    $$10\sqrt{\frac{10\text{cm}^3}{1\text{cm}^3}} = 10\sqrt{10}$$

Remember that with similar figures (figures that have the same shape, like two circles, two squares, and so on), the ratio of areas equals the square of the linear ratio (for example, a circle with a radius of 4 has an area that is 4^2, or 16, times the area of a circle with a radius of 1). The volume ratio equals the cube of the linear ratio. This concept is covered in Chapter 10.

Part V
The Part of Tens

In this part . . .

Take off your thinking cap and put on your party hat. It's time to celebrate!

This part is your reward for surviving the previous four. No brain power is required for these chapters. You don't have to work through math problems, don't have to memorize new vocabulary, and don't have to stimulate the synapses at all. These chapters are just for fun, but they do provide invaluable information. For example, where else but in *The SAT I For Dummies,* 5th Edition, can you find ways to use math to get out of doing your chores? Read on.

Chapter 21

Ten Amazing Questions I've Been Asked about the SAT

In This Chapter

- Debunking urban legends
- Proving there *is* such a thing as a "stupid question"
- Refuting what your friends tell you

In my real life, when I'm not working on writing test-prep books, I tutor SAT students. I love working one-on-one with teenagers, giving them tips, gloating when they fall for the traps I've set for them, rejoicing when they start getting paranoid and neurotic like me and *looking* for traps. Naturally, in the course of our tutorials, I encourage questions. This chapter lists ten questions I've often been asked.

Does the SAT Score Count?

Hundreds of colleges and universities demand that millions of students take the SAT. *Of course* the SAT score counts! The importance of SAT scores, however, varies from school to school. Some schools, especially the biggest ones that don't have the time to do minute evaluations of each student, assign great weight to the SAT scores. Other schools use the SAT scores only as part of your overall package, which includes your GPA (grade point average), extracurricular activities (the officially recognized ones, that is), and so on.

Is the SAT an Open-Book Exam?

You wish! No, you cannot take any books into the exam, other than those you have burned into your brain circuits. I once had a particularly insistent student who said, "But the purpose of the SAT is to see how well I'll do in college, right, and I'm going to be using books in college, so I should be able to use books to take the entrance exam." Nice try. I'd be willing to bet that kid becomes a lawyer.

Is the Same SAT Given Every Year?

No. ETS (Educational Testing Service) eventually releases most SATs. For example, a few times a year you can get what is called the Question and Answer Service. For a fee (naturally!), ETS will send you a copy of the actual exam, your answer grid, and the correct answers. If ETS were going to reuse the same SAT, any prospective test taker could just memorize the exam and get a perfect 1600 the next time.

Can You Give Me a List of All the Words That Will Be Tested on the SAT?

If I knew the exact words that will be tested on the SAT, I would sell the list for an obscenely large sum of money and be on my own coconut-trees-and-balmy-breeze island right now. (When I was in high school, I had a teacher we nicknamed Mr. Tropical Island because he was such a Bora Bora!) All anyone can do is guess at the words to be tested, based on past exams (some of the words do tend to show up repeatedly) and on *skill-level words* (words that someone entering college has been exposed to, perhaps in Shakespearean plays or other high school reading). That's why I emphasize roots, prefixes, and suffixes so much. Even if you can't define a word precisely (because you've never seen or heard it in your entire life!), you can use roots, prefixes, and suffixes to get a good enough idea of the definition to answer a question correctly.

Can I Take a Dictionary to the SAT?

As long as you leave it in your car. Having a dictionary in the exam defeats the purpose of using all these big words that are supposed to test not just your vocabulary but also your reasoning and test-taking skills. Yeah, I can just picture the room as 25 stressed-out students flip back and forth in their humongous dictionaries, an occasional scream punctuating the tense silence as yet another student suffers the searing agony of a paper cut . . . .

Does a Good SAT Score Make Me a Nerd?

No. It makes you an applicant for a good school, a success in a great career, and ultimately a gazillionaire with the best car and hottest spouse at your 20th high school reunion. Plan ahead.

Is There a Make-Up Exam?

No. If you don't get to the SAT on the assigned day, you can't sit in a room at your high school and have a teacher give you a separate SAT. Can you imagine ETS (Educational Testing Service) creating thousands of extra SATs just as make-up exams? Ain't gonna happen.

Is There Extra Credit Work?

This question has been asked several times by students who thought that they could do a report or something to get extra points added to their SAT scores. Sorry. What you see is what you get. The only way to get extra points added to your SAT score is to study harder and take the exam again.

Can My Friend Help Me?

What — a "team SAT"? Now that's an interesting concept. No, you are totally alone when you take the exam. I'll be there with you in spirit (after all the lame humor we share in this book, do you think I'd abandon you now?), but yours is the only brain clicking away on the questions. If you decide to use a little "outside" help, that's called cheating, and you don't even want to *think* about how much trouble you'd get into. Not worth the risk, believe me.

Do I Have to Take the SAT Again During College?

The SAT is an entrance exam. Schools use the SAT scores to determine whether to let you into their halls of academe. When you're in, you're back to real school exams, things like essay tests and normal multiple-choice questions without any built-in traps. Actually, I think that students who ask this question may be confused about the SAT and the GRE. The GRE is the Graduate Record Exam, which is the entrance exam to get into graduate school. It's amazingly like the SAT, with analogies, sentence completion, reading comprehension, quantitative comparisons, and problem-solving questions. It also has a few other question styles and is harder than the SAT. But for now, the GRE — four or five years in your future — is the least of your worries. All you care about is the SAT, and when it's over, it's history!

Chapter 22

Ten Bizarre Ways to Use SAT Math in the Real World

In This Chapter

- Saving time, money, and your sanity using SAT tricks
- Annoying your parents, police, and the elderly without really trying
- Tricking, conning, and duping those who haven't read this book

You have to learn this stuff, so why not get some use out of it? Teachers are notorious for saying, "Education enriches your life." Here are ten terrific techniques for making their words come true.

Getting Out of Paying for Gas

Promise your parents that if they let you borrow the car, you'll fill up the gas tank if you increase the car's mileage by 1 percent or more. The amount sounds so small to your parents, they'll probably agree . . . and you'll get away with your wallet intact. Suppose, for example, that your parents' car has 60,000 miles on it. You can do this one in your head: 10 percent (or $\frac{1}{10}$) of 60,000 is 6,000; 1 percent is $\frac{1}{10}$ of that, or 600 miles. You'd need to have a heck of a date to put 600 miles on the car in one evening; chances are good that you won't have to part with a penny. So who says percentages are useless?

Saving Money Dining Out at Fine Establishments

Tell the waiter at your favorite pizza parlor that you want a (circular) pizza with the longest chord of 10 inches — but if he'll give you a discount, you'll settle for a pizza with a circumference of 10 (pizza?) π. Laugh at him behind his back as he struggles to figure out which one would cost you more. *You,* of course, know that the two pizzas would be the same. (The longest chord, in case you've forgotten, is the diameter. The circumference of a circle is πd, making the two pizzas identical.)

Making Your Parents Clean Up Your Mess

Strike a bargain with your parents over who must do the dinner dishes. Persuade them to agree that whoever first gets the right answer to a Pythagorean theorem problem can go watch TV while the other has to clean up the table. Act as though you're doing them a favor by reminding them that the Pythagorean theorem is $a^2 + b^2 = c^2$, where a, b, and c are the sides of a right triangle. Bluster and say that they can use a calculator, but *you'll* do the problem in your head to give them an advantage. (Remind them that they need an advantage because the last time *they* did math, they were scribbling on papyrus scrolls.) Then make up a problem in which the sides are 14:48:x. While they're punching in numbers, you know that these figures are simply a variation on the ratio 7:24:25, with each number being doubled. You'll know in a flash, therefore, that $x = 50$ (double the 25).

Getting Out of Chores

Annoy your family by finding the area and perimeter (circumference) of objects around the house as you're cleaning. Announce your findings in a loud voice: "Dad, did you know that the total surface area of our refrigerator is *xx* square units?" "Mother, you'll be delighted to know that the volume of your top desk drawer is *xxx* cubic units." Your parents won't want to stifle your enthusiasm for learning, but if you get on their nerves enough, they'll kick you out of the house and finish the cleaning themselves.

Annoying the Elderly

Whenever your Great Aunt Tootsie — the one who always forgets your name at the family reunion — asks you how old you are, you can blithely answer, "Letting x equal my father's age at the time he married my mother, in $x + 30$ years from now I will have evinced a 200 percent increase in my age — although, of course, my father will have increased his age by only 125 percent." Skip away and watch Great Aunt Tootsie self-destruct as she tries to figure out the numbers.

Talking Your Way Out of a Speeding Ticket

Suppose a cop pulls you over and asks you, "Kid, do you have any idea how fast you were going?" You can look at the cop innocently and say, "Well, Officer, let's see. I left Point A at 3 p.m., driving west, and drove for 30 minutes. My friend Skip left point B at 4:15 p.m., driving east, and going 30 miles in 45 minutes. If we are now 75 miles apart, I guess that makes my speed . . . well, Officer, what do *you* think? I'd value your opinion." Either you'll frustrate the poor cop and get out of the ticket — or you'll be in even bigger trouble for being a smart aleck. Are you willing to take the risk to have the fun?

Making Your Parents Think Your Grades Are Better Than They Are

Unless your parents are mathletes, they probably still solve an average problem by dividing the sum of the numbers they see by how many numbers there appear to be. Not having had the benefit that you have of being burned repeatedly by this book, they aren't paranoid enough to look for a weighted average problem. If you tell your folks that on your tests you scored six 70 percents, three 90 percents, a 98, and a 100, they'll probably add 70 + 90 + 98 + 100, divide by 4, and get 89.5 and think they have a real A student in the family. Only you will know that you had to add the 70 six times, the 90 three times, and the 98 and 100 only once for a total of 888 and an average of 80.7.

Rejecting a Date without Destroying an Ego

Suppose that someone asks you to go to a dance. You smile gently and say, "The probability of my attending this function with you is the same as the difference between the probability of tossing a 3, 4, 5 on consecutive tosses of a die and the probability of tossing 1, 1, 1 on consecutive tosses of a die." Only you know that the probabilities are the same, making the difference between them exactly zero, the same as the chances of your actually going out on a date with someone who can't even figure that much out. After you've mastered the math in this book, you're too good for that person anyway.

Confusing Your Parents about Where the Money Went

Parents have an annoying habit of wanting you to account for how you spend your allowance, the money you get for chores, or even the money you earn yourself at a part-time job. When you run a little short of money and ask for a few dollars so that you can get the newest CDs, you may be met with an exasperated, "What did you do with all the money you got this month?" Here's how you bamboozle your folks. Reply, "The first week of this month, my school expenses went up 20 percent. The next week, they went down 25 percent, but in the last two weeks, they went up 11 percent again." Your parents will think your costs rose 6 percent (because $20 - 25 + 11 = 6$). Because you've worked through the percentages material in this book, you know that your costs have remained the same. If you have real class, you'll take your parents' money but use it to help someone less fortunate than you — buy copies of this book for students who can't afford it because their parents aren't as mathematically challenged as yours.

Stiffing a Waiter on a Tip

Tell the waiter that he can either have a 15 percent tip or get $x^0 \cdot 100\%$ as a tip, where x equals the value of your meal. Because most poor fools who haven't had the joy of going through this book will naturally think that any number to the zero power equals zero, he'll be thrilled to get a 15 percent tip. He'll never know that $x^0 = 1$ and that he could have gotten the entire amount of the bill (100 percent!) as a tip. The next time you go to that restaurant, why don't you give the waiter a copy of this book?

Chapter 23

Ten Wrong Rumors about the SAT

In This Chapter (Remember: These suggestions are wrong!)

- Disproving the so-called "time and geography advantages"
- Evaluating the meaning of scores and multiple scores
- Suggesting the best scheduling

Sure, you've heard them: the horror stories about the SAT. Rumors abound, growing more wild with each telling: "You have to write an essay!" (Absolutely not.) "It's an open book test this year!" (You wish!)

As a test-preparation tutor, I get calls all the time from students and their parents trying to check out the latest scuttlebutt. Here are ten of the most common stories that make the rounds every year.

Filling In All A's Is Better Than Jumping Around, Filling In A, B, C, D, E

You have a one-in-five chance of getting a random guess correct (one-in-four in Quantitative Comparisons because the answers there are only A, B, C, and D, without an E). Each new problem starts over again with that same chance. Whether you fill in all As or jump around makes no difference; your chances are still one in five.

You Can't Have Three A's in a Row

You *can* have three A's or B's or whatever in a row. It's highly unlikely, but not absolutely impossible, that you may even have *four* in a row. But counting how many of the same answers in a row you have is the last thing you should worry about. Suppose that you check your answer grid and discover that you have three A's in a row. Which one are you going to change? You may change the *wrong* one — who knows? You waste time and gray matter when you try to outsmart the test makers with thoughts such as: "Well, I put down a C last time, and I haven't had a D in a while, so I'd better put down a D."

"Lesser-Taken Tests" Are Easier

Many students take the SAT in October, May, or June. These dates seem to be the most popular times to take the test. Tests given in December, for example, often are taken by fewer students. Some students have heard a rumor that the test makers are trying to encourage more people to take the December exam by making that exam easier. Wrong. The exams are all designed to have the same basic level of difficulty. They often test the same concepts "forward and backward." A test in October, for example, may use PULCHRITUDE: BEAUTY as a question, whereas a test in May may use the same pair of words as an answer choice. That's why looking over your old test before retaking the exam is a good idea. (Yes, you can get a copy of your old tests, at least for some test dates. When you fill out your registration form, under "Fees" check Question and Answer service. You'll be charged at least $10, and ETS will send you a copy of the test and its answers.)

Tests in Different Parts of the Country Are Different

No way. You can't fly out to Snakes Navel, Kansas, to take the test, thinking that the kids there get to take easier exams than do the kids in big cities, such as Detroit or New York City. Everyone gets the same thing. All exams are the same — or at least at the same level of difficulty.

You Can't Study for the SAT

Why would I be writing this book if that were so? Studying can be done two ways, each advantageous in its own right. First is the last-minute cram — a review in a few weeks of the types of questions, the approach to each question, and the tricks and traps involved in the questions. (Sound familiar? This method is used throughout this book.) Second is the long-range study program in which you learn vocabulary and work on math questions from your sophomore year on. Obviously, if you have a year or two to put into this, you should get a dynamite score. Most people, however, benefit greatly from even a few weeks or months of intense study.

You Must Pass Certain Classes to Take the SAT

Although taking classes such as Latin or Greek is useful, let's get real here: Not many people take those courses today. If you are reading this book as a freshman or sophomore and have the option of taking Latin, excellent. Doing so will help you to learn the roots, prefixes, and suffixes that are such a big part of the vocabulary tested on the SAT. But you certainly don't *need* to know any Latin or Greek to do well on the test. As far as math goes, the SAT tests basic algebra, geometry, and arithmetic. A semester of algebra and a semester of geometry are sufficient. In short, there are no "required courses" or "prerequisites" for the SAT.

You Must Write an Essay

No. The SAT II — the new name for the single-subject tests that used to be called the Achievements — tests writing. The SAT I (your basic SAT — what you're studying for now) does not.

Your Score Won't Improve if You Keep Retaking the SAT

Although having your score jump hundreds of points is uncommon, it has happened. Your score's improvement depends on the reason your score was low in the first place and on how much you study before retaking the test. If your score was low because you didn't understand the format of the exam (for example, you looked at a QC question and wondered where the answer choices were), you can certainly improve that score by taking a few practice exams and becoming more comfortable with the five question styles. If your score was low because you fell for all the traps set in the SAT, you can improve your score by going through these materials, learning to recognize those traps, and studying the tips and tricks for avoiding those traps. But it is unrealistic for a slow reader to think that a few weeks of study is going to double her reading speed, or for someone who doesn't understand algebra at all to think that she can get a semester's worth of algebra instruction in an afternoon. You do need *some* basics under your belt.

The study time that you put into preparing for the second exam also is important. If you take the exam, get back your scores, register for another exam, and then wait until just a few days before the second exam to begin studying again, you may as well forget it. Although experience helps, your score won't soar simply because you've done this before. You must *study* for the second test, or you'll simply repeat the mistakes of the first.

The SAT Has a Passing Score

You can't pass or fail the SAT, but a particular college or university may have a cut-off score that you must get to be considered for admission. This score is often based on your GPA. A school may decree, for example, that if your GPA is in the 3.0 to 3.5 range, you can get an 1100. But if your GPA is in the 2.5 to 3.0 range, your SAT must be at least a 1200. To set your goals, you want to find out the SAT ranges considered acceptable by the schools in which you are interested. Your high school counselor can help you with this. (If you're no longer in high school, check the bulletins of the colleges and universities or contact the schools directly.)

You Must Take the PSAT Before You Take the SAT

The PSAT is the Preliminary (or *Pre*) SAT. It is given to juniors (and occasionally to sophomores or freshmen) as practice for the SAT. Unless you are a whiz kid going for a National Merit Scholarship, the PSAT doesn't count. The PSAT has almost the same format as the SAT, but the PSAT includes fewer, significantly easier questions (in my opinion) and gives you more time per question to answer them. If you didn't take the PSAT and your friends did, don't panic. The PSAT is *not* a prerequisite for the SAT.

Chapter 24

Ten Types of Questions You Can Skip

In This Chapter

- Identifying the clock-killers and time-wasters
- Recognizing questions that destroy brain cells
- Bailing out of no-win situations

If this were a perfect world, you'd know in a heartbeat the answer to every question and the solution to every problem. In your dreams, friend. On the *real* SAT, some questions and problems are going to make you wish that your mother and father never met. Good test-takers recognize which problems aren't worth their time and effort and bid them good-bye and good riddance with no regrets. (***Note:*** In addition to reading this chapter, make sure you look at Chapters 4, 6, 8, 13, and 15. In those chapters, I talk about specific strategies for handling each type of question, and you should be familiar with these strategies before deciding to skip any questions.)

Killer Closers

The closing questions — the last three or four or even the entire last page — can be killers. They are intentionally written to be extremely difficult. They're definitely worth skipping because very few people get them right anyway, even after squandering time and brain cells on them. Go ahead and skim them because you never know; one of the questions may be something you just happened to learn yesterday or your favorite trick question that you "got" your best friend on. But if the answer isn't obvious, or if you haven't a clue where to start, blow off the question.

Time-Waster Math

Some of the math problems require several steps to complete. You can often look at a math question and say to yourself, "Yeah, I know how to do this problem, but it requires finding the circumference of the top of the cylinder, calculating down to the radius, finding the area, and then going back and doing the volume . . . ." You must decide whether you want to do this very time-consuming problem or just skip it. The more steps that are in a problem, the more chances you have of making a careless, pencil-pushing, or button-punching error.

Weak Third of Math

The math on the SAT is approximately one-third algebra, one-third geometry, and one-third arithmetic. By the time you've gone through this book, you should definitely know which of these is your strong suit and which is your weak suit. If you're running short on time, be absolutely certain you get to those questions that you can usually answer correctly and blow off the questions that are in your weak third.

If English is not your best language, you may want to head immediately for the algebra problems, as they are usually all numbers and much easier to understand than the long word problems. Geometry problems with figures also present few language problems.

Negative Questions

Questions in both math and verbal sections that are phrased in the negative are often traps and should be skipped. These are questions that say, "All of the following are true *except*" or "Which of the following is *not* true?" or "Which of the following is *least* likely?" You're really looking for something that isn't there or something wrong. That's contrary to the usual way of answering a question and can upset your fragile brain. If you're in a hurry, this is a great type of question to skip. (Educational Testing Service appears to have wised up to this trick; the SAT seems to have fewer and fewer of the negative questions each year.)

Note: If you decide to do this type of problem, double-check it, triple-check it, and quadruple-check it. It's chock full of tricks. (Or, as we ***pretentious pedants*** like to say, involves a ***surfeit*** of ***surreptitiousness.***)

Roman Numeral Questions

Questions with such answers as "I only," "II and IV only," and "I, III, and V only" are often time-consuming and can be skipped. They require too much work. In a critical reading passage, you must go back to the passage five times, once for each Roman numeral. You end up rereading the entire passage, which you just don't have the time to do. In math, you must figure out every Roman numeral — compare that to a regular multiple-choice problem, in which you can stop as soon as you get the right answer. (ETS appears to be reducing the number of Roman numeral questions, which is good news for you.)

Sentence Completion Questions Based Entirely on Vocabulary

Some Sentence Completion questions are entirely dependent on vocabulary, as in the following example:

Accused of being - - - -, Silas protested that he was the most generous man he knew.

You know that the word must mean "stingy" or "cheap." The entire answer completely depends on your knowing the words in the answer choices:

(A) phlegmatic

(B) magnanimous

(C) parsimonious

(D) obstreperous

(E) sanctimonious

If you don't know any of the words (the answer is C), skip the question. All you can do is make a wild guess, with the odds 4-1 against you.

Compare-or-Contrast Critical Reading Questions

On the double reading passages, the last two or three questions require you to compare or contrast the passages. Usually, these questions are impossible to answer unless you have read both passages carefully and — what's worse — actually understood them. Cheap tricks (my specialty!) don't work here. Unless you really know what you're doing, these are good questions to skip because your chances of getting them right are slim.

Double-Negative Sentence Completion Questions

Some Sentence Completion questions feature simple vocabulary . . . but incredibly twisted and convoluted sentences. If a question contains a double negative ("Not inappropriately, no one but Buck was not reluctant . . ."), that sentence usually takes quite a while to figure out. You must read it, reread it, and then reread your rereading until you're clear in your mind about what's going on. If you're in a rush, skip this type of question (which is rare, but — just your luck — still shows up occasionally).

Critical Reading Questions Based on Vocabulary

A Critical Reading question may ask you for the tone of the passage and provides answers such as *sardonic, bellicose, lackadaisical, denigrating,* and *froward.* If you don't know the words, the best you can hope for is a lucky guess; don't spend the time or risk the points.

Critical Reading Questions Based on Between-the-Lines Information

Some Critical Reading questions are very straightforward, asking you to define vocabulary in context or give a fact stated in the passage. Alas, other questions ask you to make inferences or to understand what the author implies but doesn't say. If you don't understand the passage (and who always does?), skip this question.

Chapter 25

Ten Questions Not to Skip

In This Chapter

- Recognizing a "sure thing" when you see one
- Playing the odds for your best chance at success
- Knowing which questions are worth a guess

If you saw a $10 bill on the sidewalk, you'd bend over and pick it up, right? Some SAT questions put ten points in your pocket as easily as you'd stuff in that ten bucks. Your job is to keep your eyes open and recognize opportunity when you see it.

Analogies

Throughout this book, you discover many tricks for recognizing and avoiding the traps built into Analogy questions. These tricks should enable you to get nearly every Analogy question correct. Even if you don't know the vocabulary, try an Analogy question.

First Third or First Half

Questions go from easier to harder on the SAT. The first third of the questions in each section should be relatively simple. Even the first half should be easy. Not as many traps are set for you in the first third or first half as in the rest of the section; the questions and problems are pretty straightforward.

Critical Reading's Main Idea or Best Title Questions

In Chapter 8, you discover how to answer a main idea or best title question (usually by looking at the first sentence of the passage). You also find out that this is one of the easiest types of questions to get correct. Even if you're so flustered by an impossible reading passage that you decide to skip nearly all the Critical Reading questions, at least do this one.

Critical Reading's Attitude or Tone Questions

In Chapter 8, you find out that the attitude or tone of a Critical Reading passage is usually either positive or neutral, not negative. Knowing this tip usually enables you to eliminate a few answers and at least make a good guess.

Exponents Questions

Most questions featuring exponents ask you to add, subtract, multiply, or divide numbers to various powers. You can review how to do these operations in Chapter 11. After you master these four basic operations, working with exponents is simple.

Symbolism Questions

Symbolism questions in math look intimidating and demanding, but they are very easy after you learn the tricks (as described in Chapter 11). These questions also take little work or time, especially those that merely require you to substitute numbers for symbols.

Formula Problems

Many geometry problems simply require you to write down a formula and plug in the numbers, such as when finding the interior angles of a figure or the total surface area of a figure (see Chapter 10).

Problems with Drawn Figures

Many problems that include a figure (a drawing or illustration) are pretty simple to solve. The problems on the last page of the math section are an exception to this statement, however. These problems, difficult because they are close to the end, may look like wiring diagrams, with lines running every which way.

Quantitative Comparisons

QCs offer so many opportunities for using tricks that you rarely want to skip one of these problems. Just remember, however, that you lose a *third* of a point for each wrong answer (not just a quarter, as with the other problems on this test).

Linear Algebra Questions

If the entire problem consists of a simple algebraic equation, such as $\frac{4}{5}x - 13 = \frac{5}{3}x - 10$, do it. This type of question is a gift for you — something you can do in just a few seconds.

Bonus! Because the math grid-in questions have no penalty for wrong answers (the only SAT questions that cannot cost you points for guessing), fill in something, anything. *Never* leave a grid-in question blank.

Index

• D •

• E •

• K •

• L •

• M •

• Q •

• R •

• S •

• T •

• U •

• V •

• W–Z •

Notes

Notes

Notes

Notes